Author's Profile

Paul Baweja was born in Sydney, the Commonwealth of Australia. Paul was educated at LaSalle Catholic College (Sydney, New South Wales), the College of the former Australian Prime Minister, the Right Honourable Paul John Keating of the Commonwealth of Australia (r. 1991–1996). In 2012, Paul earned the Bachelor of Commerce Degree from Macquarie University. Thereafter, in 2014, Paul attained the Graduate Diploma of Chartered Accounting from the Institute of Chartered Accountants Australia. Furthermore, Paul is the recipient of numerous academic awards, including the prestigious 'Golden Key International Honour Society' Award (Atlanta, Georgia, the United States of America).

In addition, Paul attended the Macquarie Business School (Macquarie University) to obtain the Master of Business Administration Degree in 2016. Paul further completed research-based postgraduate study at the Australian National University (Canberra, the Australian Capital Territory), graduating with the Master of Diplomacy (Advanced) Degree in 2018. Paul's Master's Degree Thesis was completed under the auspices of the ANU College of Asia and the Pacific at the Coral Bell School of Asia Pacific Affairs. Paul's Thesis was titled 'International Conflict Mediation: A Diplomatic Analysis of the U.S. Camp David Talks (1978)'.

Paul is an Australian Author, Publisher, and Writer. Paul has authored several books on Philosophy, Women's History, and English Literature. Paul has previously written and published *A Philosophical Treatise of Reality* in 2021, a 500,000-word four-volume treatise. Paul's fifth book, *The Struggle of Women: Major Female Figures throughout World History* published in 2022 is 125,000 words in length. *The Struggle of Women* has been accepted into the Department of the Prime Minister and Cabinet Library (Brisbane, Queensland). This is a Government Agency library affiliated with the Australian Government. Last but not least, Paul's *A Commentary on Shakespeare's Plays* published in 2023, is 134,000 words in length, and this is his sixth book.

On matters of theology, in 2022, Paul completed the Certificate of Catholic Theology at the Augustine Institute (Greenwood Village, Colorado, the United States of America). Also, in the same year, Paul attained the Certificate in Biblical Studies from the Biblical Training Institute (Camas, Washington, the United States of America). Finally, also in 2022, Paul achieved the Certificate in the Catechism of the Catholic Church from Catholic Distance University (Charles Town, West Virginia, the United States of America).

A Commentary on
SHAKESPEARE'S PLAYS

FIRST EDITION

PAUL BAWEJA

MMXXIII

First published in Melbourne,
the Commonwealth of Australia, 2023

Published by Paul Baweja
APTOR2021_enquiries@protonmail.com

A catalogue record for this book is available from the National Library of Australia

ISBN: 978 0 6489818 5 5 (Hardcover Book)

Cover image: William Shakespeare, the English Playwright
Image credit: The Janssen Portrait of William Shakespeare, The Folger Shakespeare Library, Washington, D.C. (USA)
Image attribution: Science History Images / Alamy
Design and typesetting by Blue Wren Books (Melbourne)
Printed and bound by Ingram Spark

Dedication

Paul Baweja dedicates this book to the memory of Sister Elizabeth Kenny (1880–1952). Kenny was an Australian nurse, who made consequential progress on the treatment of poliomyelitis. Kenny's alternative treatment of poliomyelitis, known as 'the Kenny Method', relieved the suffering of countless people across the Modern World. Indeed, the Kenny Method was one of the most effective forms of medical treatment for poliomyelitis, prior to the development of vaccines to treat this debilitating medical condition.

Acknowledgement

Paul Baweja, of Sydney, the Commonwealth of Australia, acknowledges the original and true author of these thirty-seven dramatic plays as William Shakespeare (1564–1616) of Stratford-upon-Avon, the Kingdom of England. Shakespeare's plays are in the Public Domain. This Commentary augments and elucidates on the concepts, ideas, and themes advanced by the insightful and inquisitive English gentleman. All literary writing directly pertaining to Shakespeare's thirty-seven plays are appropriately referenced throughout this book.

Contents

Preface

This book examines William Shakespeare's remarkable plays. Shakespeare's works are a timeless masterpiece of English Literature. Shakespeare continues to inspire, enlighten, and illuminate our study of the humanities. Shakespeare's works shine a light on the human condition and experience in simple and often profound ways. This English gentleman's works explore themes, concepts, and ideas of greed, faith, jealousy, fear, beauty, self-interest, mortality, death, Heaven, God, pride, love, profit, revenge, power, freedom, morality, virtue, vice, friendship, justice, liberty, marriage, destiny, good, evil, religion, war, and many more.

This book critically explores the thirty-seven plays of Shakespeare. Unlike other books written on Shakespeare, this text does not provide a structured and rudimentary secondary analysis of his plays. This book is not concerned with the main characters, the storyline, the narrative, the denouement, and the many other equally important aspects of a dramatic play. Rather, this book investigates the universal ideas, concepts, and themes alluded to above, it explores the insightful literature contained within Shakespeare's time-tested writings. The Commentary proffered by this book endeavours to shed greater human understanding and bring a newfound contemporary analysis of Shakespeare's most cherished plays.

The perusal of Shakespeare's plays will continue unabated for countless centuries to come. The entertainment and amusement of his plays evoke many emotions and feelings, both the good and the unpleasant. It is the ideal objective of this book to make an incremental contribution to the greatness of such literature. The author trusts that the reader shall find this Commentary of value in the interpretation of Shakespeare's timeless literary works.

xii

Paul Baweja
Australian Author and Writer
the Commonwealth of Australia
February 2023

Keywords

Abdicate, Affection, Ambition, Beauty, Birth, Blessing, Body, Born, Bravery, Brother, Chance, Conscience, Contemplation, Counsel, Courage, Court, Crown, Curse, Death, Debt, Deed, Desire, Destiny, Devil, Dignity, Doubt, Dream, Duke, Ego, Employment, England, Evil, Expectation, Faith, False, Fate, Father, Fear, Flesh, Fortune, Freedom, Friendship, Glory, God, Good, Grace, Greed, Grief, Happiness, Heart, Heaven, Hell, History, Honour, Hope, Husband, Interest, Jealousy, Joy, Judgement, Justice, King, Kingdom, Law, Liberty, Life, Love, Man, Marriage, Mercy, Mind, Misery, Money, Morality, Mortality, Mother, Nature, Nobility, Parliament, Passion, Patience, Peace, Philosophy, Pleasure, Politics, Power, Prayer, Pride, Prince, Profit, Proud, Queen, Reason, Religion, Remedy, Revenge, Right, Sex, Shame, Sin, Sister, Sorrow, Soul, Sovereign, Spirit, Strife, Thought, Time, Treason, True, Trust, Truth, Valour, Vice, Victory, Virtue, War, Wife, Woman, Worship, and Youth.

A Commentary on
SHAKESPEARE'S PLAYS

INTRODUCTION

Shakespeare's literary writings and dramatic plays have captivated readers of all ages across the globe for well over 400 years. Without a question, Shakespeare's works are a timeless masterpiece of English Literature. Shakespeare's works examine the nuance and finesse of the human condition, not to mention, the multitude of human emotions, sensations, and feelings associated with the complexity of life. Shakespeare's plays are both original and riveting. Shakespeare demonstrates the power of words to express the highs and lows of human life, the ebbs and flows of grief and happiness, and how literature makes good on its ability to educate and inform humanity on both the frailties and strengths of the human condition.

The Commentary within this book aims to explore the intricacies of Shakespeare's writing. It examines the original writings contained within Shakespeare's magnificent plays, verbatim. This Commentary offers newfound insight and greater depth to some of the profound assertions and propositions that Shakespeare presents in his work. Within this book, there is an independent chapter devoted to each of Shakespeare's thirty-seven plays. This Commentary engages with Shakespeare's plays to promote a deeper understanding of his writings. This book offers a newfound critique of Shakespeare's timeless writings in order to delve deeper into the intimate mysteries of the human condition, including social psychology, human speech, thought, and behaviour.

Shakespeare's works are a lynchpin of Western Literature. The countless scholarly analysis of Shakespeare's writing is a living testimony to the sheer brilliance of this gentleman's thought and insight. The author trusts that the reader will find this Commentary useful in reading Shakespeare's work, but also helpful in interpreting the many shades of meaning within his majestic plays. Last but not least, this Commentary sheds greater light on Shakespeare's perception on the existential reality of human life.

Chapter 1

ALL'S WELL THAT ENDS WELL

'Love all. Trust a few. Do wrong to none.'

SHAKESPEARE

All's Well That Ends Well is a romantic comedy. This play illustrates the true and chaste love that Helena, a poor daughter of a deceased father who was a physician, exhibits for Count Bertram. Rather than the traditional approach of courting, where a gentleman courts a gentlewoman, much of the courting in this play is performed by Helena. Helena seeks to win the favour, heart, and mind of the young Count Bertram.

Throughout the play, Helena confronts structural disadvantage. Helena is of low birth and social status. Whereas, Count Bertram is a noble gentleman of high birth, wealth, and privilege. However, all hope is not lost, and Helena's genuine admiration for Count Bertram displays a remarkable persistence. When the King becomes sick, Helena resolves to seize the initiative to aid in the King's recovery. In doing so, Helena negotiates a secret pact with the King. Helena's reward for the restoration of the King's health is that she be allowed to freely select a gentleman for marriage, without regard to her class, sex, social status, income, wealth, education, private property, or any other hindrance for that matter. When Helena is successful in performing her end of the agreement, the King is honoured to uphold his royal guarantee. Needless to say, Helena determines to wed Count Bertram. However, Count Bertram reneges the exercise of His Majesty's Royal Prerogative. Initially, all hope seems lost for Helena.

This play witnesses Count Bertram depart to foreign lands and partake in wars, perchance to start a new life filled with adventure and action. Count Bertram also comes under the persuasive influence of his close associate, Parolles, a gentleman who does not favourably assist Helena in her matters of securing courtly love. Notwithstanding, Helena does not surrender her heart's resolve to win over Count Bertram. In the fullness of time, Helena's novel schemes and clever ideas witness her secure the favour of Count Bertram, and he most willingly accedes to her true love.

> '... *persecuted time with hope, and finds no other advantage in the process, but only the losing of hope by time.*'[1]

Sometimes one can feel overwhelmed by the multitude of challenges and obstacles that life presents. A person may perceive that hope is near at hand, only to find that it is diminishing with the passage of the very finite time in the course of human life. The weight of the force of circumstance is difficult to withstand in life. Indeed, transcending grief can appear as a perpetual struggle.

> '*He was likely to have lived still, if knowledge could be set up against mortality.*'[2]

If only human knowledge could provide the unyielding defence against our mortality, we may live for eternity. However, no worldly

---

1   Shakespeare, William. (1623). *All's Well That Ends Well.* Act 1, Scene 1.
2   Shakespeare, William. (1623). *All's Well That Ends Well.* Act 1, Scene 1.

knowledge can protect humans from the inevitable process of death. Not to mention, it is totally beyond the very finite capacity of secular knowledge to secure our liberty from death. For death is the price each and every person owes for their birth.

> '... *moderate lamentation is the right of the dead, excessive grief the enemy of the living.*'[3]

Once human life has passed, the dead no longer have a reason to grieve. The dead have left this material world behind. Therefore, the deceased people can only ever purport to construe a moderate perception of worldly sorrow. In stark contrast, the living people are directly subject to the endless tribulations of this world. Thus, living people hold every reason to experience perpetual bouts of grief, that shall only pass away with the end of life.

> '*Love all. Trust a few. Do wrong to none.*'[4]

This is a universal maxim of how humans ought to treat one another in civilised society. This proposition is grounded in morality, and it establishes a superior precedent of exemplary normative conduct in everyday social relations between members of an organised society, or a close-knit social group. Every person is categorically entitled to love and to be loved in return. However, it is important that trust is established between consenting parties. Trust is earnt through repeated social interactions and interpersonal exchanges between two or more people. For trust to endure, all parties must demonstrate a commitment to upholding higher values, such as honesty, integrity, sincerity, faithfulness, confidentiality, human dignity, respect, and privacy.

Lastly, humans must wrong none. At the very least, we ought to treat others how we would like to be treated. Just as we do not

---

3   Shakespeare, William. (1623). *All's Well That Ends Well*. Act 1, Scene 1.
4   Shakespeare, William. (1623). *All's Well That Ends Well*. Act 1, Scene 1.

expect any person to wrong us. Thus, we ought not to wrong another member of a social group or community, regardless of our affiliation, or lack thereof, to such an individual. Indeed, if every human followed these three moral principles, the Modern World shall be a considerably better place.

'Under thy own life's key: be checked for silence, but never taxed for speech.' [5]

People need to appreciate there is an opportune time for silence, and equally, an appropriate time for entertaining dialogue. When engaging in speech, humans ought to exercise reason and good judgement in their choice of words. Often times, mastery in the discretion of language is the key to one's own fortune. Quite literally, the employment of words can enhance or diminish a person's reputation.

'Man is enemy to virginity; how may we barricado it against him?' [6]

Shakespeare explores the nature and condition of the male sex. Man is a creature subject to sensual passion, sexual desire, physiological drives, bodily urges, and an insatiable attraction towards the female sex. The noble quandary the female sex confronts is how to resist the male's unwanted advances or unceasing demands for sexual gratification. Beyond the fascinating and observant piece of literature, this question gives rise to very real concerns for the treatment, dignity, and respect of gentlewomen in the contemporary world.

---

5   Shakespeare, William. (1623). *All's Well That Ends Well.* Act 1, Scene 1.
6   Shakespeare, William. (1623). *All's Well That Ends Well.* Act 1, Scene 1.

'... it is not politic in the Commonwealth of Nature to preserve virginity. Loss of virginity is rational increase, and there was never virgin got till virginity was first lost.' [7]

It is within the bounds of human nature to increase and multiply the human population. Procreation is a very natural act of the human condition. Procreation leads to the preservation and increase of the human species. Not to mention, Shakespeare highlights that it is not possible for a virgin to exist, had her parents not engaged in the natural act of copulation. In the final analysis, it is by the undeserved grace of God, that a minority of the human population come to abstain from sexual relations, and pursue a truly chaste and spiritual life. Sexual abstinence is not a suitable moral pursuit for every person in the world.

'Our remedies oft in ourselves do lie, which we ascribe to Heaven. The fated sky gives us free scope, only doth backward pull our slow designs when we ourselves are dull.' [8]

This is the classic and intractable question of whether human life is subject to destiny or free will? Shakespeare asserts that humans possess agency and capacity to create the life they desire. Humans ought to exercise the instrument of reason to effectuate a conventional reality which mirrors their internal world of thoughts, beliefs, ideas, and values. Yet, for a significant portion of the human population in the early twenty-first century, the Modern World exhibits the real issues of wealth inequality, abject poverty, inequality of private property, the disparities of school and higher education. Not to mention, the distinguishing factors of sex, race, colour, social class, religion, gender, and age, which often cause the marginalisation and discrimination of select people in our modern society.

---

7   Shakespeare, William. (1623). *All's Well That Ends Well.* Act 1, Scene 1.
8   Shakespeare, William. (1623). *All's Well That Ends Well.* Act 1, Scene 1.

While this positive assertion concerning free will is ideal in the sense that humans ought to seize the initiative to create the life they desire, it is also an 'over-simplification' that does not adequately address the multitude of challenges that humans confront in the Modern World. Perhaps, the correct answer resides somewhere along the 'destiny' and 'free will' continuum. While humans are born into certain traits and characteristics, for example, consider sex, colour, and parentage, humans also have the capacity to learn knowledge, attain a quality university education, master life's interpersonal skills, get married, have children, create a family, and become an honourable member of a reputable profession.

'My project may deceive me … but my intents are fixed, and will not leave me.' [9]

A strong determination, unwavering resolve, and an unshakeable faith in one's abilities shall witness a person succeed in life. Often times it appears that a person's plans are too grand, too far-fetched, or simply inconceivable. However, one needs to strive forward through the inevitable struggle and obstacles, if such a person is to stand any chance at achieving success.

The pursuit and accomplishment of self-actualisation is not possible without a myriad of challenges in life. The Biblical story of David and Goliath is an enduring example of how, on the surface, the odds may appear to be totally against a person. However, with an unbreakable belief in the favour of God, all things are possible, no matter how negligible the likelihood, or how unfortunate the circumstances may appear to us. Belief is everything.

---

9   Shakespeare, William. (1623). *All's Well That Ends Well.* Act 1, Scene 1.

> *'Such a man might be a copy to these younger times; Which, followed well, would demonstrate them now.'* [10]

In the Modern World, humans have discarded the treasures of good neighbourly relations, high moral conduct, tradition, custom, the pursuit of virtue, honour, reputation, and the belief in God. The contemporary world is constructed in accordance with the philosophy of secularism, materialism, consumerism, hedonism, capitalism, neoliberalism, and individualism. The ancient history of human civilisation remains an example of how to live an honourable and meaningful life, in today's complex, digital, fast-paced, inter-connected, virtual, and globalised world.

> *'Let me not live, after my flame lacks oil.'* [11]

Life is not worth living after one is incapable of demonstrating the passion, energy, vigour, intellect, movement, and action of human life. For a vegetative life is characterised by the inability to experience the fullness of human life.

> *'I fill a place. I know it.'* [12]

Often times life appears as though each and every one of us occupy a position, and are not more than what our birth, title, occupation, or position ascribe to us. For example, consider the titles of king, queen, mother, husband, lecturer, chief executive officer, president, duke, prince, medical doctor, lawyer, civil engineer, princess, lieutenant, or a member of parliament. From a strict legalistic perspective, the Common Law of Obligations and Contracts confers duties, responsibilities, and rights to each and every person according to their position, rank, or enforceable undertaking in modern society.

---

10   Shakespeare, William. (1623). *All's Well That Ends Well*. Act 1, Scene 2.
11   Shakespeare, William. (1623). *All's Well That Ends Well*. Act 1, Scene 2.
12   Shakespeare, William. (1623). *All's Well That Ends Well*. Act 1, Scene 2.

> *'I am driven on by the flesh; and he must needs go that the Devil drives.'* [13]

Humans are constructed of the flesh, and they are subject to the limitations and desires of the flesh. People are more likely than not to surrender to their sensual desires. The five senses (i.e., sight, sound, smell, taste, and touch) can become a hindrance to the pursuit of a more rewarding and meaningful life. When Shakespeare says 'must' he is making the representation that people do not have the freedom, nor capacity to resist temptation, and therefore, are helpless victims in the furtherance of sin. Thus, it is only by God's grace, favour, mercy, and goodness that humans turn away from sin.

> *'It is the show and seal of Nature's truth, when love's strong passion is impressed in youth.'* [14]

Nature runs its course with every human life. From pregnancy to palliative care. From birth to death. Nature has its way. During the phase of youth, the human body experiences significant change, including physiological, emotional, chemical, sexual, biological, and psychological. During the stage of puberty, hormones and chemical messengers are produced, namely estrogen, progesterone, and testosterone. Thereby, creating fundamental changes in the human body. Most importantly, these changes initiate a newfound impetus for strong attraction towards the opposite sex. During this phase of human life, the emotion of love is powerful, passionate, and profound.

---

13   Shakespeare, William. (1623). *All's Well That Ends Well.* Act 1, Scene 3.
14   Shakespeare, William. (1623). *All's Well That Ends Well.* Act 1, Scene 3.

'My friends were poor, but honest; so is my love.' [15]

A person does not require wealth, education, social status, income, private property, privileged birth, or any other social, political, or economic prerequisite to give and receive love. Love is a universal human emotion, sensation, and feeling. Love is understood and exchanged between humans, without regard to material or worldly characteristics. The language of love transcends all boundaries. The highest form of love that one can proffer to another person is unconditional love.

'Oft expectation fails, and most oft there where it most promises, and oft it hits where hope is coldest and despair most fits.' [16]

All people have hopes, desires, dreams, and goals, however, they do not always come to fruition or accomplishment. When a person has most expectation to believe their endeavours will be successful, one falls short. Yet, it is when a person has a minimal chance at accomplishing success, when the odds are next to none, it is then, that our success defies our expectations. In everyday life, managing expectations, navigating feelings, sensations, and emotions, and resolving difficult conversations, not only ours, but also of the important people in our lives, are all crucial ingredients of living a fulfilling life.

'Man assured of an uncertain life and sure death.' [17]

Without question, the human condition is defined by mortality. The course of human life is not fixed and static. Although a person may plan and devise what type of life they wish to create and how to live. The only certainty each and every person has is in the finality of this life. That is to say, certainty in the face of death.

---

15   Shakespeare, William. (1623). *All's Well That Ends Well.* Act 1, Scene 3.
16   Shakespeare, William. (1623). *All's Well That Ends Well.* Act 2, Scene 1.
17   Shakespeare, William. (1623). *All's Well That Ends Well.* Act 2, Scene 3.

The juxtaposition here is conspicuous. Shakespeare masterfully compares and contrasts how life and death are at odds. While people entertain certainty in the course and events of life, they are only sure of the one thing they most dread, and that is death.

'Strange it is that our bloods, in colour, weight, and heat, poured all together, would quite confound distinction, yet stands off in differences so mighty.' [18]

The human experience is not without prejudice in this world. While humans are very similar in their internal composition, for example, consider that we are comprised of oxygen, hydrogen, nitrogen, carbon, calcium, phosphorus, sulphur, potassium, sodium, chlorine, and magnesium, people tend to judge one another on their phenotypes (i.e., a person's observable traits, such as eye colour, hair colour, or height). Not to mention, other notable differences, such as race, colour, gender, ethnicity, age, occupation, employment status, religion, and sex are often factors that create the underlying basis for discrimination amongst the members of modern society, a voluntary association, or community group.

'From the lowest place when virtuous things proceed, the place is dignified by the Doer's deed.' [19]

All humans proceed from nought. Virtue is always earned and rewarded. Virtue is not bequeathed upon a person at birth, nor is it passed down from generation to generation. Nobility may be guaranteed by birth right; however, any individual can become a virtuous person. Virtue is secured through the performance of meritorious and noble actions. The well-known idiom, 'Actions are more important than words', succinctly expresses the essence of Shakespeare's writing.

---

18   Shakespeare, William. (1623). *All's Well That Ends Well.* Act 2, Scene 3.
19   Shakespeare, William. (1623). *All's Well That Ends Well.* Act 2, Scene 3.

'Think upon patience.' [20]

This is an elegant and beautiful statement. One that is often overlooked for its immeasurable wisdom. In a world that is defined by time constraints, endless responsibilities, duties, obligations, and commitments, patience, among many other admirable attributes, is an important virtue that creates the ground for our worldly success. Nothing great or noble is achieved overnight. Patience guides the time. As a steady pair of hands guide a naval ship, a commercial aeroplane, or a passenger train, from its place of departure to its intended final destination.

'My heart is heavy. My age is weak. Grief would have tears, and sorrow bids me speak.' [21]

This is a classic representation of the frailty of all human life. Without a doubt, worldly pain and suffering create a number of psychological burdens that humans carry within them through the course of life. Inevitably, as we advance in age, daily living activities become difficult to complete, for example, consider walking, drinking water, eating food, having a good night's rest, and many more. Although this is easier said than done, every person ought to strive to secure an inner peace that is not contingent upon external conditions of the material world, nor the unreliable state of the human body. If one can find peace in this broken world, one has secured a treasure that is rarer than the finest gold.

'But that the merit of service is seldom attributed to the true and exact performer.' [22]

It is not always the case that the individual who performs a valiant deed or noteworthy action is the person who is rewarded for their

---

20   Shakespeare, William. (1623). *All's Well That Ends Well.* Act 3, Scene 2.
21   Shakespeare, William. (1623). *All's Well That Ends Well.* Act 3, Scene 4.
22   Shakespeare, William. (1623). *All's Well That Ends Well.* Act 3, Scene 6.

meritorious conduct. Sometimes it is the unfortunate case, that acknowledgement and reward are impressed upon another party, due to circumstance, power, influence, prestige, wealth, agency, position, or rank. Disappointing as this scenario is, one must not cease from being the best version of oneself. Ultimately, God is the True Vindicator and Judge of all people.

> 'I know not what the success will be, My Lord, but the attempt I vow.' [23]

Courage, confidence, and conviction are the essential elements to achieve success in life. Although success is an uncertain outcome of human endeavours, this is not a plausible reason to deter one from the pursuit of one's worldly ambitions. As the ancient Chinese philosopher, Lao Tzu famously remarked, 'The journey of a thousand miles begins with a single step.' Therefore, success can only be accomplished by proceeding boldly on the uncertain path that is before us.

> 'It is not the many oaths that makes the truth. But the plain, single vow that is vowed true.' [24]

The very act of pronouncing oaths does not automatically render that one will keep them. As the Dutch botanist, Herman Boerhaave once remarked, 'The great seal of Truth is simplicity', and so Shakespeare emphasises the importance of plainness in undertaking our vows. For a vow must be 'vowed true' for it to have the requisite strength to survive temptations, trials, and tragedies. The unshakeable Truth of a vow is its foundation and impregnable basis for validity. Indeed, vows and oaths are not matters to be administered lightly. Vows ought to be guided by the spirit, body, mind, and heart.

---

23 Shakespeare, William. (1623). *All's Well That Ends Well.* Act 3, Scene 6.
24 Shakespeare, William. (1623). *All's Well That Ends Well.* Act 4, Scene 2.

'The web of our life is of a mingled yarn, good and ill together. Our virtues would be proud, if our faults whipped them not; and our crimes would despair, if they were not cherished by our virtues.' [25]

Human life is not completely good, nor completely evil. Life consists of a combination of the good and evil, such is the conventional reality of the material world. There are no perfect people in the world. Each and every person has their unique combination of virtues and vices. Thus, success resides in identifying our core strengths, and living life according to them. Whereas, weaknesses ought to be rectified or curtailed to the extent possible or reasonable. No matter which continent, culture, or country, no person has everything in their favour. Every person in this world is a 'work in progress'. In any art, science, practice, academic discipline, or profession, the attainment of perfection takes a lifetime to accomplish.

'Simply the thing I am shall make me live.' [26]

Every person embodies a 'will' (this term is also closely associated with an inner drive, spirit, being, essence, soul, or the faculty of mind). The will is the very immortal phenomenon that sustains human life. The very substance of 'being' defines a person and it determines 'what' they become in this world. We exist by virtue of what and who we are, not by what we idealise to become, or imagine to accomplish in our finite lifetime on Earth.

With respect to the discipline of psychology, the American psychologist, Abraham Harold Maslow's *Hierarchy of Needs Theory* posits the highest human need as 'self-actualisation', and in this category one strives to achieve their highest potential in life. Self-actualisation is the conscious process by which a person successfully creates their reality. A state of being in which one's internal world

---

25   Shakespeare, William. (1623). *All's Well That Ends Well*. Act 4, Scene 3.
26   Shakespeare, William. (1623). *All's Well That Ends Well*. Act 4, Scene 3.

is in harmony with their external world. This is a condition of existence, in which the embodiment of one's personal will becomes an accurate representation of one's conventional reality.

'All's well that ends well yet, though time seem so adverse and means unfit.'[27]

Hope is an essential component to living a content and positive life. For their shall arise a multitude of challenges, obstacles, and difficulties that are bound to eventuate in one's lifetime. Thus, hope serves to sustain a person through the dark and difficult times. Humans ought to keep faith, that in the end, all things will work towards a greater and universal good. Although faith is beyond the finite capacity of human reason (and the intellect, ego, or mind) of the self-centred person to accept, it is not entirely conceptual or abstract thinking.

'... natural rebellion, done in the blaze of youth, when oil and fire, too strong for reason's force, overbears it and burns on.'[28]

The period of life between childhood and adulthood is characterised by dramatic change. In the adolescence years of life, teenagers are sometimes characterised by an outright defiance to authority figures, such as justices, chief justices, police officers, judges, lawyers, parents, medical doctors, caregivers, religious leaders, or legal guardians. Minors experience a powerful psychological battle between reason and passion. Not to mention, the teenager's desire to create a separate and independent identity from their parents, the inherent need to construct a positive 'self-image' to secure acceptance from their peers, friends, or close-knit social group is of vital importance to them. The moments of life transition make or break a person's destiny.

---

27   Shakespeare, William. (1623). *All's Well That Ends Well*. Act 5, Scene 1.
28   Shakespeare, William. (1623). *All's Well That Ends Well*. Act 5, Scene 3.

'Praising what is lost, makes the remembrance dear.' [29]

Humans tend to cherish what they have lost or relinquished more than what they presently have in their immediate possession. At times, individuals are too focused on what has become a relic of modern history, and it is this very constant and unabating thought of what no longer is, that makes the loss more cherished, or most prized in a person's finite lifetime.

'Oft our displeasures, to ourselves unjust, destroy our friends, and after weep their dust.' [30]

People need to be careful, not to take too great an offence at minor mistakes. For the state of being unforgiving can lead to the loss of invaluable friendships. Thereafter, we are left alone to mourn the important relationships that are now no more. Good counsel herein is, to be liberal with our compliments, and be prudent with our complaints. After all, our commitment to a vocation, enjoyment of pastimes, and security in our relationships, these are all important factors in ageing well.

---

29   Shakespeare, William. (1623). *All's Well That Ends Well*. Act 5, Scene 3.
30   Shakespeare, William. (1623). *All's Well That Ends Well*. Act 5, Scene 3.

Chapter 2

ANTONY AND CLEOPATRA

'Fortune knows we scorn her most when most she offers blows.'
SHAKESPEARE

Antony and Cleopatra is a romantic tragedy. This Shakespeare's play is filled with intense passion, emotion, and drama. This play narrates the romance of one of the three rulers of the Roman Empire, Mark Antony, and the Queen of Egypt, Cleopatra. This brave and charming solider, Antony is captivated by the remarkable beauty of Queen Cleopatra. Antony entertains several visits to Egypt, in order to spend time with his beloved Egyptian mistress, Cleopatra. The two lovers spend countless days and nights together in the intimate company of each other. The push and pull of emotions, the dynamic tension of romance, and the tug of the heart strings is all too evident between the two lovers.

While Mark Antony is a courageous Roman leader and soldier, he often clashes with his Roman counterpart, the great Octavius Caesar. As a diplomatic solution to the strong rivalry and constant trouble between Antony and Caesar, a marriage proposal is put forward between Caesar's sister, Octavia and Antony. Unfortunately, the marriage is short-lived and Octavia returns home to be with her brother. Antony and Caesar continue their military battles on the high seas. On two separate occasions of their formidable naval campaigns, Caesar defeats Antony.

Following Antony's military defeats at sea, the fever pitch love between Antony and Cleopatra takes a turn for the worst. Antony receives false news that Cleopatra is dead, and thereafter, he takes his own life. While Cleopatra had only intended to 'calm the storm' between the two lovers, irreversible damage has now been done. Following the circumstantial suicide of Antony, Cleopatra resolves to take her own life. In addition, Cleopatra's two female royal accomplices also commit suicide.

Antony and Cleopatra is a remarkable piece of English literature. This play explores themes of love, power, empire, romance, trust, marriage, courage, bravery, honour, pride, and many more. Love is often bittersweet, and the greatest romance stories often end in tragedy. For example, consider the narrative of Helen of Troy in Greek mythology which led to the *Trojan War.* Much can be learnt about human nature, desire, emotions, feelings, sensations, and the bitterness of personal rivalries from the perusal of this play.

> '*Thus, did I desire it. What our contempt doth often hurl from us, we wish it ours again.*'[31]

During our lifetime, we experience countless negative and positive forces at play in the world. A dynamic push and pull, that is, opposing and contending energies that impact our pattern of thought, speech, and behaviour. As a result, at times, it is within our human nature to feel disdain for a person or object. However, this irrational interplay of emotions, moods, sensations, feelings, and impressions, are most fluid in experience, and therefore, subject to constant change.

---

31   Shakespeare, William. (1607). *Antony and Cleopatra.* Act 1, Scene 2.

Once we disassociate ourselves from the chaotic influence of feelings, emotions, and sensations, we then have the opportunity to consciously reflect upon them, from a more rational and impartial perspective. This can lead us to reconceptualise our cognition, and afford greater merit to more positive or favourable attributes in our perception, that were once all too quickly overlooked. Indeed, 'desire' and 'aversion' are extreme attributes across the spectrum of the human cognition.

'Hear me, Queen. The strong necessity of time commands. Our services awhile; but my full heart. Remains in use with you.' [32]

The reality of duty and responsibility transcends the emotional push and pull of one's heart strings. The strong and emotive force of passionate love must be abated, in order for a person to fulfil their destiny or mission. Fundamentally, humans are driven forward by passions, sensations, reason, cognition, judgement, thought, feelings, ideologies, beliefs, ideas, and values. Often times, these competing elements come into unavoidable conflict with one another during our lifetime. Thus, it is not always possible to simultaneously fulfil competing ambitions.

In the course of our life, certain decisions are mutually exclusive. Thus, difficult choices must be made, in order for a person to realise the fullness of their innate potential. In the final analysis, personal values do not neatly reside along a linear continuum, they are not all 'equal' in their significance. Values are ordered and subject to a hierarchy. Therefore, one must thoughtfully determine the importance and assignment of personal values in one's life, in order to guide one's thought, speech, and action in this world. Discernment is a most necessary element in organising the many competing priorities of our life.

---

32   Shakespeare, William. (1607). *Antony and Cleopatra.* Act 1, Scene 3.

'Equality of two Domestic Powers breed scrupulous faction.' [33]

In an organised and structured body politic, for example, consider the Commonwealth of Athens, it is not possible for two sovereigns to concurrently exist. There is a hierarchy in every empire, nation-state, dukedom, kingdom, and world order. A pecking order so to speak, that must be respected, in which every person, nation, sovereign, king, queen, prince, duke, and head of state has a rightful place. While the aspirational and theoretical notion of the equality and independence of sovereign nation-states is a democratic and liberal idea, it is fundamentally flawed in practice. There is much truth and wisdom in the self-explanatory Chinese idiom, 'Two tigers cannot share the same mountain.'

'It only stands our lives upon to use our strongest hands.' [34]

Humans must exercise agency to create a meaningful life in this world. Shakespeare's symbolic reference to our hands demonstrates the necessity of initiative and action in life. It is within the purview and responsibility of the individual to enact change and construct their own external reality. A person cannot leave life's all too important endeavours solely to the instruments of luck, fate, or chance, nor delegate personal responsibility to another individual in matters of great import and heavy consequence.

'That truth should be silent I had almost forgot.' [35]

The Eternal Truth, the Everlasting Truth is not of this world. Therefore, the most Noble Truth is rarely, if ever uttered or spoken in this world. Regardless, if the Truth be acknowledged or affirmed, the Truth will remain the Truth for all time, throughout all ages, and for eternity. Shakespeare's sharp prose and literary

---

33   Shakespeare, William. (1607). *Antony and Cleopatra.* Act 1, Scene 3.
34   Shakespeare, William. (1607). *Antony and Cleopatra.* Act 2, Scene 1.
35   Shakespeare, William. (1607). *Antony and Cleopatra.* Act 2, Scene 2.

writing highlights how this world, and the people of this world, and more attuned and accustomed to falsehood. In fact, falsehood reigns supreme, to such an extent that Honesty and Truth are not the foundation for relations between individuals.

In the Modern World, morality, ethics, and religion have diminished in their standing, and in their place, the contemporary world is governed by commercial trading interests, profit, rents, dividends, capital gains, private property, royalties, interest income, annuities, and personal wealth accumulation. The advent of Truth rarely facilitates far-reaching fame and notable success for a person whose perception of this world is defined by commercial and monetary pursuits.

'Who seeks, and will not take when once it is offered, shall never find it more.' [36]

Seldom do humans receive invaluable opportunities twice in their lifetime. Individuals need to accept the blessings they receive and make full use of them. A wasted opportunity is a source of much personal regret in life. Being opportunistic is the key to success and progress in this world. If a person requests something, and then receives it, only to reject it, such an individual should not harbour the unreasonable expectation of securing such an item, favour, or objective again. The present moment is all that each person has. The future is always indeterminate. The knowledge of the future is denied to humankind.

'If I lose mine honour, I lose myself.' [37]

A person's life stands upon their very honour and reputation. In ancient times, a life devoid of honour and reputation was one not worth living. The *Old World* held in high regard the esteemed

---

36   Shakespeare, William. (1607). *Antony and Cleopatra.* Act 2, Scene 7.
37   Shakespeare, William. (1607). *Antony and Cleopatra.* Act 3, Scene 4.

principles of religious tradition, God's Sovereign Place in Creation, familial relations, faith and worship, morality, personal character, custom, and noble conduct.

The birth of the *New World* has given ground to such aforesaid foundational principles and tenets governing the human civilisation, and replaced them with science, technology, secular education, liberty, freedom, reliance on reason, advances in human knowledge, a strong sense of the Self, the pursuit of security, pleasure, and happiness. Not to mention, the procurement of extraordinary profits and private property. The contemporary world is fast diminishing the grand importance of honour and integrity, replacing them with an unequal world devoid of social justice. This Modern World is governed by the ideologies of secularism, individualism, consumerism, atheism, neoliberalism, constitutionalism, and materialism.

> *'Be you not troubled with the time, which drives over your content these strong necessities. But let determined things to destiny. Hold unbewailed their way.'* [38]

The course of time can become unfavourable towards any person. Fortitude, forbearance, and faith are necessary elements for one to overcome the multitude of challenges along the journey of life. If we are destined to affirm witness, to the achievement or accomplishment of certain grand endeavours, then we must remain resolute that they will come to effectuate. No person will achieve their destiny without confronting (and surpassing) difficulties in life. Often times we overlook the hidden meaning in the idiom, 'Adversity is a blessing in disguise.'

---

38   Shakespeare, William. (1607). *Antony and Cleopatra*. Act 3, Scene 6.

'It is ashamed to bear me. Friends, come hither. I am so lated in the world, that I have lost my way for ever: I have a ship. Laden with gold; take that, divide it; fly, And make your peace with Caesar.' [39]

After a significant loss, or a personal experience with bereavement, a person can feel overwhelmed with feelings of helplessness, grief, and sorrow. During this time, the gravity of human emotions can lead one to become ambivalent and chaotic in their demeanour. As a result, a person can become irrational and illogical in their thinking, and make rash decisions with far-reaching consequences. The immeasurable value of wise counsel is often in limited supply when a person requires it most.

'Fortune knows we scorn her most when most she offers blows.' [40]

Each person's lot with fortune is comprised of good and evil. At times, fortune favours us, and we ought to be pleased for this outcome. Equally, at other times, we are subject to the undeserved misery and unexpected suffering of events or circumstances guided by the hand of mischance. It is during the latter phase that we feel injustice thrust upon us. What we cannot escape, we are left to treat with utmost contempt and detestation.

'I see men's judgements are a parcel of their fortunes, and things outward do draw the inward quality after them. To suffer all alike.' [41]

Rarely do individuals perceive the material world accurately and objectively, as we ourselves are within and a part of this world. The human civilisation's very existence is dependent and contingent upon the material world. Therefore, there is no causal basis of an independent vantage point of perception or cognition to ascertain

---

39   Shakespeare, William. (1607). *Antony and Cleopatra*. Act 3, Scene 11.
40   Shakespeare, William. (1607). *Antony and Cleopatra*. Act 3, Scene 11.
41   Shakespeare, William. (1607). *Antony and Cleopatra*. Act 3, Scene 13.

the material world for what it truly is. Thus, regardless be it by virtue, or the force of sheer necessity, our encounter with fortune performs an inordinate role in the exercise of human judgement.

Where Shakespeare asserts, '… things outward do draw the inward quality', the Master Playwright is asserting how the outer world is a reflection and representation of our inner will. Shakespeare portrays how countless sense impressions from the five senses (i.e., sight, sound, smell, taste, and touch) that are impressed upon the human mind are a mirror representation (and confirmation) of our thoughts, beliefs, values, and ideas. In practical effect, we all perceive the material world from a partial and biased perspective. Reality cannot be otherwise.

> *'It is your noblest course. Wisdom and fortune combating together,*
> *if that the former dare but what it can, no chance may shake it.'* [42]

Both wisdom and fortune perform a pivotal function in each person's life journey. The power and insight of wisdom assists humans to make better informed decisions in life. Wisdom can overcome the damaging effects of chance or misfortune. At the very least, the great power of wisdom can serve to limit the negative consequences that arise from the cruelty of malignant fate. Fortune is an indifferent arbitrator. However, the good discernment of wisdom is within us, to guide the course of our life to accomplish grand objectives, ideas, endeavours, and missions.

> *'When valour preys on reason, it eats the sword it fights with.'* [43]

One can never secure total victory in a battle against oneself. A person's action, speech, and thought require total internal alignment if such an individual is to succeed in their undertaking. When courage, action, and reason lack congruency, then the very

---

42   Shakespeare, William. (1607). *Antony and Cleopatra*. Act 3, Scene 13.
43   Shakespeare, William. (1607). *Antony and Cleopatra*. Act 3, Scene 13.

instruments for our battle are rendered weak and ineffective. Before a person can defeat their external enemies, one needs to conquer the internal psychological battles and exhibit total mastery over the Self. Therein one establishes the ground for total victory over one's opponents. The Patron Saint of France, Joan of Arc summarises the reality of worldly success succinctly, 'All battles are first won or lost, in the mind.'

'Never anger made good guard for itself.' [44]

Humans experience a wide array of emotions in the course of life. Anger is an emotion just like any other, for example, consider joy, shyness, guilt, grief, fear, shame, disgust, sadness, happiness, or surprise. Yet the point in case is that anger can lead to irrational actions, poor choices, and regrettable behaviour. Therefore, one ought not to trust or seek counsel whilst under the undue influence of anger. The unintended consequences of anger are often discovered well after the effectuation of one's irrational actions.

'O Sovereign mistress of true melancholy, The poisonous damp of night disponge upon me. That life, a very rebel to my will, May hang no longer on me. Throw my heart, Against the flint and hardness of my fault; Which, being dried with grief, will break to powder, And finish all foul thoughts.' [45]

The course of life rarely proceeds as envisaged. Although humans create a number of plans and schemes, our intentions do not always align with the outcomes that we secure. The reality is that uncertainty and risk are omnipresent throughout all stages of the human life cycle. From birth until death, humans are engrossed in emotions, feelings, sensations, thoughts, ideas, sense impressions, desires, values, and beliefs. In vain, individuals seek to find an

---

44   Shakespeare, William. (1607). *Antony and Cleopatra.* Act 4, Scene 1.
45   Shakespeare, William. (1607). *Antony and Cleopatra.* Act 4, Scene 9.

organised and systematic structure in a chaotic and disparate world. When a person attempts to impose their will onto the world, there is resistance and conflict. Rarely does a person attain their way in all things, great and small.

'His taints and honours waged equal with him.' [46]

When we examine a person, the good and evil components, we realise that no one is perfect. Humans have both virtues and vices. Such is the fixed reality of the human condition. Most importantly, we should be balanced in our perception of other people. We ought not to assign a greater subjective proportion of criticism towards a person's unfavourable attributes, while being careful not to overly praise their merits and desirable traits. Being subjective and partial often serves to distort our observation of reality. Subjectivity hinders our accurate introspection of the people within our vicinity.

'Make not your thoughts your prisons.' [47]

Humans ought to exercise proper discernment over their thoughts. The quality of a person's thoughts has a considerable bearing on the quality of their life. We can become trapped by our thoughts, which can create very profound and real [negative] externalities for our life. Not to mention, thoughts lead to actions, which have good and evil consequences. Thoughts serve to construct our conscious reality of the world that we inhabit. There is much wisdom in the American writer, Ernest Holmes proposition, 'Change your thinking. Change your life.' The only difficulty is that Holmes' assertion is easier spoken than effectuated.

---

46   Shakespeare, William. (1607). *Antony and Cleopatra*. Act 5, Scene 1.
47   Shakespeare, William. (1607). *Antony and Cleopatra*. Act 5, Scene 2.

'You must think this. Look you, that the worm will do his kind. Look you, the worm is not to be trusted, but in the keeping of wise people.' [48]

All animals have their innate nature and are creatures of instinct and habit. An animal cannot consciously behave against its nature, which is innate, and not learned. For example, consider that it is in the very nature of a venomous snake to utilise its fangs to bite another person or animal as an object of prey. Consequently, the snake's muscles force venom from its glands through a duct into the fangs, which inject the venom into its intended target. Such is the fixed nature of a snake. A snake cannot be trained or instructed to act against its natural instinct, which forever determines its behaviour.

'Bravest at the last. She levelled at our purposes, and, being Royal, took her own way.' [49]

Suicide is not a rational resolution to one's difficulties, problems, and issues in life. This literary assertion makes the case that when we are out of plausible options, and we are unable to exercise agency or self-determine the course of our lives, then suicide gives us a sense of complete control over our life. That is to say, suicide presents a means, a method, to direct our [immoral] actions, in the vain and fallible exercise of [human] reason, subject to an illusion, that we have the final say, and that we can freely choose between life and death. Suicide purports to create a fictitious sense of control, a false sense impression upon the human mind, that we can self-determine our own destiny, by being the final arbitrator over our uncertain life.

---

48   Shakespeare, William. (1607). *Antony and Cleopatra*. Act 5, Scene 2.
49   Shakespeare, William. (1607). *Antony and Cleopatra*. Act 5, Scene 2.

'High events as these strike those that make them, and their story is no less in pity than his glory which brought them to be lamented.'[50]

Important and significant events determine one's destiny. Sometimes for the better, and other times for the worse. At times, high events, such as the death of a king, the royal coronation of a queen, the swearing-in ceremony of a prime minister, or the cessation of a world war, create the causal basis for both pity and glory. Such is the dynamic state of this material world. In the final analysis, the wise words of the ancient Greek philosopher, Heraclitus define the true state of this world, 'There is nothing permanent except change.'

---

50   Shakespeare, William. (1607). *Antony and Cleopatra*. Act 5, Scene 2.

Chapter 3

AS YOU LIKE IT

'Who ever loved that loved not at first sight?'
SHAKESPEARE

As You Like It is a romantic comedy. In this full-of-passion play, Shakespeare masterfully narrates the classic story of inter-family rivalries and the tell-tale twists and topsy-turvy turns of love. The head of a valuable and wealthy estate, Sir Rowland de Bois has passed away. In Rowland's will, he has relinquished the family inheritance to his eldest son, Oliver. Sir Rowland's youngest son, Orlando was promised a good education and a just entitlement to the family estate. However, Oliver denies his younger brother, Orlando his rightful privilege.

While Orlando is the younger son, he has admirable qualities and inherent traits, including beauty, sharp judgement, good sense, compassion, loyalty, politeness, courage, and maturity. Oliver despises and resents the favour upon the life of his younger brother. Oliver seeks to deny Orlando his rightful place in society. As the story develops, Orlando challenges Charles, a wrestler from the Court of the Duke of Frederick to a duel. Against all odds, Orlando is victorious, however, he receives unfair scorn from the Sovereign of the State, due to his parentage, that is being a son of Sir Rowland de Bois.

Two gentlewomen were in attendance at the aforesaid contest, namely, Rosalind and Celia. Following the duel, Orlando and Rosalind develop a mutual liking and profound fondness for one another. Both Orlando and Rosalind are banished from the State. However, Celia, Rosalind's close and sincere companion, voluntarily determines to escape with Rosalind. To assure their personal safety, Rosalind takes upon the disguise of a gentleman, and the two ladies flee to the Forest of Arden.

The remainder of this play narrates adventures of wooing a gentlewoman, and the manners and proper courtesies of courtship that lovers ought to adhere to. Ultimately, Rosalind's disguise as a gentleman comes to its finality. In the end, Rosalind marries her true love, Orlando. This play is a remarkable love story. *As You Like It* demonstrates how true love overcomes the odds to transcend the artificial social, economic, legal, and political structures of nobility, birth right, parentage, education, social class, personal wealth, private property, income, and aristocracy. Indeed, true love knows no boundaries.

'Nay, now thou goest from Fortune's Office to Nature's. Fortune reigns in the gifts of the world, not in the lineaments of Nature.' [51]

The institutions of Fortune and Nature compliment and contrast one another. The 'gifts' of this world refer to private property, education, personal wealth, the legal right to an inheritance, access to political power, enjoyment of social influence, high social status, and noble birth. On the other hand, the 'lineaments' of nature refer to one's beauty, intelligence, ability, and strength. It is often the case that no person has it all. Thus, a person endowed with many of nature's wonderful blessings, is more likely than not to be subject to fortune's cursed invisible hand. Fortune can recalibrate the highs

---

51   Shakespeare, William. (1599). *As You Like It*. Act 1, Scene 1.

and lows of an individual's life experience. Nonetheless, inequity and inequality are an unquestionable fact of life.

'Young gentleman … your spirits are too bold for your years.' [52]

This statement proffers wise counsel. In the years of one's youth, personal experience, formal learning, and knowledge are rudimentary. A youngling still has a lifetime ahead of them, and a lot to learn. Often times, in the adolescent years of life, the passions, emotions, sensations, and feelings are strong.

In youth, we often tend to overestimate our abilities, qualities, and capacities. What we are 'actually' capable of performing, and what we subjectively 'perceive' ourselves to be, they are two very different states of being. Much more physiological, intellectual, emotional, psychological, and biological development is required for the full maturity of one's judgement, understanding, sensibility, reason, and expertise.

'If you saw yourself with your eyes, or knew yourself with your judgement, the fear of this adventure would counsel you to a more equal enterprise.' [53]

Humans can be overconfident in their ability to accomplish a lofty endeavour. We all have the presence of unconscious bias in our thought patterns. Therefore, it is necessary that we accurately assess our inherent capacities, so that we may secure the intended fruits of our labour. It is not a sign of weakness, but rather wisdom, for a person to acknowledge their true strengths and weaknesses. With the proper discernment of one's abilities, one ought to strive to become the best person they can be, by factoring into consideration one's innate talents, natural endowments, and God's gift of grace.

---

52   Shakespeare, William. (1599). *As You Like It*. Act 1, Scene 2.
53   Shakespeare, William. (1599). *As You Like It*. Act 1, Scene 2.

> *'I shall do my friends no wrong, for I have none to lament me;
> the world no injury, for in it I have nothing. Only in the world
> I fill up a place, which may be better supplied when I have made
> it empty.'* [54]

We all have an inner emptiness. A spiritual void that can only be filled with our personal connection to God. At times, the world can be a lonely place, and one can feel displaced from the surrounding reality of one's external environment. Philosophically speaking, Shakespeare is making the pessimistic case that it is better 'not to exist', than 'to exist' in this world. In any case, each person shall depart this material world, and leave behind all that is in it, regardless, be it treasured friendships, loved ones, family, education, prized possessions, social status, spouse, children, material items, private jets, personal valuables, personal wealth, luxury vehicles, intangible assets, or private property.

> *'Master, go on, and I will follow thee. To the last gasp, with truth
> and loyalty.'* [55]

This is the exemplary demonstration of a faithful and honest servant till the very end of life. This servant displays high integrity and noble character in honouring the high place of a Master. Regardless of one's social class or position in society, virtuous conduct is within the reach of every person on Earth. This is unconditional service in action. Service that is defined by distinction and merit. The servant displays no personal regard for commercial or trading interests, pecuniary gain, self-interest, or the security of wealth, power, profit, income, fame, private property, reputation, inheritance, or any other material or immaterial comfort of this world.

54　Shakespeare, William. (1599). *As You Like It*. Act 1, Scene 2.
55　Shakespeare, William. (1599). *As You Like It*. Act 2, Scene 3.

> *'But as all is mortal in nature, so is all nature in love mortal in folly.'* [56]

Nothing in and of this world is a permanent fixture. Everything is subject to change. All worldly phenomena arise and depart. Birth, deterioration, and death are inevitable phases of the state of being. Humanity shall not expect anything to be everlasting, especially in the affairs of love, where 'happily ever after' is a far-fetched maxim. With the accumulation of wisdom, knowledge, suffering, and personal experience of a lifetime, one must understand the true reality of nature. That is to say, nature is indifferent to the individual's concerns. Nature only concerns itself with the survival of the human species vis-à-vis copulation.

> *'Thy gentleness shall force more than thy force move us to gentleness.'* [57]

Shakespeare's masterful insight into human nature illustrates that humans are more likely than not to be swayed by compassion than the arbitrary exercise of force. The Doctrine of 'the Use of Force' can result in unintended consequences. Not to mention, force can strengthen a person's resolve to revolt, as opposed to submit to the sovereign authority of political power.

There are remarkable similarities and comparisons that can be deduced between Shakespeare's philosophy and Eastern philosophical thought. For example, consider the Chinese philosopher, Lao Tzu, who asserted, 'Water is fluid, soft, and yielding. But water will wear away rock, which is rigid and cannot yield.' As an observation, phenomenon which is fluid, dynamic, and malleable has the inherent capacity to overcome phenomenon that is durable, inflexible, and seemingly solid. In essence, what

---

56   Shakespeare, William. (1599). *As You Like It*. Act 2, Scene 4.
57   Shakespeare, William. (1599). *As You Like It*. Act 2, Scene 7.

may appear weak on the outside, can be remarkably strong on the inside.

'All the world's a stage, and all the men and women merely players.' [58]

Shakespeare's metaphor symbolises this world as a grandstand for the unique performance of all people on Earth. Every person performs their individual part in the grand scheme of the world, before their inevitable death and departure. All people are actors in this world, some are criminal lawyers, economists, civil engineers, statisticians, others are medical doctors, writers, dentists, psychologists, poets, dancers, nurses, authors, surgeons, or professors. Regardless of one's vocation or profession, and the duration of one's limited lifetime, the play of this world shall proceed forward!

'Besides, the oath of a lover is no stronger than the words of a tapster.' [59]

Lovers are not to be trusted. The very phenomenon of love is founded on the push and pull of heart strings, chaotic emotions, the chemistry of sexual attraction, and the endless pursuit of limitless sensual desires. The weight and worth of the words of a tapster, that is a bartender, are roughly equivalent to that of a lover. For both are more likely than not to convey empty promises. Furthermore, lovers and tapster's verbal communication is strongly influenced by their environment. Lovers and tapsters are both likely to make statements that are in the 'heat of the moment'.

---

58 Shakespeare, William. (1599). *As You Like It*. Act 2, Scene 7.
59 Shakespeare, William. (1599). *As You Like It*. Act 3, Scene 4.

'Who ever loved that loved not at first sight?' [60]

This is the classic and timeless statement that love is felt on the basis of romantic attraction. Love is a powerful feeling that is swayed and dictated by the physical appearance or outward characteristics of an individual, for example, consider eye colour, lips, hair colour, height, or personal grooming. While the 'physical' dimension of love is difficult to deny, there is considerably more to intimacy, in particular, when it comes to long-term and fulfilling relationships (i.e., *de facto* relationship or marriage).

Beyond the chemical and physical attraction, love between two mutually consenting people must also include the dimensions of personal safety, sense of belonging, self-expression, unconditional acceptance, respect, dignity, managing expectations, personality compatibility, personal responsibility, and many other important aspects. Initial chemistry between two lovers is the spark that serves to excite mutual attraction, but will the spark sustain the relationship through its many highs and lows?

'Then, to have seen much and to have nothing, is to have rich eyes and poor hands.' [61]

Each person lives their life according to their own philosophy. If a person has witnessed much in their lifetime, then they have a vast array of personal experiences, which Shakespeare refers to as 'rich eyes'. On the contrary, if a person is lacking in many material possessions, then they have 'poor hands'. Meaning such a person does not have significant personal wealth, income, or private property, to show for their lifetime of existence in this world.

Unfortunately, only a minority of the human civilisation in this Modern World shall enjoy the high privilege to experience the 'fullness' of life, in terms of travelling around the world, owning a

---

60   Shakespeare, William. (1599). *As You Like It*. Act 3, Scene 5.
61   Shakespeare, William. (1599). *As You Like It*. Act 4, Scene 1.

sizeable portfolio of private property, pursuing personal interests, engaging in the love of hobbies, being absorbed in intellectual passions, receiving a world-class tertiary education, becoming a distinguished member of a noble and honourable profession, and cherishing a stress-free and peaceful retirement in one's advanced years.

'Why, can one desire too much of a good thing?'[62]

The fundamental nature of desire is its insatiability. It is irrational, beyond the parameters of reason, to seek too much of any phenomenon. In all matters, great and small, moderation is the key to an optimal life. Medical knowledge confirms that, 'Where there is no homeostasis, there is death.' Also, it is important to acknowledge that 'quantity' is not everything. 'Quality' also matters. For example, consider that friendships are a 'good thing', however, success in the realm of durable and dependable friendships cannot be measured by, 'how many' friends one has, but rather, 'how reliable' such friends are in one's time of tribulation.

'Well, time is the old justice that examines all such offenders, and let time try. Adieu.'[63]

The Truth shall eventually come to light. Every now and then, it appears that a person has not received the punishment that was rightly due for their unlawful actions or crime. Yet no person escapes the true scales of justice. For the passage of time ensures that each person is ultimately held accountable for their actions. All actions have consequences. Yet, long-term thinking is seldom practiced when a person is in the frame of mind to make expeditious personal gains or exorbitant profits. Ultimately, every person will reap what they sow.

---

62   Shakespeare, William. (1599). *As You Like It*. Act 4, Scene 1.
63   Shakespeare, William. (1599). *As You Like It*. Act 4, Scene 1.

'My affection hath an unknown bottom, like the Bay of Portugal.'[64]

Love knows no bounds. Often the emotions and feelings of love are irrational. Figuratively speaking, a person is prepared to climb mountains and cross oceans in order to demonstrate their true love for their spouse or secret admirer. Love can make a person ambivalent in thought, speech, and action. Such is the human condition, for rarely is love ordered, rational, balanced, and reasoned. What a person is prepared and willing to do, in order to secure the love of another person, is often without a second thought for the foreseeable consequences, nor with the proper care and due regard for oneself.

'But O, how bitter a thing it is to look into happiness through another man's eyes.'[65]

Humans feel resentment when they witness the worldly success and happiness of another person. Yet the greater point is for one to be content with their lot in life. Every person has their fair share of troubles in this world. Often times we do not perceive the complete picture, when we simply witness the surface-level happiness of another person. The best counsel herein is to cease focusing on other people's life trajectory and their achievements. We must run our Race! In the final analysis, God has given us the requisite grace, to become who we were destined to be. We must not lose sight of our hidden potential to accomplish our life's mission. We must not engage in unfounded comparisons to other people's lives.

---

64   Shakespeare, William. (1599). *As You Like It*. Act 4, Scene 1.
65   Shakespeare, William. (1599). *As You Like It*. Act 5, Scene 2.

Chapter 4

THE COMEDY OF ERRORS

*'We came into the world like brother and brother,
now let's go hand in hand, not one before the other.'*

SHAKESPEARE

The Comedy of Errors is a hilarious tale of two identical twins situated in a quirky city. As the title of this play suggests this is a drama of mistaken identities. The long-lost twins end up serving each other's Masters. The twins are innocently left confused, when instructed to complete their Master's errands and instructions. Often times the Masters' end up bearing the burden for their servant's incompetency, including disastrous dinners, mismatched marriages, the presence of seemingly unwarranted or misplaced affection, a failure to fulfil contractual obligations, and spiritual warfare. This riveting play has it all covered.

This entire story is captivated by amusement, suspense, disorder, and confusion. The narrative sustains the mysteries of the mistaken identities of the twins and their Masters till the very end of this play. The conclusion of this play is both memorable and positive. A gentleman by the name of Egeon, a merchant of

Syracuse, who was on death row for violating the City's law on a travel ban between Ephesus and Syracuse, is finally pardoned by the City's Sovereign, the Ephesian Duke, Solinus. In addition, Egeon is reunited with his long-lost wife, the town's Abbess, Emilia. Subsequently, the identity of the twins is also confirmed.

In addition, Andriana is reunited with her true husband, Antipholus of Ephesus. Last but not least, the once illegitimate romance of Antipholus of Syracuse and Luciana is now legitimised. This intriguing story is a timeless masterpiece of romance, fun, misadventure, travel, comedy, and suspense. It is a play that appeals to people of all ages, young and old alike. A play that can be watched or read countless times over, and it still succeeds in entertaining the fascination of the viewer or reader.

> '*Yet this my comfort. When your words are done, my woes end likewise with the evening Sun.*'[66]

Death is the finality of all worldly pain and suffering. Humans shall confront privations, loss, heartache, mishaps, challenges, and problems during their lifetime in this world. However, death is the final and irreversible event that ceases all conscious activity, both the physical and metaphysical. Humans can take some comfort in the knowledge that all of human life is mortal. One day, we shall cease to exist, cease to be. Therefore, all our sources of misery and sorrow shall no longer be capable of inflicting pain upon our mind and body.

> '*He that commends me to mine own content. Commends me to the thing I cannot get.*'[67]

We all seek contentment in life. That is to say, the ideal state of satisfaction with our current state of affairs. A higher sense of

---

66   Shakespeare, William. (1594). *The Comedy of Errors*. Act 1, Scene 1.
67   Shakespeare, William. (1594). *The Comedy of Errors*. Act 1, Scene 2.

fulfilment with our personal achievements, intimate relationships, and material possessions. However, contentment is one of the most difficult things to secure in life. If we carefully examine our lives, only a minority of people are actually satisfied with what they have attained, who they are in a relationship with, and what they have accomplished in life.

In reality, there is always an underlying residual sense of the need to improve things. The cognitive need to accomplish more. The esteem need to acquire some expensive or valuable material possession, to prove one's external worth. The social need to project a self-image of worldly success. Sensible wisdom resides in being able to accept ourselves, for who we truly are, with our strengths and limitations. No one has it all, but we can all have contentment.

'Well, Sir, learn to jest in good time. There is a time for all things.' [68]

This is a statement on the importance of worldly wisdom. In life, there is a time for seriousness. A time for laughter. A time for sadness. A time for mourning. A time for joy. A time for reflection. Also, a time for leisure. Humans need to be mindful of the right time to express the right emotion. One needs to consider what is appropriate according to the context and target audience. Indeed, emotional intelligence takes a lifetime to truly master. The fine art of a good conversation is full of nuance and finesse.

'Small cheer and great welcome makes a merry feast.' [69]

Shakespeare highlights the importance of formalities and intro-ductions in greeting people to an organised event or social occasion. How we make people feel on arrival can result in a significant impact on the ambience and mood of the event or occasion. One must not underestimate the ability of small things to produce a larger

---

68   Shakespeare, William. (1594). *The Comedy of Errors*. Act 2, Scene 2.
69   Shakespeare, William. (1594). *The Comedy of Errors*. Act 3, Scene 1.

than anticipated impact. The key here is to do the small things well. In order that the important things come together. Do not leave the minute details to chance.

'Ill deeds are doubled with an evil word.'[70]

Our actions and speech work in tandem. If we speak good and perform good actions in the world, we often compound the positive effects of our conduct. Likewise, if we speak ill and perform ill actions in the world, we inadvertently compound the negative effects of our conduct. The highest morality of human conduct ought to refrain from vice, and promote virtuous actions, wherever and whenever this is possible.

'I cannot, nor I will not, hold me still. My tongue, though not my heart, shall have his will.'[71]

Sometimes, people's emotions can get the better of them. Our actions can become contingent and consequential to the events around us. Not to mention, our partial perception and subjective impression of important events influence our behaviour. It is important to carefully reflect on our thoughts, beliefs, ideas, values, and also consider the foreseeable consequences of our conduct, before proceeding in our speech or action. For anger or rage rarely make a situation any better, however, they surely have the potential to make matters worse. Regrettably, the majority of humans are an irrational and emotive species. People seldom employ good judgement and the power of reason, in forming well-thought-out conclusions, prior to the performance of action.

---

70   Shakespeare, William. (1594). *The Comedy of Errors.* Act 3, Scene 2.
71   Shakespeare, William. (1594). *The Comedy of Errors.* Act 4, Scene 2.

*'Have you not heard men say, that time comes stealing on by night
and day? If it be in debt and theft, and a Sergeant in the way, hath
he not reason to turn back an hour in a day?'* [72]

We are all prisoners of time. Time keeps us. We do not keep time. In all things, time is a constant factor, regardless of the century, decade, year, season, month, day, hour, minute, or second. Time ceases for no person's troublesome necessity, nor to attend to any person's immediate circumstances. Even if we could present a convincing and persuasive argument for the rewinding of time, the natural laws governing its movement and conduct are fixed and static.

*'Hath not else his eye strayed his affection in unlawful love?
A sin prevailing much in youthful men, who give their eyes the
liberty of gazing.'* [73]

Love is a mysterious phenomenon. One that is often emotional, passionate, irrational, and sensual in nature. While there are moral, religious, and legal principles that attempt to govern love, it is within our human nature, to rebel and transcend the parameters which seek to regulate love's behaviour and outward expression in society. In particular, the younger generation are more likely than not to consciously look upon the opposite sex with lustful motives and sensual pleasure-filled intentions.

*'The venom clamours of a jealous woman poison more deadly than
a mad dog's tooth.'* [74]

Jealousy is a negative emotion that hinders both gentlemen and gentlewomen. According to the time and tradition of Shakespeare's writing, when gentlewomen were primarily domestic servants and

---

72 Shakespeare, William. (1594). *The Comedy of Errors*. Act 4, Scene 2.
73 Shakespeare, William. (1594). *The Comedy of Errors*. Act 5, Scene 1.
74 Shakespeare, William. (1594). *The Comedy of Errors*. Act 5, Scene 1.

housewives were ruled by their husbands, Shakespeare makes the comic illustration that the female sex is stern in the use of her speech, when it comes to responding to heart-felt jealousy. In the final analysis, jealousy only serves to destroy a person's character. Jealousy steals the inner joy, peace of mind, and sense of satisfaction with one's life.

> 'The consequence is then thy jealous fits have scared thy husband from the use of wits.'[75]

Shakespeare is making the hyperbolic illustration that in order to escape the passionate and emotional wrath of the wife, the husband is likely to refrain from the exercise of reason. For if the husband attempts to reason out emotion, it will only serve to ignite unbridled emotion in the wife. Thus, the husband will simply acquiesce to the wishes of his wife, for dare he create conflict and chaos in the household. This is an outdated and stereotypical representation of gentlewomen in modern society. This prose reflects the perception of gentlewomen during the time of Shakespeare.

> 'We came into the world like brother and brother, and now let's go hand in hand, not one before the other.'[76]

Humans are all equal. Each and every person has God-given dignity. No person is above or below another person. Brothers and Sisters alike, everyone is born into this world, and so it is that each person will confront his or her destined demise in this world. The journey of life is all that we have. The very immediate experience and finite knowledge of a lifetime. Therefore, we all ought to share our experience, knowledge, learning, judgement, reason, and

---

75   Shakespeare, William. (1594). *The Comedy of Errors*. Act 5, Scene 1.
76   Shakespeare, William. (1594). *The Comedy of Errors*. Act 5, Scene 1.

understanding of life on this sacred and special journey. Life is a fulfilling, pleasant, and wonderful experience, for the people that embrace it.

Chapter 5

CORIOLANUS

'Let deeds express what's like to be their words.'

SHAKESPEARE

Coriolanus is the full expression of human tragedy. This play examines the noble conduct and spectacular speech of the formidable Roman leader, Caius Marcius Coriolanus. Without question, Coriolanus is a noble Roman statesman. He has fought wars and made Rome proud by his victories and battlefield scars. However, this highly decorated Roman soldier lacks the insightful ability to make good and persuasive speech. Coriolanus has a sharp and shrewd tongue, that slanders more often than it praises.

Coriolanus is a straight-forward and very matter-of-fact leader. Without harbouring any ill-intention, Coriolanus damages important relationships with the influential and learned Senators of Rome. This most uncourtly conduct is to Coriolanus' great disadvantage, and it has profound consequences for his standing amongst the Roman people and his place in the Roman Senate.

The noble Senators of Rome are more than willing to turn the Roman people against Coriolanus. This tragic turn of events witnesses Coriolanus exiled from his nation-state. Till the very end, Coriolanus is a gentleman that is true to his nature, he demonstrates high moral principles, courage, discipline, integrity, steadfastness, righteousness, and honour. Regrettably, Coriolanus' unpolished speech overshadows his vast collection of virtues, and ultimately it leads to his downfall and unbecoming as the great leader that he was destined to become.

This exemplary play explores family ties, the art of politics, the themes of power, love, jealousy, virtue, vice, and the very essence of human nature. Indeed, the saying, 'Change our thinking, and Change who we are', is always easier said than done. This remarkable play demonstrates how difficult it is to change a person's inborn nature, thinking, character, vices, and virtues. Even at the high cost of one's own life. In the final analysis, each person has a combination of the good and evil within them. No person is perfect in every aspect of life. Such is the human condition.

'What he cannot help in his nature, you account a vice in him.' [77]

It is incredibly difficult for a person to act against their innate nature, to supersede their inner nature, the very essence of who they are. Therefore, it is questionable for us to account as a 'vice' or 'fault', what essentially is a fundamental trait in a person, that makes them truly who they are as an individual. It is nigh impossible for a person to 'become' against their nature of 'being'.

'It will in time win upon power and throw forth greater themes for insurrection's arguing.' [78]

We must preserve the faith in our ability to secure the promised victory, to prevail over the challenges and difficulties in life. Even in the midst of a difficult situation, where the odds are against us, surrendering is not an option that leads to 'mission accomplished'. Make no mistake, enemies will come against our endeavours, and

---

77   Shakespeare, William. (1608). *Coriolanus*. Act 1, Scene 1.
78   Shakespeare, William. (1608). *Coriolanus*. Act 1, Scene 1.

we will confront challenges that we once thought insurmountable. However, if our belief is strong, then it is possible to 'Turn Mountains into Molehills'.

'He is grown. Too proud to be so valiant.' [79]

Pride is the root cause of a person's downfall. While we must celebrate our successes, cherish our victories, and be proud of our accomplishments, these are God's beautiful gifts to us, which are all contingent on God's goodness, mercy, favour, grace, and power. We must not let our ego dictate our inflated sense of self-worth.

In the end, all humans are mortal. We can only truly celebrate God's Eternal Glory. For the Sun shall set on each person's pride. Just as surely each person will return to naught, to dust, to dirt, and to nothing. All human accomplishments are to amplify the Eternal Glory of God.

'For thy revenge wrench up thy power to the highest.' [80]

It is within the bounds of human nature to seek revenge for the performance of any wrong done to us. However, it takes courage, wisdom, and maturity to transcend the base instinct, to right a wrong with another wrong. For two wrongs never made a right. It is timely to reflect upon the quote most often associated with the Indian nationalist and freedom fighter, Mahatma Gandhi, 'An eye for an eye makes the whole world blind.' Rarely, if ever, does the act of retribution resolve the underlying cause of human conflict.

79　Shakespeare, William. (1608). *Coriolanus*. Act 1, Scene 1.
80　Shakespeare, William. (1608). *Coriolanus*. Act 1, Scene 8.

'I thank you, General; But cannot make my heart consent to take a bribe to pay my sword: I do refuse it; And stand upon my common part with those. That have beheld the doing.'[81]

Humans ought to aspire to live a life according to the highest moral ideals. That is to say, live a life that strives to be virtuous in thought, speech, and conduct. Human nature consists of 'good' and 'evil' parts. Herein Shakespeare demonstrates how a virtuous person overcomes temptation and desire to commit a wrong by declaring an irrevocable oath against partaking in transgression. It is within our agency and free will, to act with regard to the consequences of our actions. Therefore, deliberation, good judgement, reason, knowledge, and wisdom must guide one's actions in this material world.

'He has in this action outdone his former deeds doubly.'[82]

Actions always speak louder than words. Noble, courageous, and selfless actions, are more worthy of praise and recognition, than self-interested, narrow-minded, and commercially motivated actions. Virtuous conduct is a way of thinking, a way of living, and above all, seeking to advance the Kingdom of God. There are no perfect people. However, each and every person ought to strive to become the best version of themselves. This is a moral duty that every person is capable of achieving in this lifetime.

'Death, that dark spirit, in its nervy arm doth lie, which, being advanced, declines, and then men die.'[83]

Death is an inevitable and inescapable reality for all people. Such is the human condition. Human life is defined by birth, infancy, youth, old age, pain, suffering, procreation, degeneration, and finally,

---

81   Shakespeare, William. (1608). *Coriolanus*. Act 1, Scene 9.
82   Shakespeare, William. (1608). *Coriolanus*. Act 2, Scene 1.
83   Shakespeare, William. (1608). *Coriolanus*. Act 2, Scene 1.

death. Since the question of death has a fixed and unchangeable answer, the most important obligation we have is to make the journey and experience of life a meaningful one. That is to say, every person ought to make the most out of their finite time on this planet. The greatest life is one of community service, charity, positive contribution to society, spiritual reflection, honourable conduct, righteousness, love, and moral excellence.

'It is held that valour is the chiefest virtue, and most dignifies the haver.' [84]

Valour, that is courage, is a supreme and admirable virtue. This is because courage is the outward expression of boldness, and it is commonly associated with selflessness. Often times, an individual shall fight for a higher cause that is greater than themselves, greater than life. The performance of courage, whether as a soldier on a battlefield, or a civilian rescuing a child from a burning house, symbolises that one has risked their own personal safety, and accepted that their selfless actions may result in their very death. However, such a person has proceeded forward on their course, resolved to seek victory in their just cause.

'Looked upon things precious as they were the common muck of the world.' [85]

All the things of this world, we shall leave behind. Regardless, they be highly-prized gold bullion bars, or alternatively, inconsequential grains of sand. Nothing is truly ours, but our possession of present time, which is slipping away constantly as we further move towards death. It is only the subjective and biased human assignment of an 'economic' value towards a particular phenomenon, that creates the basis for its commercial worth.

---

84   Shakespeare, William. (1608). *Coriolanus*. Act 2, Scene 2.
85   Shakespeare, William. (1608). *Coriolanus*. Act 2, Scene 2.

It is only within the purview of a minority of people to perceive the material world without distinction, without judgement, and without partiality. In the final analysis, all of Creation is God's Good Work. Everything within Creation serves God's Divine Purpose.

'Think upon me! Hang them! I would they forget me, like the virtues which our divines lose by them.' [86]

Coriolanus is a noble gentleman. He does not seek any glory or high praise for his virtue. Good actions, performed quietly, without the thought of recognition or merit, are always witnessed by God. Those individuals who are committed to the service of God's Sovereign Will, do not boast about their insignificant works, or inconsequential accomplishments.

One shall not perform virtuous deeds for the praise that they bring, for that is representative of a most shallow intention for one's conduct. For to seek security in the opinion of the common people is as uncertain as the forecast of the weather. Public opinion is always subject to the whims and fancies of the season. An honourable person ought to place unconditional trust in God, that they receive grace sufficient for their assignment. In the final analysis, all our names will inevitably be erased from the surface of this Earth. However, the Name of God shall dwell forever and ever, beyond the finite realm of the Universe.

'Why in this wolvish toge should I stand here, to beg of Hob and Dick, that does appear, their needless vouches? Custom calls me to it.' [87]

Often times our actions are dictated by the bounds of tradition. We perform or partake in certain rituals, socially accepted rites of passage, or entertain ceremonies, in order to secure social approval

---

86   Shakespeare, William. (1608). *Coriolanus.* Act 2, Scene 3.
87   Shakespeare, William. (1608). *Coriolanus.* Act 2, Scene 3.

from our peers within a community or institution. Normative behaviour serves to sustain the cultural practices and traditions of a society, however, where 'groupthink' is challenged and there is a sudden deviation from the status quo, then conflict and discord result. Coriolanus is fiercely independent and strong-willed. Thus, Coriolanus does not willingly submit to the mainstream Roman customs, conventions, traditions, and practices of his time.

'Let deeds express what's like to be their words.' [88]

Any person can express themselves sufficiently in speech. However, a minority of people let their actions dictate their thoughts and intentions, writ large. Furthermore, words can have 'double meaning'. Thus, there is the opportunity for considerable ambiguity in writing. As a result, the spoken or written word is subject to interpretation. On the contrary, actions are concrete, final, and irreversible. In any case, if we have the option to discern a person based on their deeds or words, the former is the 'gold standard' of the measurement of a person's true character.

'What is the city but the people?' [89]

A city consists of many attributes and properties, for example, consider commercial buildings, cultural monuments, high-rise apartments, court houses, prisons, hospitals, people, nursing homes, retirement villages, juvenile correction facilities, cemeteries, retail shops, restaurants, libraries, parliament, shopping centres, sports complex, churches, public parks, scenic walkways, outdoor reserves, museums, stadiums, auditoriums, gymnasiums, concert venues, universities, and historical sites. But most importantly, it is the 'people' that constitute a city. For a city can exist without all

---

88   Shakespeare, William. (1608). *Coriolanus*. Act 3, Scene 1.
89   Shakespeare, William. (1608). *Coriolanus*. Act 3, Scene 1.

the aforementioned things, albeit in an inferior state of anarchy, however, a city cannot exist, without the presence of its people.

'By the consent of all, we were established the People's Magistrates.'[90]

It is necessary to secure the consent of the people in order to derive legitimacy to govern in a democratic and liberal nation-state. The preordained 'Divine Right' of Kings and Queens no longer possesses the supreme authority to issue royal decrees, as a means of ruling the people. Rather, in the British Westminster system, political power is vested across the two Chambers of Parliament, the Prime Minister, the Cabinet, and the elected Members of Parliament. In the specific case of the Commonwealth of Australia, the Chief Justice and the Justices of the High Court of Australia are not elected by the consent of the people, rather, they are appointed by the Governor-General, acting upon the advice of the Executive Council and the Attorney-General.

Shakespeare is referring to 'magistrates' as the term was known and used during the time of Ancient Rome. The Roman Magistrate was a powerful and influential government officer. Such a learned person was vested with both judicial and executive powers. Even in Ancient Rome, the 'consent of the people' was a democratic principle that was upheld. Indeed, much of the modern Western Civilisation's Laws are founded upon the legal principles, doctrines, and maxims contained within Roman Law.

---

90   Shakespeare, William. (1608). *Coriolanus.* Act 3, Scene 1.

'Why do you wish me milder? Would you have me false to my nature? Rather say I play. The man I am.'[91]

Humans seek to enact change in other people through influence and persuasion. Perhaps, to make other individuals more like themselves. Yet, people need to unconditionally accept other individuals, for who they truly are. This approach leads to the creation of authentic relationships and genuine conversations.

A person can only ever 'become' the person they were meant to be. A person may not have God's Grace in every area of their life. In some areas a person may exhibit grace, for example, consider intelligence, beauty, or personal wealth. Whereas, in other areas, grace may be non-existent, for example, consider a person's biological children, personal relationships, or vocation. In the final analysis, it is not our place to pass judgement on God's Creation. However, we are to unconditionally accept God's Sovereign Will in action, in all things, and upon all people.

'You might have been enough the man you are, with striving less to be so.'[92]

Each person needs to accept themselves for who they are. We ought to be content with our unique gifts, abilities, skills, and natural endowments. It is excellent and commendable to strive to become the best version of ourselves. However, when we attempt to become what we are not, then we begin to run another person's race. A race that we are not equipped to run. As a result, we only finish achieving less than the 'fullness' of our capacity. Each individual is unique and original. No person is a replica of another person.

---

91 Shakespeare, William. (1608). *Coriolanus*. Act 3, Scene 2.
92 Shakespeare, William. (1608). *Coriolanus*. Act 3, Scene 2.

'Where is your ancient courage? You were used. To say extremity was the trier of spirits. That common chances common men could bear. That when the sea was calm all boats alike showed mastership in floating.'[93]

When life is proceeding according to our plans, and all of our personal affairs are in order, we have little cause for concern. People truly distinguish themselves according to the difficult circumstances they confront, and how they respond to such life-changing circumstances. It is only during the upheavals, the challenges, the difficult life issues, and during the 'do' or 'die' battles that we realise our full potential. Our remarkable inner capacity for resilience. Our determination and total resolve to surmount the insurmountable. Tenacity will test us, however, it will also enhance our personal growth and moral development.

'We are all undone, unless the noble man have mercy.'[94]

Justice and mercy ought to go hand in hand. Indeed, the deliverance of justice must be tempered by mercy. A noble person ought to have regard for and deference to the basic principles of jurisprudence. However, the undeserved allowance of compassion is the supreme virtue of a noble, learned, and courteous person. For without the presence of mercy and compassion, humanity shall lose its conscience.

From a purely legal perspective, one can peruse the detailed doctrines and critical discourse on 'Natural Law Theory' versus 'Legal Positivism'. However, without morality, there can be no humanity. Morality is the fundamental ground, not a consequential or secondary factor in the good governance of modern society. The ideal promotion of responsible government, and the furtherance of peaceful relations between individuals, is founded on morality.

---

93   Shakespeare, William. (1608). *Coriolanus*. Act 4, Scene 1.
94   Shakespeare, William. (1608). *Coriolanus*. Act 4, Scene 6.

'All bond and privilege of nature, break! Let it be virtuous to be obstinate.' [95]

We are all born with certain automatic relationships at the time of our birth, for example, consider mother, father, aunt, and uncle. However, inflexibility in relationships can result in detrimental damage to the relationships provisioned to us by our family heritage. At times, certain relationships can become 'unmanageable' or 'dysfunctional'. Thus, it becomes necessary, that the only course forward is to part ways. It is not entirely plausible that to be 'obstinate' is considered a virtue. However, Shakespeare has employed this term to reflect the strong and steadfast character of Coriolanus.

'Plough Rome and harrow Italy, I'll never. Be such a gosling to obey instinct, but stand. As if a man were author of himself. And knew no other kin.' [96]

Pride constitutes an impediment in our ability to make rational and sensible decisions. Here we witness the finality of Coriolanus' life, as he is tragically murdered in a duel. Coriolanus is true to his nature and character, till the very end of his life. Coriolanus does not sway or bend in his convictions or high moral principles. Coriolanus is determined to die for who he truly is, rather than to live, to become who he is not, by nature, supposed to be. Such is the heavy price to exact for an unyielding spirit, body, and mind. However, Coriolanus has exercised his agency to always live true to himself. True to the very last moment of his life.

---

95   Shakespeare, William. (1608). *Coriolanus.* Act 5, Scene 3.
96   Shakespeare, William. (1608). *Coriolanus.* Act 5, Scene 3.

Chapter 6

CYMBELINE

'Fortune brings in some boats that are not steered.'
SHAKESPEARE

Cymbeline is a compelling play that explores the themes and ideas of love, trust, seduction, integrity, deception, betrayal, morality, and forgiveness. The King of Ancient Britain, Cymbeline, is angered by the reality that his daughter, Imogen has married Posthumus. This marriage was against the goodwill of King Cymbeline. In response, King Cymbeline banishes Posthumus. While Posthumus is exiled, he strikes a wager on Imogen's faithfulness. Iachimo is the devious Roman gentleman with whom Posthumus makes his grand bargain. Iachimo is a cunning person, who attempts to seduce Posthumus' wife through dishonest means, and thereby, falsely prove that Imogen is an unfaithful wife.

While Imogen performs no wrong doing in her conduct with Iachimo, Iachimo gets his way with her through treachery. Most notably, Iachimo is able to perfectly describe Imogen's body, and he makes claim to the possession of her most treasured bracelet, which all but confirms, Iachimo has been in bed with Imogen. The remainder of this play deals with Imogen restoring her good name and regaining her esteemed reputation in society. In addition,

Imogen also discovers her long-lost brothers at the very end of this play.

In the final scenes of *Cymbeline*, Imogen is reunited with her faithful husband, Posthumus. To make the ending more memorable and honourable, the King enters into a peace pact with Rome. Once trust is damaged, it is often difficult to re-establish and repair one's prized reputation. Thus, quite rightly, Iachimo repents for his ignoble conduct and countless misdeeds. Posthumus is a compassionate and merciful person, and he forgives Iachimo for his immoral behaviour. Posthumus shows undeserving mercy towards Iachimo, and he lets Iachimo live. In the hope that Iachimo becomes a reformed person, and does good towards other people.

Cymbeline is a fascinating play that explores how human conduct is governed by jealousy, desire, lust, mercy, and betrayal. Importantly, this play also examines how the cherished bonds of marriage are tested, to their absolute limits.

'As I my poor self did exchange for you, to your so infinite loss, so in our trifles I still win of you.' [97]

It is possible that the institution of marriage be sealed between two unequal partners. That is to say, unequal by birth right, education, parentage, socio-economic class, status, political power, private property, personal wealth, vocation, personal income, and other distinguishing factors. However, each spouse brings something unique and special to a marriage. It is not the mere material factors that make love complete and perfect. Rather, it is the importance of non-material factors, that create the basis for a fulfilling and enduring relationship of equals, for example, consider intimacy, good conversation, attraction, respect, and admirable personality traits. What a person lacks in their material worth, such a person can account for in their character, demeanour, conduct, virtue, moral principles, and etiquette.

---

97 Shakespeare, William. (1611). *Cymbeline*. Act 1, Scene 1.

*'I am the Master of my speeches and I will undergo what's spoken.
I swear.'* [98]

The importance of thinking before speaking cannot be overstated.
A minority of people are true masters of their speech, for to be so,
one must speak with the use of reason, and not simply from how
one feels, or the unjust sway and power of emotions. Furthermore,
for a person to keep their spoken word on oath is a sign of trust
and integrity. This is an admirable and praiseworthy virtue. The
discharge of personal commitment requires the acceptance of
personal responsibility.

*'Blessed be those, how mean so ever, that have their honest wills,
which seasons comfort.'* [99]

Honesty is a noble quality that any person can express and practice,
without regard to sex, gender, faith, colour, personal wealth, level
of education, income, private property, social status, religious
affiliation, or any other distinguishing factor. However, while the
embrace of honesty is open to each and every person, it is seldom
practiced and rarely kept in the Modern World. A world which is
defined by greed, profit, self-interest, jealousy, wealth, and private
property. It is a perfect paradox, that honesty is open to all people,
yet it is only within the reach of a minority of people.

*'I'll write against them. Detest them. Curse them. Yet it is greater
skill in a true hate, to pray they have their will.'* [100]

Each person attempts to impose their will, on those people who are
around them. This dismal reality inevitably leads to much discord
and conflict amongst the members of a community or society.
No matter if a person harbours disdain for another person, it takes

---

98   Shakespeare, William. (1611). *Cymbeline.* Act 1, Scene 4.
99   Shakespeare, William. (1611). *Cymbeline.* Act 1, Scene 6.
100 Shakespeare, William. (1611). *Cymbeline.* Act 2, Scene 5.

a high level of maturity and remarkable sensibility to let another person effectuate their will, or simply, have their way in the day-to-day affairs of life. This approach can be a source of much inner peace and tranquillity. Indeed, one can save a significant quantity of time and energy, by being shrewd and selective in the exercise of judgement, when it comes to determining which battles to engage in, and which battles to disassociate from. Wisdom resides in discernment.

'Though those that are betrayed do feel the treason sharply, yet the traitor stands in worse case of woe.' [101]

This is an interesting statement by Shakespeare which highlights how injustice effects both the victim and the perpetrator. While the victim has much cause to feel saddened by the consequence of personal loss or damage to material possessions, physical harm to a person's body, or the infliction of psychological trauma, Shakespeare incorporates a second thought for the perpetrator of a criminal act. In the extreme case, the case of woe for the perpetrator may be capital punishment, or second to that, a life sentence of imprisonment, without the possibility of parole.

'Prithee, fair youth, think us no churls, nor measure our good minds by this rude place we live in.' [102]

Often humans are quick to reach an ill-informed conclusion, or to form an imprudent judgement concerning another person, simply on the basis of outward appearances or external observations. The force of circumstance may determine much about a person's life; however, it never defines who a person is (i.e., ideas, beliefs, values, character, faith, moral principles, and personality traits), or what a person is capable of accomplishing. To suspend judgement is a

---

101 Shakespeare, William. (1611). *Cymbeline.* Act 3, Scene 4.
102 Shakespeare, William. (1611). *Cymbeline.* Act 3, Scene 6.

sign of wisdom, albeit it is seldom practiced in modern society. In the contemporary age, people are all too quick to determine the importance of a person based on the ownership of material possessions that signify an exorbitant economic value, for example, consider the ownership of luxury motor vehicles, legal title to luxury penthouses, or the possession of luxury-branded personal goods.

'Society is no comfort to one not sociable.' [103]

By the interconnected function of nature, nurture, personality, parenting style, environment, genetics, and culture, some people are more accustomed to being alone. Certain people prefer their own company, rather than the company of other people. For some people, the state of solitude is preferable to society. After all, seclusion is for select people only.

On the other hand, some people are highly sociable individuals. Such individuals thrive when they are in the association of countless people at a birthday party, formal work function, wedding ceremony, sporting event, cultural festival, or in attendance at a music concert. It is important to acknowledge, that being 'alone' and 'loneliness' are two separate matters. A person can be accompanied by a group of a several dozen people and still feel lonely. For loneliness is an internal psychological state of being, it is a feeling. On the contrary, a person can be alone, however, not feel lonely.

There are several factors that contribute to how sociable a person is, such as genetics, personality, emotions, childhood development, intelligence, personal experiences, competing personal and professional priorities, self-esteem, employment, sporting commitments, and the individual requirement for personal belonging to an institution, association, or community.

---

103 Shakespeare, William. (1611). *Cymbeline*. Act 4, Scene 2.

'Our very eyes are sometimes like our judgements, blind.' [104]

Humans are quick to perceive, however, slow to examine. Accurate perception requires detailed observation, and sometimes repeated observation. Shakespeare makes a similar comparison with respect to human judgement. When we determine a judgement, it is not always correct and factual. We may have limited information in our possession. We may rely upon imprecise knowledge that is not grounded upon empirical evidence. Alternatively, we may determine judgements that do not concur with the fundamental principles and laws of natural science. Therefore, it is important to pause and reflect upon our initial impressions. Personal reflection gives us the opportunity to ruminate and better discern the assumptions that undergird our elementary analysis of the world, and all that is within it.

'Fortune brings in some boats that are not steered.' [105]

There are many different words for fortune, such as luck, chance, coincidence, and fate. While it is true that fortune does perform an inevitable and uncontrollable role in the determination of our life trajectory, we must exercise our agency and free will to steer our life trajectory, into the direction that we desire it to proceed. A person cannot leave the all-too-important course of life to the tides of chance and the winds of fortune. In the final analysis, 'uncertainty' and 'risk' are variables that will always be present in all major life decisions. Prudence resides in managing the presence of such inherent risk and assured uncertainty in our life.

---

104 Shakespeare, William. (1611). *Cymbeline*. Act 4, Scene 2.
105 Shakespeare, William. (1611). *Cymbeline*. Act 4, Scene 3.

'What pleasure, Sir, find we in life, to lock it from action and adventure?' [106]

Action is the basis of human life. For without action, we cease to be. We cease to exist. We also cease to create progress and move forward in our life. A life without adventure is both monotonous and unexciting. Adventure engenders passion, exhilaration, feeling, emotion, sensation, and the fullness of living life. Although action and adventure are essential ingredients for a life well-lived, it is equally important to stress the necessity of rest and recuperation. For the latter serves to prolong the human life span, but also increase the quality of life. Which, in turn, considerably enhances one's ability to experience greater action and adventure.

'Yourself so out of thought, and so overgrown, cannot be questioned.' [107]

Humans often tend to judge other individuals based on visible factors, such as age, sex, gender, race, colour, ethnicity, vocation, personal wealth, and many others. Shakespeare exposes the fallibility and frailty of human judgement. Often times, we are more likely than not to accept the spoken or written assertions of an elderly person. A person advanced in age. On the unfounded premise, that a wealth of life experience dictates unquestionable accuracy and perfect wisdom in a person's speech or writing. Unfortunately, the fullness of a person's natural lifespan alone, does not necessarily equate to genuine wisdom, learning, knowledge, expertise, or sound logic. We must look to the quality of a person's judgement and ability to reason.

---

106 Shakespeare, William. (1611). *Cymbeline.* Act 4, Scene 4.
107 Shakespeare, William. (1611). *Cymbeline.* Act 4, Scene 4.

'By medicine life may be prolonged, yet death will seize the Doctor too.' [108]

No person can escape the destined reality of death on Earth. All people are mortal, and this is a categorical fact, one that cannot be refuted or negated. Such is the fixed condition and unchangeable state of all life forms on Earth. Shakespeare makes clever use of an oxymoron. For it is the very moral duty and legal responsibility of Medical Doctors to save the lives of their patients. However, even the Medical Doctor, who provides life-saving medicine, surgery, and specialist treatment, such a learned and noble person is also subject to the reality of death. In the final analysis, no person is above or beyond the domain of death.

'Heaven mend all.' [109]

At times, extenuating events and unfortunate circumstances are wholly beyond the scope of human understanding. During such a scenario, we must pray to God, to grant us grace and undeserved mercy, so that we shall see ourselves through such tribulations and find reconciliation in our lives. In the interim, we must content ourselves with the unconditional promise found in the *Holy Bible*, specifically, in the *Book of Philippians* at Chapter 4, Verse 7: 'The Peace of God, which surpasses all understanding, will guard your hearts and your minds through Christ Jesus.'

'I am sorry for thee, by thine own tongue thou art condemned and must endure our law.' [110]

The importance of prudence in speech cannot be overstated. We need to exercise considerable care and proper judgement in what we say. Not to mention, our very speech can be used as testimony

---

108 Shakespeare, William. (1611). *Cymbeline*. Act 5, Scene 5.
109 Shakespeare, William. (1611). *Cymbeline*. Act 5, Scene 5.
110 Shakespeare, William. (1611). *Cymbeline*. Act 5, Scene 5.

against us in legal proceedings. It is essential that we take a moment to adequately reflect upon a question that is placed before our consideration. If unsure, we must clarify what is being asked of us, and then provide an adequate answer that does not put oneself in jeopardy.

Shakespeare brings to our conscious attention that 'self-incrimination' is not just a hypothetical idea, or a theoretical concept of jurisprudence. Self-incrimination is a very plausible scenario that any person can be subject to during court proceedings. Therefore, vigilance and attentiveness are the best safeguards to prevent such a legal tragedy from occurring.

> *'Kneel not to me. The power I have on you is to spare you. The malice towards you, to forgive you. Live! And deal with others better.'* [111]

To show forgiveness and mercy unto another person, when they have done us wrong is a brave act. This is not an act for the faint-hearted. For it is always more convenient to hold on to the sense of injustice and the thought of being wronged. It takes considerable maturity and practical wisdom to ascertain, that by the very act of forgiving a person, we have ended the destructive psychological cycle, whereby, the person who has hurt us once, can continue to hurt us countless times in our subconscious thoughts. In genuine forgiveness, all parties can secure peace over conflict. It is an honourable virtue to create a sincere and lasting peace.

---

111 Shakespeare, William. (1611). *Cymbeline*. Act 5, Scene 5.

Chapter 7

HAMLET

'Lord, we know what we are, but know not what we may be.'
SHAKESPEARE

Shakespeare's *Hamlet* is one of the most popular and well-known of his outstanding plays. This brilliant play is a tragedy. *Hamlet* narrates the story of the spirit of the deceased King of Denmark, which instructs his beloved son, Prince Hamlet, to avenge the King's unjust death at the hands of Claudius. Regrettably, Claudius is a mischievous gentleman and traitor to the sovereign state of Denmark. Claudius has murdered the King of Denmark, in order to secure his illegitimate accession to the Danish Throne.

Once Claudius murders the King of Denmark, he is crowned the new Sovereign of Denmark. Shortly thereafter, Claudius marries Gertrude, who is the Queen of Denmark. This arrangement is a 'marriage of convenience'. Far beyond the artificial appearance of love, marriage allows Gertrude to remain the Queen of Denmark, and it also serves to legitimise Claudius' rise to power.

This story is a fascinating account of the twists and turns as Prince Hamlet seeks to exact his revenge, for the cruel death of his father, the late King of Denmark. Upon Hamlet's mind, we witness the great psychological burden of the cold-blooded murder of his father. Often times, Prince Hamlet is delusional, ambivalent, and disoriented. Not to mention, Hamlet is misunderstood by his close friends. Throughout the entire course of this play, King Claudius harbours his suspicions of Prince Hamlet. Thus, Claudius conceives to plot the death of Hamlet. As an interim solution, Claudius decides to banish Hamlet to England.

In the finality of this play, we witness the ultimate triumph of tragedy in human affairs. In the last scene, there is a duel in which Prince Hamlet and Laertes are both killed, along with the death of King Claudius and Queen Gertrude. Thus, it is so, that the spirit of the former King of Denmark can now rest in peace. The drama of *Hamlet* is a remarkable story of what we sow is what we reap. Furthermore, each person is personally responsible for their actions. While justice might be deferred, it is never discarded.

'Let not thy Mother lose her prayers, Hamlet. Stay with us. Go not to Wittenberg.' [112]

A mother always desires to keep her children close to her. The love of a mother transcends all boundaries, natural and artificial. The highest love in this world is the love of God. The second highest love is that established between a mother and her beloved children.

'Foul deeds will rise. Though all the Earth overwhelm them, to men's eyes.' [113]

On the surface level, a person can purport to hide their unlawful or immoral conduct. However, sooner or later, the Truth is bound to arise. This is an inevitable fact of life. A person can proceed to extreme lengths to cover up their misdeeds. Yet, some trace or element of a crime is always left at the scene. Thus, it is only a matter of time, before the perpetrator of ill deeds comes to light.

---

112 Shakespeare, William. (1603). *Hamlet.* Act 1, Scene 2.
113 Shakespeare, William. (1603). *Hamlet.* Act 1, Scene 2.

Before committing an evil deed, a person ought to think twice. Perchance, reason oneself out of executing such a hideous act.

> *'His greatness weighed; his will is not his own. For he himself is subject to his birth.'* [114]

Humans are a product of their will, the inner essence of a person, the true foundation of the being of a person. A person's will can never be their own. Rather, it is that a person is the complete expression of their will. The latter component of this proposition acknowledges that each person is born into their worldly reality. For example, consider a person is born into their gender, genetics, colour, deoxyribonucleic acid, sex, race, ethnicity, family environment, parentage (i.e., mother and father), social class, culture, language, heritage, religion, society, and nation-state. While a person's life trajectory is not completely determined at the time of birth, the aforementioned factors provide a substantial contribution in the stages of infancy and early childhood development of a person.

> *'Beware of entrance to a quarrel. Give every man thy ear, but few thy voice. Take each man's censure, but reserve thy judgement.'* [115]

A person must exercise prudence in becoming involved in the internal affairs of other people, for it can lead to unintended consequences. A sagacious person will listen to all people, however, is selective to whom their speech is given. To provision every person our hearing results in much learning and gathering of information. On the other hand, to give every person our speech can result in situations where there is a breach of trust, or one is taken advantage of. The final part of this assertion proposes, that it is wise to listen to the disapproval of other people. For in doing so, we will gain an awareness of our shortcomings. On the contrary, we ought to be

---

114 Shakespeare, William. (1603). *Hamlet.* Act 1, Scene 3.
115 Shakespeare, William. (1603). *Hamlet.* Act 1, Scene 3.

modest in our criticism of other individuals. This approach avoids unnecessary quarrels in society.

> '*Neither a borrower nor a lender be, for loan oft loses both itself and friend, and borrowing dulls the edge of husbandry.*'[116]

Dealing in financial capital always leads to problems. It does not matter if one borrows or lends money. For in the case one borrows money, one confronts financial difficulties, such as being unable to repay personal debts. In the other scenario, where one is a lender of money, one may not earn interest revenue, and in the worst case, not recover the principal amount of money that was lent. Thus, both borrowing and lending comes with considerable financial risk. Shakespeare employs an interesting metaphor in his literature. Shakespeare suggests borrowing money 'dulls the edge' of husbandry. More likely than not, Shakespeare makes the case that the financial stresses and endless burdens of debt can inadvertently impact marriage and cause spousal conflict.

> '*This above all. To thine own self be true.*'[117]

This is one of the simplest quotes of Shakespeare's entire literary canon, however, it is immensely profound in its meaning. First and foremost, each person has a moral obligation to be true to themselves. We cannot become someone else, other than who we are destined to be. In order to realise one's destiny, a person must truly embrace themselves, with their faults, shortcomings, weaknesses, strengths, skills, aptitude, talents, beliefs, values, motivations, personality traits, psychological drives, abilities, gifts, natural endowments, and capacities.

In all things, we have to be true to who we are. Authenticity is the key to a life well-lived. In the final analysis, we must create

---

116 Shakespeare, William. (1603). *Hamlet*. Act 1, Scene 3.
117 Shakespeare, William. (1603). *Hamlet*. Act 1, Scene 3.

a meaningful life that affirms our identity, and promotes a sense of acceptance of who we are. It is wholly within the initiative and agency of each and every person to construct their external reality. A reality which reflects an individual's inner will.

'If thou didst ever thy Dear Father love … revenge his foul and most unnatural murder.'[118]

Prince Hamlet's deceased father, the King of Denmark, is giving Hamlet the clearest instruction to avenge his most cruel and unjust cold-blooded murder. The spirit of Hamlet's father cannot find peace, nor rest, until it has secured its vengeance. While Hamlet's father's spirit is rightly aggrieved, one has to disassociate from the destructive cycle of seeking revenge and inflicting endless destruction in the world. The curse of murder can never be removed by inflicting another murder. Only forgiveness and mercy can set one free from the far-reaching boundaries of sin that enmesh this world in endless conflict and war.

'There are more things in Heaven and Earth, Horatio, than are dreamt of in your philosophy.'[119]

A person's philosophy reflects their unique cognition, beliefs, views, ideas, knowledge, ideologies, values, and experiences. It is an important reflective learning exercise to appreciate that each person's perception of the material world is limited to their thoughts. It is not possible for a person's philosophy to capture the entirety of the Universe, Heaven, or Earth for that matter.

The human imagination knows no bounds. However, the true essence of existential reality is always subjective, it is never objectively perceived. This is the case, because in the final analysis, we are not independent of our particular perception of the external

---

118 Shakespeare, William. (1603). *Hamlet*. Act 1, Scene 5.
119 Shakespeare, William. (1603). *Hamlet*. Act 1, Scene 5.

world. However, we are in and of this world. That is to say, we are dependent upon the very world that we wish to examine and understand. Therefore, we can never perceive the world for what it truly is, for we are reliant upon it for our very existence. Put another way, human life is contingent upon the material world for its survival. Therefore, the human civilisation is unable to perceive this world impartially and objectively.

'I assure you my good liege. I hold my duty as I hold my soul, both to my God and my King.' [120]

Based on our position, rank, and status in modern society, we all have duties and obligations, some are moral, while others are legal, or fiduciary in their nature. Our first and foremost duty is to God, and second to that, to the King or Queen of our sovereign nation-state. From a strictly legal perspective, the Law of Obligations and Contracts, defines how parties ought to conduct themselves in fulfilling the agreed terms of a legally enforceable covenant or contractual undertaking.

Legal agreements have the 'Force of Law' and must be discharged in good faith. In the event that one party breaches the articles of an agreement, then remedies, or penalties can be sought by the wronged party, for damage or loss that is suffered. In a similar manner, there are also moral duties in the function of modern society. For example, consider the duty of love and affection that parents owe to their children.

'And yet in my youth, I suffered much extremity for love.' [121]

During the adolescence stage of life, emotions, passions, feelings, and desires for the opposite sex are heightened. Often times, a person is prepared to proceed to extreme lengths in order to

---

120 Shakespeare, William. (1603). *Hamlet.* Act 2, Scene 2.
121 Shakespeare, William. (1603). *Hamlet.* Act 2, Scene 2.

demonstrate their love and affection for the person they truly admire. Courtship requires much persistence and tenacity, however, during this protracted process, one can experience much suffering from heartbreak, rejection, and uncertainty.

The pursuit of love is irrational. Once love is found, it is most uncertain to last. A person may suffer considerable psychological distress from the pursuit of love. However, while the observable behaviour of courtship is somewhat irrational at times, one is almost always willing to continue the pursuit. Indeed, to love is to live a life filled with passion, desire, emotion, sensation, and feeling.

'For there is nothing either good or bad, but thinking makes it so.'[122]

An object in and of itself is not good or evil, however, it is the partial cognition of the subject (i.e., the perceiver), that makes it appear so. Often, our thought gives rise to judgement which is biased. In fact, the entire world is a subjective perception of the individual. The world is what we make of it. The outer world is the complete expression of our inner will.

For example, consider the socio-economic phenomenon of financial capital in modern society. Now financial capital can be utilised for good ends, that is to alleviate poverty, eliminate hunger, prevent sickness, cure diseases, secure medical treatment, or make charitable donations. Alternatively, financial capital can be utilised for evil ends, such as the purchase of weapons, terrorism, illicit substance abuse, or the promotion of violence and crime. Thought gives rise to action, and so it is in the aforesaid example, that our particular thought of financial capital, determines our utility of it.

---

122 Shakespeare, William. (1603). *Hamlet.* Act 2, Scene 2.

'The spirit that I have seen may be a Devil, and the Devil hath power to assume a pleasing shape.' [123]

Humans must be vigilant of the Devil's clever schemes, contrived tricks, and most deceptive plots. The Devil has the powerful agency to deceive the individual, and mislead a person. What is extremely pleasing to the eyes, makes a beautiful sense impression on the individual's mind, and this can cause a person to undertake actions, without the proper exercise of reason. Indeed, the power of the Devil challenges the finite capacity of the power of human judgement. In all scenarios, it is best advice to execute an action with proper consideration for its consequences.

'To be, or not to be? That is the question—whether it is noble in the mind to suffer the slings and arrows of outrageous fortune, or to take arms against a sea of troubles, and by opposing end them? To die ... to sleep ... no more, and by a sleep to say we end the heartache ... and the thousand natural shocks that flesh is heir to, it is a consummation devoutly to be wished. To die ... to sleep.' [124]

Shakespeare is addressing one of the fundamental existential questions of philosophy. Is it desirable for humans to exist? Alternatively, is the state of non-existence more desirable? For existence, that is, the state of being, provisions humanity with a plethora of vexations, disturbances, pain, and suffering, which are all part and parcel of the human condition. Whereas, in the alternative scenario. Not to exist. Not to be. This reality ceases all the known and possible tribulations associated with the human condition.

In the final analysis, suffering is an inevitable part of human reality. However, a person can exercise the sensibility of reason and good judgement, to alleviate or minimise the incidence of suffering

---

123 Shakespeare, William. (1603). *Hamlet*. Act 2, Scene 2.
124 Shakespeare, William. (1603). *Hamlet*. Act 3, Scene 1.

in this world. In addition, there are many positive dimensions of the human condition, which are equally important to emphasise. For example, consider joy, happiness, serenity, excitement, love, inspiration, and above all, hope.

'Or if thou wilt needs marry, marry a fool. For wise men know well enough what monsters you make of them. To a nunnery, go, and quickly too. Farewell.' [125]

This is a significant and life-changing question that each person must answer for themselves: To marry, or not to marry? The female and male sex are more likely than not to entertain disagreements and possibly the incidence of spousal (or partner) conflict during the course of a marriage, or any other type of intimate relationship. Having said that, disagreements can also constitute the ground for a fundamental change of perceptions and personal growth of both partners in a relationship. It is best counsel for both parties to constructively work together and through the personal challenges and relationship issues that they confront. Where appropriate, the parties can seek professional guidance.

Regardless of the type of issues confronting a married couple, active listening, unconditional love, and non-judgemental support are the critical success factors in the creation of a loving and enduring marriage. These aforementioned factors are often overlooked in today's fast-paced, super-connected, and information-rich Modern World of social media, the internet, smartphone applications, endless technology, and virtual reality. Yet, for some people, marriage is simply not an option, it never was, and it never will be. Each to their own.

---

125 Shakespeare, William. (1603). *Hamlet.* Act 3, Scene 1.

*'For thou hast been as one, in suffering all, that suffers nothing.
A man that fortune's buffest and rewards hast taken with equal
thanks, and blest are those whose blood and judgement are so
well commeddled that they are not a pipe for fortune's fingers to
sound what stop she pleases.'* [126]

Humans need to appreciate the hands of fortune impact their lives
for good and evil. It is easier said than done, however, humans need
to control their response and reaction to the swings of fortune.
It is within the agency of all people, however, only a minority of
people exercise control over their mind, to regulate their response
to fortune's most cruel blows, and this is what Shakespeare signifies,
when he writes, 'blest are those … they are not a pipe for fortune's
fingers to sound what stop she pleases.'

For a wise person does not react to the highs and lows that
fortune posits before such a person. A sagacious person shall not
'play the sound', nor the specific 'musical note' at which fortune's
'fingers stop'. This is a simple metaphorical illustration, however,
such mastery over body, mind, speech, thought, and action is
often considerably difficult to demonstrate. For humans have their
emotions, sensations, and feelings, that are capable of swaying
the rationality of reason towards the irrationality of strong sense
impressions.

*'Give me that man that is not passion's slave, and I will wear him
in my heart's core.'* [127]

It is a mark of rarity for a person to transcend the human condition.
Each person has their desires, feelings, sensations, impressions,
emotions, ideas, and thoughts. A person that is not a slave to
passion has, in effect, overcome the base instinct, the animality,
the concupiscence that constitutes a troublesome reality for much

---

126 Shakespeare, William. (1603). *Hamlet*. Act 3, Scene 2.
127 Shakespeare, William. (1603). *Hamlet*. Act 3, Scene 2.

of the human civilisation. Such a sagacious person is most worthy of wearing in a person's heart. For that person is the epitome of a moral and noble life.

> *'In the corrupted currents of this world offences gilded hand may shove by justice, and oft it is seen the wicked prize itself buys out the law.'* [128]

In this world, the deliverance of natural justice is not always weighed by the set of impartial and blind scales. There is considerable income, personal wealth, and private property inequality in modern society. The institution of law can be circumvented, and the scales of justice weighed in favour of the unjust party. The presence of social injustice is a fact and reality. For all the laws of a sovereign nation-state constitute a social, economic, legal, and political construction.

Laws represent a set of formal and codified rules that are formed and interpreted by learned jurists, magistrates, justices, practicing lawyers, honourable senators, and learned professors. The function of Legal Positivism reigns supreme in this world. Unfortunately, the all-too-ideal Doctrine of Natural Law is a theoretical fiction. A fiction that is far beyond the finite capacity of human nature (and reason) to realise on Earth.

> *'There the action lies in his true nature, and we ourselves compelled, even to the teeth and forehead of our faults to give in evidence.'* [129]

Every individual acts in accordance with their innate nature. It is very difficult, almost nigh impossible, for a person to act outside of their true nature. Humans are partly 'instinctual' and partly 'rational' in their behaviour. However, instinct always comes first. Instinct is the natural disposition of the two distinct dispositions

---

128 Shakespeare, William. (1603). *Hamlet.* Act 3, Scene 3.
129 Shakespeare, William. (1603). *Hamlet.* Act 3, Scene 3.

of human behaviour. Instinct is innate, it is not learned, nor does it require the use of human thought, or the higher powers of the mental faculties. On the contrary, the powers of reason, logic, and judgement need to be refined and developed, this can only be achieved through their repeated employment and exercise, combined with knowledge, learning, experience, and wisdom.

> *'Confess yourself to Heaven. Repent what's past. Avoid what is to come, and do not spread the compost on the weeds to make them ranker.'* [130]

Humans are imperfect. We all make mistakes in the course of our life. Therefore, it is imperative that we reflect upon and learn from our experiences, assume personal responsibility for our actions and their consequences. Confession is a spiritual form of self-disclosure to God. Confession also allows us the opportunity to reflect on our shortcomings and improve our self-awareness. Confession helps to build a person's character and sense of moral integrity. In order to find forgiveness, first we need to humble ourselves and sincerely confess our countless transgressions.

Shakespeare proceeds one step further by mentioning, 'avoid what is to come'. Herein Shakespeare is referring to the conscious process of 'learning from one's mistakes'. By the accumulation of experience, knowledge, education, reflection, and wisdom, we can all exercise prudence. This will allow us to refrain from participating in evil deeds, or engaging in questionable actions in the future. Last but not least, figuratively speaking, we must not allow 'weeds' to flourish in our life. We must not provide 'weeds' with the requisite opportunity to proliferate and strengthen.

---

130 Shakespeare, William. (1603). *Hamlet.* Act 3, Scene 4.

'I must be cruel only to be kind.' [131]

This is an interesting idiom, for it possesses a double meaning and it is open to interpretation. On face value, it is irrational for a person to employ cruel means, in order to secure a good outcome. However, there are a narrow and finite set of circumstances, where such thought deserves some merit. For example, consider the following scenario in the specialist field of Emergency Medicine. If a patient is confronting the prospect of their imminent death, due to the advanced stages of a deadly disease, or the presence of a debilitating medical condition, then the execution of 'extreme measures' shall be entirely necessary and may represent the only plausible option to save that patient's life.

Now with respect to the aforementioned medical scenario, considered in complete isolation, without proper regard to the patient's personal circumstances, the medical emergency context, and the provision of sound medical advice by an experienced and qualified surgeon, then the undertaking of 'extreme measures' may constitute a cruel act. However, the end result herein is to prolong the patient's life. To save an individual's life. This is a good outcome, one which wholly justifies the means. Therefore, in certain circumstances, it may be permissible to be cruel, if, and only if, the desired objective is to perform a greater good, that promotes a benefit which exceeds the total incidence of harm to the patient.

'What is a man if his chief good and market of his time be but to sleep and feed?' [132]

Each and every person must strive to accomplish some significant endeavour in their finite lifetime. To find and pursue one's passion and purpose is the fulfilment of human life and spirit. The simple regenerative and biological processes of sleeping, consuming

---

131 Shakespeare, William. (1603). *Hamlet.* Act 3, Scene 4.
132 Shakespeare, William. (1603). *Hamlet.* Act 4, Scene 4.

adequate hydration and nutrition, they only represent the fulfilment of our basic survival needs. A person must live for much more than the satisfaction of the physiological needs of human life.

Each person has the unprecedented opportunity to 'leave their mark' on this world, to actively, in the present moment, in the here and now, take conscious steps to 'create their legacy'. In the words of American psychologist, Abraham Maslow, 'self-actualisation' constitutes the ultimate fulfilment of human life. Self-actualisation is an ideal every person ought to strive towards accomplishing. It is within us, indeed, it is our obligation, to ensure that we reach our inherent potential in life. It is incumbent upon us, to ensure that our life is well-lived. That our existence is made meaningful.

> '*Now, whether it be bestial oblivion, or some craven scruple of thinking too precisely on the event, I do not know why, yet I live to say, this thing's to do. Sith I have cause, and will, and strength, and means to do it.*'[133]

A firm personal conviction, strength of spirit, and an unyielding mind. These are the essential elements to successfully accomplishing a desired mission or intended objective. From the outset, a person cannot know the exact outcome of their efforts, however, the attempt must be made. Otherwise, the achievement of success is not a plausible outcome.

At times, it is best not to over-analyse our decision-making process. We ought to consciously reflect on our instinct, judgement, reason, and seek the counsel of a trusted advisor in our affairs. Most importantly, we must do what is right. Right in thought, speech, and action. Simply because we possess the 'cause, will, strength, and means' to execute an action, does not constitute sufficient ground for such an action to be performed. The execution of action must be contingent upon good moral intentions.

---

133 Shakespeare, William. (1603). *Hamlet*. Act 4, Scene 4.

'Rightly to be great is not to stir without great argument, but greatly to find quarrel in a straw when honour's at the stake.' [134]

According to medieval custom, honour is worth fighting for, and if need be, dying for. Learned and honourable people will attend to matters of significant importance, and shun concerns of inconsequential or no importance. However, for the defence of honour, even a trivial matter is worth the duel. For honour is a most noble virtue. One that is worthy of protection in and of itself. The preservation of honour is not contingent upon any particular phenomenon or action that gives rise to a concern between two or more parties.

'Lord, we know what we are, but know not what we may be.' [135]

A person is the reflection of their moral, genetic, hereditary, and intellectual constitution. However, we do not consciously know what we may be, for that is contingent upon the very act, or conscious process of becoming, or the conscious realisation of one's true being. This is a psychological process of Discovery of the Self. It can take a lifetime to realise one's true and final potential. To accomplish what we may be. To discover and embrace the Self. This is the complete expression and the actualisation of the fullness of human life. If one knows and becomes what one may be. That is the privilege of a lifetime.

'We must be patient, but I cannot choose but weep.' [136]

Shakespeare's writing reflects the dismal reality of human life. Shakespeare's clever employment of a simple juxtaposition opposes and contrasts human nature. It is ideal and admirable to think upon patience, when our affairs do not align with our inner will

---

134 Shakespeare, William. (1603). *Hamlet.* Act 4, Scene 4.
135 Shakespeare, William. (1603). *Hamlet.* Act 4, Scene 5.
136 Shakespeare, William. (1603). *Hamlet.* Act 4, Scene 5.

or personal intentions. However, more often than not, we become aggrieved by our circumstances. We can feel overwhelmed by a lack of control over our life trajectory. While we desire and pray for patience, we cannot help but fall to the surface reality of the human condition. A worldly reality that is sometimes defined by grief, sorrow, pain, suffering, and heartache.

> *'When sorrows come, they come not single spies but in battalions.'* [137]

Shakespeare's intelligent employment of a metaphor demonstrates the distressing reality of grief. Rarely, if ever, is grief compartmentalised and contained. Grief is more often than not, overwhelming and made worse by a multitude of factors that create sorrow in our lives. The causes of bereavement in our life are limitless. Some of these include, death of a loved one, divorce, abortion, diagnosis of a life-threatening medical condition, loss of employment, bankruptcy, imprisonment, late intrauterine fetal death, entering into a new phase of life (for example, consider the onset of retirement), or an unexpected event or personal crisis (for example, a motor vehicle accident).

> *'Nature is fine in love, and where it is fine, it sends some precious instance of itself after the thing it loves.'* [138]

The intricacies and depths of nature are revealed to us in love. For in the act of love and attraction, the natural act of copulation is effectuated. Thus, reproduction takes place. This is wherein the secrets of nature, 'send some precious instance of itself after the thing it loves.' The very intimate act of copulation is nature's art, and it ensures the survival of the human species.

---

137 Shakespeare, William. (1603). *Hamlet.* Act 4, Scene 5.
138 Shakespeare, William. (1603). *Hamlet.* Act 4, Scene 5.

'And where the offence is let the great axe fall.' [139]

This is a self-explanatory statement. One that can be interpreted as a platitude. In order for justice to be discharged, then the lawful punishment must be inflicted upon the offender, in accordance with the gravity of the criminal offence. Although not expressly stated by Shakespeare, there is also the real possibility of 'the great axe falling, where the offence is not'. As a consequence, we confront the legal dilemma known as a 'miscarriage of justice'.

'No place, indeed, should murder sanctuarise. Revenge should know no bounds.' [140]

The immoral (and illegal) act of murder must never result in a place being sanctified by such a horrendous act. No place should be sanctified by the shedding of innocent blood. No place ought to be sanctuarised by the act of murder, period. When attempted murder does effectuate, it can give rise to an ill-thought, within the aggrieved party's mind to seek revenge. Regrettably, the pursuit of revenge has no limits, until its mission has been fulfilled. Therefore, the best advice herein is, never give evil a foothold in our thoughts.

'Nature her custom holds. Let shame say what it will.' [141]

The enduring institution of nature acts out of purpose. Nature has no regard for the presence of ignominy. A classic example is the natural act of copulation amongst the members of the human species. A person may feel shame discussing the topic of sexual intercourse. For sex is still considered a taboo topic across some countries, continents, and cultures in the contemporary world.

Furthermore, in almost all countries, continents, and cultures, both within the civilised world, and the remaining uncivilised or

---

139 Shakespeare, William. (1603). *Hamlet*. Act 4, Scene 5.
140 Shakespeare, William. (1603). *Hamlet*. Act 4, Scene 7.
141 Shakespeare, William. (1603). *Hamlet*. Act 4, Scene 7.

natural societies, a person's sexual organs of reproduction are covered and concealed from the public sphere of society. For one ought to feel shame for one's nakedness. Nonetheless, nature has its way with all the species. Thus, the overriding force, the powerful natural instinct of sexual attraction decrees, that members of the human species copulate, and thereby, reproduce.

'Alexander died. Alexander was buried. Alexander returned into dust. The dust is Earth, of Earth we make loam ... Imperious Caesar, dead and turned to clay, might stop a hole to keep the wind away.' [142]

Ultimately, all the things of this world, and all the people belonging to the human civilisation pass away and turn into dust. Such is the inevitable outcome of all transient matter in this world. In the end, everything on the Earth shall perish. Nothing is permanent, enduring, or destined to last for eternity. Even the most remarkable members of the human civilisation, Alexander the Great, Aristotle, Boudica, Julius Caesar, Catherine the Great, Cleopatra, Elizabeth I, Queen Hatshepsut, Paul the Apostle, Plato, and Socrates, are no more. They are nothing, but ashes mixed with the Earth. From whence they came, they return. All of humanity is returned to naught, for all humans are mortal. No person shall escape the predestined reality of birth and death.

'Let us know, our indiscretion sometimes serves us well when our deep plots do pall.' [143]

At times, a person's indiscretion can perform to their advantage. In particular, when such a person's malignant or deceptive plots are spoiled. In any case, one shall reap what they sow. The Universal Law

---

142 Shakespeare, William. (1603). *Hamlet.* Act 5, Scene 1.
143 Shakespeare, William. (1603). *Hamlet.* Act 5, Scene 2.

of *Karma* is an inescapable reality for all people. Individuals need to think and act with prudence. For all actions have consequences, both intended and unintended.

'But to know a man well were to know himself.' [144]

Humans are often fearful to explore their inner psychology. The intricate working of the heart and mind of the Self. The complex constitution of being is often shunned from thorough introspection and detailed examination. Therefore, it is only a minority of the human population that come to ascertain who they truly are. The majority of people circumvent the great depths of the human condition with mindless amusement, entertainment, and trivial activity. Indeed, it is not for the faint-hearted to enter into the abyss of the human condition. To know and understand oneself, truly and wholly, this is an astounding accomplishment of a lifetime. The entire human life is a struggle against the Self. To overcome the Self. To conquer the Self. To make peace with the Self. This is the greatest victory.

'For me, with sorrow I embrace my fortune.' [145]

The dismal reality for some people is that chance or fate has not dealt them with a favourable 'deck of cards' in this lifetime. Regardless of the operation of fate or destiny, it is within our agency and capacity to determine how we respond, and therefore, make the most out of our lot in life. We can accept our lot in life with sorrow and misery, or we can accept it with joy, optimism, and hope. The wisdom resides in how we perceive our fortune. Our mindset has the power to shape our worldly reality, for the better, or for the worse.

---

144 Shakespeare, William. (1603). *Hamlet*. Act 5, Scene 2.
145 Shakespeare, William. (1603). *Hamlet*. Act 5, Scene 2.

Chapter 8

HENRY IV (PART ONE)

'*The better part of valour is discretion.*'

SHAKESPEARE

Shakespeare's *Henry IV* is a two-part play. The first part focuses on the reign of His Majesty King Henry IV of England. This play covers English History from the *Battle of Homildon Hill* (1402), and it ends with the *Battle of Shrewsbury* (1403). This captivating play incorporates a variety of themes, including honour, nobility, wealth, prestige, power, war, deception, pride, and rebellion.

His Majesty King Richard II is deceased, and Henry Bolingbroke has now been crowned as King Henry IV. However, King Henry IV has many troubles and domestic concerns to attend to, which threaten the very existence of his rule as the newly appointed Sovereign of England. The Honourable Percy Family, which assisted Henry to the throne, are now proving to be newfound opposition to Henry's rule. Aside from the unavoidable quarrels with the nobility, Scotland and Wales now openly threaten rebellion against King Henry IV. Furthermore, King Henry's condescending treatment of Henry Percy, the Earl of Northumberland's son, who is known as Hotspur, only serves to add to the ever-growing list of problems that King Henry IV now confronts.

This play narrates how a sovereign's grip on power is ever-diminishing and fleeting. Conflict and hostility are an inevitable and inescapable reality that King Henry IV has to contend with throughout his reign. In this play, Shakespeare brings to the forefront of our conscious mind, the very inner essence of our human nature. Our unending desire for power, wealth, property, influence, and fame. We witness the very self-centredness of egoistic behaviour. The tragedy of conflict. The outbreak of war. The testing of loyalty. Not to mention, the heart-breaking realities of the betrayal of trust. A great deal is learned about the basic principles of anthropology, from carefully perusing this masterpiece of English Literature.

'I will from henceforth rather be myself.' [146]

This statement signifies what we all ought to do, but often neglect to do well. The majority of people are conscious, perhaps over-conscious, of what other people think about them. While self-image, perception, and managing expectations matter, we have a superior obligation to be true to ourselves. In order to realise our full potential, and to embrace the fullness of our individual being, we must walk in our footsteps and tread the unique path of our own journey. A person can never realise their full potential, as long as they let the changing perceptions and unfounded opinions of other people define them.

'When we need your use and counsel, we shall send for you.' [147]

Such is the reality of a commercial, transactional, secular, corporate, and commoditised modern society. For we only tend to

---

146 Shakespeare, William. (1598). *Henry IV, Part One.* Act 1, Scene 3.
147 Shakespeare, William. (1598). *Henry IV, Part One.* Act 1, Scene 3.

think of someone when we have a requirement for their service or advice. Benevolence is fast-diminishing in our Modern World. The hospitable thought and sincere regard for one another, for our dear brothers and sisters, is being demoted to the concept of 'economic utility'.

Rational economic thought is fast replacing the universality of love in the Modern World. The narrow-mindedness of humanity, coupled with the finite limits of the human intellect, have supposedly forgotten the ancient and common thread of humanity. That is to say, we are all equal members of the human civilisation. The heart of humanity must always triumph over the coldness of commerciality. When it comes to social relations between individuals, humanity must never forget its conscience.

'Imagination of some great exploit drives him beyond the bounds of patience.' [148]

The human imagination has no real boundaries. In our minds, we can explore limitless opportunities to create and manifest our external worldly reality. It is imperative to acknowledge that the imagination can be utilised for both good and evil. Therefore, we must act with diligence and exercise care to ensure our thoughts and actions have a positive moral grounding. We must make this world a better place.

'Instinct is a great matter.' [149]

Instinct is definitely not an inconsequential matter. For instinct informs our thought, speech, and behaviour. Instinct guides our interactions with other people. Instinct is responsible for our initial reaction to external stimuli, or our immediate response to an unexpected event. The modern civilised world has suppressed

---

148 Shakespeare, William. (1598). *Henry IV, Part One.* Act 1, Scene 3.
149 Shakespeare, William. (1598). *Henry IV, Part One.* Act 2, Scene 4.

the operation of instinct in human affairs. Now humans are more commonly guided by the instruments of reason, logic, and judgement.

The application of international law, commercial practices of trade, established rules of commerce, the indispensable function of multinational corporations, standardised employment contracts, and criminal and civil codes in sovereign nation-states, all collectively function to render human behaviour more predictable, routine, rational, and consistent.

In the contemporary world, people are guided in their decision-making by an understanding and awareness of rewards and punishment. Expectations of the performance of a contract. Actions that are lawful and unlawful. The receipt of profits, royalties, salary, interest income, wages, annuity payments, rent, pecuniary gains, employer superannuation contributions, and the payment of fines, taxes, duties, and penalties. Indeed, money makes the world go around.

'The hope and expectation of thy love is ruined, and the soul of every man prophetically doth forethink thy fall.' [150]

As we think and act, so does our external reality come into fruition. Above all, hope and expectation must never be discarded. A person can lose everything in life, however, if one retains hope, faith, and love, then no obstacle or difficulty is insurmountable. How we perceive ourselves has a significant influence and bearing on our rise or fall. The most sensible counsel one can receive is to be careful with the thoughts, beliefs, ideas, values, emotions, and feelings that one possesses. For these matters come to define a person's life.

---

150 Shakespeare, William. (1598). *Henry IV, Part One.* Act 3, Scene 2.

'Then with the losers let it sympathise. For nothing can seem foul to those that win.' [151]

There are countless meticulous and detailed 'Rules of Engagement' when it comes to conflict between belligerents. There exist codified Laws of War. Laws which incorporate all aspects of warfare. These include a declaration of war, the lawful effect of a ceasefire, the execution of a surrender instrument, treatment of prisoners of war, treatment of civilians, the unrestricted passage of humanitarian assistance, enforcement of a no-fly zone over a country's airspace, ceding of sovereignty over territory, the demarcation of state borders, settling questions of territorial integrity, and the treatment of 'protected persons' under International Humanitarian Law. Unfortunately, belligerents do flout international laws, norms, rules, treaties, and conventions. In order to secure the advantage in a military conflict, and ultimately, to secure victory on the battlefield.

'And God befriend us, as our cause is just!' [152]

For those people that believe in the existence of God, we all seek the support of God in our affairs. God's unfathomable mercy, goodness, divine grace, and favour are infinite, and available to each and every person. No person is beyond the reach and assistance of God. On a more subjective note, each person prefers to think that their cause is most just, however, this is not necessarily so. We all have our unconscious bias, personal ambitions, prejudices, errors, and fallacies.

---

151 Shakespeare, William. (1598). *Henry IV, Part One.* Act 5, Scene 1.
152 Shakespeare, William. (1598). *Henry IV, Part One.* Act 5, Scene 1.

'O Gentlemen, the time of life is short! To spend that shortness basely were too long, if life did ride upon a dial's point, still ending at the arrival of an hour. And if we live, we live to tread on Kings!' [153]

Shakespeare's employment of a platitude signifies the obvious. That is to say, life is a fleeting, transient, and momentary experience. We must not waste away the seconds, minutes, hours, days, months, years, and decades of our precious lifetime in the pursuit of trivial activities. Although this is a self-evident hyperbole in Shakespeare's literature, where he mentions, 'and if we live, we live to tread on Kings!', he is referring to our higher duty to accomplish the fullness of life. We must strive to live a grandiose life. We ought to live a life that is marked by unchecked ambition, self-determination, and the will to power.

'Now, for our consciences, the arms are fair, when the intent of bearing them is just.' [154]

Intention and action, work hand in glove. The conscience of a person is reflective of their character and integrity. For example, consider that the pursuit of social justice is a worthy cause. It is a moral cause that is worth fighting and dying for. Intention determines the basis for our actions. Indeed, intention is equally as important as the action itself. The intention serves to justify the action. The intention is the primary cause for the action to come into effect in this world. By the very performance of action, we affirm our sense of being in this world.

---

153 Shakespeare, William. (1598). *Henry IV, Part One.* Act 5, Scene 2.
154 Shakespeare, William. (1598). *Henry IV, Part One.* Act 5, Scene 2.

'Let each man do his best.' [155]

People are different. Nature does not equally endow every member of the human species. Humans have distinct talents, virtues, knowledge, skills, abilities, and gifts of nature. Thus, each person ought to perform to the best of their individual capacity. In the context of Shakespeare's writing, he is referring to military battles, however, this statement is readily and equally applicable to civilians in everyday life. Regardless of our occupation, status, or rank in society, we all ought to strive to do our best in everything that we undertake.

'All is done! All is won! But thought's the slave of life, and life ... time's fool. And time itself, that takes survey of all the world, must have a stop.' [156]

Our thoughts determine the trajectory, experience, and quality of our life. Humans do not have complete freedom to disassociate life from thought. For action, the very basis of human life, commences with cognition. On the contrary, life is always subject to the force of circumstance and the necessity of time. A person cannot escape the boundaries of space and time. All of our experiential and existential reality is confined within space and time. The very substance of being in this world, is not permeable to a conventional reality existing outside the parameters of space, time, energy, and matter. This cannot be so.

'The better part of valour is discretion.' [157]

The effectuation of irrational decisions is not a demonstration of courage or bravery. Discretion must be utilised in order to ascertain the right time and proper place to execute our next

---

155 Shakespeare, William. (1598). *Henry IV, Part One.* Act 5, Scene 2.
156 Shakespeare, William. (1598). *Henry IV, Part One.* Act 5, Scene 4.
157 Shakespeare, William. (1598). *Henry IV, Part One.* Act 5, Scene 4.

significant decision. For the presence of discretion can extend a person's successes and victories in life. Good judgement is the key to increasing one's probability of securing the objective of 'mission accomplished'.

> 'And since this business so fair is done, let us not leave till all our own be won.'[158]

Once we have commenced a significant project, or initiated a major endeavour, we must not cease our pursuit, until we have accomplished all that we have set out to do. A person's resolve shall be tested, but if a person persists through the highs and lows, through the heights and depths, through the ebbs and flows, then they have a strong chance to secure total victory in their desired objectives.

---

158 Shakespeare, William. (1598). *Henry IV, Part One.* Act 5, Scene 5.

Chapter 9

HENRY IV
(PART TWO)

*'Is it not strange that desire should so many years
outlive performance?'*

SHAKESPEARE

Henry IV (Part Two) continues the developments of *Henry IV (Part One)*, following on from King Henry IV's victory at the *Battle of Shrewsbury*. In this play, King Henry suffers from debilitating illness and he is beyond cure. King Henry's youngest son, Prince John of Lancaster engages in military battle with the rebels. Prince Hal is King Henry IV's destined successor, and when King Henry IV dies, Hal is enthroned the King of England. Once Hal is proclaimed Sovereign of England, he banishes Sir John Falstaff from the Royal Court, and prepares England to wage war against France.

This play is filled with important themes, such as English History, royal succession, rebellion, competing claims for power, mortality, significant questions of war and peace, and the inevitability of animosity. The protracted nature of military conflict in the History of England is difficult to deny. This play is constantly embroiled in military battle after battle. The grand paradox here is that while a King (or Queen) may feel secure in the power and legitimacy of the English Crown, the continued possession of power, is all but certain. Conflict is a fundamental aspect of human nature. This play captures the essence of how effortless it is to 'breach the peace', and yet, just how difficult it is to 'preserve the peace'.

In this play, Shakespeare's use of the English language and employment of literary techniques is second to none. Throughout this play, Shakespeare employs a wide variety of rhetorical and literary techniques, such as hyperbole, irony, juxtaposition, metaphor, metonymy, motif, oxymoron, paradox, simile, soliloquy, and tragicomedy, to illustrate a vividly captivating narrative of royalty, war, power, pride, ego, mortality, and strained loyalties.

'A good wit will make use of anything.'[159]

Humans ought to make effective utility of the resources they have within their immediate possession. A clever and optimistic person maximises the return from the resources at their disposal. Whereas, a pessimistic person thinks of the many barriers and limitations that stand in the way of their desired goal achievement. To be original, inventive, and creative is a way of thinking. A positive mindset can reorient a person's perception, fortune, and accomplishments.

'We are time's subjects, and time bids be gone.'[160]

Every person's life, their very existence, is subject to the confines of time. Time keeps us. It is time that decides when we are to be no more in this world. We cannot exercise control over how much time we have remaining on Earth. Therefore, we must focus on what is in our control. Namely, what we do with the finite time that we possess. Time is the most precious commodity that a

---

159 Shakespeare, William. (1600). *Henry IV, Part Two*. Act 1, Scene 2.
160 Shakespeare, William. (1600). *Henry IV, Part Two*. Act 1, Scene 3.

person has. For without time, we cease to exist. We cease to be. We cannot become.

'Sir John, I am well aware of your manner of wrenching the true cause the false way.' [161]

Humans ought to exercise caution in believing the speech of other people. Words can be manipulated and falsely construe the facts, or even distort our perception of worldly reality. As the ancient saying asserts, 'Actions speak louder than words.' When we are in doubt, we must examine the actions over the words of a person. For the performance of action shall always reveal the true character, integrity, conscience, morality, and intention of a person.

'Well, thus we play the fools with the time, and the Spirits of the Wise sit in the clouds and mock us.' [162]

Humans like to think they are in control of their destiny. However, the very idea of control is an illusion. Humans cannot control many of the fundamental and basic aspects of their existence. From a medical perspective, for example, consider that we are subject to the involuntary and automatic forces that control our heart rate, pulse, thirst, appetite, blood pressure, basal metabolic rate, red blood cell regeneration, respiration, sexual arousal, sleep patterns, and the endocrine glands secretion of hormones.

Furthermore, the autonomic nervous system is directly responsible for the regulation of the aforementioned physiological processes that take place within the human body. To use Shakespeare's language, 'the spirits of the wise' ascertain the very real limitations of the human body. They ridicule our inability to realise, to perceive, to witness, beyond the human condition and the fabrication of conventional reality.

---

161 Shakespeare, William. (1600). *Henry IV, Part Two.* Act 2, Scene 1.
162 Shakespeare, William. (1600). *Henry IV, Part Two.* Act 2, Scene 2.

'Is it not strange that desire should so many years outlive performance?' [163]

Desire is the very essence, the true heart of being. For to live, is to desire to exist. Even in old age, when we are advanced in our years, and no longer capable of the stellar performance that we could achieve in our youth, we still desire to relentlessly strive. To become even a quarter of what we were capable of accomplishing several decades ago. Nonetheless, all humans are mortal, and subject to the fixed reality of birth, growth, degeneration, and death. No person shall escape the worldly reality of human existence.

'Uneasy lies the head that wears a Crown.' [164]

The esteemed position of a sovereign is always admirable from a distance. What we often fail to factor into consideration is the dismal reality that a sovereign is consumed with a multitude of problems, such as the all-important questions of peace and war, civil unrest, internal rebellion, royal succession planning, taxation, the safeguarding of royal wealth, private property, and vast estates, the management of relations with foreign heads of state, and many other important duties. The tremendous burden of this consequential personal responsibility, duty, loyalty, honour, and power, make for much discomfort and anxiety in the affairs of a sovereign.

'Death is certain.' [165]

Death is the inescapable reality of human life. All humans are subject to the finality of death. The future is unknown and uncertain in all respects, including private wealth, personal income, education, employment, family, children, retirement, marriage, and

---

163 Shakespeare, William. (1600). *Henry IV, Part Two*. Act 2, Scene 4.
164 Shakespeare, William. (1600). *Henry IV, Part Two*. Act 3, Scene 1.
165 Shakespeare, William. (1600). *Henry IV, Part Two*. Act 3, Scene 2.

private property. However, death is guaranteed. In the final analysis, all humans are mortal. We cannot escape our date of destiny with death.

'We see which way the stream of time doth run. And are enforced from our most quiet there. By the rough torrent of occasion.' [166]

The vicissitudes of time can have a significant impact on our life trajectory. To continue with Shakespeare's analogy, sometimes the current of the stream is favourable, and at other times it is unfavourable. For example, consider the occurrence of financial crises, epidemics, world wars, civil wars, military rule, the forced internal displacement of people within a sovereign nation-state, food shortages, climate extremes of bushfires, cyclones, Earthquakes, and floods, political instability, economic recessions, and global pandemics. All these scenarios, and many more, create disorder in our lives. In all cases, we must adapt to the circumstances of the present time.

'And have the summary of all our griefs, when time shall serve, to show in articles.' [167]

Grief is part and parcel of the human condition. All humans experience grief, and none are exempt from it. The only variation resides in the type of grief, and thereafter, the degrees to which we suffer in our grief. To overcome grief is a must, if a person is to move forward and embrace their future. For to be trapped in grief is to lose sight of one's destiny. The universality of grief is a common experience to all of humanity. However, our grief is so personal, that often times, no one can completely understand how we truly feel in our hardest hour of grief.

---

166 Shakespeare, William. (1600). *Henry IV, Part Two.* Act 4, Scene 1.
167 Shakespeare, William. (1600). *Henry IV, Part Two.* Act 4, Scene 1.

'Construe the times to their necessities, and you shall see indeed it is the time, and not the King, that doth you injuries.' [168]

The necessity of time determines much in the realm of human affairs. Time teaches every person to endure. To be patient. To trust in God's Word. To keep faith. To love. To hope in all that we do. Injuries will come—this is an apodictic truth of life. We will be wronged from time to time. However, it is within our power to forgive. To relinquish the psychological pain and suffering. To move forward with our life. 'Letting go' of the hurt and pain, and 'moving forward' are important aspects of living. These are profound treasures, that no person can confiscate from us.

'A peace is in the nature of a conquest, for then both parties nobly are subdued, and neither party loser.' [169]

For a conquest to be permanent, both belligerents must come out of the battle with an acceptable outcome. It is true, the victor will be in a position to determine the 'terms of peace'. However, it is important to acknowledge that all belligerents have exhausted valuable 'blood and treasure' in their endeavours. A permanent peace ought to reflect justice, equity, and fairness. Otherwise, the peace will be a temporary agreement.

'Therefore, my grief stretches itself beyond the hour of death.' [170]

At times, we witness the irrationality and absurdity of human behaviour. There is a time and place to grieve our losses. However, the sway of strong emotions and feelings often do surpass human understanding and make us somewhat ambivalent. The human condition is chaotic at times. Thus, for some people, recovery

---

168 Shakespeare, William. (1600). *Henry IV, Part Two*. Act 4, Scene 1.
169 Shakespeare, William. (1600). *Henry IV, Part Two*. Act 4, Scene 2.
170 Shakespeare, William. (1600). *Henry IV, Part Two*. Act 4, Scene 3.

is a protracted and painful process. Unfortunately, not all of life is characteristic of reason, logic, and good judgement.

'Will Fortune never come with both hands full, but write her fair words still in foulest letters?' [171]

Shakespeare describes the paradox of the twists and turns of fortune. We can never have what we require, and when we desire it most in this world. The dismal reality is that fortune is indifferent, and often cruel. The practical solution, one that is within our immediate control, is to be content with our present condition in life. No matter how much or how little is within our possession. For contentment is a state of mind that is reflective of our perception of what we have. Contentment has naught to do with the given quantity or external value of what we have in our possession.

'O foolish youth! Thou seekest the greatness that will overwhelm thee.' [172]

When a person is young, they are inexperienced and lack knowledge of the world. Yet such a person is full of life, emboldened with confidence, and ready to demonstrate to the world their natural prowess. Thus, a young person seeks fame, greatness, glory, success, and worldly accomplishment. However, a youngling wholly lacks the wisdom of how to handle such majestic achievements.

Before a person can wear the Crown, one must serve others. One must be properly trained. One must be adequately prepared to inherit the Crown. If one inherits the Crown before one is mature and ready, that person will surely lose it just as quickly. After all, fortitude is a test of character. Greatness is achieved after a lifetime of experience.

---

171 Shakespeare, William. (1600). *Henry IV, Part Two.* Act 4, Scene 3.
172 Shakespeare, William. (1600). *Henry IV, Part Two.* Act 4, Scene 5.

*'More would I, but my lungs are wasted. So that strength of speech
is utterly denied me.'* [173]

The will-to-live is within us, however, the human lifespan is limited.
We have finite powers and capacities. We cannot live forever. Even
though the desire to exist, the will to endure life is always present
within us. The frailty of all human life is an undeniable fact.
We all have to come to terms with our mortality. At some point,
we become aged and the vital strength is sapped from within us.
Thus, the Old has to give way to the New. This is the way of Nature.

'Therefore, let men take heed of the company they keep.' [174]

Humans needs to be mindful of the people they associate with.
For the people within our environment influence us, both for good
and evil. It is also important that we take note, who we share our
thoughts, desires, future plans, expectations, and hopes with. For
information is an invaluable commodity in this world. The very
real possibility of betrayal is also a cause for concern. Thus, we
ought to exercise prudence and shrewdness of judgement, in order
to determine who we place our trust in.

*'He's walked the way of nature, and to our purposes he lives no
more.'* [175]

Nature will have its course with every human life. There is no
question to entertain or examine here. One day, every person on
Earth will cease to exist. We shall be no more. We need to accept
that our position, rank, power, influence, prestige, knowledge,
learning, intelligence, education, accomplishments, experience, and
relationships, the entire lot of it, will be swept away into the endless

---

173 Shakespeare, William. (1600). *Henry IV, Part Two*. Act 4, Scene 5.
174 Shakespeare, William. (1600). *Henry IV, Part Two*. Act 5, Scene 1.
175 Shakespeare, William. (1600). *Henry IV, Part Two*. Act 5, Scene 2.

pages of history. We shall be forgotten and seldom remembered. The only enduring entity that shall survive for eternity is God's Name, and in that respect, God's Eternal Glory shall live on forever.

'How ill white hairs become a fool and jester. Know the grave doth gape for thee thrice wider than for other men.' [176]

We all ought to reflect on our mortality. Our forthcoming and unavoidable death in this world. The latter half of Shakespeare's statement is ill-founded and unwarranted. For death does not discriminate. No matter if one is wealthy or destitute, a criminal or a priest, young or old, a company director or a cleaner, a medical doctor or a school teacher, death comes to every person.

We need to accept our fate with boldness. For it could not have been any other way, except for the way that events did come to proceed in our lifetime. Therefore, we ought to embrace the reality that we have been dealt. Indeed, a minority of people can live life where they come to wholly and truly accept the 'love of one's fate'. In all respects, this is a profound idea to affirm.

The German philosopher, Friedrich Wilhelm Nietzsche explores the idea of *amor fati* (love of one's fate) in his existentialist philosophical discourse known as *Ecce Homo: How One Becomes What One Is* (1908). Nonetheless, the sombre reality of suffering in this world is undeniable. Regardless of its particular form, type, or degree, suffering is inevitable. In essence, debating the individual variation of suffering, and ultimately the phenomenon of death in human life is futile. Human suffering is a universal fact. Rather, one ought to concentrate on reconciling oneself with the inevitability of suffering and the finality of death. Death constitutes the permanent and irreversible cessation of consciousness.

---

176 Shakespeare, William. (1600). *Henry IV, Part Two.* Act 5, Scene 5.

Chapter 10

HENRY V

'We are in God's Hand, brother, not in theirs.'

SHAKESPEARE

Henry V is a captivating play which is entrenched in the depths of English and French Military History. This play is written in the context of the *Hundred Years' War* (1337–1453). Thus, it narrates the story of King Henry V's military forces fighting France. For Henry V has made a bold claim to exercise his rule as Sovereign over France as well as England. The French King, Charles VI meets with King Henry V's Royal Ambassador, the Duke of Exeter. However, the French King unanimously rejects Henry V's claim to sovereignty over French territory. A peaceful transfer of power was never on the horizon. As a consequence, armed conflict between England and France is the end result.

At face value, the odds appear to favour the French forces over the English. The morale of the English armed forces is in total disarray. Sickness among the English troops, and the presence of poor weather does not aid their cause. On the other hand, the French forces appear confident. Not to mention, they possess the added benefit of home battle-field advantage, with this conflict taking place in Northern France. The major fighting within this play takes place at the *Battle of Agincourt* (1415). King Henry V mobilises his troops, giving them a resounding speech to boost morale, before advancing them into battle against the French armed forces.

In a sincere act of humility, King Henry V places the trust of his troops in the Hand of God. In addition, King Henry V calls upon God to deliver him with a definitive military victory. With God's Grace, King Henry V is victorious over the French military forces. The English forces suffer negligible losses on the battlefield. To seal this military victory with an unwavering rule as Sovereign over France, King Henry V wins the heart and mind of the French Princess Katherine. The Union of King Henry V of England and Princess Katherine of France serves to link these two great nations together, through the institution of marriage.

Henry V is a remarkable play infused with conflict, history, warfare, love, politics, and marriage. It dramatises the endless human desire for power, territory, influence, property, wealth, and love. This play will leave readers with a critical impression of English and French History. More importantly, this play illustrates the importance and power of speech to bolster courage and confidence. Lastly, this play showcases that all is not lost in our grandest pursuits. For even when the chances are negligible, and the odds are against us, if we believe in God, preserve our faith, and hold on to hope, then anything is possible.

'We are blessed in change.' [177]

Sometimes in our life, it is difficult to accept change. However, change is a fundamental law of all life forms on Earth. With respect to the human species, from the very first moments of a baby's birth, when the newborn is delivered from the mother's uterus, till the very final stages of life marked by death, all of human

---

177 Shakespeare, William. (1600). *Henry V*. Act 1, Scene 1.

life is a process of change. Change takes place within our body throughout the course of the human lifespan on a number of levels, including cellular, psychological, physiological, biological, chemical, molecular, and the human reproductive capacity.

Aside from the involuntary and unconscious internal changes taking place within our body, there are the countless external changes to the human-made environment. Not to mention, the profound social, political, legal, technological, and economic changes in our Modern World. For example, consider rising global sea-levels, melting of glaciers, deforestation, the rise of social media, the advent of the internet, mobile phones, changes to monetary and fiscal policies of the nation-state, the Abolition of Slavery, the Emancipation of Women, World Wars, Decolonisation of Asia and Africa, changes in elected governments across the Democratic World, and the advent of electric vehicles.

We cannot exert total control over the many processes of change in our life and the world, writ large. However, we can determine how we personally respond to change. Our positive perception and constructive attitude towards change, will assist, rather than hinder, our future progress in the Modern World, where change is not only inevitable, but the rate of change is rapidly increasing. Those people that embrace change as part and parcel of human life are truly blessed.

'Faith, I will live so long as I may, that's the certain of it, and when I cannot live any longer, I will do as I may.'[178]

Shakespeare's clever play with words expresses that the duration of our lifespan is most uncertain. However, it is certain that we will live as long as we do live. The employment of a pun makes it clear how there is no certainty to be found in uncertainty. One can extend Shakespeare's thought, beyond the duration of life, to

---

178 Shakespeare, William. (1600). *Henry V*. Act 2, Scene 1.

also incorporate the course of life in modern society. For much is uncertain in the organisation of human affairs, for example, consider employment, wealth, marriage, income, education, health, finances, and private property ownership.

'A sword is an oath … and oaths must have their course.' [179]

Custom and tradition guided the majority of human behaviour in the *Early Modern Period* (1500–1700). Swords were utilised as a means to swear an oath. In keeping with this solemn practice, it was imperative that oaths be faithfully sworn and honourably discharged. A person's character, reputation, honour, integrity, and esteem were held on credit. On the basis that one fulfilled their obligation, in accordance with their oath.

'Self-love, my liege, is not so vile a sin as self-neglecting.' [180]

Humans must love themselves. Although self-love can induce feelings of guilt and indulgence, however, it is a necessary ingredient to ensure a life well-lived. A life with dignity, honour, and respect. First, love God. Second, love our neighbour. Third, love ourselves. Love is a fundamental component of the human condition. A life without love is devoid of all purpose and meaning.

The *Holy Bible*, within the *Gospel of Matthew*, Chapter 22, Verses 37 to 40, define the importance of love in all that we do, 'Jesus replied: Love the LORD your God with all your heart and with all your soul and with all your mind. This is the first and greatest Commandment. And the second is like it: Love your neighbour as yourself. All the Law and the Prophets hang on these two Commandments.'

---

179 Shakespeare, William. (1600). *Henry V.* Act 2, Scene 1.
180 Shakespeare, William. (1600). *Henry V.* Act 2, Scene 4.

*'A night is but small breath and little pause to answer matters of
this consequence.'* [181]

Matters of heavy consequence require much thought and
deliberation. Significant decisions must be weighed and debated
with careful consideration. To not adequately ponder over a
significant event or major decision is more likely than not to lead
to a poor or careless determination. Therefore, we ought to take
the required time to carefully reflect on our thoughts, beliefs, and
values concerning major life determinations, prior to reaching an
informed decision.

*'In peace, there's nothing so becomes a man. As modest stillness
and humility.'* [182]

The world oscillates between the opposing forces of peace and
conflict. Peace, equality, faith, charity, community service, and
social justice bring out the best in humanity. With respect to peace,
this is the finest and highest state of humanity on Earth. Peace
represents a transcendent tranquillity that surpasses the finite
capacity of human reason. While peace is the preferred state of
affairs in the Modern World, the reality is much more sombre. With
seemingly unending conflict scattered across the globe, such is
the fixed nature of humanity. What is desirable and amenable to all,
is yet, so difficult to achieve.

*'Would I were in an alehouse in London. I would give all my fame
for a pot of ale and safety.'* [183]

The basic elements of life are always of prime importance. These
include love, a sense of belonging, personal safety, nourishment,
hydration, clothing, and housing. Human rationality confirms that,

---

181 Shakespeare, William. (1600). *Henry V.* Act 2, Scene 4.
182 Shakespeare, William. (1600). *Henry V.* Act 3, Scene 1.
183 Shakespeare, William. (1600). *Henry V.* Act 3, Scene 2.

one exchanges the fulfilment, or realisation of higher desires, for the fundamental need to survive. In this statement, Shakespeare illustrates how fame means naught to an individual, if such a person's life is in immediate danger.

> '*For Nym, he hath heard that men of few words are the best men.*'[184]

This statement represents both the tragedy and paradox of humanity. For the more we speak, the better we ought to be understood, however, the opposite is the case. The more we speak, the more likely we are to say something that is disagreeable, create grounds for offence, or a cause for concern. The people of few words are most likely to avoid the presence of rancour in their relationships.

> '*Fortune is painted blind, with a muffler afore her eyes, to signify to you that fortune is blind, and she is painted also with a wheel, to signify to you, which is the moral of it, that she is turning, and inconstant, and mutability, and variation.*'[185]

Shakespeare paints a beautiful picture with words to portray the characteristics and attributes of fortune. While humans would like to assert that they are in control of their affairs and the course of their lives, the reality is that the hands of fortune can change our circumstances, either for good or evil, at any point in time. In this world, no person can escape the mischance or favour of fortune. While we may exercise free will, personal agency, and self-determination in a number of our life's important decisions, it is an illusion to think that we are in complete control of our lives.

---

184 Shakespeare, William. (1600). *Henry V.* Act 3, Scene 2.
185 Shakespeare, William. (1600). *Henry V.* Act 3, Scene 6.

'Advantage is a better soldier than rashness.' [186]

In the course of military conflict, for a belligerent to possess the advantage is always desirable to all other factors. For advantage in a military campaign creates the grounds for total victory. Rashness, second to indecisiveness, must always be avoided on the battlefield. Poor judgement can be costly, and result in heavy casualties, strategic errors, or total defeat. A sound mind and good use of judgement are prerequisites for a Field Marshal to accomplish an assigned mission.

'We are in God's Hand, brother, not in theirs.' [187]

This is a truism that defines the reality of all humans on Earth. Regardless of one's steadfast beliefs, values, thoughts, and ideas, every person is subject to the Sovereign Will of Almighty God. God has the final say with respect to our destiny and life trajectory. While it might temporarily appear that we are held captive to the will of another person, God is in control. Thus, God determines the final course and future trajectory of the Universe, and all that is contained within it.

Within the *Holy Bible*, in the *New Testament*, in the *Second Book of Corinthians*, Chapter 11, Verses 32 and 33, we witness the Eternal Glory and Unrivalled Power of God. In this particular situation, Paul (Saul of Tarsus) is trapped in the City of Damascus surrounded by his enemies who threaten him deadly harm, 'In Damascus the Governor under King Aretas had the City of the Damascenes guarded in order to arrest me. But I was lowered in a basket from a window in the wall and slipped through his hands.'

---

186 Shakespeare, William. (1600). *Henry V.* Act 3, Scene 6.
187 Shakespeare, William. (1600). *Henry V.* Act 3, Scene 6.

> *'Tis good for men to love their present pains upon example,*
> *so the Spirit is eased.'* [188]

Pain is an unavoidable reality of human life. There is pain in child birth. Pain in recovery from surgery on the human body. Pain in processing memories concerning tragedies and accidents in life. Not to mention, much psychological pain in conversing about traumatic events and distressing experiences. While not every person is capable of wholly embracing their pains, we all ought to consciously reflect upon our pains, so that we shall find our inner healing. Reality cannot be ignored indefinitely. Therefore, reality must be embraced. Always know that in the remembrance of God's Name, our Spirit is comforted and assured.

> *'I am afeared there are few die well that die in a battle.'* [189]

A soldier's death is never pleasant. For one can die from a fatal wound, excessive blood loss, body parts becoming dismembered, loss of a limb, and many more deadly methods. It is a rarity for a soldier to have died a good death on the battlefield. The best counsel to reflect upon is this: Hope for the best, however, be prepared for the worst. In the end, no amount of training, knowledge, learning, or experience can prepare a person for military life. It is impossible to foreknow the perilous journey that a soldier will confront in the theatre of war.

> *'The King is not bound to answer the particular endings of His*
> *soldiers.'* [190]

There is a hierarchy to any ordered and civilised society. With the poor and illiterate people, at the base of a social structure (or order), answerable to the affluent and learned people at the very

---

188 Shakespeare, William. (1600). *Henry V.* Act 4, Scene 1.
189 Shakespeare, William. (1600). *Henry V.* Act 4, Scene 1.
190 Shakespeare, William. (1600). *Henry V.* Act 4, Scene 1.

top. Rarely, if ever, are the aristocratic, noble, learned, privileged, and affluent people, at the very top of a social order, answerable to their subjects. With respect to a monarchy system of political rule, the King or Queen's subjects have a duty, an oath, a responsibility to serve their sovereign. In fact, to disobey the direct command or published decree of a sovereign is considered an act of treason. However, in stark contrast, the King or Queen may or may not entertain the pleadings of their subjects, for a sovereign is not bound in duty.

A good-hearted King or Queen may adhere to the argument that they are bound in conscience, to consider the petitions of their noble subjects. Still there is no fixed mandate, or legal, or moral obligation for a sovereign to do so. For example, consider the request for a Queen to pardon a criminal offender who is Her subject. Now it is at the Queen's sole discretion to grant or deny the requested pardon. The Queen can determine to act upon expert counsel from Her Majesty's Royal Staff and Learned Advisors. However, equally, Her Majesty may determine not to attend to such a request. Such a Royal Prerogative of Mercy is solely at the behest of Her Majesty's Pleasure.

> *'Now, if these men have defeated the law and outrun native punishment, though they can outstrip men, they have no wings to fly from God.'* [191]

Select citizens of a nation-state may have the means and ability to circumvent the application of the law of a sovereign nation-state. Therefore, justice may not be served, where it is rightly due. For example, consider that a convicted criminal may escape police custody and travel beyond the jurisdiction of that particular nation-state in which the criminal offence was committed. Now, if there is a ratified extradition treaty in force, the legitimate government

---

191 Shakespeare, William. (1600). *Henry V.* Act 4, Scene 1.

of that nation-state, in which the crime was committed, may make an application for the lawful extradition of the convicted offender to the legitimate government of that foreign nation-state, where the perpetrator is currently residing. However, if this extradition request is rejected, then the possibility of pursuing justice has been denied.

While the justice of this world is not always just and true, God's Justice cannot be escaped. God's Justice is perfect and final. Within the *Holy Bible*, in the *New Testament*, in the *Book of Galatians*, Chapter 6, Verses 7 to 10, the Word of God makes it known that Justice will be delivered, 'Do not be deceived. God cannot be mocked. A man reaps what he sows. Whoever sows to please the Flesh, from the Flesh will reap destruction. Whoever sows to please the Spirit, from the Spirit will reap Eternal Life. Let us not become weary in doing Good, for at the proper time we will reap a harvest if we do not give up. Therefore, as we have opportunity, let us do Good to all people, especially to those who belong to the Family of Believers.'

> *'Every subject's duty is the King's, but every subject's soul is his own.'* [192]

Every subject is bound to the performance of duty to the King or Queen of a nation-state, by virtue of the unbreakable bonds of sworn allegiance. However, a subject has a higher duty. A duty of conscience. Namely, obedience to the Divine Command of God. Shakespeare makes a fine distinction in a person's duty to a sovereign, but also personal responsibility for their own conduct and actions. No matter the decree of a Head of State, each person is individually responsible for the good and evil that they commit in this world. Thus, a person must exercise their agency and reason, within the proper and righteous bounds of moral conscience, to ensure their soul is not tainted with the negative externality of sin.

---

192 Shakespeare, William. (1600). *Henry V.* Act 4. Scene 1.

'All things are ready, if our minds be so. Perish the man whose mind is backward now!' [193]

When a person is determined on a particular course. That is to infer, one possesses a resolved mind. Then all obstacles, challenges, and difficulties become surpassable and surmountable. If a person proceeds with total resolution towards the fulfilment of their significant endeavour, then all things can work towards one's advantage. On the contrary, a person who harbours doubt, fear, uncertainty, hesitation, indecisiveness, or confusion. Such a person who is double-minded in their thoughts. That person shall never succeed in their most noble endeavours.

'God be with you all! And how thou pleasest, God, dispose the day!' [194]

No matter where we are situated on Earth, or what we do in life, the most important activity is that the remembrance of God be in our heart, spirit, and mind on our journey of life. God's Sovereign Will shall always come to pass, in all things, great and small. Thus, each and every day shall effectuate as it pleases God. In vain, the majority of humans strive and struggle to impose their individual will upon this material world.

However, it is only ever a rare minority of the human population, those select individuals that are blessed by God, who voluntarily accept God's Will and submit to God's Will. This noble act pleases God. God's People listen to God's Word. In the *Holy Bible*, within the *New Testament*, the *Gospel of Luke*, Chapter 22, Verse 42 affirms the importance of accepting God's Will in all matters, 'Father, if You are willing, take this cup from me. Yet not my will, but Yours be done.'

---

193 Shakespeare, William. (1600). *Henry V*. Act 4, Scene 3.
194 Shakespeare, William. (1600). *Henry V*. Act 4, Scene 3.

'The empty vessel makes the greatest sound.' [195]

Those individuals with limited knowledge, personal experience, education, formal learning, economic resources, and attainment are often the people who speak the loudest. One with much formal learning, knowledge, understanding, and wisdom is often a reflective person. For the learned person is consciously aware of how little they have mastered in life, and how so much of reality remains forever unknown to them. That is to say, beyond the finite confines of human reason, judgement, logic, understanding, and consciousness. It is an enlightening paradox, that the learned person who has mastered a significant quantum of worldly knowledge, truly knows, how little they know.

'Let life be short, else shame will be too long.' [196]

Life must be lived in accordance with the moral principles and noble virtues of courage, honesty, love, kindness, compassion, respect, loyalty, fairness, equality, brotherhood, sisterhood, integrity, temperance, moral excellence, justice, wisdom, tolerance, mercy, and moderation. It is a purposeful life, to have lived a short life, that was in accordance with one's honourable creed, being virtuous and good-hearted. As opposed to living a long life, that was dishonourable and full of vice. It is true indeed, shame casts a drawn-out, dreadful, and dark shadow.

'I tell thee truly, Herald, I know not if the day be ours or no.' [197]

Before we go into battle, we can never be totally assured of our victory. How events effectuate on the day will be determined on the battlefield. While Shakespeare is referring to military conquests and armed conflict, the aforementioned statement is readily applicable

---

195 Shakespeare, William. (1600). *Henry V.* Act 4, Scene 4.
196 Shakespeare, William. (1600). *Henry V.* Act 4, Scene 5.
197 Shakespeare, William. (1600). *Henry V.* Act 4, Scene 7.

to many other aspects of our everyday life. In the sense that, certainty is beyond the scope of all human action and endeavours. What we must do is take the initiative and brave the attempt. In the words of the famous Roman poet, Horace, *carpe diem* (seize the day)!

'Praised be God, and not our strength, for it!' [198]

All praise belongs to the Creator—the Most High God. While we may witness extraordinary human actions that demonstrate remarkable courage, intellect, scholarship, talent, wisdom, community service, humanity, charity, justice, forgiveness, leadership, love, sacrifice, hope, perseverance, faith, and kindness. The source of all the goodness of these virtues is God. Our strength is negligible and inconsequential. It is the Divine Providence of God which allows humanity to accomplish all great endeavours.

'There is more good toward you peradventure, than is in your knowledge to dream of.' [199]

We can never be certain of the future outcomes of the present decisions that we make in life. Probability and risk can be reduced; however, they can never be wholly eliminated. In any case, we must be prepared to act upon the rare chances and unique opportunities that life presents us with. In all things, courage, confidence, and conviction are the prerequisites to proceed forward, in order to secure our dreams and create the future in our image.

---

198 Shakespeare, William. (1600). *Henry V.* Act 4, Scene 7.
199 Shakespeare, William. (1600). *Henry V.* Act 4, Scene 8.

'All offences, My Lord, come from the heart.' [200]

The heart gives rise to good and evil. In effect, what the tongue speaks is sourced from the deep reservoir of the heart. Offences may be effectuated in speech or action; however, they originate from the heart. In the *Holy Bible*, within the *Old Testament*, the *Book of Proverbs*, Chapter 4, Verse 23 affirms the importance of keeping a watchful eye over the heart, 'Above all else, guard your heart, for everything you do flows from it.'

'But a good heart, Kate, is the Sun and the Moon, or rather, the Sun, and not the Moon, for it shines bright and never changes, but keeps his course truly.' [201]

A good-hearted person is virtuous, noble, and morally righteous. Not to mention, such a person's speech and actions radiate throughout the four corners of the Earth, shining light like the Sun's powerful ultraviolet radiation. Likewise, a sincere person can illuminate the world with the brightness of love, mercy, kindness, empathy, and compassion. A sincere person is constant in their demeanour and well-mannered towards all people. For a sincere individual's strength resides within themselves, and it is not reflective of external conditions, wealth, power, social status, property, or fame.

'God, the Best Maker of all marriages, combine your hearts in one, your realms in one!' [202]

We must place our unconditional trust in God when it comes to the selection of our spouse. The institution of marriage is a sacred and consensual relationship between a husband and wife. Marriage is where two become one, through a divine union in

---

200 Shakespeare, William. (1600). *Henry V*. Act 4, Scene 8.
201 Shakespeare, William. (1600). *Henry V*. Act 5, Scene 2.
202 Shakespeare, William. (1600). *Henry V*. Act 5, Scene 2.

God's Creation. For a married couple, marriage is one of the most important relationships in life. Marriage is the foundation stone for a family, children, home, a lifetime of memories and experiences, the sharing of grief and happiness, spiritual union, devotion, and the remembrance of God.

> *'That never may ill office, or fell jealousy, when troubles oft the bed of blessed marriage, thrust in between the Paction of these Kingdoms, to make divorce of their Incorporate League; That English may as French, French Englishmen, receive each other. God speak this. Amen.'* [203]

Division in unity is a very real possibility in human affairs. Through the presence and working of sin, human nature is corrupted. The vices of jealousy, prejudice, insecurity, envy, lust, anger, pride, covetousness, and hatred are omnipresent throughout the world. It is essential that humanity turn its heart towards God to confess, repent, and seek God's goodness and blessing in our life. God's mercy is infinite. God's mercy is open to every person who is willing to seek and receive it.

---

203 Shakespeare, William. (1600). *Henry V*. Act 5, Scene 2.

Chapter 11

HENRY VI (PART ONE)

'I have no power to let her pass.
My hand would free her, but my heart says no.'

SHAKESPEARE

Following the death of King Henry V, the youthful Henry VI is proclaimed King of England. Notwithstanding Henry VI's ascent to power, it is the Duke of Exeter and Duke of Gloucester that wield the real power in the Kingdom of England. War with France is a dominant theme throughout the entirety of this play. With General Lord Talbot leading the English forces against the French forces. Meanwhile *Joan la Pucelle* (Joan of Arc) is the Captain of the French armed forces.

In a higher claim to the transcendent forces of divinity, Joan of Arc asserts the profound blessing of the Virgin Mary to liberate France from English rule. In addition, the English General, Lord Talbot is accompanied by his brave and loyal son, John Talbot. The young John Talbot makes a courageous and unforgettable final stand on the battlefield, alongside his father. Both father and son are unable to stop the onslaught of the superior might of the French soldiers, and they are slain on the battlefield. The distinguished valour of the Talbot's serves to dignify their place in the eternal memory of English Military History.

On this occasion, the military power of the English armed forces cannot prevail against the French armed forces. For the English have a myriad of internal problems. Not to mention, their aristocratic houses are not in order, and their most powerful kingdom is lacking in unity. The noble English Houses begin to divide and entertain conflict amongst themselves. The two main warring factions being, the House of York and the House of Lancaster.

There is the continuation of in-fighting amongst the English elite for the prized English Crown and Throne. The Bishop of Winchester is of the perspective that Gloucester intends to seize power from King Henry VI. This leads to conflict on the outskirts of the Tower of London. Not to mention, Richard Plantagenet asserts his claim to the English Crown. Subsequently, Richard has a major disagreement with the Duke of Somerset.

During the course of this play, the fortunes of the French armed forces take a turn for the worst, and Joan of Arc is captured. King Henry VI is persuaded to seek a peace treaty with the French, and he does so through the traditional institution of marriage. The Earl of Suffolk arranges King Henry VI's royal marriage to a beautiful French Princess by the name of Margaret of Anjou. King Henry VI's agreement to this marriage proposal makes Margaret of Anjou the newfound Queen of England. This play demonstrates the timeless themes of love, power, marriage, royalty, rivalry, succession, and conflict.

'O, let no words, but deeds, revenge this treason.' [204]

Actions always speak louder than words. Shakespeare's aforesaid statement closely follows the *Code of Hammurabi*, which established

---

204 Shakespeare, William. (1591). *Henry VI. Part One.* Act 3, Scene 2.

the legal foundations for equal justice and punishment in the Ancient World. The spirit of the Code is summarised by the well-known expression, 'An eye for an eye. A tooth for a tooth.' The unlawful act of treason is a matter of considerable gravity and heavy consequence in the affairs of State. In most jurisdictions, the crime of treason is punishable by death, or imprisonment for life.

'A braver soldier never couched lance, a gentler heart did never sway in Court, But Kings and mightiest Potentates must die, For that's the end of human misery.' [205]

All humans have to confront the inevitable reality of death in this world. Death cannot be circumvented, regardless of a person's rank, nobility, high birth, parentage, personal wealth, income, private property, social class, political status, influence, or power. Some people may find solace and security in death, knowing that it will end all their troubles, tribulations, and tragedies, with an irreversible and unwavering finality.

'Care is no cure, but rather corrosive for things that are not to be remedied.' [206]

What is beyond repair is not worth the concern. If something cannot be remedied, in effect, a person is wasting their valuable time, resources, energy, and efforts in order to rectify, what is beyond rectification. In most cases, this unproductive action can result in further damage and unintended harm. For nothing good eventuates from a destructive process. Therefore, the real possibility of an adverse outcome is most plausible. In particular, where a person irrationally attempts to fix things that are beyond correction.

---

205 Shakespeare, William. (1591). *Henry VI. Part One.* Act 3, Scene 2.
206 Shakespeare, William. (1591). *Henry VI. Part One.* Act 3, Scene 3.

'Strike those that hurt, and hurt not those that help.' [207]

This is a war-time or battlefield reality for all soldiers. In a state of armed conflict, enemy combatants who hinder our success and impede our objectives must be struck down. Whereas, soldiers in allegiance to our great cause, those who serve to advance our aims, must be given our protection from harm, and every care that can be reasonably afforded to them. Comrades in arms must be supported physically, with military resources, medical supplies, food, water, equipment, but also psychologically, namely, through ensuring high morale, cheerful spirits, the equal right to worship of one's faith, and the provision of compassionate care in times of distress.

> *'When first this Order was ordained, My Lords, Knights of the Garter were of noble birth, Valiant and virtuous, full of haughty courage, such as were grown to credit by the wars; Not fearing death, nor shrinking for distress, But always resolute in most extremes.'* [208]

Historically, the unequal qualities of tradition, parentage, custom, and high birth were the pre-determining factors to a person's status, influence, honour, prestige, rank, power, and standing in the Early Modern Society. Admirable virtues were closely associated with aristocratic people of noble parentage and high birth. To be a Knight was no inconsequential matter. For such an honourable person was resolutely committed to the cause of duty, demonstrating utmost regard for personal responsibility, allegiance, loyalty, and sacrifice for the Order.

---

207 Shakespeare, William. (1591). *Henry VI. Part One.* Act 3, Scene 3.
208 Shakespeare, William. (1591). *Henry VI. Part One.* Act 4, Scene 1.

'The quarrel toucheth none but us alone, betwixt ourselves let us decide it, then.' [209]

In the Pre-Modern World, a duel was the most appropriate and honourable manner in which to resolve an outstanding conflict. When two or more parties disagreed over an intractable issue, they settled it amongst themselves, with the perspective to determining the matter with finality. The Modern World has witnessed a fundamental paradigm shift in how conflicts are resolved.

The institution of Common Law is how disputes are resolved in the contemporary world. With dissensions now taking place in Law Courts. In civilised society, conflicts are settled with proper regard to court procedure, rules of evidence, persuasion of argument, representation by accredited lawyers, thoughtful deliberation and a verdict by jurors, followed by sentencing by the learned and noble judges of the Court. Once upon a time, justice was determined by anarchy and tyranny. Nowadays, justice is determined by power, private property, and personal wealth.

'My tender years, and let us not forego. That for a trifle, that was bought with blood.' [210]

Humans need to exercise good judgement and prudence to ensure their trade, commerce, or any other form of exchange with another party is equitable in its value. It is absurd to exchange a prized possession, a most valuable item of possession, a cherished ornament, or a remarkable treasure, which was secured through sacrifice, toil, the exertion of labour, or bloodshed for a meagre commodity. Think twice, for once an exchange is done, it cannot be undone. *Caveat Emptor* (Let the Buyer Beware)!

---

209 Shakespeare, William. (1591). *Henry VI. Part One.* Act 4, Scene 1.
210 Shakespeare, William. (1591). *Henry VI. Part One.* Act 4, Scene 1.

'It is much when sceptres are in children's hands, but more when envy breeds unkind division. There comes the ruin. There begins confusion.' [211]

Sovereigns are appointed young and old. Age is no barrier to Royalty and the Throne. The lack of worldly knowledge, formal learning, good judgement, and personal experience are matters of serious concern for a youthful sovereign. Therefore, it is best that a young ruler is surrounded by mature, competent, learned, and honourable advisors, who offer excellent counsel in the affairs of State.

Shakespeare candidly points out that the areas of far greater concern herein are resentment and jealousy, which create discord and conflict amongst the subjects of a kingdom. During disunity, subject's loyalties are tested and strained. Competing forces and factions emerge, with ruthless leadership contests for seizing political power and the royal prerogative to govern the people.

'God and Saint George, Talbot and England's Right, Prosper our colours in this dangerous fight!' [212]

Victory is only ordained by the blessing of God. As with the passage of English custom and tradition, we witness English soldiers assert their allegiance by raising their flag and proclaiming a battle cry to God and their Saint, namely, Saint George for a resounding victory on the battlefield.

Beyond the noble practice of adhering to an English war-time tradition, such an art of rhetoric, combined with distinguished emblematic action, have a profound effect on boosting the soldier's morale. Thereby, reinforcing courage, conviction, and confidence amongst the brave soldiers of a battalion. Such motivational speech instills a sense of unity and higher purpose for the soldiers to proceed forward in defence of their just cause.

---

211 Shakespeare, William. (1591). *Henry VI. Part One.* Act 4, Scene 1.
212 Shakespeare, William. (1591). *Henry VI. Part One.* Act 4, Scene 2.

'No more my fortune can. But curse the cause, I cannot aid the man.' [213]

To a considerable degree, humans are the products of their fortune or destiny. This is a reality that can often be difficult to accept in and through the course of life. Humans do not embody the Sovereign Will of God to make determinations in all areas of their life. The finite power of our free moral choice is often more constrained than we think, or would like it to be the case. Sometimes, it is not within the very scope of our power, or narrow parameters of personal agency to make significant determinations. From time to time, we are all subject to the force of circumstance. Not to mention, the social, economic, legal, and political forces that construct our everyday reality in this Modern World.

'There is no hope that ever I will stay. If the first hour I shrink and run away.' [214]

At the immediate outset of a journey or battle, during its initial commencement, the temptation to shirk one's personal responsibility or neglect one's sworn duty is a danger that must be overcome. If we withdraw within the first hour of a battle, then all hope is unequivocally lost. We have no chance to hold our ground. Make significant territorial gains. Secure major strategic advances. Thus, win the battle at the eleventh hour. The dark forces of fear, temptation, doubt, confusion, uncertainty, anger, hesitation, and disloyalty must be overcome in the soldier's mind. Only then can the soldier's body act for the accomplishment of the mission positioned before it.

---

213 Shakespeare, William. (1591). *Henry VI. Part One.* Act 4, Scene 3.
214 Shakespeare, William. (1591). *Henry VI. Part One.* Act 4, Scene 5.

'If thou wilt fight, fight by thy Father's side, and commendable proved, let's die in pride.' [215]

General Lord Talbot reluctantly accepts his son's unwavering resolve to fight and die alongside him on the battlefield. Lord Talbot's son, John Talbot is a brave, courageous, and honourable young gentleman, who fights until the very end. Even though there is no hope of victory and death stares him down from above, Lord Talbot earnestly entreats his young son to flee the battlefield, and save his precious life. To live. To fight another day. To seek revenge. To seek retributive justice, on another, more auspicious occasion.

Nonetheless, the young and noble John is defiant. Thus, John makes his last stand on the battlefield, dying in the arms of his distinguished father. As a consequence, the Talbot family name is ingrained in English Military History, for the Talbot's unflinching bravery and first-class gallantry.

'Ay, marry, Uncle, for I always thought it was both impious and unnatural that such immunity and bloody strife should reign among professors of one faith.' [216]

There is no denying it, the dismal reality is that members of the same faith group do have much disagreement and heated conflict amongst one another. This dismal reality is most reflective of the evil, immoral, and imperfect nature of humans. Not to mention, examine the greater distrust and protracted disputes amongst the numerous denominations of the major established and institutionalised faiths, for example, consider Christianity and Islam.

One method to respond to widespread religious division is inter-faith dialogue. Inter-faith dialogue is one instrument that shall aid the noble cause of religious reconciliation. With respect

---

215 Shakespeare, William. (1591). *Henry VI. Part One.* Act 4, Scene 6.
216 Shakespeare, William. (1591). *Henry VI. Part One.* Act 5, Scene 1.

to the Christian faith, *Ecumenism* serves to bridge the long-standing differences between the numerous Christian denominations.

'I shall be well content with any choice tends to God's Glory and my Country's weal.' [217]

When a person makes a decision that gives God Glory and serves their sovereign nation-state, this is most reflective of an honourable undertaking. Therefore, such a person ought to be satisfied with their conduct, both morally and legally, for they have performed a meritorious deed. This action is representative of most selfless conduct, and it rightly brings deserving praise to the individual. Indeed, it is difficult to imagine a more noble deed. Therefore, true contentment is the ripened fruit of one's honest labour.

'Of all base passions, fear is most accursed.' [218]

Fear functions to paralyse the individual. Fear prevents the performance of action, real progress, and major accomplishments in our life. Second to fear is the existence of doubt. Doubt makes a person double-minded. Doubt inhibits the construction of a resolute and firm mind. Fear must be overcome. Fear cannot be allowed to seize the mind. Fear must never gain a foothold in a person's cognition. Fear restricts the creation of a positive mindset. Fear prevents a person from experiencing the 'fullness' of human life.

'I have no power to let her pass. My head would free her, but my heart says no.' [219]

Most, if not all, of love is irrational. The desire for the opposite sex is strong and difficult to transcend. Sexual attraction is a natural

---

217 Shakespeare, William. (1591). *Henry VI. Part One.* Act 5, Scene 1.
218 Shakespeare, William. (1591). *Henry VI. Part One.* Act 5, Scene 2.
219 Shakespeare, William. (1591). *Henry VI. Part One.* Act 5, Scene 3.

instinct. Shakespeare masterfully narrates how the 'head' represents the instrument of reason. The fountain of rational thought. The seat of logic. The storehouse of judgement. Last but not least, the capacity of intellect. On the contrary, the 'heart' represents the push and pull of human emotions, feelings, and sensations.

Both the 'head' and the 'heart' are powerful, dynamic, and opposing forces in the human. For the 'head' is willing to execute the bold decisions and effectuate the difficult determinations to relinquish an intimate relationship. Whereas, the 'heart' is swayed by emotion and passion. The heart surrenders to the power of desire. The heart is unable to forsake the powerful grasp of love that it so intently cherishes. The learned Scottish philosopher, David Hume made an enlightening assertion in his profound work, *A Treatise of Human Nature* (1739), in which Hume states, 'Reason alone cannot be a motive to the will, but rather is the slave of the passions.'

'Aye, beauty's princely majesty is such, confounds the tongue and makes the senses rough.' [220]

The phenomenon of beauty is captivating and alluring. For beauty captures and amazes the sight of a person. Beauty has the power to dull the function of reason. Beauty overpowers one with the strong emotion of love. At times, a gentlewoman's mesmerising physique and natural beauty may lead a gentleman to become startled, and therefore, unable to maintain his eloquence or fluency in speech. Not to mention, the proper functioning of the remaining senses of the gentleman may become slightly diminished as he is awestruck by the pleasant sight of a beautiful gentlewoman. Such is the unrivalled power of nature. In all matters great and small, nature has its own special *modus operandi*.

---

220 Shakespeare, William. (1591). *Henry VI. Part One.* Act 5, Scene 3.

'Marriage is a matter of more worth than to be dealt in by attorneyship.' [221]

The sacred institution of marriage is of too great importance to be placed in the hands of lawyers. In the event of a disagreement, conflict, or dispute, a married couple must seek the Sovereign Counsel of God in all respects. Seek out pastoral care. Speak to a religious minister, or a trusted member of the clergy. Alternatively, consider other secular and professional support services, such as the care and guidance of a social worker, medical practitioner, counsellor, therapist, or clinical psychologist. Lawyers should only become involved in the internal affairs of a married couple as a matter of last resort.

'For what is wedlock forced but a Hell, an age of discord and continual strife?' [222]

Marriage, just like any other relationship, can become strained at times. Within intimate relationships, including that of marriage, change is constant and inevitable. For example, consider that disagreements emerge from time to time. There is a widening gap in the expectations that spouses have of each other. Communication breaks down. The priorities of husband and wife change over time. Children come into the family paradigm. Children mature into adulthood and eventually move out of the parental home. Employment and personal health changes occur. Also, there are special requirements for home residence with advanced age and the elderly stages of life. Not to mention, activities that were once favourite hobbies and cherished pastimes, are no longer the source of passion and excitement that they once were.

In all the aforementioned scenarios and cases, change is a constant factor. Thus, perspective always matters. For example,

---

221 Shakespeare, William. (1591). *Henry VI. Part One.* Act 5, Scene 5.
222 Shakespeare, William. (1591). *Henry VI. Part One.* Act 5, Scene 5.

consider that some people will observe a glass with 50 per cent water in it and assert, 'the glass is half full'. While other people will observe the identical glass, and mention, 'the glass is half empty'. Now, both are correct answers. Therefore, the purpose of this illustration is not to signify which person is correct or incorrect. Rather, this example demonstrates that the unique 'perception' of the individual determines their construction of worldly reality.

'Grief, I fear me, both at first and last.' [223]

The feeling of grief is part and parcel of our worldly reality. Grief is an undeniable aspect of the human condition, it cannot be negated. Therefore, the only plausible option that we have is to confront the undeniable presence of grief in our life. Within the *Holy Bible*, in the *Gospel of Matthew*, at Chapter 5, Verse 4, the sacred Scripture informs us that, 'Blessed are those who mourn, for they will be comforted.' Grief, just like a variety of other emotions, is a most natural psychological response to the events that we experience in our lifetime. Grief must be acknowledged and processed to move forward in life.

---

223 Shakespeare, William. (1591). *Henry VI. Part One.* Act 5, Scene 5.

Chapter 12

HENRY VI (PART TWO)

'Trust nobody, for fear you be betrayed. The trust I have is in mine innocence. Therefore, am I bold and resolute.'

SHAKESPEARE

Henry VI (Part Two) is a continuation of the events that unfolded in *Henry VI (Part One)*. The newfound peace between the Kingdom of England and the Kingdom of France holds for the time being. The English Court remains divided and the desire for power amongst the nobles is as strong as ever. Within the Kingdom of England, Suffolk's influence, prestige, and power are fast-growing. Suffolk is now a Duke, an honourable member of the English Court, and a passionate lover of Queen Margaret.

The English nobles unite in their ill-founded quest to eliminate the good influence of the Duke of Gloucester, an esteemed figure amongst the King of England and the English people. Meanwhile, Somerset who had been in France, returns home to England, bearing the unpleasant news that the English territories in the Kingdom of France have been lost. Upon hearing this terrible news, the Duke of York becomes opportunistic. York exploits this disastrous news to blame Gloucester for England's prized territorial losses in France. Gloucester is accused of high treason. Shortly thereafter, Suffolk, Margaret, York, and the Bishop of Winchester collude to plot the murder of Gloucester.

With respect to England's territorial possessions closer to home, there is a rebellion against English rule in Ireland. Thus, York departs England to quell the unrest in Ireland and put an end to this crisis. Now York has his own ambitions and desire for limitless power. York seeks to make his bold claim to the English Throne. Thus, York encourages a Kentish rebel by the name of Jack Cade to stir up a revolt in the great City of London. This rebellion is ultimately unsuccessful, and public order is restored in London. This failed rebellion does not mark the conclusion of York's determined quest for the English Crown.

Towards the final stages of this play, York returns to England to assert his bold claim to the English Crown. York is wholly supported by his three sons, Edward, George, and Richard. In addition, York has the favour and confidence of Salisbury and Warwick. Meanwhile, King Henry is assisted by Buckingham, the Cliffords, Margaret, and Somerset. In a historic battle, the armed forces of the House of Lancaster and the House of York confront each other at St Albans. The English King and Queen flee for their safety. Now York's armed forces take the momentum and they inch ever closer towards capturing London.

'Welcome, Queen Margaret. I can express no kinder sign of love than this kind kiss.' [224]

Actions serve to express our intention and gratitude towards one another. A sincere and loving kiss is an expression of love from one person to another. Regardless of rank, birth, wealth, nobility, parentage, education, faith, income, private property, or social class,

---

224 Shakespeare, William. (1594). *Henry VI. Part Two.* Act 1, Scene 1.

love is a universal language. Love can be exchanged, shared, and disseminated throughout all the countries, continents, and cultures of this world. Material poverty or low socio-economic status are not impediments to a person's ability to love another person.

'O Lord, that lends me life, lend me a heart replete with thankfulness.' [225]

All life comes from God. God is the Provider, Sustainer, and Redeemer of humanity. While we have life, we forget to reminisce on the very goodness of God. The very existence of humanity on Earth is contingent upon God's mercy, grace, goodness, and favour. We must take the time to thank and praise God for the opportunity to experience life on Earth. Often times we become engrossed in the midst of our personal issues and significant life challenges. We must practice contentment. We ought to be thankful to God for the blessing of life. The privilege to experience a lifetime is priceless.

'Let not his smoothing words bewitch your hearts. Be wise and circumspect.' [226]

People can select their words carefully, both for the effectuation of good and evil actions. A person can utilise their speech to misconstrue or fabricate actions, not to mention, conceal deception. Therefore, we must be vigilant and not trust a person's use of words on face value. It is essential that we examine a person's motives, intentions, actions, and thoughts, in conjunction with their speech. This will assist us to ascertain a complete and comprehensive assessment of 'what' and 'who' an individual truly is. That is to say, accurately ascertain a person's character, reputation, honour, integrity, morality, and credit, before we place our trust and confidence in their words.

---

225 Shakespeare, William. (1594). *Henry VI. Part Two.* Act 1, Scene 1.
226 Shakespeare, William. (1594). *Henry VI. Part Two.* Act 1, Scene 1.

'Pride went before, ambition follows him.' [227]

Every person is a unique combination of particular strengths and weaknesses. Such is the fixed reality of the human condition. No person on Earth is complete and perfect unto themselves. Pride is an emotion that ought to be regulated and managed. Pride is not necessarily a 'good' or 'evil' emotion. Pride can become either 'good' or 'evil', based on how a person consciously associates their self-image among other members of an institution or community. A sensible perception of pride is having a 'quiet confidence' in one's knowledge, skills, learning, abilities, experience, and aptitude, celebrating one's successes, and obtaining satisfaction from one's accomplishments.

On the other hand, an egoistic perception of pride is most dangerous to one's ability to flourish and relate to other people in modern society. In this particular case, pride is likely to demonstrate conceit, and result in a person's downfall. Within the *Holy Bible*, in the *Old Testament*, the sacred Scripture contained within the *Book of Proverbs*, Chapter 16, Verse 18, forewarns us that, 'Pride goes before destruction, and a haughty spirit before a fall.'

In a comparable manner, ambition is a favourable desire that must be managed throughout the course of life. Being overly ambitious can result in the situation, where we are unable to manage and meet our expectations. Therefore, we ought to establish goals that develop and further our abilities. However, we need to be realistic and factor into consideration our circumstances, abilities, skills, knowledge, resources, and priorities. Pragmatism will ensure that we position ourselves for success.

---

227 Shakespeare, William. (1594). *Henry VI. Part Two.* Act 1, Scene 1.

'My troublous dreams this night doth make me sad.' [228]

We must not ponder over negative thoughts. Extensive reflection shall alter our cognition, mood, feelings, emotions, and accurate perception of reality. While sadness, much like grief, anger, joy, interest, surprise, disgust, contempt, fear, shame, shyness, guilt, and happiness, is a natural emotion, it must be regulated and kept in balance.

All people are likely to feel sad at some point in their lives. Sadness may be due to missing out on a university scholarship. Finishing second place in a prestigious swimming competition. Navigating the pain of a divorce. Working through issues concerning child custody arrangements. Loss of an important relationship. Missing out on that prized promotion at work. Not passing a final exam for a course at university. The death of a loved one. Loss of employment. Struggles with personal finances. Addiction with gambling or alcohol. Complications with pregnancy, resulting in a caesarean section. Not being able to attend our children's school graduation ceremony. Incarceration for being found guilty of first-degree murder. Receiving a conviction for an indictable offence. Being the victim of family and domestic violence. Being subject to sexual assault. The death of a close friend due to suicide. Receiving the unwelcome news of a loved one being diagnosed with Pancreatic Cancer. The self medication of non-lethal drugs to manage the effects of depression. During such unimaginably difficult times, a person should seek professional care, support, and guidance. Help is available. Help is at hand. God's Grace be with you. Peace be with you.

---

228 Shakespeare, William. (1594). *Henry VI. Part Two.* Act 1, Scene 2.

'But God in mercy so deal with my soul, As I in duty love my King and Country!' [229]

We ought to pray to God for mercy, and not for justice. If we sought the Administration of Justice in God's Court, then no person would secure their undeserved Salvation. Human nature is such that we would all fall short, through our sinful conduct in the flesh. Indeed, the battle with the flesh is a challenge, even for the greatest of all people. For example, consider the *Letters of Paul* contained within the *Holy Bible*, in the *New Testament*, specifically, in the *Book of First Corinthians*, Chapter 15, Verse 31, for it states: 'I face death every day—yes, just as surely as I boast about you in Christ Jesus our Lord.' More commonly, Paul the Apostle's words are translated as, 'I die daily.' Such is the fierce battle with the flesh. The corrupting nature of sin is a protracted battle that continues unabated throughout the entire course of human life.

In the final analysis, it is essential that we forgive other people who sin against us. So that God shall forgive us. Love is the highest good that we shall express on Earth. To love God. Also, to love our brothers and sisters. There are a plethora of Scripture verses that emphasise the importance of love during our time here on Earth. For example, consider the following Scripture verse within the *Holy Bible*, in the *Book of First Peter*, Chapter 4, Verse 8, 'Above all, love each other deeply, because love covers a multitude of sins.'

'I prithee, Peace, Good Queen, and whet not on these furious Peers, for blessed are the Peacemakers on Earth.' [230]

This world revolves around the extremes of war and peace. Given the vast magnitude of differences in human thought, speech, and behaviour, it is relatively effortless to entertain a quarrel or escalate a conflict. A blessed minority of the human population understand

---

229 Shakespeare, William. (1594). *Henry VI. Part Two.* Act 1, Scene 3.
230 Shakespeare, William. (1594). *Henry VI. Part Two.* Act 2, Scene 1.

the principle that, 'Peace is the highest good, second only to love.' Those people who seek to create and preserve the basis for peace in this world are mindful and virtuous in thought, speech, and action.

'The winds grow high, so do your stomachs, Lords.' [231]

All humans are subject to physiological drives, psychological responses, emotions, feelings, sensations, sensual desires, spiritual yearning, contemplation, and biological requirements. These include nutrition, hydration, sleep, copulation, personal safety, companionship, acceptance, love, pain, suffering, sorrow, happiness, joy, interest, and surprise.

The aforementioned basic human needs and responses must be acknowledged and attended to. Thereafter, we can pursue more lofty endeavours in life. For example, consider attaining a university degree. Participating in a marathon. Competing in the Olympics. Engaging in software development. Writing a book. Learning how to drive a motor vehicle. Becoming a scientist. Travelling around the world. Getting married. Purchasing real property. Completing a doctorate degree. Securing employment. Learning a foreign language. Alternatively, attaining the prestigious rank of Professor at a world-class university.

'How irksome is this music to my heart! When such strings jar, what hope of harmony?' [232]

The five human senses (i.e., sight, sound, smell, taste, and touch) all have an influence on the mind. Sometimes for the better, and at other times, for the worst. External stimuli induce excitatory and inhibitory sensations in the human brain that result in desirable or undesirable feelings, emotions, and thoughts. We must not permit our external environment to determine our internal state of mind.

---

231 Shakespeare, William. (1594). *Henry VI. Part Two.* Act 2, Scene 1.
232 Shakespeare, William. (1594). *Henry VI. Part Two.* Act 2, Scene 1.

It is important that we preserve our inner joy and safeguard our precious peace during our finite time on Earth.

'Now, God be praised, that to believing souls gives light in darkness, comfort in despair.' [233]

God is the ultimate basis for our salvation and redemption. Without God, humanity shall have no hope, love, or faith. God's mercy, favour, grace, and goodness allow humanity to transcend the struggles, privations, tribulations, and difficulties of human life. God is our one and only True Source. God is the Provider, and God is the Redeemer of all humanity. We can all seek divine union with God through sincere acts of devotion, worship, community service, charity, penance, reading Scripture, and prayer.

'Thus got the House of Lancaster the Crown. Which now they hold by force and not by right.' [234]

According to Shakespeare, the House of Lancaster has usurped the English Throne. This is not an anomaly in the history of power struggles for the English Crown. Some people acquire what belongs to them through rightful inheritance and legitimate succession. While other individuals engage in the act of misappropriation in order to illegitimately secure the private property, personal wealth, and real estate that belong to another person. 'The Use of Force' is not a novel doctrine. The employment of force has been around since the earliest known history of humanity. Regrettably, 'the Use of Force' is very much a part and parcel of humanity's existence in the twenty-first century.

---

233 Shakespeare, William. (1594). *Henry VI. Part Two.* Act 2, Scene 1.
234 Shakespeare, William. (1594). *Henry VI. Part Two.* Act 2, Scene 2.

'I beseech Your Majesty, give me leave to go. Sorrow would solace and mine age would ease.' [235]

Extreme circumstances can warrant us being excused from our professional duty and legal responsibility. Often times, in the midst of unexpected difficulty, we are burdened with dismal feelings and consequential tribulations, coupled with the onset of advanced age, which diminishes the inherent capacity of the mind and body to discharge our contractual obligations, to the very best of our ability. We must be acutely aware of our limitations and accept that sometimes, it is beyond our finite capacity to perform in a certain position. In contrast, this engenders the newfound opportunity for another individual to occupy our position. With earnest hope and belief, the successor shall go further than their predecessor.

'God shall be my hope, my stay, my guide, and lantern to my feet.' [236]

Whom so ever places their unconditional trust in God shall be protected and blessed. For an individual who positions their trust in another person may be betrayed, deceived, misled, or falsely accused. On the contrary, God honours sacred covenants and promises, even when we fall short and do not fulfil our end of the agreement. For God overlooks our faults and inadequacies, through undeserving acts of mercy, forgiveness, love, and kindness.

Indeed, God's Grace is the inexplicable cause for our abilities, accomplishments, possessions, education, personal wealth, spouse, income, private property, and many other worldly blessings. No matter who helps us along our life journey, we must always remember that God is our Source. Within the *Holy Bible*, in the *Book of Job*, Chapter 19, Verse 25, we are reminded that God's Presence is eternal and always accessible to us, 'I know that my Redeemer lives, and that in the end, He will stand on the Earth.'

---

235 Shakespeare, William. (1594). *Henry VI. Part Two.* Act 2, Scene 3.
236 Shakespeare, William. (1594). *Henry VI. Part Two.* Act 2, Scene 3.

'Here let them end it; and God defend the Right!' [237]

God is always on the side of those who are righteous. We must look to God as our Source of inspiration, hope, faith, and love. There are many difficulties that we have confronted in the past. There are challenges that are before us, at this present moment in time. There will be issues that we have to address in the uncertain future. In all things, we must place our unconditional trust, belief, faith, and hope in God.

'O God, have I overcome mine enemies in this presence?' [238]

In every person's life, there will be opposition. There will be enemies. There will be difficulties. Also, there will be betrayals. Nonetheless, we must proceed forward, with the hope and conviction that our endeavours shall be prosperous. Positioning our unconditional trust in God, we have the inner confidence, that God shall keep a watchful eye over us and our affairs.

'Thy greatest help is quiet. I pray thee, sort thy heart to patience.' [239]

We shall always keep God in our heart, mind, thoughts, and prayers. The remembrance of God does not require any boasting, fanfare, public display, grand ostentation, or flamboyance. After all, God is the Searcher of hearts and Keeper of souls. We can trust in God to resolve our complex personal affairs in the manner that God perceives it best.

The heart shall always be restless in our present human condition. The heart is detached from God. The great theologian, philosopher, writer, preacher, and bishop of Roman North Africa, Saint Augustine, imparts to us much wisdom in his theological masterpiece, *Confessions*, 'Thou hast made us for Thyself, O Lord,

---

237 Shakespeare, William. (1594). *Henry VI. Part Two.* Act 2, Scene 3.
238 Shakespeare, William. (1594). *Henry VI. Part Two.* Act 2, Scene 3.
239 Shakespeare, William. (1594). *Henry VI. Part Two.* Act 2, Scene 4.

and our heart is restless, until it finds its rest in Thee.' Through the good acts of repentance, confession, charity, community service, and prayer, we can bring ourselves ever closer to God.

> *'Smooth runs the water where the brook is deep, and in his simple show he harbours treason. The fox barks not when he would steal the lamb.'* [240]

Appearances are deceptive and misleading. Therefore, we ought to exercise discretion in whom we place our trust. By employing the metaphor of a river, Shakespeare cleverly illustrates that where the surface water in a river appears smooth, it is often concealing deep water. Thus, we cannot readily perceive what is beneath the surface. As a consequence, appearances are imprecise, and not truly illustrative of the substance, or essence they conceal beneath them. In a similar manner, Shakespeare employs the analogy of a fox, which can alter its behaviour, when in pursuit of its prized end.

> *'The care you have of us, to mow down thorns that would annoy our foot, is worthy praise.'* [241]

The care we demonstrate towards other people is a reflection of our values, character, integrity, and personality. More importantly, we must be detached from the outcome of our good actions. That is to say, we must not perform virtuous conduct in anticipation of praise, affection, thanks, gifts, or any other material or immaterial advantage, or benefit. Our thought, speech, and action, collectively, define who we are. Therefore, we must use these instruments for the betterment and service of humanity.

---

240 Shakespeare, William. (1594). *Henry VI. Part Two.* Act 3, Scene 1.
241 Shakespeare, William. (1594). *Henry VI. Part Two.* Act 3, Scene 1.

'The purest spring is not so free from mud. As I am clear from treason to my Sovereign.' [242]

At times, we may be accused of a civil wrong, or criminal charges may be laid against us in a court of law or tribunal. However, setting aside legal procedure and deference to the ideal principles of jurisprudence, our conscience matters most of all. If we are truly innocent in the contentious matter before us, then our conscience shall not be troubled by the accusations that are presented before us.

As an example, consider the inspirational story of Paul the Apostle. Paul was a learned gentleman of faith, and a Roman citizen. Paul faced unfounded accusations, trials, shipwrecks, imprisonment, and torture on his remarkable journey of Discipleship throughout the Roman World. Above all, Paul's conscience was sincere, and his heart was pure. For Paul's Conversion transformed him into a beloved Disciple of God.

'I say no more than truth. So help me God!' [243]

In times of difficulties, we must call upon God's Name to assist us in the pursuit of our endeavours. Only God can render the assistance that we require to hold onto the Truth. To speak the Truth. Also, to act Truthfully. Our highest allegiance is always to God. Subsequently, to His Majesty the King, or Her Majesty the Queen, the Head of State, and also to our fellow citizens within our sovereign nation-state. In all matters, great and small, God is our True Helper.

---

242 Shakespeare, William. (1594). *Henry VI. Part Two.* Act 3, Scene 1.
243 Shakespeare, William. (1594). *Henry VI. Part Two.* Act 3, Scene 1.

'Ah, Gracious Lord, these days are dangerous. Virtue is choked with foul ambition ... and charity chased hence by rancour's hand.' [244]

In the contemporary world, people are not all what they purport to be. Virtue is a masquerade for lofty desires, selfish ambitions, the illustrious pursuit of self-interest, the acquisition of private property, the accumulation of vast profits, and seeking exorbitant quantities of personal wealth. Not to mention, the moral concepts of community service, charity, and compassionate care are rapidly becoming extinct throughout the Modern World.

This world has a value-system and culture that is increasingly defined by individualism, materialism, capitalism, consumerism, nihilism, secularism, liberalism, and hedonism. The overly inflated sense of attaching a grand importance to one's own affairs, and neglecting the welfare of the disadvantaged people of modern society, is starting to destroy the very heart and foundation of our society.

'A staff is quickly found to beat a dog.' [245]

Shakespeare is utilising colourful language to make a point. That if a person is determined to inflict pain or punishment upon another person, they will find a suitable method, instrument, technique, or manner to make that happen.

'My heart is drowned with grief, whose flood begins to flow within mine eyes. My body round engirt with misery, for what's more miserable than discontent?' [246]

The emotion of grief can be overwhelming at times. Thus, we can feel psychologically burdened with unbearable sadness. It is essential that we keep a 'balanced' mind. That we do our best to

---

244 Shakespeare, William. (1594). *Henry VI. Part Two.* Act 3, Scene 1.
245 Shakespeare, William. (1594). *Henry VI. Part Two.* Act 3, Scene 1.
246 Shakespeare, William. (1594). *Henry VI. Part Two.* Act 3, Scene 1.

position grief in 'perspective'. Loss is inevitable in this broken world. Therefore, grief is a most natural reaction to adversity, suffering, and pain. The best counsel that can be proffered herein is, that while grief is very personable, however, it can be shared and communicated with other people. Yet, no person can share our exact experience of grief, in the manner that we felt and experienced it. Each person needs their own time and space to work through the challenges associated with grief. To make one's peace with reality.

Towards the end of the aforesaid proposition, Shakespeare puts forward a rhetorical question. For the state of discontent is the most miserable condition in our life. Sometimes, it is best for a person to count their blessings. To seek contentment with what they do have. For the human condition is such, that desire is insatiable. No matter how much, or how little one has, the very state of satisfaction with one's life, always appears to be beyond attainment.

'For things are often spoke and seldom meant.' [247]

Language is a medium used to convey thoughts, ideas, facts, stories, concepts, and much more. However, at times, we find our speech to be unintelligent. Sometimes, our speech is out of synchronisation with our actions. Alternatively, in the heat of the moment, we may say something that we did not mean. We may regret having spoken the words that we did in the first place. This is not a reflection of language being imprecise, but rather, the limitations of human communication. The incredible complexity of human personality, emotions, feelings, cognition, and sensations, are beyond the complete human understanding. The human condition has its limitations. Our speech does not always come to reflect our intended or desired reality.

---

247 Shakespeare, William. (1594). *Henry VI. Part Two.* Act 3, Scene 1.

'No, not to lose it all, as thou hast done. I rather would have lost my life betimes. Than bring a burden of dishonour home. By staying there so long till all were lost.' [248]

Some battles are won and some battles are lost. Yet honour, integrity, and reputation can rarely, if ever, be recovered once they are forfeited. Shakespeare is illustrating the point that it is more acceptable for a person to surrender their life, rather than relinquish one's most prized honour. For to have lost it all, and to remain alive is a dishonourable act. Now there is nothing left to live for. Life is temporal; however, dishonour and shame will endure in perpetuity. Indeed, the long-lasting memory of human history, while imperfect and sometimes imprecise, is often harsh and cruel.

'O Thou that judgest all things, stay my thoughts, my thoughts that labour to persuade my soul.' [249]

God is the True Judge of all human actions. In all things of importance, we must call upon God's Sovereign Name and Eternal Word, to guide our thoughts. God's Counsel shall facilitate our wise decisions, that further the cause of social justice, community service, peace, charity, love, equality, brotherhood, sisterhood, faith, marriage, family, and human dignity. We must make earnest appeals to God, for the requisite spiritual guidance, to direct the trajectory of our thoughts towards wholesome, positive, good, and constructive endeavours.

'If my suspect be false, forgive me, God, for judgement only doth belong to Thee.' [250]

We ought to refrain from passing false judgement upon other people. It is well and truly possible that we be mistaken in our

---

248 Shakespeare, William. (1594). *Henry VI. Part Two.* Act 3, Scene 1.
249 Shakespeare, William. (1594). *Henry VI. Part Two.* Act 3, Scene 2.
250 Shakespeare, William. (1594). *Henry VI. Part Two.* Act 3, Scene 2.

partial judgement. Therefore, rightly so, we must ask God for forgiveness. The right to judge another person only belongs to God. While we have the institution of Common Law and numerous remedies to seek justice on Earth, this is an imperfect world. For example, consider the concepts of miscarriage of justice, fabricated evidence, compounding a felony, misfeasance in public office, misprision of felony, obstruction of justice, perjury, perverting the course of justice, false witness testimony, and juror bias. Whereas, God's Justice is perfect and true in all respects. Indeed, God's Justice is the highest and final 'Court of Appeal'.

'So, get thee gone, that I may know my grief. For it is surmised while thou art standing by.' [251]

Grief is a very personal emotional suffering. A person can attempt to express grief in words. However, it is nigh impossible, to accurately share one's psychological impression of profound loss, experience of tragedy, anguish, lamentation, negative externality from a national crisis, or immeasurable heartache. In most cases, our personal experience of grief illustrates how our mental (or psychological) pain, is almost always greater than the physical pain, that we suffer from a tragic event, or traumatic experience in life.

We can only come to know ourselves better, through personal experience which entails grief. As a result, we grow and learn from such life-changing experiences. Importantly, we can communicate our grief with other people. We can share our grief in a constructive and meaningful manner. This approach has two profound benefits. First, sharing grief is a conscious reminder that we are not alone in our grief. Second, talking through our grief can help, rather than hinder, other people who are confronting similar life challenges. To express conscious awareness that we are only human is an important

---

251 Shakespeare, William. (1594). *Henry VI. Part Two.* Act 3, Scene 2.

reminder for all of us. Last but not least, grief is a universal attribute of human life. Grief is experienced in different degrees, however, in underlying substance, our grief is almost identical.

'Ah, what a sign it is of evil life, where death's approach is seen so terrible!' [252]

Death is an unchanging reality of human life. At some point in time, every living person on Earth will experience death. Therefore, what matters most is our 'perception' of death. We must accept death as a fact of life. Death is part and parcel of existence in this broken world. The end-to-end human lifespan, which is governed by the stages of fertilised ovum, foetus, neonate, baby, toddler, child, teenager, mature adult, and elderly person, all these stages contain traces and elements of pain and suffering. In the final analysis, mortality is an indisputable fact of human life. We must make our peace with being mortal.

'Forbear to judge, for we are sinners all.' [253]

This phrase expresses an undeniable reality of the human condition. No person is perfect. While we have the temptation to judge other people, to highlight their shortcomings, inadequacies, and imperfections, the fact is, that we are no better ourselves. The sinful conduct resides in our universal human nature, not in the different challenges, inclinations, and struggles that we confront in the course of our life. To demonstrate mercy towards people for their mistakes. To grant forgiveness to those people who have done us wrong. These are noble symbols of good character.

---

252 Shakespeare, William. (1594). *Henry VI. Part Two.* Act 3, Scene 3.
253 Shakespeare, William. (1594). *Henry VI. Part Two.* Act 3, Scene 3.

> *'Suffolk's imperial tongue is stern and rough, used to command, untaught to plead for favour.'* [254]

Humans have different personalities, traits, facial expressions, temperaments, ideas, emotions, thoughts, and behaviours. While we are all similar, we are not identical. The inexact art of physiognomy attempts to ascertain a person's character from their facial expression. According to the ancient wisdom of the Greek physician, Hippocrates, there are four primary temperaments: Choleric, Melancholic, Phlegmatic, and Sanguine.

The reality is that some people are soft-spoken and amiable. While other people are pertinacious and brusque. Shakespeare makes the point, that it is not within the pertinacious and brusque person's intrinsic nature, to plead for favour or good-treatment. For such a person is naturally inclined to instruct, direct, and order. In any institution or community, there will always be natural leaders. Those who encompass the requisite traits to command other people's attention and obedience.

> *'True nobility is exempt from fear.'* [255]

Nobility is the opposite of fear. The highest nobility is comprised of honesty, courage, and kindness. Thus, it does not matter what rank, parentage, birth, ethnicity, race, or social class a person has originated from. Any person can develop their personal character to possess nobility. Nobility requires discipline, conscientiousness, honesty, integrity, steadfastness, righteousness, and commitment. Nobility allows a person to take a stand for what is right, just, and proper conduct, even in the midst of adversity or adverse consequences, without the fear of reprisal. Indeed, morality is the basis for true nobility. Such profound nobility is rare and exceptional in the Modern World. For this is a broken world, where humanity

---

254 Shakespeare, William. (1594). *Henry VI. Part Two.* Act 4, Scene 1.
255 Shakespeare, William. (1594). *Henry VI. Part Two.* Act 4, Scene 1.

is overly defined by and concerned with, the ideological forces of materialism, consumerism, individualism, secularism, hedonism, liberalism, and capitalism.

'Come, Soldiers, show what cruelty ye can. That this my death may never be forgot! Great men oft die by vile bezonians.'[256]

The documented narrative of ancient and modern history, all too often illustrates, how great fighters and heroic leaders are often killed at the hands of mercenaries, lowly beggars, common soldiers, assassins, traitors, and scoundrels. The possession and exercise of power, influence, and authority in respectable leaders often breeds jealousy, mistrust, deception, and envy in their governed subjects. The Italian diplomat, philosopher, and author, Niccolò Machiavelli, advanced an insightful observation regarding leadership in his famous political treatise, *The Prince* (1532), 'It is better to be feared than loved, if you cannot be both.'

'The first thing we do is kill all the lawyers.'[257]

This statement is clearly a hyperbole. The greater point Shakespeare asserts is that lawyers and the institution of Law is full of complex language, formal procedures, bureaucratic structures, endless rules, difficult to navigate hierarchies, absurd formalities, and traditional customs. These legal intricacies are almost impossible for the lay person to accurately comprehend. The ordinary person is inevitably going to confront confusion and frustration with the legal profession, when seeking natural justice to resolve their quandary.

---

256 Shakespeare, William. (1594). *Henry VI. Part Two.* Act 4, Scene 1.
257 Shakespeare, William. (1594). *Henry VI. Part Two.* Act 4, Scene 2.

'And you that love the Commons, follow me. Now show yourselves men, it is for liberty.' [258]

The common lot of people must be prepared to make a stand for their freedom from tyranny and for the security of their human rights. Freedom, like sovereignty, needs to be fought for and secured. A life without liberty is not worth living. Put another way, for the sake of liberty, we must be prepared to forsake our life. For both life and liberty are precious. Nevertheless, a life without liberty, is no life at all.

Each and every person in modern society possesses several inalienable rights. The right to civic participation in the political affairs of the sovereign nation-state. The right to a quality school and university education. The right to access affordable housing. The human right to food, water, and essential medication. The right to protection of private property. The right to equal access to an impartial and fair justice system. The economic right to receive equal access to support services by the Federal Government (i.e., disability support or pension payments). The social right to access public amenities (i.e., recreational facilities, libraries, hospitals, national parks, and swimming pools). The economic right to earn a living wage, which reflects a person's expertise, skill, knowledge, qualifications, learning, and abilities. The moral right to freedom of conscience. Freedom of religion. Freedom of worship. Freedom of thought. The fundamental human right to be treated with dignity and respect. The legal right to be presumed innocent, unless proven guilty. Last but not least, the human right to be treated without discrimination of any kind.

The philosophical concept of an egalitarian society must be transformed from the 'ideal' to the 'real'. Only then can each and every member of modern society be assured peace, love, happiness, security of private property, safety of person, harmony, and liberty.

---

258 Shakespeare, William. (1594). *Henry VI. Part Two.* Act 4, Scene 2.

'We will keep heart and courage, proceeding forward bold and resolute.' [259]

We shall confront countless challenges, troubles, privations, and injustices throughout the course of our life. Yet, in all matters, we must keep faith and never surrender hope. Moving forward allows us to experience the fullness of human life, to secure our God-given potential. Always remember, that all things are possible. However, we have to dare to believe. Belief is the cornerstone that becomes the basis for our positive thoughts, which lead to action. In the end, it is action that creates our worldly reality.

On the other hand, if we fail to move forward, we only deprive ourselves of the 'once-in-a-lifetime' opportunity to create the life that we desire. The life that we conceptualised within our mind. There is no benefit to be gained from being fixated upon the past. For the past only serves to diminish the value of the present moment. The present time is all that we have. The present time is all that we need, to create our future. In the final analysis, the sooner a person moves forward from a personal tragedy, loss, or difficult event, more likely than not, the easier it is. The passage of time, in and of itself, rarely resolves anything, in matters of great grievance and personal loss.

'Trust nobody, for fear you be betrayed. The trust I have is in mine innocence. Therefore, am I bold and resolute.' [260]

This proposition posits a quandary. It is indeed a matter of 'heavy consequence' to trust another person, with one's personal affairs, private and sensitive information, inner secrets, and genuine concerns. Such exposure of personal and confidential information creates a high degree of vulnerability. This in turn, positions a person in a precarious state. As a result, an innocent individual's

---

259 Shakespeare, William. (1594). *Henry VI. Part Two*. Act 4, Scene 4.
260 Shakespeare, William. (1594). *Henry VI. Part Two*. Act 4, Scene 4.

trust may be betrayed. An unsuspecting person can be exploited and taken advantage of, to serve the interests and ends of a malevolent person.

> *'Thou hast appointed Justices of Peace, to call poor men before them about matters they were not able to answer. Moreover, thou hast put them in prison; and because they could not read, thou hast hanged them; when, indeed, only for that cause they have been most worthy to live.'* [261]

Regrettably, there is inequity and inequality in every social order. Modern society is ordered and structured along the socio-economic principles of income, personal wealth, race, ethnicity, gender, sex, colour, private property, tertiary education, and many others. In the pre-eminent institution of law, not to mention, medicine, the learned, honourable, affluent, wealthy, powerful, and influential aristocratic class often have the unfettered opportunity and access to economic resources to gain the requisite learning, education, knowledge, qualifications, and experience, in order to hold positions of high office or prestige in society, such as a judge, lawyer, magistrate, justice, chief justice, medical doctor, or surgeon.

On the contrary, it is the most destitute people in our society, the illiterate individuals, those people who are unskilled labourers, unlearned, without a tertiary education, those people that are earning the minimum wage, that are subject to the force of circumstance to survive. Such disadvantaged people are truly bound by their confrontation with necessity. Socio-economically disadvantaged people lack the requisite financial capital to fulfil their inherent potential.

The poor people's life is determined by the whims of economic crises and financial shocks. Thus, poor people quite often find themselves on the wrong side of the law. While every person is

---

261 Shakespeare, William. (1594). *Henry VI. Part Two.* Act 4, Scene 7.

equally responsible for their actions, injustice in our modern society is all too common. Not to mention, injustice most impacts the unlearned people of low socio-economic class.

'And seeing ignorance is the Curse of God. Knowledge the wing wherewith we fly to Heaven.' [262]

It is only through God's undeserving mercy that people have the profound opportunity for redemption. If we possess specialist knowledge, or have completed any profound works, it is not of our own power, initiative, or accord, but rather it is a manifestation of the Power of God that works through the Holy Spirit. For what end and purpose is humanity's limited knowledge and good work? To reveal God's Eternal and Majestic Glory.

'The Proudest Peer in the Realm shall not wear a head upon his shoulders, unless he pay me tribute.' [263]

We all owe our duties and taxes to the sovereign of the nation-state, or in more contemporary times, to the democratic government of the nation-state. The proper and effective administration of the State requires the contribution of all its citizens. A federal taxation system must be fair and equitable. The tax system serves many important functions, such as the funding of hospitals, schools, childcare facilities, libraries, national parks, essential services (i.e., waste collection and management), the construction and maintenance of public roads and major highways, the protection of private property, the maintenance of a police force, ambulance fleet, fire stations and brigades, armed forces (i.e., army, navy, and air force), and the many other important aspects of a sovereign nation-state.

---

262 Shakespeare, William. (1594). *Henry VI. Part Two.* Act 4, Scene 7.
263 Shakespeare, William. (1594). *Henry VI. Part Two.* Act 4, Scene 7.

Indeed, it is the legal obligation of every citizen to make a contribution to their sovereign nation-state. This objective promotes the proper maintenance and good standing of the State. The English philosopher, Thomas Hobbes, in his magnificent work, *Leviathan* (1651), explores the concept of a 'Social Contract' between the people and the Commonwealth. Hobbes' Social Contract will not be fulfilled, unless both parties, citizen and nation-state, rightly and faithfully, uphold their obligations and duties.

'I thought you would never have given out these arms, till you had recovered your ancient freedom. But you're all recreants and dastards, and delight to live in slavery to the Nobility. Well, let them break your backs with burdens.' [264]

The majority of humanity desires their cherished freedom. However, it is only ever a minority of the human population that consciously self-determine what to do with their invaluable freedom. For with freedom comes personal responsibility. Yet, most people do not desire to accept the duty of personal responsibility that is associated with freedom. To position the above assertion differently, individuals desire their rights, liberties, and privileges, not their obligations, duties, and responsibilities in modern society.

The productive utility of true freedom requires considerable thought. A higher quality of thought in a person. A person has to consciously inquire and deeply reflect upon the difficult questions concerning freedom, such as:

- What type of life do I want to create?
- What do I want to become?
- How do I best utilise my time?
- What shall be my legacy?
- What do I want to leave behind?
- What are my motives, intentions, and ambitions?
- What constitutes a successful life?

---

264 Shakespeare, William. (1594). *Henry VI. Part Two.* Act 4, Scene 8.

These questions are both significant and personal. More importantly, there are no 'right' or 'wrong' answers to the aforementioned consequential questions. Each person is an individual. Thus, each person is unique. For people have different personalities, emotions, backgrounds, faiths, personal beliefs, personal experiences, life priorities, and personal endeavours. In the final analysis, it is the people who confront the difficult questions of life, that will not only come to know themselves better, but also understand what motivates them, and what their true passions are in life.

'God on our side, doubt not of victory.' [265]

Success in a person's endeavours starts with their beliefs. How a person thinks about themselves, their capacities, abilities, talents, and strengths. We need to believe that God is with us in our struggles, privations, and challenges. The presence of doubt, confusion, fear, hesitation, and indecision are some of the greatest hindrances in human life. These hindrances not only serve to paralyse a person's good thinking, they also diminish an individual's capacity for action. Furthermore, these hindrances also decrease the finite and valuable time that a person has on Earth. The sooner one dispels with doubt, the better they will be in life. The same is inferred about fear.

In the *Holy Bible*, within the *Old Testament*, in the *Book of Genesis*, Chapter 43, Verse 10, we witness how doubt hinders action and defers progress in our affairs, 'As it is, if we had not delayed, we could have gone and returned twice.' The presence of time is limited in life. The concept of time is comparable to the numerous grains of sand in an hourglass. One day there will be no time in the remainder. Therefore, we ought to make the most of the opportunities and moments, that life presents us with.

---

265 Shakespeare, William. (1594). *Henry VI. Part Two.* Act 4, Scene 8.

*'Was ever King that joyed an Earthly Throne and could command
no more content than I?'* [266]

While Kings and Queens revel in royalty, honour, privilege, wealth, private property, influence, prestige, and power, the sombre reality is that their extrinsic joy conceals the countless and complex layers of troubles, concerns, responsibilities, and worries that a sovereign is responsible for. Ultimately, contentment is a state of mind. Contentment has naught to do with a person's wealth, material possessions, number of relationships, status, accomplishments, achievements, accolades, and successes.

Contentment is about perception, emotion, and feeling. Contentment is about how a person perceives their life. Whether a king, queen, or private citizen, each person is rightly entitled to their inner state of contentment. The cherished prize of contentment is not an exclusive prerogative of the aristocratic class. Therefore, the correct and difficult question is: Can a person accept and be content with their life?

*'No sooner was I crept out of my cradle. But I was made a King,
at nine months old.'* [267]

Some people are born to rule, and thus, some people are born into greatness. Destiny is an indisputable factor in the life trajectory of everyone. For some people, destiny's presence is favourable. Whereas, for other people, destiny deals an unfavourable result. Regardless of one's country of birth, parentage, socio-economic status, class, gender, sex, race, ethnicity, faith, sexual orientation, age, profession, education, income, personal wealth, and private property, each person is entitled to the 'fullness' of human life.

This 'fullness' includes a life of love, friendship, happiness, liberty, the attainment of one's sporting and intellectual aspirations,

---

266 Shakespeare, William. (1594). *Henry VI. Part Two.* Act 4, Scene 9.
267 Shakespeare, William. (1594). *Henry VI. Part Two.* Act 4, Scene 9.

personal ambitions, formal learning, education, employment, family, devotion to God, and adequate rest from one's (almost endless) labours.

'Was never subject longed to be a King. As I do long and wish to be a subject.' [268]

We cannot always self-determine our place, prosperity, power, property, prestige, and position in society. Some people personally disapprove of their position in a social order, and this harbours them with considerable resentment in their life. Most importantly, confronting reality starts with 'acceptance'. The acceptance of where one is at in the present moment of life is essential. Now a person may not approve of their present circumstances, accomplishments, and position in modern society. However, a reasonable person must accept this as their starting point. From this starting point, a discontent individual can begin the conscious process of initiating genuine change and creating real progress.

'I am resolved for death or dignity.' [269]

To position this assertion another way, a life without dignity is not worth living. For human dignity is the entire basis of affirming life. Dignity is the 'foundation stone' upon which our character, reputation, confidence, standing, and honour reside. Therefore, this assertion holds, that if one cannot possess human dignity, then death is the only viable alternative. For to live in shame, is no meaningful life at all. Life defined by indignity is a darkened, dead, dreadful, and dull existence in this world.

---

268 Shakespeare, William. (1594). *Henry VI. Part Two.* Act 4, Scene 9.
269 Shakespeare, William. (1594). *Henry VI. Part Two.* Act 5, Scene 1.

> *'Fear frames disorder and disorder wounds where it should guard.'* [270]

Very similar to the case with doubt, fear also hinders our objectives and progress in life. Fear confuses and disorients a person's thoughts. Fear limits a person's ability to perceive the world and reality around them in a thoughtful, logical, rational, and systematic manner. Inevitably, such a disoriented and deluded mind, sets into motion the creation of negative causes, which shall lead to our downfall, rather than our triumph. As the well-known saying goes, 'Victory begins in the mind.' What we often first conceptualise in our mind, that does come into creation in our worldly reality.

> *'Let no soldier fly. He that is truly dedicate to war hath no self-love, nor he that loves himself hath not essentially but by circumstance the name of valour.'* [271]

Soldiers must be 'at the ready' for the call of military duty. A valiant soldier, positions their country and sovereign ahead of themselves. Above all, the duty of a soldier may require the ultimate sacrifice. The soldier must be prepared for this inopportune moment. While moderate self-love is important in life, Shakespeare is specifically referring to a soldier's duty. In this case, the concept of 'self-love' must not be allowed to interfere with a soldier's oath of allegiance. True bravery on the battlefield requires a soldier setting aside one's own concern for welfare and personal safety. To ensure the mission or objective of their battalion is successfully accomplished.

---

270 Shakespeare, William. (1594). *Henry VI. Part Two.* Act 5, Scene 2.
271 Shakespeare, William. (1594). *Henry VI. Part Two.* Act 5, Scene 2.

'God knows how long it is I have to live.' [272]

God is the one and only True Keeper of souls. God determines our birth in this world, our life trajectory, and when it is our time to depart this broken world. The entire Creation is for the expression of the Majestic Glory of God. Therefore, the most important relationship we will have in our lifetime, is our relationship with God. Furthermore, the most important action we will perform in our lifetime is to love God. Peace be with you.

---

272 Shakespeare, William. (1594). *Henry VI. Part Two.* Act 5, Scene 3.

Chapter 13

HENRY VI
(PART THREE)

*'To say the truth, so Judas kissed his Master and
cried "All hail!" when as he meant all harm.'*

SHAKESPEARE

Henry VI (Part Three) is the third and final part of the Henry VI trilogy. This play is characterised by a fierce struggle between the House of York and the House of Lancaster for the English Crown. In a continuation of the events from *Henry VI (Part Two)*, the Duke of York, Richard Plantagenet is victorious at the epic battle of St Albans. As a result, Richard Plantagenet is now enthroned the King of England.

Following an interesting turn of events, the dethroned King Henry VI is forced to acquiesce to King Richard's demand, that Henry VI disinherit his legitimate son, Edward, the Prince of Wales, from the line of Royal Succession to the English Crown. King Henry VI's wife, Queen Margaret is furious and enraged that Henry VI has acquiesced to this seemingly unjust demand of King Richard Plantagenet. Queen Margaret is of the firm mind, that Edward, the Prince of Wales, shall not bear the punishment, nor the inequity for Henry VI's inadequacies and incompetency. Thus, Queen Margaret secures the confidence and support of Lord Clifford to raise an army.

Queen Margaret's armed forces confront York's armed forces at the *Battle of Wakefield* (1460). York's youngest son, Rutland is brutally slain by Lord Clifford. Subsequently, York is captured by Lord Clifford and the Earl of Northumberland. York is mocked and tormented with the horrific details of Rutland's murder, before York is killed by Lord Clifford and Queen Margaret. As a result, more bloodshed and revenge are all but on the horizon. Edward and Richard learn of their father's death at the hands of the enemy. The two gentlemen join forces with Warwick. Furthermore, Edward is proclaimed the new Duke of York, thereafter, to be enthroned King Edward IV of England.

The House of York, led by Edward and Richard, with the assistance of Warwick, raise an army and proceed into battle against the House of Lancaster at Towton. The Yorkists are victorious. As a result, Henry VI, Queen Margaret, and their young son are forced to flee. In the endless shedding of blood for blood, Lord Clifford is killed in revenge for the death of Rutland and York. Henry VI is captured and he is brought to London, at the command of newly crowned King Edward IV. Thereafter, Henry VI is imprisoned in the Tower of London.

Meanwhile, Queen Margaret and the Earl of Warwick are in France, where they are attending the Royal Court of His Majesty King Louis. The Earl of Warwick and King Louis of France join forces, with Queen Margaret, to turn against King Edward IV. Towards the close of this play, King Edward IV and the Earl of Warwick's armed forces meet at Barnet, and Warwick is slain. Queen Margaret has now arrived back in England. Queen Margaret's forces encounter King Edward IV's forces at Tewkesbury. After a long and fierce campaign, the *Battle of Tewkesbury* (1471) witnesses the House of York as victors.

There is much English and French History, and significant military battles condensed in this monumental play. Shakespeare explores several themes, including love, war, revenge, betrayal, power, corruption, allegiance, and many more. This play will leave readers with a critical impression on the fragility of power.

'But thou preferrest thy life before thine honour.' [273]

This is the reverse perspective of the traditional statement, wherein a person prefers 'their honour, before their life'. In many respects, both life and honour are valuable. However, a life without honour is a life without reputation, character, integrity, good standing, and merit. In the final analysis, in this contemporary world, it is each person to their own, when the ordering of values and beliefs are concerned.

The hierarchy of values is no longer universal and fixed in the Modern World. What one person considers of prime importance, might be of total inconsequence to another person. We live in a contemporary world that is governed by liberalism, individualism, secularism, consumerism, hedonism, materialism, and capitalism. These ideologies have witnessed a transformational shift in human thought, speech, behaviour, relationships, culture, language, and identity.

'About that which concerns your grace and us, the Crown of England, Father, which is yours.' [274]

If we are to secure a grand achievement or major accomplishment in life, first, we must believe that it will happen. For the power of belief is the precursor, which sets into motion the chain of events that ought to transpire, in order for success to be realised. Any major victory or triumph in life commences with the belief that

---

273 Shakespeare, William. (1595). *Henry VI. Part Three.* Act 1, Scene 1.
274 Shakespeare, William. (1595). *Henry VI. Part Three.* Act 1, Scene 2.

we can accomplish what we set our mind to attain. In the *Holy Bible*, within the *New Testament*, the *Gospel of Mark*, at Chapter 11, Verse 24, affirms the unparalleled importance of belief, 'Therefore, I tell you, whatever you ask for in prayer, believe that you have received it, and it will be yours.'

> *'I took an oath ... But for a Kingdom any oath may be broken.*
> *I would break a thousand oaths to reign one year. No, God forbid*
> *your grace should be forsworn.'* [275]

Shakespeare eloquently demonstrates the comparison and contrast between the selfish desires of humanity, and the noble duty of humanity, to preserve one's word that is given under oath. The temptation is ever-present for a person to discard an oath, where significant self-interest, fame, wealth, income, prestige, profit, power, or vast pecuniary gain is at stake, however, to do so, one has disowned their very reputation, integrity, conscience, and character. Indeed, the immaterial loss of breaking an oath, is far greater than the material gain of worldly treasures.

> *'The sands are numbered that make up my life. Here must I stay,*
> *and here my life must end.'* [276]

Each and every person's days on this Earth are numbered, much like the strands of hair on a person's head. Shakespeare utilises a classic metaphor to illustrate the concept of 'human mortality'. Without question, our time on Earth is limited. At one point in time or another, we must confront our inevitable demise. Such is the fixed reality of the human condition. No person is beyond, or exempt from, the all-encompassing jurisdiction of death.

---

275 Shakespeare, William. (1595). *Henry VI. Part Three.* Act 1, Scene 2.
276 Shakespeare, William. (1595). *Henry VI. Part Three.* Act 1, Scene 4.

'My ashes, like the phoenix, may bring forth a bird that will revenge upon you all.' [277]

The power of blessings and curses endure long after their originator has deceased and departed this world. The evil desire to inflict harm and revenge upon other people only serves to perpetuate a vicious cycle of sin that becomes unbreakable, but for God's grace, goodness, forgiveness, favour, and mercy. All of us are personally responsible for our free moral actions.

In the event that we mistakenly escape the natural justice of this world, the *Holy Bible*, within the *Book of Galatians*, Chapter 6, Verse 7, affirms that God's True Justice is inescapable, 'Do not be deceived. God cannot be mocked. A man reaps what he sows.' In the final analysis, it is best counsel to forgive. Demonstrate mercy unto those people that have done us wrong. So that God forgives us, and also shows mercy to us.

'It is war's prize to take all vantages, and ten to one were no impeach of valour.' [278]

In the time of war, it is the end result that matters most. The means can be discarded to claim the decisive victory. For if we do not act upon all the advantages that are presented to us, throughout the course of a war, chances are the opposing belligerent shall stand to benefit from our loss. Battle tactics, military strategy, disinformation (or misinformation) campaigns, intercepting military signals code, and false flag operations, entertaining diplomatic negotiations for peace (when there is no intention to pursue peace). These are just some of the many means and methods by which ambiguity and confusion are introduced into a war, for the grand purpose of securing total victory.

---

277 Shakespeare, William. (1595). *Henry VI. Part Three.* Act 1, Scene 4.
278 Shakespeare, William. (1595). *Henry VI. Part Three.* Act 1, Scene 4.

'It is beauty that doth oft make women proud. But, God, He knows, thy share thereof is small. It is virtue that doth make them most admired.' [279]

Humanity is captivated by the astonishing beauty of a gentlewoman. However, there is considerably more to a gentlewoman's value and worth, than simply her appearance and physique. A gentlewoman who demonstrates warmth of heart, service of humanity, the fear of God, honesty, integrity, good character, honourable conduct, discernment, justice, charity, pure conscience, and community service, all serve to amplify her immeasurable value. For these intangible, immaterial, and often unseen virtues contribute towards the character of a gentlewoman. Needless to say, these virtues are often much more significant and enduring than the surface-level physical attraction towards the female sex.

'Nor can my tongue unload my heart's great burden. For self-same wind that I should speak withal. Is kindling coals that fires all my breast. And burns me up with flames that tears would quench.' [280]

At times, it feels like our words cannot give adequate expression to our sorrow, pain, suffering, grief, heartache, agony, burden, and privation. There is a considerable amount of nuance in the complexity of human emotions, sensations, and feelings. Yet, even the great finesse of human language cannot sufficiently express our all-too-human sentiments. The natural expression of emotions, sensations, and feelings is part and parcel of human life. Nevertheless, a 'balance' is needed in the proper regulation and management of them.

---

279 Shakespeare, William. (1595). *Henry VI. Part Three.* Act 1, Scene 4.
280 Shakespeare, William. (1595). *Henry VI. Part Three.* Act 2, Scene 1.

'To weep is to make less the depth of grief.' [281]

Weeping is a physical expression of human grief. Yet, to weep does not always do justice to our inner state of being and feeling of grief. Often times, weeping does not complete the psychological process of grief and suffering. To weep, is but one component of the human expression of grief. Grief is a very personal experience. Thus, each person has their own 'coping mechanism' to address the tragedy of grief. In one sense, Shakespeare emphasises the point that to express one's grief openly is to make less of it. There is some truth in this expression. For no other individual can wholly understand our grief, its circumstances, its impact on our life, its particular context, and our unique response to grief.

'Withhold revenge, Dear God! It is not my fault, nor wittingly have I infringed my vow.' [282]

This statement demonstrates the remarkable paradox in human thought. When we make a mistake, we desire mercy, leniency, and forgiveness for our shortcomings. However, when another party infringes upon our rights, entitlements, and liberty, we desire revenge and demand justice. The German philosopher, Immanuel Kant, has written extensively on Moral Philosophy. In Kant's remarkable work titled, *Groundwork of the Metaphysic of Morals* (1785), Kant introduces the Doctrine of 'Categorical Imperative' which provides a considered response to this dilemma. In plain language, Kant's moral principle proposes that, 'We ought to treat others, how we would like to be treated.'

---

281 Shakespeare, William. (1595). *Henry VI. Part Three.* Act 2, Scene 1.
282 Shakespeare, William. (1595). *Henry VI. Part Three.* Act 2, Scene 2.

'The smallest worm will turn being trodden on, and doves will peck in safeguard of their brood.' [283]

Shakespeare illustrates the fundamental essence of animal nature. In comparison, much can be inferred about human nature. Although the institutions of law, religion, government, and morality serve to constrain and regulate human affairs in our modern society, the reality is that some aspects of human conduct are totally innate, by the very fact of our belonging to the human species. For example, consider the functioning of the autonomic nervous system that regulates the involuntary physiologic processes of the human body (i.e., heart rate, blood pressure, respiration, digestion, and sexual arousal). In the final analysis, human behaviour is defined by a combination of 'animality' and 'rationality'. Not to mention, much absurdity.

'But, Clifford, tell me, didst thou never hear that things ill-got had ever bad success?' [284]

It is not only the end result itself, but also the means and methods that we utilise to attain the end result that matters. Humans, as moral agents with a finite capacity for the expression of free will, are all responsible for their conduct. If a person has an evil intention, and acquires wealth, private property, income, worldly success, influence, power, fame, material possessions, or any other invaluable items through immoral or dishonest means, this demonstrates that such a person does not have the fear of God in their heart. It is possible that the deliverance of justice in this broken world may be circumvented. However, God is the Supreme and Sovereign Witness to all of our actions. We cannot escape the True Justice of God's Righteous Court.

---

283 Shakespeare, William. (1595). *Henry VI. Part Three.* Act 2, Scene 2.
284 Shakespeare, William. (1595). *Henry VI. Part Three.* Act 2, Scene 2.

'And learn this lesson. Draw thy sword in right.'[285]

We must not utilise the sword as an instrument of injustice and oppression against other people. Rather, the sword shall be a symbol of social justice and preserving the peace in society. To utilise a sword for an illegitimate purpose is not only morally wrong, but also unlawful conduct. Humans have a moral and legal duty to preserve all human life. To ensure the safety of other individuals (i.e., do no harm to another person). Not to shed the blood of another human. To uphold the liberty and dignity of all human life. Also, to protect the private property of all the citizens within a sovereign nation-state.

'To whom God will, there be the victory!'[286]

It is God's Sovereign Will that determines the trajectory and final outcome of events in this world, and the Universe, writ large. The endless and fragmented record of history has demonstrated that human motivation, will power, effort, ambition, intelligence, and ability are important factors in influencing the course of events on Earth, however, God always has the final say. Thus, it is of grand importance, in all that we do, that we keep God in our hearts and minds. We shall pray to God for success and victory in our endeavours. Yet, more importantly, we ought to trust in God for our redemption and salvation.

'Would I were dead! If God's Good Will were so. For what is in this world but grief and woe?'[287]

At times, our grief may appear inconsolable. However, the notion of suicide and entertaining the immoral thought of an early death is no 'real' solution to our numerous problems on Earth. It is an

---

285 Shakespeare, William. (1595). *Henry VI. Part Three*. Act 2, Scene 2.
286 Shakespeare, William. (1595). *Henry VI. Part Three*. Act 2, Scene 5.
287 Shakespeare, William. (1595). *Henry VI. Part Three*. Act 2, Scene 5.

indisputable fact of human existence that privations, challenges, and difficulties will arise throughout the course of our life. The opposing reality is that there is also a considerable amount of good to be experienced in this world. For example, consider the blessings of joy, laughter, adventure, wonder, surprise, amazement, happiness, and success. Thus, it is advisable to have a well-balanced mind, and a pragmatic perspective of the world. It is true, there is both good and evil in this world.

'Pardon me, God! I knew not what I did!' [288]

We will all make mistakes in life. We will unintentionally cause offence against other people. There is no difference between humans in this regard. For we are all born through sin. It is important to acknowledge, that many Saints were once sinners too. It is not that one is born without sin, and therefore, a Saint by the privilege of birth right, but that sinners become Saints. For example, consider the thought-provoking writing of Christian theologian, Saint Augustine of Hippo, specifically his grand work, *Confessions*, which is a soul-examining read on the human condition. Ultimately, God has the Power to forgive transgressions. What is required from humanity is meekness and humility. We must be able to come before God and earnestly beseech God for forgiveness.

'Away! For death hold us in pursuit.' [289]

We can escape the agony of a military battle. However, we cannot indefinitely escape the authority of death. The dominion of death will always hang over our head, so long as we are confined to the human body. The real possibilities concerning our natural death are endless. How and when our death shall arrive, will take many people by surprise. In the final analysis, all of human life is to reveal the

---

288 Shakespeare, William. (1595). *Henry VI. Part Three.* Act 2, Scene 5.
289 Shakespeare, William. (1595). *Henry VI. Part Three.* Act 2, Scene 5.

Eternal Glory and Supreme Power of God. In the *Holy Bible*, within the *Book of Exodus*, Chapter 14, Verse 4, God repeatedly reveals to us how God hardens the heart of Pharaoh to reveal God's Glory, 'And I will harden Pharaoh's heart, and he will pursue them. But I will gain glory for Myself through Pharaoh and all his army, and the Egyptians will know that I am the LORD.'

'Measure for measure must be answered.' [290]

In a perfect world, one that is governed with justice, morality, and equality, there will be no need to answer actions, measure for measure. However, in this broken world, governed by sin, pride, envy, jealousy, profit, gain, greed, hate, and evil, the flesh desires to exact retributive justice, that is measure for measure. This narrow-minded approach to justice only serves to further the endeavours of the flesh. Thus, ignoble individuals continue the exploitative path of furthering sin on Earth. It is only the person who has overcome evil with good, that has transcended the limitations and constraints of the flesh, such a person peacefully dwells in the power, perfection, and presence of the Spirit.

'Yield not thy neck to fortune's yoke. But let thy dauntless mind still ride in triumph. Over all mischance.' [291]

No matter the unfavourable odds in an opportunity or endeavour, we must never voluntarily submit to death, damage, and destruction. For to do so would mean everything is lost, including all hope, faith, love, and belief. Perseverance and tenacity are the hallmarks to success. Whereas, doubt, confusion, hesitation, anger, uncertainty, and fear will only serve to prosper the ignoble cause of failure. Mischance is a real possibility in all events and undertakings; however, we must not afford it a second thought. Strive on and

---

290 Shakespeare, William. (1595). *Henry VI. Part Three.* Act 2, Scene 6.
291 Shakespeare, William. (1595). *Henry VI. Part Three.* Act 3, Scene 3.

march ever forward! For prosperity and success only belong to the bold and resolute people of this world.

> *'His demand springs not from Edward's well-meant honest love, but from deceit bred by necessity. For how can tyrants safely govern home, unless abroad they purchase great alliance?'* [292]

Actions are one thing; however, their motivation and intention are another. Often times, people will misconstrue their actions to serve their personal endeavours. For self-interest, in the form of the pursuit of pleasure, profit, or pecuniary gain are rarely beyond the immediate motivating force of a person's action. We must not always take a person's actions on face value. We ought to consider what is the underlying motive of a person's behaviour.

With respect to the latter half of Shakespeare's statement, in the realm of politics, rebellious factions within a sovereign nation-state almost always require the support of a foreign Great Power to aid and abet their cause. For example, consider in the *American Revolutionary War* (1775–1783), the Colonists in British America were supported by the Kingdom of France in their just cause for independence and the realisation of sovereignty from the British Crown.

> *'For though Usurpers sway the rule awhile, yet Heavens are just, and time suppresseth wrongs.'* [293]

Injustices and injuries will come against all of us during the course of our life, however, they are temporary. It is only the Sovereign Will of God that endures for eternity. Many times, people will attempt to impose their will on the world. Have their way in all things, great and small. However, no human's will shall endure forever. For the tide will eventually turn against them. For example,

---

292 Shakespeare, William. (1595). *Henry VI. Part Three*. Act 3, Scene 3.
293 Shakespeare, William. (1595). *Henry VI. Part Three*. Act 3, Scene 3.

consider that if we reflect upon some of the greatest rulers in World History, such as Abraham Lincoln, Alexander the Great, Boudica, Caesar, Cleopatra I, Cleopatra II, Edward III, Eleanor of Aquitaine, Elizabeth I, Genghis Khan, George Washington, Hammurabi, Hatshepsut, Henry IV, Ivan IV the Terrible, Mary I, Napoleon, Nero, Ramses II, Richard II, William Pitt the Elder, and William Pitt the Younger, all have turned to dust and ashes. None have surpassed the unyielding test of time. This is the fixed reality of human mortality.

'I hear, yet say not much, but think the more.' [294]

There is considerable wisdom in this concise and pertinent proposition from Shakespeare. We shall all benefit from listening more attentively to those important people around us. For we will learn more. We should also speak less often. This will allow us the requisite time and space to thoughtfully reflect upon the information within our possession. In addition, if we think more, and speak less often, we will inevitably come to the realisation that much of what humanity speaks is actually not worth the time and effort to ponder over, let alone respond to. In sum, quality over quantity of speech makes for an effective orator.

'Not I, my thoughts aim at a further matter. I stay not for the love of Edward, but the Crown. Though fortune's malice overthrow my State, my mind exceeds the compass of her wheel.' [295]

Our thoughts are often the precursor to our actions. Our select thoughts can devise a multitude of hypothetical options before us, on how to respond to a given scenario, and present us with what suitable options we can choose in a particular situation. In most cases, people's thoughts are self-centred and directed towards the

---

294 Shakespeare, William. (1595). *Henry VI. Part Three.* Act 4, Scene 1.
295 Shakespeare, William. (1595). *Henry VI. Part Three.* Act 4, Scene 3.

furtherance of one's personal endeavours. These are primarily concerned with the futile fulfilment of sensual pleasures. The attainment of material possessions. Profit-seeking behaviour. Private transactions of a commercial nature aimed at pecuniary gain. The desire for power, income, wealth, concupiscence, fame, influence, or private property.

'What fates impose, that men must needs abide.' [296]

It is not by virtue, but by the force of necessity that humanity must accept the function of fate. Gentlemen and gentlewomen have no agency to circumvent the twists and turns of fate. Some of fate is favourable. Some of fate is unfavourable. However, we must reconcile ourselves and inevitably make peace with the finality of our destiny. Ultimately, our life could not have been otherwise, but for the way it is. In seeking 'acceptance' of our life, with its good and not so good aspects, this is not to argue for a wholly fatalistic doctrine towards life.

The fundamental interpretation of *Fatalism* posits that we are helpless victims in the vacuum of this world. Rather, we ought to embrace the perspective that the acceptance of reality is a powerful 'starting point' for us to consciously examine our lives with clarity, purpose, logic, rational thought, and without being ambivalent in our thoughts. We need to consciously investigate and carefully separate the aspects of our lives that are within our control and agency, and those aspects that are beyond our control and agency.

Thereafter, we need to exert our time, energy, effort, and resources towards addressing what we can change. While what is not within our purview, agency, or scope to change, we need to 'relinquish', or alternatively, adopt a *laissez-faire* approach. This pragmatic method allows us to secure the most substantial gains and enhancements in our life. Thereby, we can maximise the result

---

296 Shakespeare, William. (1595). *Henry VI. Part Three.* Act 4, Scene 3.

and output of our tireless efforts, to create a superior worldly reality for ourselves.

'For trust not him, that hath once broken faith.' [297]

We must be highly selective in whom we trust with our personal information. For the opportunity or potential is always present for a trusted person to betray us for personal gain, exorbitant wealth, income, fame, influence, power, status, money, love, high office, private property, or gold. This is a high standard to set, however, if someone has once broken a sworn oath, or betrayed the sacred thread of trust, it is then our 'error of judgement', to subsequently trust such a person again.

'Come, therefore, let us fly while we may fly. If Warwick take us, we are sure to die.' [298]

Instinct and intuition are fundamental to the survival of the human species. If we sense the presence of imminent danger, then we must act appropriately to secure our safety. If we cannot secure victory in a battle, then consider retreat. To live. To fight another day. This is the more 'rational and measured' approach to battlefield tactics. As opposed to 'fighting till the death'. Herein one is assured of total defeat, however, confronts their death, with pride intact.

'Whilst I myself will lead a private life and in devotion spend my latter days, to sin's rebuke and My Creator's Praise.' [299]

Towards the end of our life journey, desire for the pleasures of the flesh become weak. A person is disinterested in the pursuit of gratification and indulgence in the human senses. This is an opportune time to renounce sin and focus on God's Word. As we

297 Shakespeare, William. (1595). *Henry VI. Part Three.* Act 4, Scene 4.
298 Shakespeare, William. (1595). *Henry VI. Part Three.* Act 4, Scene 4.
299 Shakespeare, William. (1595). *Henry VI. Part Three.* Act 4, Scene 6.

near death, which all of us shall at some point in time, spirituality is one of the most important aspects of life that require our conscious attention.

For all our worldly achievements, material possessions, family members, friends, loved ones, accomplishments, and cherished memories, none will go with us, but for our soul, the merits and demerits of our actions, and our character. When all is said and done, we must seek forgiveness for our shortcomings. We must thank God for the opportunity to have experienced life on Earth.

'But when the fox hath once got in his nose, he'll soon find means to make the body follow.' [300]

Once we fall prey to temptation, regardless of its outward form or deceptive appearance, then it is incredibly difficult to resist the allure of going further into sinful conduct. Once a person has been baited with the hook, the irreversible process is underway to secure the entirety of the person, both in body and mind. Therefore, it is best to destroy the presence of falsehood and the strong temptations of sin, before they gain a foothold in our mind.

We are forewarned of the power of the Devil. We must not attempt to reason with temptation. For the finite capacity of human reason is infirm. Within the *Holy Bible*, the *Book of Ephesians*, Chapter 4, Verses 26 and 27, Scripture reminds us, 'In your anger do not sin. Do not let the Sun go down while you are still angry, and do not give the Devil a foothold.' In the final analysis, we ought not to determine to reason with and entertain the presence of ignoble desires in our life. This is a spiritual battle that we are more likely than not to confront our defeat.

---

300 Shakespeare, William. (1595). *Henry VI. Part Three.* Act 4, Scene 7.

'And when the lion fawns upon the lamb, the lamb will never cease to follow him.' [301]

The struggle for power is epic and brutal. One that often ends in much bloodshed and tragedy. At times, the temptation, attraction, and desire for power can make us ill-perceive ourselves. We become overconfident in our abilities, demonstrate a false sense of security in our thoughts, and tend to overestimate our capacities to secure accomplishments and victories, that in reality, are far beyond our aptitude. Yet, such is the inferior condition of human nature. The pursuit of power is irrational. We often neglect to consider the very real possibility, that desiring [the illusion of] power, shall result in our existential demise.

'The Sun shines hot, and if we use delay, cold-biting winter mars our hoped-for hay.' [302]

Advantage belongs to the party which seizes the initiative. Often, we can make the best of preparations. However, from time to time, it is essential to recalibrate our strategy to factor into consideration the changing circumstances, resources, privations, difficulties, and environmental conditions that confront us in the noble quest to fulfil our endeavours.

Successful people are those that have their eyes set on the final destination, on the end goal, however, are prepared to incorporate flexibility and adaptability in the grand pursuit of their lofty endeavour. We must not compromise on our endeavours. However, we must be prepared to factor in adjustment, and readjustment, in how we secure the realisation of our endeavours. Always remember, that the journey of life is not all smooth sailing, nor is it a straight path.

---

301 Shakespeare, William. (1595). *Henry VI. Part Three.* Act 4, Scene 8.
302 Shakespeare, William. (1595). *Henry VI. Part Three.* Act 4, Scene 8.

'Lo, now my glory smeared in dust and blood!' [303]

The idea of human glory is a figment of our imagination. In fact, human glory is an illusion, a fiction, a fabrication, that is waiting to be shattered. Only the Glory of God is ever-present, for eternity. God's Glory shall endure without exception, qualification, condition, or modification. It is the fixed destiny of all humans to return to dust and ashes. All of human accomplishments, power, prestige, authority, influence, wealth, private property, victories, and successes, are but vanity. All human achievements shall come to naught. At most, some of the greatest names in the history of the human civilisation shall be assigned a meagre footnote in the living memory of humanity.

'My parks, my walks, my manors that I had, even now forsake me; and of all my lands, is nothing left me but my body's length! Why, what is pomp, rule, reign, but Earth and dust? And, live we how we can, yet die we must.' [304]

In the end, we shall surrender everything that we have accumulated in this lifetime. All our possessions. Our valuables. Our treasures. Our storehouse of private property and personal wealth. Our tertiary education. Our treasured friendships and prized relationships. Our beloved spouse. Also, our precious gold. For we shall be left with nothing, but our material body and our immaterial soul. Even 'our body's length', we shall have to disown and inevitably relinquish at the time of death. Death is the unquestionable destiny of all life forms on Earth.

---

303 Shakespeare, William. (1595). *Henry VI. Part Three.* Act 5, Scene 2.
304 Shakespeare, William. (1595). *Henry VI. Part Three.* Act 5, Scene 2.

> *'What cannot be avoided it were childish weakness to lament or fear.'* [305]

There is considerable truth in this simple assertion. If we have no control over an event, incident, or situation, then we are only diminishing our valuable time, energy, resources, and efforts expending much thought about it. For to ponder over something that cannot be changed, is illogical and irrational. For example, consider the phenomenon of death. We cannot circumvent death. Therefore, we must, sooner or later, confront the inevitable situation of our existential demise. After all, we are only mortal. Therefore, to express concern, anxiety, worry, apprehension, confusion, anger, fear, or doubt over death, serves no worthy purpose.

> *'Suspicion always haunts the guilty mind. The thief doth fear each bush an Officer.'* [306]

The person who is guilty of an indictable offence shall always harbour fear, doubt, and suspicion of their illegitimate actions. For immoral actions that demonstrate culpable and reckless conduct only serve to destroy a person's peace of mind. Not to mention, the dark psychology of a criminal is likely to consider, and reconsider, each scenario or event relating to a crime, with an uneasiness or concern, demonstrating an unfounded and irrational behaviour within their immediate environment. In one sense, a criminal is always 'looking over their shoulder', to make certain they do not get caught.

---

305 Shakespeare, William. (1595). *Henry VI. Part Three.* Act 5, Scene 4.
306 Shakespeare, William. (1595). *Henry VI. Part Three.* Act 5, Scene 6.

'O God, forgive my sins, and pardon thee.' [307]

As we near the end of life, mercy, forgiveness, and salvation are the most important aspects of concern. God has the Supreme Authority and Sovereign Power to forgive our countless sins and transgressions. We have to humble ourselves in God's Presence and ask for God's Forgiveness. Equally, for those people who have done us wrong, we must pardon them. So they are also forgiven for their sins and transgressions. If we forgive the people who wrong us, then God shall also forgive us.

'I am myself alone.' [308]

Many times, we find ourselves alone in life. Alone in our grief, suffering, pain, experience, thought, accomplishment, loss, adversity, setback, victory, and achievement. From time to time, our life can feel like no person entirely understands, or comprehends our unique perception of the world. Throughout the highs and lows of life, it is important that we do not forget God.

In the final analysis, anything and everything is always possible through God's Grace. However, we have to believe, pray, and perform our duty to the very best of our ability. We have to trust in God's Timing. Trust in God's Plan for our life. Even in the midst of the darkest times in our life, there is always the beacon of hope. For our part, we need to keep the Faith. We need to look beyond the immediate horizon.

The Spanish Catholic priest, mystic, and poet, Saint John of the Cross, author of *Dark Night of the Soul*, reminds us that, 'How, although this night brings darkness to the Spirit, it does so in order to illumine it and give it light.' This lifetime presents us with the unprecedented opportunity to cultivate our virtues. To strengthen

---

307 Shakespeare, William. (1595). *Henry VI. Part Three*. Act 5, Scene 6.
308 Shakespeare, William. (1595). *Henry VI. Part Three*. Act 5, Scene 6.

the resolve of our Spirit. It is incumbent upon us that we come to know God's Love and Goodness.

'To say the truth, so Judas kissed his Master and cried "All hail!" when as he meant all harm.' [309]

Judas' immoral conduct represents the evil dimension of human nature. For people are deceptive, dishonest, and deceitful. Even those very trusted individuals, whom we thought we could trust with our private property, personal wealth, income, honour, and reputation, we will be betrayed and forsaken by them. We must be vigilant in whom we position our trust. Trust can easily be fractured. Relationships on Earth are a testing ground of our character, integrity, reputation, morality, virtue, merit, and honour. Unfortunately, much of humanity will trade fine gold for base metal. Such is the selfish, egoistic, and self-centred thought and behaviour of humanity.

---

309 Shakespeare, William. (1595). *Henry VI. Part Three.* Act 5, Scene 7.

Chapter 14

HENRY VIII

*'My doing well with my well saying! It is well said
again, and it is a kind of good deed to say well.
And yet words are no deeds.'*

SHAKESPEARE

Henry VIII is an interesting and mesmerising play. This drama informs us of the dynamics of human nature, self-interest, love, power, trust, honour, integrity, morality, and character. The Duke of Norfolk informs Buckingham of a meeting between His Majesty King Henry VIII and His Majesty King Francis I of France. Cardinal Wolsey, who is King Henry VIII's right-hand man, is the mastermind behind the arrest of the Duke of Buckingham for the charge of high treason. The Queen of England, Katherine, has her own protests against King Henry VIII. However, Henry VIII has his eyes set on another gentlelady by the name of Anne Boleyn, whom he subsequently falls in love with.

Unfortunately, the Duke of Buckingham is prosecuted at Court, and he is executed for the crime of high treason. Meanwhile, the Duke of Norfolk and the Duke of Suffolk aim to position Henry VIII and Cardinal Wolsey against one another. On the affairs of love and marriage, King Henry VIII attempts to call into question the very legitimacy of his marriage to Queen Katherine. In the pursuit of this most unfaithful endeavour, King Henry VIII appoints Cardinal Wolsey and Cardinal Campeius as His Majesty's Royal Representatives within a special tribunal to determine the matter. After giving a preliminary speech at the tribunal, Queen Katherine withdraws. Katherine refuses to cooperate with the tribunal's 'corrupt agenda' to separate the King and Queen.

On the other hand, King Henry VIII's newfound lover, Anne Boleyn is appointed the Marchioness of Pembroke. Not to mention, Anne Boleyn secretly marries His Majesty King Henry VIII. At long last, with the untiring efforts of the Duke of Norfolk and the Duke of Suffolk, Cardinal Wolsey's fall from grace is effectuated into motion. Wolsey's corrupt agenda is finally exposed. As a result, Cranmer is appointed the next Archbishop of Canterbury. Not to mention, King Henry VIII divorces Queen Katherine, and in her place, Anne Boleyn is crowned the Queen of England. Last but not least, Queen Anne gives birth to a baby girl named Elizabeth. This youngling is destined for greatness. Elizabeth shall rise to become a future Sovereign of England. Namely, Her Majesty Queen Elizabeth I.

'Then in a moment, see how soon this mightiness meets misery.'[310]

The trajectory and course of our life is partially uncertain. A person's fall from grace is a plausible reality, one that cannot be discarded as some far-fetched and distant fiction. What is high, exalted, and lofty, can be brought low. Conversely, what is low can rise to unprecedented new heights. Chance, fortune, and luck have the capacity to enact sudden change, both favourable and unfavourable.

The force of circumstance, or the vicissitudes of time, can unravel a lifetime's worth of work. We must accept that certain

---

310 Shakespeare, William. (1613). *Henry VIII*. Act 1, Prologue.

life-changing events, humanitarian crises, economic shocks, world wars, natural disasters, and financial crises are beyond our control. However, the presence of peace is always within our immediate reach. Therefore, we must earnestly pray to God. We must turn our heart towards God. Pursuant to the formidable power of the Scriptures, as noted within the *Holy Bible*, the *Book of Philippians*, in Chapter 4, Verse 7, God shall grant us, 'The Peace of God, which transcends all understanding.'

'And, if you can be merry then, I'll say. A man may weep upon his wedding day.' [311]

The famous 'honeymoon' period following a wedding is destined to be short and splendid. Initially, a spouse may appear to be incredibly delighted and overjoyed with this significant occasion. With the passage of time, a sombre, experienced, knowledgeable, and learned spouse is more likely than not to perceive the institution of marriage as a matter of future concern. For example, consider some of the well-known issues associated with marriage, such as financial challenges, raising children, everyday stress, spousal miscommunication, boredom, loss of intimacy, managing expectations, undesirable friends, addictions, the division of household duties, different parenting styles, a mismatch in values and beliefs, conflicting personal schedules, changing and competing life priorities (i.e., employment, tertiary education, career change, new hobbies, retirement, or travelling around the world).

'To climb steep hills requires slow pace at first.' [312]

We all commence our most grand and lofty life endeavours at ground zero. Therefore, 'pacing' ourselves appropriately shall guide us through to the finality of our mission. Furthermore, it is essential

---

311 Shakespeare, William. (1613). *Henry VIII*. Act 1, Prologue.
312 Shakespeare, William. (1613). *Henry VIII*. Act 1, Scene 1.

to point out that 'momentum' is accumulated over a period of time in an activity, not merely upon the initial commencement of a goal. Last but not least, starting out a major activity methodically allows us to better manage the release of our energy. For the conservation of energy is an important principle in our quest to conquer the greatest of all missions. To become accomplished!

'Anger is like a full-hot horse, who being allowed his way, self-mettle tires him.'[313]

The expression of anger is a natural and normal emotion. Anger is comparable to the variety of other emotions expressed by humans, such as joy, sadness, happiness, fear, surprise, disgust, and many more. However, in extremity, the expression of anger can become detrimental to our best interests. We must not allow ourselves to be irrationally controlled by anger.

As a general rule, never make significant decisions when subject to the rashness and unpredictability of anger. For all actions have their unique consequences. The accumulation of personal experience, formal learning, and knowledge, which collectively provision invaluable wisdom through conscious reflection, combined with the power of hindsight, will better inform our reason and good judgement. We must prudently guide our actions towards a more appropriate and measured response to life's challenging situations and unexpected events.

'Be to yourself, as you would to your friend.'[314]

Shakespeare makes a simple, yet remarkably underrated statement that accurately depicts much about human interaction in modern society. That is to infer, we often treat our close and well-known friends much better than we treat ourselves. For example, consider

---

313 Shakespeare, William. (1613). *Henry VIII*. Act 1, Scene 1.
314 Shakespeare, William. (1613). *Henry VIII*. Act 1, Scene 1.

the following scenarios. We are unlikely to criticise our friends. We are more likely to provide our friends with a compliment on how they have dressed, or what they have achieved in their lifetime. We might even overlook an offence committed by our friends.

On the contrary, we are more likely than not to engage in self-criticism, if we make a mistake, or error in an activity. We are not likely to compliment ourselves on being well dressed, or celebrate our amazing achievements in life. We may even proceed as far as to devalue our accomplishments. In the final analysis, when we examine the well-known moral analogy, namely, 'Treat others, how we would like to be treated', equally, we must not forget, 'To treat ourselves, how we would like to treat others.'

'Be advised. Heat not a furnace for your foe so hot that it do singe yourself.' [315]

In our irrational, evil, sinful, and unforgiving nature, we tend to over concentrate on causing harm to those people that have done us wrong. Rather, we must demonstrate mercy, forgiveness, and compassion. If we become irrationally and dangerously concerned with exacting vengeance and inflicting retributive justice on other people, we may entertain such extreme lengths, that our very actions inflict pain and suffering upon ourselves.

In the final analysis, we must remember that we are all sinners. Before we are too quick to judge and condemn other people, we must equally and truthfully examine ourselves and consciously investigate our own shortcomings. Upon careful examination, we shall become mindful, that we are no better than any other person on Earth.

---

315 Shakespeare, William. (1613). *Henry VIII*. Act 1, Scene 1.

'We may outrun, by violent swiftness, that which we run at, and lose by over-running.'[316]

Throughout the course of life, we cannot escape from our destiny or fate. We may attempt to harbour the false illusion that we have 'outrun' ourselves. However, all we have accomplished is to have denied ourselves the fullness of life, or deferred the complete realisation of our human potential. In doing so, we have accomplished little of value or merit, except to have 'lost by over-running'.

Human life is a finite continuum of 'free moral choices', which, when put into action, have real and profound consequences. The culmination of the externalities, both positive and negative, of our moral choices, combine to create the life that we embody in the present moment. Thus, we need to carefully consider, what we run towards, and what we run away from. More importantly, that we do not attempt to outrun ourselves.

In the *Holy Bible*, specifically, in the *Book of Jonah*, we witness the importance and infallibility of God's Word. Each person must accede to their God-given destiny. The Prophet Jonah attempts to circumvent the Word of God. Jonah refuses to complete God's Calling on his life. Indeed, Jonah initially attempts to evade his divine mission, only to repent, and return to God.

In the *Book of Jonah*, Chapter 3, Verses 1 to 4, we witness Jonah obeying God's Command, 'Then the Word of the LORD came to Jonah a second time. Go to the great City of Nineveh and proclaim to it the message I give you. Jonah obeyed the Word of the LORD and went to Nineveh. Now Nineveh was a very large city; it took three days to go through it. Jonah began by going a day's journey into the city, proclaiming, Forty more days and Nineveh will be overthrown.' We may outrun ourselves, however, we cannot outrun God.

---

316 Shakespeare, William. (1613). *Henry VIII*. Act 1, Scene 1.

*'It will help me nothing to plead mine innocence for that dye is
on me which makes my whitest part black.'* [317]

Sometimes it is almost a hopeless situation for us to pursue our
own cause. Regardless be it a just, righteous, and meritorious cause.
Pleading for innocence, when we have a lack of credible witnesses,
admissible evidence, and black and white proof of our assertions,
can collectively present a challenging situation. In all circumstances
and scenarios, God has the final say. God is our Vindicator.
Therefore, we shall make our case before God. For God's Justice
is always righteous and impartial.

'The Will of Heaven be done in this and all things! I obey.' [318]

Every self-centered, rational, logical, and egoistic person shall
attempt to have their own way. To impose their will on the world.
It is the blessing of God, that a small minority of humanity express
the innate capacity to subjugate themselves to the Sovereign Will
of Almighty God (or the Divine Mandate of Heaven) in all matters,
significant and insignificant. The vast majority of humanity are ill-
prepared to acquiesce themselves to God's True Word and Supreme
Will. Humans have forgotten, that all things exist, but for one
reason, and that is to express God's Eternal and Majestic Glory.

*'If we shall stand still, in fear our motion will be mocked or carped
at, we should take root here where we sit, or sit State-statues
only.'* [319]

The presence and devastating effect of fear, uncertainty, confusion,
hesitation, and doubt only function to paralyse a person from
executing action in this world. We cannot assign too great an
importance to how other people perceive our undertakings or

317 Shakespeare, William. (1613). *Henry VIII*. Act 1, Scene 1.
318 Shakespeare, William. (1613). *Henry VIII*. Act 1, Scene 1.
319 Shakespeare, William. (1613). *Henry VIII*. Act 1, Scene 2.

endeavours. For to ponder on such ill-thoughts shall only serve to impede our future progress and total expression of boldness. We have a significant choice, an option, a decision to effectuate. Either we proceed forward, or become idle, and thereby, unintentionally permit life to pass us by.

'Things done well, and with a care, exempt themselves from fear.' [320]

Whatever valuable task or activity that we work at, we must work at it with all our heart and mind. That is to say, with passion, motivation, and intellect. If we perform our work to the very best of our ability, and with care and diligence, then we need not harbour concern for fear or negligence, or alternatively, being accused of dereliction of duty. The presence of fear is only an obstacle. A hindrance. A negative emotion. Fear must be confronted and crushed through examining our personal concerns, irrational phobias, self-limiting beliefs, unfounded weaknesses, and unhelpful thought patterns.

In almost all cases, it is the innate 'fear or failure', and 'not failure itself', that prevents us from attempting to accomplish our highest potential. Our inner action potential resides within our beliefs and thoughts. These determine the construct of our external reality. For example, consider the remarkable story of the American inventor, Thomas Alva Edison. Edison made countless attempts to create the light bulb. In doing so, Edison did not consider his unsuccessful attempts as 'failures'. Rather, Edison branded his failures as 'Successfully finding ways in which his inventions did not work as planned'. Our perception matters.

---

320 Shakespeare, William. (1613). *Henry VIII*. Act 1, Scene 2.

'I must now forsake ye. The last hour of my long weary life is come upon me. Farewell.' [321]

At some point, each and every person's life is going to come to its inevitable end. For some people, that end to life shall be after a long life, with an ideal death from natural causes. For other people, that unfortunate end to life shall be abrupt and traumatic, constitutive of a violent and harrowing death. Most regrettably, some fetuses will die prior to the advent of their live birth, during the stage of gestation in the mother's womb. That is to infer, from either a medical termination of pregnancy, or be subject to the irreversible condition of intrauterine fetal demise.

On the other hand, some infants shall die within a short period of their live birth. That is, as neonates who have prematurely come into this world. Regardless, we are only human. We are all subject to the unchanging reality of death. Thus, consider it a blessing to have lived a long, fruitful, and productive life into old age. For once we near 100 years of age, at that point in time, one has, literally, become 'ripened' for the process of death to effectuate its due course.

'There is hope. All will be well.' [322]

In the course of human life, through all the different life stages, we must keep hope that the countless ebbs and flows of life are only temporary. In many respects, the course of life is uncertain. The highs and lows that we encounter must be traversed and chartered to move forward and create the life that we truly desire for ourselves. It is most important to constantly reflect upon the essential ingredients to overcome life's challenges. These include the remembrance of God, love, work, faith, hope, charity, community service, and family.

---

321 Shakespeare, William. (1613). *Henry VIII*. Act 2, Scene 2.
322 Shakespeare, William. (1613). *Henry VIII*. Act 2, Scene 3.

'Now I think on it, they should be good men, their affairs as righteous. But all hoods make not monks.' [323]

We should not be deceived by outward appearances. For example, consider that we rightly expect all sworn and uniformed police officers to uphold the law and serve the community. Now there are a minority of cases, where police officers are charged with criminal offences, dealing with the proceeds of crime, or committing civil offences. The point in case is that a symbolic uniform does not constitute the true essence, or the inner substance of a person. In a comparable manner, a hood does not make a monk, nor does a veil make a nun. Essentially, it is the combination of character, morals, integrity, conscience, values, beliefs, ethics, and faith, that define 'who' a person is, their very living constitution.

'Truth loves open dealing.' [324]

Shakespeare expresses a platitude. Not so much on the 'necessity', but rather the 'characteristics' of Truth. In all matters and affairs, where a person is truthful in their speech, they can openly express their words amongst any person in society. For Truth does not have any hindrances or obstacles to its faithful expression. It is not a necessary proposition, that Truth be dealt with transparently and with public disclosure. For truthful matters can be expressed in private and with confidence. However, what is truthful content and honest expression, need not fear its exposure to the light of day.

'A strange tongue makes my cause more strange, suspicious.' [325]

When we speak intermittently, or appear to be tongue-tied, it can represent how we are incongruent in our cognition. Such a haphazard state of verbal communication only serves to create

---

323 Shakespeare, William. (1613). *Henry VIII*. Act 3, Scene 1.
324 Shakespeare, William. (1613). *Henry VIII*. Act 3, Scene 1.
325 Shakespeare, William. (1613). *Henry VIII*. Act 3, Scene 1.

the causal basis for confusion and breeds suspicion. Speaking in a concise manner with clarity, confidence, and conviction shall serve us well. Being well spoken ensures that we make a good first impression. Fluency also ensures that we are persuasive in our communication with people in modern society.

'Heaven is above all yet. There sits a Judge that no King can corrupt.' [326]

Every person is subject to the decrees and commands of Heaven. No person is above or beyond the jurisdiction of Heaven. Unfortunately, the Earthly realm is occupied by sovereigns, both Kings and Queens, that are only human, and therefore, corruptible by vices, such as greed, envy, jealousy, hate, anger, pride, or lust. It is entirely plausible that a King or Queen enact a Royal Decree that is not in the best interests of the subjects that the Sovereign is charged to govern. In passing a Royal Decree, the Sovereign of a nation-state may factor into consideration personal gain, family relationships, even advance motives or intentions that seek exorbitant profit, the advancement of self-interest, or the realisation of pecuniary gain.

'Nothing but death shall ever divorce my dignities.' [327]

By virtue of being a member of the human species, each person has afforded to them human dignity. Dignity is an irrevocable and unconditional characteristic of being human. Regardless of a multitude of differences across the spectrum of humanity, some biological and natural, such as race, age, colour, sex, and ethnicity, whereas, other distinctions are artificially constructed, such as gender, personal wealth, power, influence, personal income, tertiary education, private property, religion, or marital status. We all share the universality and equality of 'humanness' on Earth.

---

326 Shakespeare, William. (1613). *Henry VIII*. Act 3, Scene 1.
327 Shakespeare, William. (1613). *Henry VIII*. Act 3, Scene 1.

'You have Angels' faces, but Heaven knows your hearts.' [328]

People are not always 'what' or 'who' they purport to be. People can misconstrue their image and representation in the world, in order to conceal their true ends, motives, and purposes. We must not perceive people, solely based on their spoken words and performance of deeds. However, if we are to truly understand an individual's psychology, we must also seek to understand their motives, desires, ambitions, and intentions. Only God knows what is truly situated in each and every person's heart.

'If you will now unite in your complaints, and force them with a constancy, the Cardinal cannot stand under them.' [329]

The ordinary people, the masses of a nation-state derive their power and strength in their colossal numbers. If the masses are to make a difference, or enact fundamental change in the affairs of State, it is absolutely necessary that they come together in the expression of their grievances and speak with 'one voice'. In this endeavour, the aspirational leadership of a charismatic individual shall assist the unenlightened masses to further advance their noble cause in the body politic.

Throughout the history of the *Early Modern Period*, all too often we have witnessed how the masses (i.e., the working class) have been exploited by the elite and aristocratic class, which seek to 'divide' and 'rule' the masses, by preventing them from organising mass political movements that further the interests of the common people. The aristocratic position the masses against one another, with the allure of subsistence wages, inconsequential private assets, trivial personal wealth, and with a debt-burdened mortgage on a residential property. All this keeps the masses occupied and in check.

---

328 Shakespeare, William. (1613). *Henry VIII*. Act 3, Scene 1.
329 Shakespeare, William. (1613). *Henry VIII*. Act 3, Scene 2.

Such commercial economic activity, collectively serves to keep the masses obedient and compliant to the laws, rules, and regulations of their sovereign nation-state. That is to infer, to ensure the masses remain tirelessly working without respite, or financial freedom in sight, but only to indirectly serve and further the private interests of the royalty, the aristocracy, the privileged, and the noble classes.

'My doing well with my well saying! It is well said again, and it is a kind of good deed to say well. And yet words are no deeds.' [330]

Actions always speak louder than words. It is an admirable and virtuous trait to be well-spoken. However, equally, and more importantly, it is a person's ability to be virtuous in their conduct which matters most of all. Collectively, our actions come to determine our character and our life trajectory. Our actions express how we feel, our thoughts, beliefs, values, ideologies, and ideals. Therefore, it is imperative upon each and every individual, that they appropriately consider what type of life they desire to create, and the foreseeable consequences of their free moral actions.

'This is the state of man. Today he puts forth the tender leaves of hope. Tomorrow blossoms, and bears his blushing honours thick upon him. The third day comes a frost, a killing frost. And when he thinks, good easy man, full surely his greatness is a ripening, nips his root. And then he falls, as I do.' [331]

Shakespeare succinctly illustrates the remarkable constancy prevalent in human nature. After all, there is not an extreme difference in the 'substance' of the common person's life and their personal affairs. But rather, the difference resides in the 'degrees' of personal experience, faith, formal learning, knowledge, reasoning,

---

330 Shakespeare, William. (1613). *Henry VIII*. Act 3, Scene 2.
331 Shakespeare, William. (1613). *Henry VIII*. Act 3, Scene 2.

and judgement. We all have hopes, desires, dreams, and ambitions. We all look forward, with eager expectation, that we secure the fruit of our tireless labour. And after all is said and done, whether we accomplish much or little with our finite time on Earth, loss is inevitable in this broken world.

'And when he falls, he falls like Lucifer. Never to hope again.' [332]

Shakespeare masterfully employs figurative and metaphorical language to depict a person's fall from grace. With the fall of a person, there is an understandable loss of ambition, desire, and volition in moving forward through life. However, all can be lost and subsequently regained in life, with the added qualification that hope, belief, love, faith, and purpose remain intact. To live a life without hope for a better and brighter future. This is the worst possible outcome that a person can confront in their lifetime. Subject to the confinement and limitations of our existential reality, we must always hold on to hope. Having said that, the provision of false hope is more dangerous, than having no hope. Natural reason must operate within the boundaries of human sensibility.

'Why, well; Never so truly happy, my Good Cromwell. I know myself now. And I feel within me a peace above all Earthly dignities. A still and quiet conscience.' [333]

We can never be content with striving and persevering for more. However, we can only ever be content with what we have in our immediate and present possession, our accomplishments, achievements, and significant life events. For example, consider tertiary education, employment, marriage, the birth of a baby, first home ownership, and retirement. More importantly, and above all the material and external possessions that we may attain, the

---

332 Shakespeare, William. (1613). *Henry VIII.* Act 3, Scene 2.
333 Shakespeare, William. (1613). *Henry VIII.* Act 3, Scene 2.

greatest peace a person can find in this world, is the peace within themselves.

To be at peace with who we are. This is the greatest and highest accomplishment of all time. No person can provision us with peace. Peace cannot be learned, purchased, traded, exchanged, or sold. The Eternal Peace of God can only be found situated deep within oneself, by thoughtful reflection, critical introspection, and spiritual growth. Indeed, it is a journey of a lifetime to 'truly discover' ourselves. To 'unconditionally accept' ourselves. To secure an 'immovable peace' within ourselves.

'Had I but served my God, with half the zeal I served my King,
He would not in mine age have left me naked to mine enemies.' [334]

We must exercise care and caution in deciding to whom we pledge our allegiance and service. In all matters, we must always position God in first place. This broken world, and the people of it, may betray and deceive us, however, God's Word and Powerful Promises shall remain true for eternity.

All too often in the vanity of self-interest, the pursuit of profit, and seeking pecuniary gain, personal wealth, income, and private property, we re-organise our value system, beliefs, ideologies, and hierarchy of priorities. We must never forget that everything in and of this broken world shall be left behind. When we depart this world, only our soul, conscience, and the moral development of our character will be of lasting significance and immeasurable consequence.

---

334 Shakespeare, William. (1613). *Henry VIII*. Act 3, Scene 2.

Chapter 15

JULIUS CAESAR

*'This day I breathed first. Time is come around … and where
I did begin, there shall I end. My life is run his compass.'*

SHAKESPEARE

Shakespeare's *Julius Caesar* is a fascinating play. It is full of emotion, drama, love, friendship, betrayal, history, warfare, duty, honour, and the struggle for power. Themes which are all intertwined in the context of the high politics of Rome. This play commences with the notable tribunes of Rome, Flavius and Marullus, dispersing a public gathering of Roman citizens who are celebrating Caesar's homecoming from war. A notable figure at the victory celebrations is Caesar's *protégé*, the loyal and honourable Mark Antony.

Not all Roman citizens are pleased with the ambitious and powerful Caesar's triumphant return to Rome. In fact, Caesar is forewarned by a perceptive Roman citizen of a radical movement known as 'The Ides of March'. However, the fearless and confident Caesar dismisses any and all concerns of enemies and plots against his rule as the Sovereign of Rome.

Meanwhile, Roman Senators, Caius Cassius and Marcus Brutus harbour suspicions of Caesar's future political motives. Cassius and Brutus believe Caesar is accumulating too much power. The

Roman people are treating Caesar like a living God. In addition to these two Roman Senators, a conspirator by the name of Casca is also an active and influential figure in plotting the tragic demise and violent death of Caesar. Initially, Brutus harbours reservations of plotting against Caesar's rule. After much debate, discontent, and disagreement, Brutus is finally persuaded by the ill-motives of Cassius and Casca, to murder Caesar.

On the infamous and ill-destined morning of the 15th of March, Caesar's wife, Calpurnia, implores her husband to refrain from attending the Roman Senate. The night prior, Calpurnia experienced dreams that presented an ill-fate for Caesar at the Senate. Caesar publicly dismisses the wise counsel of his wife, and he heads for the Senate. The chain of tragic events leading to Caesar's downfall are now irreversibly set into motion. Caesar is murdered by Brutus, Casca, Cassius, and their accomplices.

Following Caesar's cold-blooded assassination, Mark Antony presents a memorable speech in the market place to publicly pay his sincere respects to the late Caesar. Antony's funeral oration for Caesar is passionate, emotional, and dramatic. More importantly, it resonates with the ordinary citizens of Rome. After much public pressure from the Roman people, Antony openly narrates Caesar's will. This will proclaims that land and money shall be allotted to every Roman citizen. As a result, the Roman people turn against the conspirators; Brutus, Casca, and Cassius are forced to flee.

The remainder of this play witnesses Brutus and Cassius recruit a powerful army in Northern Greece. They confront Mark Antony on the battlefield. Although Brutus and Cassius appear to be consolidating military gains in the early stages of this conflict, the unpredictable trajectory of this military battle suddenly turns against them. Mark Antony now appears on the verge of total victory.

Consequently, the formidable force of fear seizes Cassius. Cassius instructs one of his faithful servants to assist him to his honourable death. When Brutus learns of the death of Cassius, he is left in shock and dismay. Brutus decides that suicide is now the only honourable end in sight for him. Once the fighting is over, the victorious and humble Mark Antony, and the honourable Octavius collectively return as the next Sovereigns of Rome.

'Men at some time are Masters of their fates.' [335]

During certain periods of time in our life, it appears our choices are guided by destiny, fate, or chance. On the contrary, at other times, we have complete control of our future. We can exercise personal agency, free will, and self-determination, to create the life that we desire. The reality of human life is that the 'correct answer' resides somewhere between the two extremes of 'free will' and 'destiny'.

The former Prime Minister of India, Jawaharlal Nehru accurately describes the conventional reality of human life betwixt free will and determinism. For Nehru mentions, 'Life is like a game of cards. The hand you are dealt is determinism; the way you play it is free will.' Most importantly, this present moment is the most significant period of time to create our desired reality. All the meaningful change in our finite life trajectory, must be done in the present.

'For who so firm that cannot be seduced?' [336]

Shakespeare's literature draws out an interesting observation about human nature, in particular, about human weakness. The most morally astute, God-fearing, and ethically responsible people can hold themselves in high esteem. Yet, the sombre reality is that all humans have desires, addictions, feelings, emotions, sensations, and passions. For so long as we remain in the flesh, the Spirit will be troubled. Also, the allure of the Devil's temptation is always near at

---

335 Shakespeare, William. (1623). *Julius Caesar.* Act 1, Scene 2.
336 Shakespeare, William. (1623). *Julius Caesar.* Act 1, Scene 2.

hand. In fact, the seductive grasp of temptation is closer to us, than we consciously think or truly realise.

'The fault, Dear Brutus, is not in our stars, but in ourselves, that we are underlings.' [337]

We often look to Heaven (or the stars) to ascertain more about ourselves, to understand our shortcomings and weaknesses. However, everything that we are, is wholly within ourselves, including our emotions, sensations, feelings, thoughts, ideas, beliefs, values, personality, intelligence, genetics, perception, cognition, psychology, and philosophy.

We are all subject to the limitations of the human condition. Such is our temporal state of being in this world. We cannot transcend, nor surpass, this static and fixed worldly reality. Thus, we must come to terms with, and an acceptance of, the quality of 'humanness'. Humanity is a combination of good and evil.

'Why are you breathless, and why stare you so? Are not you moved, when all the sway of Earth shakes like a thing unfirm?' [338]

To display a stoic state of mind, whilst a person is in turmoil and subject to the vicissitudes of grief is a remarkable quality. One that we all ought to emulate. Everything within the Earth is transient, subject to change, and constantly passing away. All the life forms on Earth are not beyond birth, decay, degeneration, and death. Thus, true wisdom resides in the 'acceptance' of the nature of all Earthly phenomena. To be attached, moved, or rather seek out aversion or desire towards any material phenomena on the Earth is irrational. For all conventional reality is elusive. Change is the only universal and constant factor.

---

337 Shakespeare, William. (1623). *Julius Caesar.* Act 1, Scene 3.
338 Shakespeare, William. (1623). *Julius Caesar.* Act 1, Scene 3.

'Those that with haste will make a mighty fire. Begin it with weak straws.' [339]

As a matter of principle, strategic planning, methodological analysis, and rational deliberation, prior to the execution of one's agenda, are the foundation stones to a successful outcome. If we quickly proceed to complete or achieve a lofty endeavour, then the means and methods will not be as enduring, and may even serve to hinder the final result. While on the surface, promptitude appears attractive, it does not always constitute a durable and lasting advantage.

'Of all the Wonders that I yet have heard, it seems to me most strange that men should fear; seeing that death, a necessary end, will come when it will come.' [340]

Humans are powerless to deny death its proper and rightful place in every person's life. Just as birth is a natural process. Thus, dying and death are also natural processes. The process of dying is defined by physiological, chemical, electrical, and biological changes within the human body. Having said that, dying also encompasses psychological, spiritual, philosophical, theological, religious, moral, legal, social, and ethical dimensions.

It is the 'thought' of death that troubles the majority of people. It is the sheer uncertainty of 'how' death will confront an individual. 'When' death shall come to transpire. Also, subject to 'what' conditions and circumstances will a person confront their death. These questions are the most concerning and pressing matters of life. In all cases, regardless of the 'type' of death a person confronts, the fact of death remains wholly undeniable and irrefutable. Thus, since death cannot be prevented, nor denied its rightful and proper place, then, rationally and logically speaking, it is worthless fearing.

---

339 Shakespeare, William. (1623). *Julius Caesar.* Act 1, Scene 3.
340 Shakespeare, William. (1623). *Julius Caesar.* Act 2, Scene 2.

'My heart laments that virtue cannot live out of the teeth of emulation.' [341]

Virtues, such as courage, honesty, self-restraint, temperance, modesty, integrity, benevolence, kindness, and many more, are unique to each and every person. Virtues cannot be genuinely imitated or learned. We can only be virtuous in our strengths and qualities, not the strengths and qualities of other people. In any event, to live a life where a person attempts to emulate the virtues of another person, is an artificial and superficial life, for it lacks authenticity and originality. The characteristics of moral excellence are unique to the individual. We must be, who we were meant to be. We must become, who we were meant to become. Our very essence of being is not a replica, nor is it a duplicate of any other person on Earth.

'O mighty Caesar! Dost, thou lie so low? Are all thy conquests, glories, triumphs, spoils, shrunk to this little measure? Fare thee well.' [342]

No matter how great, learned, skilled, accomplished, or talented a person is, every person shall confront their death. Every person's trivial and inflated sense of glory shall be brought to the measure of their death. That is to say, to dust and ashes. No person is above the human condition. All those who are born of the womb, must eventually confront their demise, to return to the Earth. Only the Glory of God shall reign forever and ever, beyond the known parameters of space, time, energy, matter, and force.

---

341 Shakespeare, William. (1623). *Julius Caesar.* Act 2, Scene 3.
342 Shakespeare, William. (1623). *Julius Caesar.* Act 3, Scene 1.

> *'The evil that men do lives after them, the good is oft interred with their bones.'* [343]

Curses are passed on and through the successive generations of a family lineage. Thus, the individual harbouring or committing an evil act, fails to ascertain its enduring consequences, that continue through the individual's family line, well after the very ill-minded person's existential demise. On the contrary, good actions make the world a better place. Therefore, blessings are not only powerful in breaking curses and aiding the well-being of other individuals. In addition, the person sowing the blessing, often reaps a twofold recompense.

> *'Even so, great men great losses should endure.'* [344]

Greatness does not come without sacrifice, loss, privations, challenges, difficulties, and delayed gratification. We all endure personal loss in this world. The dismal reality is that loss is inevitable in a broken world. This world is not our permanent home. To secure worldly gains and suffer losses also serves to enhance our personal experience, knowledge, learning, and unquestionable sense of mortality. Not to mention, lethal shocks to a person's inflated ego and pride, shall serve well to attenuate the final shock of death.

> *'There is a tide in the affairs of men, which, taken at the flood, leads on to fortune. Omitted, all the voyage of their life is bound in shallows and in miseries.'* [345]

We must demonstrate good judgement and proper discernment in accurately perceiving our external environment, both the presenting threats and opportunities. Then the only key to our

---

343 Shakespeare, William. (1623). *Julius Caesar*. Act 3, Scene 2.
344 Shakespeare, William. (1623). *Julius Caesar*. Act 4, Scene 3.
345 Shakespeare, William. (1623). *Julius Caesar*. Act 4, Scene 3.

success is that of effectuating action, which is only realised by seizing the initiative. If, at the right time and place, the initiative is not taken, then the allure of hope is lost. There shall be certain opportune moments and unique events in a person's life, where one will not receive a second chance. Therefore, we must not let the fight on the battleground of 'inflection points' in our life be lost. Be prepared. Be ready. Be of the mind to secure total victory.

> *'On such a full sea are we now afloat, and we must take the current when it serves, or lose our ventures.'* [346]

When we are presented with an opportune moment, we must take the strategic advantage. We must resolutely proceed forward, with the aim of accomplishing our pursuits, goals, and endeavours. For if we lose the high ground, then the fortune of the battle is against us. The very tide is against us. What could have been accomplished with limited effort, or much convenience, shall thereafter, become an arduous struggle to regain lost ground.

> *'But, since the affairs of men rest still incertain, Let's reason with the worst that may befall.'* [347]

The life trajectory of all people contains some uncertainty that cannot be eliminated. For risk is inherent in all the activities that we undertake. Not to mention, the future itself is also uncertain. In any case, the very worst that can befall a person is the experience of a violent and tragic death. To deliberate and reason about an endless list of hypothetical scenarios of calamities and disasters that one can be struck down with, is neither helpful or productive, nor is it a constructive use of one's time. In the final analysis, we expect the best outcomes, with the application of our untiring efforts. However, we shall be psychologically prepared for the worst.

---

346 Shakespeare, William. (1623). *Julius Caesar.* Act 4, Scene 3.
347 Shakespeare, William. (1623). *Julius Caesar.* Act 5, Scene 1.

'This day I breathed first. Time is come round ... and where I did begin, there shall I end. My life is run his compass.' [348]

We are all destined to confront our existential demise. For we have no agency, free will, self-determination, or free moral choice in our confrontation with death. Our life shall end. This sombre reality is fixed for eternity. Mortality is an undeniable attribute of humanness. Then, since we cannot change our destiny with death, we ought to employ our present time and efforts towards creating the life that we truly desire in the world. Therefore, the correct question for our consideration is not one concerning our destined confrontation with death. But rather, an inquiry concerning how to best utilise the finite time in our [very limited] lifespan.

'I know my hour has come.' [349]

Unless our death is sudden and unexpected, our intuition shall provide us with some preliminary indication that we are approaching our final phase of this human life. The best counsel a person can receive herein is to make the most out of every opportunity in life. Be prepared to proceed to the grave without any resentment or regret. At the very hour of one's death, to secure an inner peace of mind within oneself, this is the greatest wish that one can desire, or hope to attain.

---

348 Shakespeare, William. (1623). *Julius Caesar.* Act 5, Scene 3.
349 Shakespeare, William. (1623). *Julius Caesar.* Act 5, Scene 5.

Chapter 16

KING LEAR

*'I will maintain my truth and honour firmly. Draw thy sword,
that if my speech offend a noble heart thy arm may do thee justice.
Here is mine. Behold, it is the privilege of mine honours,
my oath, and my profession.'*

SHAKESPEARE

King Lear is a tragedy that is filled with the raw intensity and expression of powerful emotions, such as grief, love, deceit, anger, melancholy, pain, nostalgia, sadness, confusion, and fear. This play covers several themes, including power, good, evil, loyalty, betrayal, mortality, allegiance, duty, honour, family, the dangers of ignorance, heartbreak, morality, social isolation, emotional manipulation, pride, retributive justice, and poor judgement.

This play commences with a weary and indignant King Lear who is 80 years of age. His Majesty King Lear has convened a special meeting to inform his trusted nobles of his intention to transfer the Royal Duties and Responsibilities of the English Monarchy to his three beloved daughters. King Lear's eldest daughter is Goneril. The middle daughter is Regan. The youngest one is Cordelia.

The two eldest daughters, Goneril and Regan, are well-spoken and through the use of fine speech, they flatter the aged King.

Whereas, the honest and simple words of his youngest daughter, Cordelia, cause an undue and rather abrupt rupture, between father and the youngest daughter. Consequently, King Lear divides his Royal Estate amongst his two elder daughters, Goneril and Regan. On the other hand, His Majesty King Lear banishes the youngling, Cordelia. In the fullness of time, and with the added benefit of hindsight, King Lear will come to regret his injudicious decision.

As the narrative progresses, we witness the ulterior motives and improper intentions of the two elder daughters, Goneril and Regan. The two sisters openly deceive King Lear. By King Lear transferring overwhelming authority and power to his two eldest daughters, the function of power and the dynamics of the Royal Family relationship have turned against him. The two elder daughters now refuse their father's rightful place.

Not to mention, King Lear is also denied a place of residence with either of his two older daughters. As a result, His Majesty becomes mad. King Lear begins to display signs of insanity. King Lear wonders aimlessly through an unrelenting storm. King Lear confronts the depths of despair, agony, torment, heartache, and he experiences the 'dark side' of human psychology.

The remainder of this play is concerned with the psychological battles between the two elder daughters and the younger daughter. Battles for power, fame, love, and influence. Meanwhile, King Lear has the unimpeded opportunity to carefully examine his thoughts and consciously reflect upon his irrational determinations that led to his downfall. In the extreme emotional finality of this play, the two elder daughters are overly consumed in competition for the love of the Earl of Gloucester's illegitimate son and courtier, Edmund. This love endeavour leads to Goneril and Regan's tragic death. Cordelia's life is also lost, as the assistance to save her arrives too late.

In the final scene of this play, King Lear is left with his youngest daughter, Cordelia, lying dead in his arms. His Majesty King Lear irrationally hopes to witness Cordelia live again. To speak again.

To breathe again. However, it is all in vain. The unspeakable grief, heartache, and total loss is overwhelming for King Lear. The sheer insanity of the chaotic events culminate to witness King Lear consumed by grief. As a consequence, King Lear confronts his own death.

'Come not between the dragon and his wrath. The bow is bent and drawn, make from the shaft.' [350]

It is wise counsel to take notice that to enter the path of danger is to directly position oneself in harm's way. To attempt to reason with a person in the midst of anger is not a wise strategy. Rather, one should let the chaos of anger dissipate. Once calm and peace have been restored, only then make use of the instrument of reason to persuade another person of the most appropriate course of action.

'And your large speeches may your deeds approve. That good effects may spring from words of love.' [351]

As witnessed throughout the many brilliant plays of Shakespeare, actions always speak louder than words. Persuasive, rhetoric-filled, figurative, hyperbolic, metaphorical, and colourful speeches are captivating and mesmerising. Notwithstanding, speeches do little more than inspire the hearts and minds of the audience, and stir their imagination. A well-written speech is a powerful instrument for the 'call to action', however, it must be translated into meaningful deeds to change the world. For example, consider the following remarkable speeches:

- The English Sovereign, Her Majesty Queen Elizabeth I's speech titled *The Tilbury Speech* (1588)
- The American abolitionist and civil rights activist, Sojourner Truth's speech titled *Ain't I A Woman?* (1851)

---

350 Shakespeare, William. (1608). *King Lear.* Act 1, Scene 1.
351 Shakespeare, William. (1608). *King Lear.* Act 1, Scene 1.

- The British political activist and suffragette movement leader, Emmeline Pankhurst's speech titled *Freedom or Death* (1913)
- The British Prime Minister, Winston Churchill's speech titled *We Shall Fight on the Beaches* (1940)
- The Indian Prime Minister, Jawaharlal Nehru's speech titled *A Tryst with Destiny* (1947)
- The American minister and civil rights activist, Martin Luther King Jr.'s speech titled *I Have a Dream* (1963)
- The South African anti-apartheid activist and President of South Africa, Nelson Mandela's speech titled *I Am Prepared to Die* (1964)

'Time shall unfold what plighted and cunning hides. Who covers faults, at last with shame derides.' [352]

The Truth cannot be concealed forever. People with a malignant will can proceed to extreme lengths to hide their criminal actions, fabricate evidence, source false witnesses, or misconstrue events. However, there is bound to be a true witness, or critical piece of evidence, that shall bring factual information to light. Time shall be the keeper of the scales of justice. Indeed, the deliverance of justice may be deferred. But a guilty person, who has committed a wrong, shall eventually be undone.

---

352 Shakespeare, William. (1608). *King Lear.* Act 1, Scene 1.

*'These late eclipses in the Sun and Moon portend no good to us.
Though the Wisdom of Nature can reason it thus and thus, yet
Nature finds itself scourged by the sequent effects. Love cools,
friendship falls off, Brothers divide. In cities, mutinies; in countries,
discord; in palaces, treason: and the bond cracked betwixt Son
and Father.'* [353]

Shakespeare's writing is almost an extract from a book on Anthropology. Human nature is such that the unbridled fire of love is more likely than not to overlook an offence. For the chemistry of mutual attraction and sexual desire draws lovers together in such a remarkable manner, that offences seem minor and trivial, when we gaze upon the beauty of our beloved. For in matters of true love, emotions, sensations, and feelings guide the heart. Thus, the logical, rational, and reasoning capacities of the intellect give ground. Yet, like all things in life, with the passage of time, love fades and the passions dull. The chemical and electrical signals are no longer as sharp, powerful, and full of excitement. The flame of passion becomes hollow.

In the realm of politics, the Rule of Law and the preservation of order in the body politic is an important matter of public interest and safety. For the Sovereign of a commonwealth, nation-state, or kingdom, cannot risk rebellion or revolutionary forces, that threaten its legitimate seat of Supreme Power. Indeed, preserving the peace is no trivial matter. Last but not least, as the Son comes to a ripe age, he shall remember the grievances that his Father laid upon him.

*'I see the business. Let me, if not by birth, have lands by wit.
All with me's meet that I can fashion fit.'* [354]

Some people shall acquire private property and personal wealth by virtue of possessing noble parentage. That is to infer, by the

---

353 Shakespeare, William. (1608). *King Lear.* Act 1, Scene 2.
354 Shakespeare, William. (1608). *King Lear.* Act 1, Scene 2.

unmerited prerogative of birth right. For those people that do not entertain such a lofty privilege, they shall be reliant on their hands and judgement. In other words, on their labour power and the quality of their thought, to accumulate their worldly fortune.

There is considerable economic, political, legal, and wealth inequality. Not to mention, social injustice in this world. Some people are born high. While other people are born low. Some people are illiterate and ignorant. While other people are learned and honourable. A wise person makes the best use of the resources, talents, capacities, skills, abilities, learning, knowledge, experience, and opportunities, that life presents them with.

'How sharper than a serpent's tooth it is to have a thankless child!' [355]

A loving and generous parent often goes to extraordinary lengths to provide for their beloved child. Thus, it is most heartbreaking, when a child does not adequately acknowledge the immeasurable benefit they receive from their parents. This is where the wisdom of the parent must realise the innocence of their child. For a youngling truly lacks the knowledge, experience, learning, and judgement to genuinely appreciate a parent's untold efforts and untiring sacrifices.

'How far your eyes may pierce I cannot tell. Striving to be better, often we mar what's well.' [356]

Each person needs to secure the 'right' balance between their never-ending ambitions and their true potential. An equilibrium of the Self, in which a person truly and wholly becomes who they were destined to be is ideal. However, a person shall not entertain an 'endless search' to become something, or someone they are not meant to be. For an endless striving to constantly become better,

---

355 Shakespeare, William. (1608). *King Lear.* Act 1, Scene 4.
356 Shakespeare, William. (1608). *King Lear.* Act 1, Scene 4.

only serves to diminish our contentment and satisfaction of the capacities, knowledge, experience, learning, virtues, inherent traits, and natural abilities, that are already within our possession.

'If it be true, all vengeance comes too short which can pursue the offender.' [357]

One shall never be satisfied with the effectuation of revenge upon another person. While the Flesh desires to inflict grave punishment and retributive justice upon the offender, the wronged party needs to aim at the realisation of a higher endeavour. That is to infer, peace of mind. The further development and full articulation of the Spirit must not be hindered by the limitations of the human body. The Flesh always seeks to bring the Spirit down towards the Earthly realm. To be engrossed in endless worldly matters, compelled by greed, lust, jealousy, envy, power, desire, pride, hate, and wealth. As long as we remain in the Flesh, we must not let our trivial affairs become an obstacle to our spiritual development. Let the Spirit rise high above. Always remember God's Name.

'Nothing almost sees miracles but misery.' [358]

This is an interesting thought. Why would we have any expectation of miracles, when we are in the midst of misery? The answer resides in our circumstances and expectations. When we are at our lowest point in life, from thereon, our fortunes can only rise upwards. Not to mention, when we are in the company of misery, we least expect a turnaround in our fortunes. Thus, where expectations are lowest, there resides the latent potential for unmerited success in our personal affairs and endeavours. Miracles and greatness often arise out of difficult and challenging circumstances. It is in this context that we witness the Glory of God. We must realise our

---

357 Shakespeare, William. (1608). *King Lear.* Act 2, Scene 1.
358 Shakespeare, William. (1608). *King Lear.* Act 2, Scene 2.

full potential to overcome the seemingly unconquerable mountains that are scattered along our life journey.

'Fortune, that arrant whore, never turns the key for the poor.' [359]

The poor people of this world are often overburdened with endless privations, struggles, hardships, and lack of material comforts in their life. Regrettably, there is much economic inequality and social injustice in the Modern World. Not to mention, the hands of fortune never seem to provision the poor people with any significant or enduring comfort. No matter how much, or how little a person has, the state of contentment is always within every person's proximity.

'We are not ourselves when nature, being oppressed, commands the mind to suffer with the body.' [360]

There are two distinct types of suffering that humans experience during their time on Earth. The first type is 'physical' suffering. The suffering of the human body. This consists of all types of ailments, conditions, diseases, and afflictions. The second type is 'psychological' suffering. The suffering of the mind. In this case, the tranquillity of the mind is disturbed. It is always the latter suffering which is more severe and difficult to withstand. Indeed, the prolonged effects and severe consequences of psychological suffering endure long after the physical pain of injury is no more.

'O Heavens, give me that patience, patience I need!' [361]

Patience is a virtue in short supply. Humanity can always do with a greater abundance of virtue. Moral excellence develops good character, creates better quality relationships, and cultivates

---

359 Shakespeare, William. (1608). *King Lear.* Act 2, Scene 4.
360 Shakespeare, William. (1608). *King Lear.* Act 2, Scene 4.
361 Shakespeare, William. (1608). *King Lear.* Act 2, Scene 4.

patience. These positive character traits assist us to better listen and appreciate other people's perspectives and opinions. In addition, patience can assist us to better cope with personal challenges in our lives. More importantly, the presence of patience furthers tolerance and acceptance of differences in modern society. These features are essential for peace and harmony. In a Modern World that is replete with cultural, racial, ethnic, religious, gender, and linguistic diversity, forbearance is a prerequisite to world peace.

'O Sir, to wilful men the injuries that they themselves procure must be their schoolmasters.' [362]

There are many methods of learning in this world. Some people are educated through the medium of instruction, which provides for 'formal learning' at schools, colleges, and universities. Herein students systematically examine the academic fields of ancient and modern history, the humanities, psychology, physics, chemistry, biology, clinical medicine, sociology, finance, business, commerce, political science, criminology, common law, theology, philosophy, economics, and anthropology, to 'acquire knowledge' and thus, make empirical sense of the natural world around them. Yet, in some cases, there will always be individuals who learn best from the power of 'personal experience', which is often the most perceptive and insightful method to further 'human understanding'.

'The art of our necessities is strange that can make vile things precious.' [363]

The dark twists and turns of fortune are cruel and most unfavourable in the course of our life. The unkind force of circumstance can render us with limited options in life, from which we must inevitably choose the least unfavourable course of action.

---

362 Shakespeare, William. (1608). *King Lear.* Act 2, Scene 4.
363 Shakespeare, William. (1608). *King Lear.* Act 3, Scene 2.

Thus, confronted with a sombre reality of the world, what we once looked upon as worthless and dispensable, is now considered of great personal utility and economic value. The necessity of time can transform a person's perspective of the world.

'When every case in law is right, no squire in debt, nor no poor knight.' [364]

Where there is justice, there is equity and equality for all people. However, in practice, rarely is the Common Law precise, impartial, and always correct. Legal judgements are sometimes invalid or void. Thus, there is a requirement for a new trial at a superior court, or a court of appeal. Not to mention, evidence can be fabricated and presented to a court of law. A sworn witness can provision false testimony. The expert opinions of learned and qualified medical professionals are subject to the folly of human judgement. A juror can be subconsciously influenced by racial bias in their thinking and reasoning. A Chief Justice can display human error in the rendering of a dissenting opinion.

It is for these reasons, and many more, that from time to time, the institution of Common Law exhibits a 'miscarriage of justice'. Thus, the court of law fails to correctly establish the facts pertaining to the legal case. While the existence and function of Common Law is of paramount importance to the peaceful and civilised operation of our modern society, it is an imperfect institution. The human-made institution of Common Law is a work in progress.

'But where the greater malady is fixed the lesser is scarce felt.' [365]

In the general course of things, rectifying a greater offence will often witness the minor offence overlooked. Beyond the domains of law and justice, there is an important moral point to emphasise

---

364 Shakespeare, William. (1608). *King Lear.* Act 3, Scene 2.
365 Shakespeare, William. (1608). *King Lear.* Act 3, Scene 4.

herein. Namely, that we must concentrate our attention on the 'grand picture'. We must aim to secure a firm resolution on the 'major issues' that will move our life forward. On the contrary, if we are consumed with 'inconsequential matters', then we shall never be able to realise the fullness of our life.

> '*O pity! Sir, where is the patience now. That you so oft have boasted to retain?*' [366]

It is when we traverse the trajectory of tragedy in our life, that we come to appreciate just how incredibly difficult it is to demonstrate the requisite patience to endure our countless troubles. It is most convenient to preach patience to the select people who are undergoing heartache and pain. However, the litmus test of patience is always against the Self. The positive news is that patience can be cultivated over time and through personal experiences. Not to mention, patience supports the positive development of our conscience, contentment, and character.

> '*When we our betters see bearing our woes, we scarcely think our miseries our foes.*' [367]

We all have it within ourselves to overcome the challenges and difficulties that will befall upon our life. Therefore, it is within our agency to become the best version of ourselves, and move forward. We must strive to overcome the many tall obstacles on our personal journey of life. In doing so, we will come to the enlightened realisation that our misfortunes, losses, grief, personal issues, and challenges, all function to our advantage. In the sense that, they develop our character, conscience, integrity, morality, principles, and virtues.

---

366 Shakespeare, William. (1608). *King Lear.* Act 3, Scene 6.
367 Shakespeare, William. (1608). *King Lear.* Act 3, Scene 6.

'Who alone suffers, suffers most in the mind, leaving free things and happy shows behind.' [368]

The mind configures our unique perception of reality. Our perspective of the world around us, shapes our interaction with people, nature, and society. The greatest suffering a person can experience is within their cognition, their particular way of thinking. The quality, or poverty of our thought, shapes our life experience. The irony is that we become so overly consumed in our 'psychological' suffering, that we relinquish the rare opportunities to appreciate the finer moments in our life. The simple pleasures. The thought-provoking and intellectually stimulating conversations. The importance of quality relationships. The astounding beauty of nature. The blessing of life itself.

'But then the mind much sufferance doth overskip. When grief hath mates, and bearing fellowship.' [369]

By the constitution of human nature, we are all social creatures. We thrive on good company and loyal companionship. Therefore, when we are in the midst of grief, the presence of social support and company makes the difficult times more bearable. Proceeding through grief alone is not a solution that will resolve a person's challenges. The latter approach will only defer and delay addressing the unresolved issues a person has in their life. Aside from seeking medical advice and professional support, having a strong social support network is a powerful and positive coping mechanism for when we confront adversity and sorrow.

---

368 Shakespeare, William. (1608). *King Lear.* Act 3, Scene 6.
369 Shakespeare, William. (1608). *King Lear.* Act 3, Scene 6.

'How light and portable my pain seems now, when that which makes me bend, makes the King bow.' [370]

When individuals belonging to a higher social class or superior noble rank than ourselves, share in the difficulties and challenges that we confront, our personal hardship and individual suffering subjectively feels of less importance, and therefore, more bearable. The commonality of shared pain, that is borne by all members of an institution, or community, serves to lessen the burden of pain upon any particular individual.

'Thy comforts can do me no good at all, thee they may hurt.' [371]

We can entertain all the material comforts and expensive pleasures of this world. However, we still lack the two most crucial components for a quality life. Namely, contentment and peace of mind. In fact, the countless comforts and purposeless pleasures of this world, only serve to hinder our spiritual progress and the pursuit of moral excellence. Therefore, it is necessary to live a life that is not overly consumed, nor wholly absorbed by, worldly endeavours and material aspirations. Being engrossed in worldly matters only serves to impede our service to humanity, commitment to charity, spiritual development, and the remembrance of God.

'Full often it is seen our means secure us, and our mere defects prove our commodities.' [372]

The greatest instrument to achieve success is to believe in ourselves. Believe in our abilities, capacities, talents, natural endowments, intelligence, imagination, and creativity. If we proceed forward in life, secure in our beliefs, with unflinching boldness and firm resolution, then we shall witness, that we have the means within

---

370 Shakespeare, William. (1608). *King Lear.* Act 3, Scene 6.
371 Shakespeare, William. (1608). *King Lear.* Act 4, Scene 1.
372 Shakespeare, William. (1608). *King Lear.* Act 4, Scene 1.

us, and the necessary instruments at our disposal, to achieve our desired ends. Not to mention, what we may seemingly attribute as a shortcoming, or deficiency within us, can perform to our untold advantage.

'It is the time's plague, when the madmen lead the blind.' [373]

For the most part of human history, the contours of civilised society have been defined, organised, and guided by the educated, affluent, learned, noble, and aristocratic class. In using the archaic language of the past, lunatics, maniacs, and psychotic people were institutionalised in psychiatric hospitals or mental health prisons. *Elitism* is still a major guiding force in the future development of the contemporary world.

'So distribution should undo excess, each man have enough.' [374]

The Indian nationalist and freedom fighter, Mahatma Gandhi once asserted, 'Earth provides enough to satisfy every person's needs, but not every person's greed.' There is plentiful supply in the Modern World of water, oxygen, food, medicine, clothing, education, housing, and energy. However, the supply is ill-distributed amongst the billions of citizens of this Modern World.

The tragedy of the unequal global distribution of resources is that the affluent people in the First World, who possess an abundance of wealth and private property, are not incrementally happier, or more satisfied in life. For oversupply in the Western World has its own set of unique issues, such as excessive waste, obesity, the rise of non-communicable diseases, depression, and a myriad of social and health problems, for example, consider alcoholism and dementia. On the contrary, the poor people in the Third World, who do not have sufficient resources, are confronted

---

373 Shakespeare, William. (1608). *King Lear.* Act 4, Scene 1.
374 Shakespeare, William. (1608). *King Lear.* Act 4, Scene 1.

with life-threatening, or major developmental issues, such as malnutrition, illiteracy, destitute poverty, or dehydration. Not to mention, the real possibility of death from preventable diseases, such as malaria, diarrhoeal diseases, tuberculosis, or pneumonia.

'O you mighty Gods! This world I do renounce, and in your sights shake patiently my great affliction off.' [375]

In most cases, we are knowledgeable of religious persons observing the Doctrine of Renunciation across a number of major faith groups, for example, consider the vowed monks and nuns in Buddhism. With respect to Christianity, within the *Holy Bible*, in the *Book of John*, Chapter 18, Verse 36, we witness the *Messiah's* perception of this material world. When the beloved Son of God decrees, 'My Kingdom is not of this world.'

Indeed, everything in and of this material world is perishable and changing. Nothing is permanent and enduring, but for the Word and Glory of God. Therefore, in a deeper spiritual and philosophical sense, renouncing this material world, only serves to save ourselves. To extract ourselves from great pain and untold suffering. In this broken world, we are irrationally and illogically attempting to construct and fixate a permanent reality on temporary ground, that sooner or later, will surely disintegrate.

'O ruined piece of nature. This great world shall so wear out to naught.' [376]

This is a broken world. This world is only our home for a temporary period of time. This material world, and everything in and of it, will eventually diminish to naught. For it is the very course of nature with all living things, that they have a limited lifespan. A lifespan which is marked by birth, growth, sexual reproduction,

---

375 Shakespeare, William. (1608). *King Lear.* Act 4, Scene 6.
376 Shakespeare, William. (1608). *King Lear.* Act 4, Scene 6.

degeneration, and death. We shall not position our hopes on this world. We shall entrust God with our endeavours.

'See how yond justice rails upon yond simple thief.' [377]

Often it is the case, that the thief who steals a loaf of bread, receives the harshest punishment for the crime executed by the force of necessity. Whereas, on the opposite end, a white-collar criminal, who has misappropriated client funds and mismanaged private assets, is rarely seen to have received a punishment, that fits the scale and severity of the financial crime. The ways of worldly justice appear to inflict a greater severity of punishment upon the poor people of the Modern World. In Common Law jurisdictions, the use of penalties and sanctions are rarely equal in value, when one considers the empirical realities of socio-economic status, private wealth, private property, education, employment discrimination, and income inequality.

'Now, Good Sir, what are you? A most poor man made tame to fortune's blows, who, by the art of known and feeling sorrows, am pregnant to good pity.' [378]

Every person will be subject to the twists and turns of fortune. No one is above the human condition of feeling grief, sorrow, pain, and misery. Regrettably, this sombre and dismal reality makes us seek out pity for our sake. However, pity from other people rarely serves to improve our condition, or advance our recovery. In the final analysis, we must not let our Self be defined by the sorrow, pain, suffering, trauma, and tragedy of this world. Every person has psychological scars and battle wounds, however, we must rise above them. We must experience the fullness of this life. We must not become beholden to pity, like a person sinking in quicksand.

---

377 Shakespeare, William. (1608). *King Lear.* Act 4, Scene 6.
378 Shakespeare, William. (1608). *King Lear.* Act 4, Scene 6.

'I will maintain my truth and honour firmly. Draw thy sword,
that if my speech offend a noble heart thy arm may do thee justice.
Here is mine. Behold, it is the privilege of mine honours, my oath,
and my profession.' [379]

In the Ancient World, disagreements were decisively settled with a duel. For the righteous shall defend their honour with the sword and overcome false charges levied against them. To have lived a life, maintaining one's integrity and conscience is a good life, that has refined one's character, to the fullest extent possible. In the contemporary day and age, people look to secure vast pecuniary gains, accumulate exorbitant profits, and advance their self-interest, at all costs, without due regard to the time-tested principles of morality and ethics.

'But his flawed heart—Alack, too weak the conflict to support—
betwixt two extremes of passion, joy, and grief, Burst smilingly.' [380]

The human condition is comprised of a range of emotions. These include joy, happiness, amusement, disgust, surprise, sadness, anger, and many more. Often the expression of these emotions is a natural part of human life. However, the occurrence of unfortunate incidents, or unforeseeable events, can serve to disrupt the harmony and proper regulation of our emotions. This can cause us to become ambivalent in our thinking, incoherent in our judgement, or chaotic in our behaviour.

---

379 Shakespeare, William. (1608). *King Lear.* Act 5, Scene 3.
380 Shakespeare, William. (1608). *King Lear.* Act 5, Scene 3.

'I have a journey, Sir, shortly to go. My Master calls me, I must not say no.' [381]

We are all bound to the call of duty, both in conscience and in law. Thus, we must not be deterred in the fullest performance of our legal duties and moral obligations. However, it is important to infer a distinction herein. Our first and foremost sacred duty is to God, and thereafter, to our Sovereign and Country. In reality, we all have a unique life journey. Our life is shaped by our parentage, education, heritage, language, experience, family, learning, faith, beliefs, thoughts, values, profession, knowledge, and ideas. However, regardless of individual differences and distinctions, we all have a destiny to fulfil on Earth.

In the final analysis, the numerous ethnic and racial variations found across the human civilisation determine peoples unique experience of life. The expression of symbolism, the social, legal, and political construction of meaning, and the formation of personal identity, is conditioned through the spectrum of distinct cultural practices, heritage, religion, language, history, customs, traditions, nationhood, and ideologies.

'The weight of this sad time we must obey, speak what we feel, not what we ought to say.' [382]

Tragedy and error will befall us. At times, we have no agency in denying the occurrence, or impact, of tragic events in our lives. During these difficult times, we are often guided by our emotions, feelings, sensations, and thoughts, all of which can be irrational and illogical. Often, we ourselves know better. However, it is the self-mastery of a minority of the human population, that can move forward with the exercise of logic, reason, and good judgement, when in the midst of confronting crises and troubled times.

---

381 Shakespeare, William. (1608). *King Lear.* Act 5, Scene 3.
382 Shakespeare, William. (1608). *King Lear.* Act 5, Scene 3.

'The oldest hath borne most. We that are young, Shall never see so much ... nor live so long.'[383]

That person who has lived to witness advanced age, has perceived and endured a considerable quantum of feeling, suffering, pain, loss, and grief, throughout their lifespan. The generation of adolescents has not yet experienced the calamities and troubles of life. For personal experience, knowledge, wisdom, judgement, formal learning, and character, take a lifetime to reach maturity. Indeed, a young person may truly be talented, gifted, ambitious, and driven, however, such a person is yet to become accomplished.

---

383 Shakespeare, William. (1608). *King Lear.* Act 5, Scene 3.

Chapter 17

THE LIFE AND DEATH OF KING JOHN

*'What surety of the world, what hope, what stay,
when this was now a King, and now is clay?'*

SHAKESPEARE

The Life and Death of King John is a play characterised by an eternal power struggle to secure the English Crown. His Majesty King John, who is the younger brother of the deceased King Richard I, is calculated, cold, and cunning in his quest for absolute power in the Kingdom of England. The King of France and the Duke of Austria support John's nephew, Arthur, to become the next Sovereign of England. To make matters more complex, Philip Faulconbridge, the illegitimate son of the late King Richard I, also makes his claim to the English Throne.

A state of war has been declared between England and France. The armed forces of both nations meet outside the strategic City of Angers in France. Initially, the local citizens of Angers deny entry to the armed forces on both sides of the conflict. Until the all-important question is settled: Who is the 'rightful' and 'legitimate' King of England?

Negotiations for peace are entered into between the belligerents. A marriage proposal is put forward, as a means to settle the conflict and unite the two warring countries. The heir to France, Lewis the Dauphin (also known as Prince Lewis), and John's niece, Lady Blanche, are the two lovers who create a short-lived peace pact between England and France.

Religious considerations are not far away from the important questions of war and peace. Cardinal Pandulph attempts to persuade John of England for the appointment of Rome's preferred Archbishop of Canterbury. King John refuses to accede to the demands of Cardinal Pandulph. As a result, King John is excommunicated from the Roman Catholic Church. The Catholic Cardinal masterfully plays off the English and French against each other. Pandulph increases his influence and power in matters of State. Before long, the English and French resume war.

During the upheavals and turmoil of war, the English armed forces capture young Arthur. King John gives the order to Hubert to murder the young boy. Hubert follows his conscience in the matter, and finally decides against killing Arthur. While Arthur is allowed to live at the hands of Hubert, tragedy strikes shortly thereafter. The young Arthur takes his own life. To make matters worse for King John, his beloved mother, Queen Elinor has passed away in France, placing His Majesty's French territories in jeopardy.

With the tide of fortune now in full swing against King John, he hastily entertains entreaties to Cardinal Pandulph for peace with Rome. The Roman Catholic Cardinal agrees to broker peace with the French, in exchange for King John submitting the English Crown's political authority to Rome. The necessity of fortune has checked King John's strategic options. Thus, King John agrees with Cardinal Pandulph. Unfortunately, the Catholic Cardinal is unsuccessful in persuading Lewis the Dauphin to the just cause of peace. Now the French armed forces refuse to lay down their arms against England. The charismatic, charming, and clever Cardinal Pandulph has overplayed his hand. Pandulph is now undone.

The final stages of this play witness Prince Lewis leading the French armed forces into battle against the English armed forces who are represented by Philip Faulconbridge. His Majesty King John falls ill during the course of this military battle and he is taken to Swinstead Abbey. There are heavy casualties on both sides of the war. Towards the end of this play, King John passes away. The English armed forces are left to confront the next battalion of French soldiers. Regrettably, the anguish of war between England and France has no end in sight.

'But truth is truth. Near or far off, well won is still well shot.' [384]

No matter the context or the content, if something is true, then it is true for all time. That is to say, true for eternity. For the Truth is not contingent, nor conditional, upon the presence of another cause or fact. The Truth is true, in and of itself. The Truth is always self-sustaining. The latter half of Shakespeare's proposition demonstrates that, 'a victory is still a victory', no matter if the means and methods were not perfectly executed. In all cases, we must always be grateful for our victories, and celebrate our accomplishments.

'By long and vehement suit, I was seduced. To make room for him in my husband's bed. Heaven lay not my transgression to my charge!' [385]

Humans are by their very nature imperfect and subject to countless temptations and desires. We must always be vigilant and exercise forethought, that we do not fall into the illusion and grasp of sin. In the instance that we do fall short, we must seek forgiveness for our shortcomings and repent for our sins. For repentance and forgiveness, not only bring our mistakes to our conscience, but also

---

384 Shakespeare, William. (1623). *The Life and Death of King John.* Act 1, Scene 1.
385 Shakespeare, William. (1623). *The Life and Death of King John.* Act 1, Scene 1.

assist us in taking personal responsibility for our shortcomings. We must have every confidence in God's infinite love and mercy. We must not fear to come to God. For nothing is beyond the Sovereign Power of Almighty God to forgive. The secret to Communion with God, resides within the sincerity of our heart.

> *'But thou art fair, and at thy birth, Dear Boy, Nature and Fortune joined to make thee great.'* [386]

Every person is endowed with some measure of greatness. Nature distributes her gifts and prized abilities unevenly and impartially to all members of the human species. Therefore, it is within our power to discover our hidden talent and latent capacity for greatness. The most important and critical element in life is belief. For our beliefs come to define our cognition, and shape our worldly reality. Indeed, our beliefs establish the parameters of our thoughts. Our beliefs determine the height of our potential to achieve untold greatness.

> *'To me, and to the state of my great grief, let Kings assemble; for my grief's so great. That no supporter but the huge firm Earth. Can hold it up. Here I and sorrows sit.'* [387]

The experience of grief is very personal. Often times, a person can feel overwhelmed or inconsolable by the occurrence of tragic or negative events in life. We can discuss how we feel with other people, and this is a sensible idea. However, it is incredibly difficult for another person to truly understand our grief. In any case, good companionship and social support, can serve to shorten the unwelcome season of grief.

---

386 Shakespeare, William. (1623). *The Life and Death of King John.* Act 3, Scene 1.
387 Shakespeare, William. (1623). *The Life and Death of King John.* Act 3, Scene 1.

'O Lewis, stand fast! The Devil tempts thee here. In likeness of a new untrimmed bride.' [388]

Temptations are difficult to resist, let alone transcend. We must keep our vows and be faithful to God's Eternal Word. The protracted battle between the 'Flesh' and 'Spirit' rages on in this world, and this is a battle sooner lost, than won. Humans require a soldier-like discipline, to stand guard against the allure of temptation. Even at our finest moments, it is important to acknowledge that we are always vulnerable to sin.

'Exceptionalism' does not exist when it comes to desire, passion, emotion, or temptation. It does not matter if we are a priest, pastor, nurse, author, politician, economist, professor, surgeon, theologian, bishop, medical doctor, teacher, lawyer, or engineer. We are all human. It is the case that the human condition is imperfect. Therefore, we must strive to quash the very presence of temptations at first sight. For entertaining the very thought of a temptation only breeds the ground for its further development in the mind. This gives rise to the undesirable condition for our fall into the dark trap of temptation.

'You are as fond of grief as of your child. Grief fills the room up of my absent child.' [389]

Every person's experience with grief is personal. Not to mention, grief is often difficult to narrate to other people. It is important to acknowledge that grief is a natural emotion and appropriate response to express during the tragic times of loss, trauma, heartbreak, suffering, and pain. It is a sombre reality; however, we must accept, that we shall all come to experience grief at some point in our life. Thus, it is not a matter of if, however, it is only a matter of when, we shall experience grief in our life. It can be

---

388 Shakespeare, William. (1623). *The Life and Death of King John.* Act 3, Scene 1.
389 Shakespeare, William. (1623). *The Life and Death of King John.* Act 3, Scene 4.

incredibly challenging to examine grief with a rational, logical, and empirical mind. After all, we are only human. The strong forces of emotions, feelings, passions, and sensations, can easily obstruct our better judgement.

While it can be challenging, we have to 'let go' of the grief, hurt, and pain, in order to move forward. There is a season for grieving, and a season to move forward. We must not let the expression of grief become our life narrative. Grief has the supreme power to consume our thoughts, beliefs, and life. If left unchecked, grief will diminish this precious opportunity of the present moment, which we now have, to create the future that we truly desire.

In all things concerning grief, the sooner we move forward, the easier it is. In reality, the passage of time does not address the underlying causes of grief. It is the conscious recalibration of a person's perception of reality, and confronting the true essence of human nature, and realising the brokenness of this world, that provides an adequate explanation. Our life could not have been otherwise.

'There's nothing in this world can make me joy.' [390]

Strong parallels can be deduced between Shakespeare's despondent assertion and the German philosopher, Arthur Schopenhauer's pessimistic philosophy in his grand work, *The World as Will and Representation* (1818). While the world has its fair share of challenges and troubles, hope is always near at hand. Hope leads us to the possibility, that we can make this world a better place for all people. There is considerable joy to be found in working towards the construction of a better world. All of worldly reality, resides in our unique perception of it.

---

390 Shakespeare, William. (1623). *The Life and Death of King John.* Act 3, Scene 4.

'Life is as tedious as a twice-told tale. Vexing the dull ear of a drowsy man; and bitter shame hath spoiled the sweet world's taste, that it yields nought but shame and bitterness.' [391]

The *Doctrine of Original Sin* is the simplest, and yet the most profound theological explanation, as to why this world is the way it is today. This world contains a multitude of unresolved problems, far beyond the presence of shame, guilt, anger, evil, conflict, and bitterness. Nevertheless, the once-in-a-lifetime opportunity to experience life is a special gift from God. We must not neglect, impair, or diminish our life, in the entertainment of self-interested and futile pleasures, or the pursuit of trivial endeavours.

'Strong reasons make for strong actions.' [392]

We must possess a powerful motivating force that propels us into action. Indeed, sound reasoning is not only persuasive and noble, however, reason also makes for a bold and valiant determination, to resolutely proceed forward with our ambition and drive to accomplish our life's grand mission. Actions performed without natural reason, are often deceived by strong emotions, feelings, sensations, or disoriented cognition. It is advisable to carefully re-examine our thought and philosophy, before we decide upon a particular course of action. We must be measured and merited in our judgement.

---

391 Shakespeare, William. (1623). *The Life and Death of King John.* Act 3, Scene 4.
392 Shakespeare, William. (1623). *The Life and Death of King John.* Act 3, Scene 4.

'When workmen strive to do better than well, they do confound their skill in covetousness; and oftentimes the excusing of a fault doth make the fault the worse by the excuse. As patches set upon a little breach discredit more in hiding of the fault. Than did the fault itself, before it was so patched.' [393]

To perform an activity or task, to the best of one's ability. This is more important than the attempt to achieve perfection. For the pursuit of perfection does not necessarily lead to a better outcome. In endlessly addressing the shortfall in our expectations, we often find ourselves expending much valuable time, energy, and resources, in an effort to rectify perceived defects in our quality or artisanship. If we complete an assignment to the best of our ability, and with all our heart, body, spirit, and mind, consider it well done.

'There is no sure foundation set on blood. No certain life achieved by others' death.' [394]

The obligation is upon each and every individual, to utilise their unique talents, abilities, endowments, resources, and gifts, to create the life that they desire. We can have no certainty in other people's convictions and deeds to create our ideal life. It is within ourselves, and upon ourselves, to ensure we live a life, where at the end of it, when all is said and done, we shall gladly pronounce, 'Mission Accomplished.'

---

393 Shakespeare, William. (1623). *The Life and Death of King John.* Act 4, Scene 2.
394 Shakespeare, William. (1623). *The Life and Death of King John.* Act 4, Scene 2.

'Our griefs, and not our manners, reason now. Our sadness is talking now, not our manners. But there is little reason in your grief. Therefore, it were reason you had manners now. But your sadness is unreasonable, so there's good reason for you to have manners now.' [395]

The human condition is a function of the constant friction between the opposing forces of 'reason' and 'emotion', or to put it another way, 'rationality' versus 'animality'. On the one hand, we are guided by the higher powers of our faculties, such as judgement, intellect, cognition, logic, will, memory, perception, observation, intuition, and imagination. On the other hand, we are subject to the irrational forces of feeling, emotion, sensation, pleasure, desire, passion, temptation, and ignorance. Wisdom resides in the moderation between the two extremes of Epicureanism and Stoicism.

'But wherefore do you droop? Why look you sad? Be great in act, as you have been in thought. Let not the world see fear and sad distrust.' [396]

There are no perfect people in the world, period. Sometimes, emotions and feelings get the better of people who have good intentions and a generous heart. We must not let doubt, fear, uncertainty, unbelief, anger, hate, confusion, or any other negative emotion, or destructive thought, hinder our steady progress towards our life mission, or higher purpose. If we are to proceed from thought to action, we must execute and act upon our good thinking. We cannot permit negative beliefs to become an obstacle to our worldly success.

Thus, we need to carefully reflect upon our subconscious thoughts. This method of introspection shall assist us, to bring to the attention of our conscious mind, our true beliefs, desires,

---

395 Shakespeare, William. (1623). *The Life and Death of King John.* Act 4, Scene 3.
396 Shakespeare, William. (1623). *The Life and Death of King John.* Act 5, Scene 1.

motives, and intentions. We must replace the 'Old' with the 'New'. We must make space for positive beliefs, visualisation of success, and the reinforcement of good ideas. Most importantly, we must always remember, in all that we do, that we always keep God first place.

> *'May know wherefore we took the Sacrament. And keep our faiths firm and inviolable. Upon our sides it never shall be broken.'* [397]

In times of hardship, challenges, privations, loss, heartache, and difficulties, we must always search deep within ourselves to identify and re-associate with our values, beliefs, ideals, faith, and oaths. For collectively, these factors constitute our personal identity. In matters of faith, we must remind ourselves of our life-long commitment to our faith. We must preserve our everlasting trust and hope in God.

The Saints of Old have set the true precedent on how to live a meaningful and purposeful life marked by the love of God, devotion to community service, and generous giving to charity. For example, consider the monumental legacy of Saint Cecilia, Saint Brigid of Kildare, Saint Catherine of Siena, Saint John of the Cross, and Saint Teresa of Ávila. At a moment's notice, we must be prepared to surrender our life for our faith. However, the Faith must be kept under all circumstances.

> *'What surety of the world, what hope, what stay, when this was now a King, and now is clay?'* [398]

Everything in and of this world is transient in nature. No matter if one is a wealthy King, a powerful Queen, or a destitute beggar, each person shall one day depart this Earth. We are all situated on Earth for a temporary period of time. What matters most, during our time on Earth, is the perfection of our character. Our unconditional

---

397 Shakespeare, William. (1623). *The Life and Death of King John.* Act 5, Scene 2.
398 Shakespeare, William. (1623). *The Life and Death of King John.* Act 5, Scene 7.

love of God. Also, our steadfast commitment to moral excellence. It is inevitable, that we shall all return to dust and ashes. However, we must strive forward, with boldness, ambition, determination, and a sense of urgency, to advance God's Kingdom on Earth.

Chapter 18

LOVE'S LABOUR'S LOST

'Yet how can that be true love if falsely attempted?'
SHAKESPEARE

Love's Labour's Lost is a brilliant comedy. This play symbolises the disruptive desire and limitless longing for love in our life. Indeed, love adds much colour, emotion, humour, joy, sadness, grief, and happiness in our lives. The human condition is not the same without love. This play narrates the story of the King of Navarre and his three close companions, namely Berowne, Dumaine, and Longaville. These gentlemen commit themselves to a high-minded and noble life of study, seclusion, and scholarship. The four gentlemen swear an oath, to abstain from discourse and intercourse with gentlewomen.

Without further delay, the King receives news that the Princess of France and her three close companions, namely Katharine, Maria, and Rosaline, are about to visit the Royal Court. The King of Navarre instructs the gentlewomen to reside outside of the Court's Royal Residence for the duration of their stay. However, physical distance is no barrier to the pull of the heart strings and the push of romantic emotions.

This play witnesses how the four gentlemen gradually come under the charm of the gentlewomen's beauty. The gentlemen's longing for love cannot be stopped by an oath to abstain from intimate relations with noblewomen. Thus, the gentlemen follow their all-too human nature of instinct, passion, and emotion. The gentlemen discard their higher pursuit of scholarship, guided by the powers of reason, logic, good judgement, intellect, and discernment, in the pursuit of their 'happily ever after' love life.

As a result, the affluent gentlemen set their minds to win the hearts of the four gentlewomen. This play is totally captivating. It is complete with a series of miscommunications between the opposite sexes. The writing of love letters and romantic poems, that illustrate the grand quest for successful courtship. The speaking of confessions of the heart, and much comical entertainment, as the gentlemen attempt to woo the four gentlewomen. This play is humorous and colourful. *Love's Labour's Lost* illustrates the lengths and extremities that a gentleman is prepared to undertake, in order to impress a gentlewoman. This play is remarkable in its accurate characterisation of traditional courtship in Early Modern Society. Furthermore, this play depicts how a gentleman's untiring efforts at courtship are always incalculable.

In many respects, this play draws out the nuances between the male and female sex. Shakespeare brilliantly showcases, not only how both sexes are different to one another in emotions, feelings, sensations, thought, speech, and behaviour, but also how the male and female perception of the opposite sex is not always what is seems.

The closing of this play is not marked by a cheerful resolution to the gentlemen's persistent romantic advances towards the gentlewomen. The Princess of France receives the tragic news that her father has passed away, and she must immediately return home to ascend to the French Throne. The four gentlemen swear to remain faithful to the gentleladies they dearly love and whole-heartedly admire. However, the gentleladies are not wholly convinced, and they assert that the gentlemen must wait one year and one day to prove their faithfulness to them. Thus, the gentleladies depart. The four gentlemen are now left to entertain a most uncertain future.

'What is the end of study? Let me know. Why, that to know which else we should not know. Things hid and barred, you mean, from common sense? Ay, that is study's God-like recompense.' [399]

Scholarship is a life-long journey. Scientific scholarship is a constant exploration and re-exploration of the existing paradigms, ideologies, principles, laws, and doctrines of the Natural World, in the quest to expand the known parameters of human knowledge. Throughout the course of modern history, the human civilisation has witnessed great minds, including Sir Isaac Newton, Albert Einstein, Nikola Tesla, Leonardo Da Vinci, Marie Curie, Pablo Picasso, Pierre Curie, Jean Piaget, Johannes Kepler, Robert Boyle, Charles Darwin, René Descartes, Rosalind Franklin, Nicolaus Copernicus, Niels Bohr, Francis Bacon, Ada Lovelace, and Galileo Galilei. Human civilisation has learnt much about the Earth, the Solar System, and the Universe in the former 500 years through the natural sciences. Yet, much more remains to be discovered and understood.

'Light, seeking light, doth light of light beguile. My Spirit grows heavy in love.' [400]

The presence of light illuminates its surroundings. The presence of love is difficult to dismiss. For love weighs down the heart. Love distracts the mind. Love makes the Spirit restless. Love is an emotional guiding force. Love brings a gentleman and gentlewoman together, into a civil union, for the purpose of mutual fulfilment in each other's physical, social, emotional, intellectual, and spiritual

---

399 Shakespeare, William. (1598). *Love's Labour's Lost.* Act 1, Scene 1.
400 Shakespeare, William. (1598). *Love's Labour's Lost.* Act 1, Scene 1.

association. Furthermore, the institution of marriage serves as the basis of creating a family, deference to God's Word, and living a productive and harmonious life in society.

'Such is the simplicity of man to hearken after the flesh.' [401]

The nature and constitution of a gentleman is such, that he is driven by the desires, temptations, and demands of the flesh. The common gentleman entertains an insatiable desire to satisfy the longings of the flesh, however, this is not possible. For an unenlightened life guided by the worldly demands of the flesh is a life beyond fulfilment and satisfaction. It is only through the continued cultivation of the Spirit, and our connection with God, that both gentlemen and gentlewomen come to ascertain their true purpose. To experience the fullness of life on Earth.

'Yet how can that be true love if falsely attempted?' [402]

For true love to be true, it must be attempted and gained by means most true. True love need not hide in the midst of shadows, nor make its pursuit behind veils and silhouettes. True love must dare to be open and bold in pursuit of total victory for the lover's heart and mind. The traditions and customs of courtship demonstrate an earnest and genuine method to win over a lover. While love is guided by the emotions of the heart, over the logic of reason, a lover secured by honest and transparent means, is more likely than not, to make for a trusted relationship.

---

401 Shakespeare, William. (1598). *Love's Labour's Lost.* Act 1, Scene 1.
402 Shakespeare, William. (1598). *Love's Labour's Lost.* Act 1, Scene 2.

> *'Good Lord Boyet, my beauty, though but mean, needs not the*
> *painted flourish of your praise. Beauty is bought by judgement*
> *of the eye, not uttered by base sale of Chapmen's tongues.'* [403]

The very idea of beauty is beyond the finite capacity of language to demonstrate its true worth. Even the countless nuances of linguistics shall never do justice to the expression of beauty. The value of beauty is perceived. Beauty is in the eye of the beholder. Thus, beauty is a subjective sense impression. What one person finds beautiful, another person may find lacking in beauty altogether. Nonetheless, beauty is not adequately expressed through speech. Beauty secures its merit, in our most subjective visual perception of it.

> *'My vow was Earthly. Thou, a Heavenly love. Thy grace being*
> *gained cures all disgrace in me. Vows are but breath, and breath*
> *a vapour is. Then thou, fair Sun, which on my Earth dost shine,*
> *exhalest this vapour-vow. In thee, it is. If broken then, then it is*
> *no fault of mine. If by me broke, what fool is not so wise to lose*
> *an oath to win a Paradise?'* [404]

People employ the limitations and errors of human reason, to negate and circumvent, the once-firm resolutions of their seemingly eternal vows. Being captivated by the Earthly beauty of a gentlewoman witnesses a gentleman surrender to the temptations of desire and relinquish his vows for the [attempted] satisfaction of the flesh. The most attractive allure of 'instant gratification' witnesses a gentleman engage in an inferior trade. The ignoble gentleman surrenders his character, integrity, conscience, reputation, and morality, in exchange for the irrational and endless pursuit of pleasure.

---

403 Shakespeare, William. (1598). *Love's Labour's Lost.* Act 2, Scene 1.
404 Shakespeare, William. (1598). *Love's Labour's Lost.* Act 4, Scene 3.

'But love, first learned in a Lady's eyes, lives not alone immured in the brain. But, with the motion of all elements, courses as swift as thought in every power; and gives to every power a double power above his function and his offices. It adds a precious seeing to the eye. A lover's eye will gaze an eagle blind. A lover's ear will hear the lowest sound when suspicious head of theft is stopped. Love's feeling is more soft and sensible than are the tender horns of cockled snails. Love's tongue proves dainty Bacchus gross in taste. And when love speaks, the Voice of all the Gods makes Heaven drowsy with the harmony.' [405]

Shakespeare paints a beautiful and colourful picture of love. The power of love is truly captivating. For love seizes the spirit, body, heart, and mind, like no other force on Earth. As we advance in age, and we reflect upon our personal experiences concerning love, we all have fond and cherished memories of our first love. In particular, for a gentleman, his first experience of 'falling in love' with a gentlewoman revolves around aspects of physical beauty, not to mention, the strong attraction to the properties and attributes of a gentlewoman's body, most notably, the facial appearance and physique.

'The blood of youth burns not with such excess as gravity's revolt to wantonness.' [406]

For the majority of the human species, when a person is in their adolescent years, life is driven on by the unparalleled exigencies of the flesh. The strong desire for the opposite sex, motivates humans towards activities aimed at courtship, love, romance, affairs, copulation, and the like. Indeed, to transcend the base demands of the flesh and be in harmony with the Spirit is a life-long endeavour.

---

405 Shakespeare, William. (1598). *Love's Labour's Lost.* Act 4, Scene 3.
406 Shakespeare, William. (1598). *Love's Labour's Lost.* Act 5, Scene 2.

The supreme spiritual quest to assert self-control requires the cultivation of patience, discipline, forgiveness, thought, prudence, courage, resistance, and reason. In all things, it is through God's mercy, blessing, favour, goodness, and grace, that we transcend the challenges of life.

'Rebuke me not for that which you provoke. The virtue of your eye must break my oath.' [407]

We tend to misappropriate blame for our shortcomings and inadequacies upon those people who are around us. Unfortunately, influential people can provoke us into the terrible traps of temptation. We must rise above the fallacies of securing false promises and empty rewards through the irrational pursuit of temptation. The power of beauty is often irresistible to the human eye. Therefore, we must not solely rely upon our finite capacities to overcome concupiscence. We must earnestly pray to God for mercy, goodness, grace, favour, and blessings. God's Goodness shall assist us to transcend the corruptness of sin, and become morally righteous people.

'Since to wail friends lost is not by much so wholesome profitable as to rejoice at friends but newly found. I understand you not. My griefs are double. Honest plain words best pierce the ear of grief.' [408]

Life is too short to indefinitely reflect upon our losses. There is an appropriate season for grieving. Yet no matter the adversity or heartbreak, we always need to move forward through life. Move forward to the creation of a better and brighter future. Where there is loss, there is also the untold opportunity to make newfound gains. At times, the reality of life can be sobering and

---

407 Shakespeare, William. (1598). *Love's Labour's Lost*. Act 5, Scene 2.
408 Shakespeare, William. (1598). *Love's Labour's Lost*. Act 5, Scene 2.

grim. However, we must confront the hard truths and engage in the difficult conversations, if we are to make an honest assessment of our life. Time does not stand still for any person. We must make a bold determination to seize the future, which belongs to us.

Chapter 19

MACBETH

'Your Son, My Lord, has paid a soldier's debt.
Your cause of sorrow must not be measured
by his worth, for then it hath no end.'

SHAKESPEARE

Macbeth is a play that vividly illustrates a pivotal and often overlooked message concerning the affairs of gentlemen and gentlewomen in society, and that is, 'We reap, what we sow.' In the early stages of this play, three witches make a bold prophecy, asserting that Scottish General Macbeth will become the next King of Scotland. With the endless and over-powering persuasion of his beloved wife, Lady Macbeth, Lord Macbeth resolves to murder King Duncan in His Majesty's bedroom chamber. Thereafter, Lord Macbeth is proclaimed the new Sovereign of Scotland.

Immediately after murdering King Duncan, Lord Macbeth shows considerable remorse and immense regret for his evil actions. Lord Macbeth's wife comforts him, and she makes persistent efforts to revive his sanity. With the twists and turns of fate, the late King Duncan's two sons, Donalbain and Malcolm, hurriedly flee in genuine concern for the safety of their lives. Lord Macbeth portrays the late King's sons hurried departure as proof of their guilt and a sign of their involvement in King Duncan's death. In reality, the late King's two sons are wholly innocent in the matter. Donalbain and Malcolm vow to return to their homeland, to make amends for this great injustice inflicted upon their deceased father.

Throughout King Macbeth's rule as Sovereign of Scotland, he is overwhelmed by feelings of guilt, doubt, fear, anger, confusion, uncertainty, and insecurity. In a desperate bid by Lord Macbeth to keep his illegitimate place on the Scottish Throne secure, he plots the murders of individuals that are deemed an existential threat to his rule as Sovereign. Nonetheless, Lord Macbeth remains restless. Once again, Lord Macbeth seeks out the three witches for further advice and counsel on what the future holds for him.

Meanwhile, Malcolm overcomes his own doubts and insecurities to lead an army into battle against King Macbeth's rule. On the other hand, Lady Macbeth is distraught and distressed with the insecurities of how the Macbeth's came to inherit the Scottish Throne. Lady Macbeth's physical and mental condition deteriorates. In a twist of fate, Lady Macbeth commences sleep walking and she discloses her inner secrets to her physician. Despite the countless pleas and appeals by Lord Macbeth, the physician has no medicine that can restore Lady Macbeth's peace of mind. Eventually, Lady Macbeth commits suicide. This tragic news imposes an unprecedented psychological burden upon King Macbeth's state of mind.

In the final scenes of this play, Macduff takes the high ground to revenge the killing of his family at the hands of His Majesty King Macbeth. In the closing duel of this play, Macduff defeats King Macbeth, and brings Macbeth's head to Malcolm. As a result, Malcolm declares a state of peace across the Kingdom's territory. Malcolm is set to be enthroned the next legitimate King of Scotland. Now Malcolm embarks for Scone to attend to his official coronation ceremony.

'If you can look into the seeds of time and say which grain will grow and which will not, speak, then, to me, who neither beg nor fear. Your favours, nor your hate.' [409]

The future is most uncertain and unpredictable. We can make educated estimates and informed decisions on how our life trajectory may proceed. However, it is almost impossible to know the fruits of our labour, until the opportune time has arrived that the fruit is ripened, and it is the appropriate time for a harvest. For when we harvest, we shall come to know, which grain bore fruit, and which grain was spoiled. In all things, fortune favours the bold. We must make the most of our resources, time, abilities, talents, learning, endowments, knowledge, gifts, experience, and education that we possess, to create the life that we desire.

'But it is strange and oftentimes, to win us to our harm, the instruments of darkness tell us truths; win us with honest trifles, to betray us in deepest consequence.' [410]

Our beliefs define and create our living reality. We must be vigilant not to let an evil-minded person misconstrue the Truth, to serve their illegitimate ends and create a fabricated sense of reality. Therefore, we must be attentive, not only in 'what' we entrust, but also 'whom' we trust in. For an evil person's intention to employ the Truth against us, can be persuasive when we are positioned in a vulnerable situation. Not to mention, a person with a malignant will is only employing the Truth to gain our trust, in order that we be deceived. The instrument of vigilance, deters the presence of evil.

---

409 Shakespeare, William. (1623). *Macbeth.* Act 1, Scene 3.
410 Shakespeare, William. (1623). *Macbeth.* Act 1, Scene 3.

'Present fears are less than horrible imaginings.' [411]

Often people exaggerate their fears to be considerably worse than what they truly are. Psychology is a complex and important component of each person's life. Psychology is the scientific and empirical examination of a person's world perception, cognition, emotions, feelings, sensations, thought, speech, and behaviour. The psychology of an individual assists to explain one's unique perspective of doubt, fear, and a range of other emotions.

A person's imagination can function both as a blessing and as a curse, depending on how it is employed. There is no pre-defined end, or established limit, to a person's imagination. It is essential that our imagination be utilised to construct or visualise success, interest, joy, happiness, surprise, and amazement. The emotions of 'positive psychology'. As opposed to pondering on fear, doubt, sadness, anger, guilt, confusion, hesitation, and loneliness. The emotions of 'dark psychology'.

'Come what come may, time and the hour runs through the roughest day.' [412]

No matter the consequential difficulties, privations, hardships, pain, or suffering that we confront in this world, the function of time is an equal and constant factor in all things. Regardless, be it the most 'positive' or 'negative' day of our life, it shall not endure forever. While this is easier said than done, we need to preserve equanimity of mind in all of our personal affairs. We must not become attached or attempt to fixate upon reality. For the desire or aversion to any external phenomenon in this transient world is against the very nature of true reality. Attachment and aversion only cause us considerable pain and untold suffering. Peace be with you.

---

411 Shakespeare, William. (1623). *Macbeth*. Act 1, Scene 3.
412 Shakespeare, William. (1623). *Macbeth*. Act 1, Scene 3.

'There is no art. To find the mind's construction in the face.
He was a gentleman on whom I built an absolute trust.' [413]

We can learn a considerable amount about a person through close observation. In particular, through non-verbal communication. Non-verbal communication is self-evident through a person's facial expressions, but also their hand movements, symbolic gestures, eye contact, sitting posture, and alertness to their surrounding environment. In fact, non-verbal communication constitutes the majority component of a person's communication.

'Stars, hide your fires. Let not light see my black and deep desires.
The eye wink at the hand; yet let that be, which the eye fears,
when it is done, to see.' [414]

We are all sinners. Some people greater than others. However, no person is keen to shine light on their darkest thoughts and twisted intentions. The fear of judgement and retribution keeps a person from becoming the best version of themselves. In the final analysis, we are all responsible for our actions. Our free moral actions have real consequences, both intended and unintended. Therefore, we must consciously reflect upon our desires, motives, intentions, beliefs, values, and sincerity of mind, before we commit to a particular course of action. Where the exercise of human agency is concerned, the 'means' matter as greatly as the 'ends'.

To live a life filled with regret, grief, guilt, fear, doubt, confusion, hesitation, anger, and disbelief, only serves to diminish the beauty and value of life itself. Thus, we ought to carefully and methodically think through our actions. Equally consider the 'good' and the 'evil' consequences, before committing to our actions. In all things, in the fullness of time, we must be prepared to reap the harvest, of what our actions have merited.

---

413 Shakespeare, William. (1623). *Macbeth*. Act 1, Scene 4.
414 Shakespeare, William. (1623). *Macbeth*. Act 1, Scene 4.

'Only look up clear. To alter favour ever is to fear.' [415]

A person who believes in God, with all their heart, need not question or doubt God's Favour. Disbelief only serves to negate a person's confidence and conviction in God. When we place our total trust in God, then we shall proceed forward with an iron-like resolve, an unwavering boldness, and a firm determination.

Within the *Holy Bible*, in the *Book of James*, Chapter 1, Verses 6 to 8, we are told how the presence of doubt destroys hope, 'But when you ask, you must believe and not doubt, because the one who doubts is like a wave of the sea, blown and tossed by the wind. That person should not expect to receive anything from the LORD. Such a person is double-minded and unstable in all they do.'

'The love that follows us sometimes is our trouble, which still we thank as love.' [416]

Love is a complex and multi-faceted emotion. We all experience, share, receive, and express love in our daily interactions with humanity. At times, in particular concerning the institution of marriage, love can be misunderstood, or poorly received. This unpleasant reality can cause serious issues in a marriage. Sometimes a spouse's expectations are not met or managed, and this can cause major friction in a marriage. Such pressing marriage issues and concerns must be acknowledged and worked through between the husband and wife in a calm, considerate, and cooperative manner. All things considered, we shall still be thankful for the precious and priceless opportunity to love. For a world without love, is a world without hope.

---

415 Shakespeare, William. (1623). *Macbeth*. Act 1, Scene 5.
416 Shakespeare, William. (1623). *Macbeth*. Act 1, Scene 6.

'Art thou afeard to be the same in thine own act and valour as thou art in desire?' [417]

The dark and destructive emotion of fear is a paralysing hindrance to the complete realisation of our full potential. It is only the performance of action that can bring to reality our desired life. For doubt and fear are the two major obstacles to the true manifestation of our ideal life. At times, our imagination desires greatness that is too far-fetched for our courage and conduct, however, it is all a matter of belief. For if we believe it is possible, then we can accomplish all that we desire.

'If we should fail? We fail! But screw your courage to the sticking place, and we'll not fail.' [418]

We need to possess a single-minded determination in our thoughts. We must be resolved to witness our envisioned mission through to its completion. Half-heartedness is not sufficient material to accomplish success in our chosen vocation, profession, sport, or career. Perhaps, the greatest failure in life, is not attempting an endeavour which we are passionate about, due to a lack of courage, the presence of inhibition, infirm volition, or paralysing fear and doubt. We must not create the future grounds for regret and remorse in our life, by diminishing the immense power of the present moment, to create our desired reality.

'Away, and mock the time with fairest show. False face must hide what the false heart doth know.' [419]

When circumstances are corrupt, we must bide the time. However, to chide another person shall never resolve our dilemma. Thus, a person can misconstrue their appearance and hide the Truth in

---

417 Shakespeare, William. (1623). *Macbeth.* Act 1, Scene 7.
418 Shakespeare, William. (1623). *Macbeth.* Act 1, Scene 7.
419 Shakespeare, William. (1623). *Macbeth.* Act 1, Scene 7.

their heart. However, the Truth is bound to come to light sooner or later. For the fragile fabric of falsehood cannot endure the litmus test of time. In the final analysis, one can be false towards other people, in order to portray an image that is not true. However, a person cannot be false towards God. God is the Searcher of hearts and Keeper of souls.

'Be not lost. So poorly in your thoughts.' [420]

Our thoughts and beliefs determine our perception of reality. The quality of our thoughts is the precursor to what type of life we shall create during our time on Earth. It is possible for a person to become overwhelmed in their thoughts. The key to positive thinking resides in self-esteem. The very subjective and personalised concept of the Self, determines our essence of being in this world.

Individuals who exercise a strong degree of control over their thoughts and create their ideal reality possess an 'internal locus of control'. On the other hand, individuals who feel they are unable to control the circumstances, forces, and events that determine the trajectory of their life demonstrate an 'external locus of control'. While no person can assume total control in this chaotic and often unpredictable world, we must find a balance, harmony, and peace within ourselves.

'Shake off this downy sleep, death's counterfeit, and look on death itself!' [421]

We must not permit life to pass us by. We have a very limited time on Earth, and when we consciously 'look on death itself', we know that we are only mortal. Therefore, to be inactive or idle, is a waste of our very existence. When we consciously reflect on death, it

---

420 Shakespeare, William. (1623). *Macbeth.* Act 2, Scene 2.
421 Shakespeare, William. (1623). *Macbeth.* Act 2, Scene 2.

shall serve as the impetus and prime motive, for us to create a life that is meaningful and purposeful.

We must strive to create a life that involves genuine commitment to community service and provision for charity. When we are nearing our life's full and natural course, we can then infer, we are accomplished. It is within our present agency to create a fulfilling life. Thus, in our advanced age, when we reflect on our life with the power of hindsight, rather than be full of regret, we are full of satisfaction.

'Our separate fortune shall keep us both the safer. Where we are there's daggers in men's smiles.' [422]

It is not always possible to trust the people that are around us. A person's body language, and other demonstrable forms of non-verbal communication can be manipulated. As a result, a person's true intentions become concealed from our sight. At certain times in our life, it is best counsel to err on the side of caution in the exercise of our judgement. The force of circumstance can turn the tide against us. Thus, our vulnerabilities may leave us exposed to danger, which other people may take advantage of, or seek to benefit from. For such is the shallow nature of the rational, self-interested, exploitative, calculated, liberal, and egocentric person in our contemporary society.

'Naught's had, all's spent, where our desire is got without content.' [423]

It is in vain that we tirelessly attempt to fulfil our insatiable desires. However, we never secure a sense of complete satisfaction in the irrational pursuit of our desires. In the end, we shall exhaust all our resources, and have nothing to show for our labour in attempting

---

422 Shakespeare, William. (1623). *Macbeth.* Act 2, Scene 3.
423 Shakespeare, William. (1623). *Macbeth.* Act 3, Scene 2.

to create a happy and pleasure-filled life. Upon conscious reflection, we realise that contentment is one of the most difficult emotional states to obtain in life. For whosoever is truly content, needs nothing more. A content person has found the precious treasure of satisfaction deep within themselves. A content person is truly blessed and most rare indeed.

> *'Better to be with the dead. Whom we, to gain our peace, have sent to peace. Than, on the torture of the mind, to lie. In restless ecstasy.'* [424]

Shakespeare makes the classic philosophical argument, that it is advisable to embody a state of 'non-existence', compared to the inferior state of 'existence' in this world. This broken world is full of troubles, traumas, tragedies, and tribulations that are unceasing and unyielding, till death does us apart. In all cases, the worst type of suffering is that of the mind. For the mind's tortures and disorders are often incurable. Mental disorders are representative of life-long psychiatric conditions, that witness one lose the sanity of their mind, to live a purposeful, peaceful, and productive life.

> *'Things bad begun make strong themselves by ill.'* [425]

The forces of evil self-perpetuate considerable darkness in this broken world. Therefore, the proliferation of sin continues unabated. It is only God's power, goodness, mercy, favour, and grace that can destroy the perpetual chain of sin. For once a person commences on the ill-fated journey of evil, such a person proceeds further down the route, and only commits greater evils in order to seek a false sense of refuge in their mind. However, all the function of sin ever achieves is to lose a person's peace of mind, and disturb a person's serenity.

---

424 Shakespeare, William. (1623). *Macbeth*. Act 3, Scene 2.
425 Shakespeare, William. (1623). *Macbeth*. Act 3, Scene 2.

In *Macbeth*, we witness first-hand the evil nature of humanity. We witness how ill deeds ultimately yield corrupt fruit. The psychological burden of Lord Macbeth murdering His Majesty King Duncan has a profound impact on Lady Macbeth's life, and she eventually commits suicide. Not to mention, Lord Macbeth cannot escape the constant torment of insecurity and fear as the newfound King of Scotland. As a consequence, Lord Macbeth continues to plot the murder of other notable figures who pose an existential threat to his rule as sovereign. Regrettably, Lord Macbeth confronts his destined fate. Lord Macbeth is subject to a dishonourable death by beheading.

'When our actions do not, our fears do make us traitors.' [426]

This statement captures the dilemma of the human condition. Sometimes we are paralysed betwixt thought and action. The presence of fear, confusion, and doubt only serve to obstruct our resolve on a particular course of action. If we are paralysed by fear, then, by default, we become traitors to the execution of the very proposed action that we intended to perform. We must not let the 'fear of fear' inhibit our thinking, and defer our actions. The wise words of Terence, the Ancient Roman playwright, makes the construction of our worldly reality self-evident, 'Fortune favours the bold.'

'But cruel are the times when we are traitors and do not know ourselves; when we hold rumour from what we fear, yet know not what we fear.' [427]

The presence and function of fear, confusion, hesitation, anger, uncertainty, and doubt only serve to turn ourselves against ourselves. If we perform good, honourable, virtuous, and noble

---

426 Shakespeare, William. (1623). *Macbeth*. Act 4, Scene 2.
427 Shakespeare, William. (1623). *Macbeth*. Act 4, Scene 2.

deeds, then we need not fear their repercussions. On the contrary, if we perform sinful, evil, egocentric, and selfish deeds, then we have every reason to be concerned for our future. There is one phenomenon to fear for every person on this Earth, and we must all know what we ought to fear, it is God. Throughout the *Holy Bible*, we repeatedly witness the message of fearing God. For example, consider in the *Book of Revelation*, Chapter 14, Verse 7, 'Fear God and give Him Glory, because the hour of His Judgement has come. Worship Him who made the Heavens, the Earth, the Sea, and the Springs of Water.'

> *'But I remember now … I am in this Earthly world, where to do harm is often laudable, to do good sometime accounted dangerous folly.'* [428]

Humans confront the paradox of having self-interested, egocentric, and evil actions rewarded. On the other hand, to perform good may not reap instantaneous rewards, nor always be awarded its due and proper recognition. Furthermore, to perform good works, may at times go beyond our personal interests. In any case, we must always remember that our free moral actions have real consequences. It is possible that we may escape the uneven scales of justice in this broken world. However, no person escapes the True Justice of God's Sovereign Court.

> *'Angels are bright still, though the Brightest fell; though all things foul would wear the brows of grace, yet grace must still look so.'* [429]

Even the most Perfect Angels are susceptible to the powerful temptation of sin. Needless to infer, no living person on Earth is beyond the temptation of sin. The Devil was once a 'Perfect' Angel. However, in seeking God's Glory and Power, the renowned Lucifer

---

428 Shakespeare, William. (1623). *Macbeth*. Act 4, Scene 2.
429 Shakespeare, William. (1623). *Macbeth*. Act 4, Scene 3.

fell from grace and was banished from the Kingdom of Heaven. Thus, it is essential that we know our place as Servants of the Most High God. Our life mission is to advance the Kingdom of God.

'But there's no bottom, none, in my voluptuousness. Your wives, your daughters, your matrons, and your maids, could not fill up the cistern of my lust, and my desire all continent impediments would overbear that did oppose my will.' [430]

Shakespeare masterfully illustrates the dark reality of human nature and the great challenge humanity confronts whilst in the flesh. The worldly temptations of the flesh are numerous. The protracted battle with concupiscence is one of the primary sins that turn humanity away from God's Presence and Love. Nevertheless, humanity's endeavour to fulfil their Earthly desires is an irrational and impossible undertaking. For by its very nature, desire is always insatiable. In the final analysis, no matter how much we personally experience during our time on Earth, the quantum of formal learning and knowledge we obtain, or the material possessions that we own, it will always be insufficient. The state of contentment is always found within ourselves, not without.

Within the *Holy Bible*, the *Book of Romans*, Chapter 7, Verses 14 to 25, Paul narrates his profound and protracted struggle with sin. Paul most precisely demonstrates, just how incredibly difficult it is, to transcend our sinful human nature. Despite our best intentions to perform good in this world. 'We know that the law is spiritual; but I am unspiritual, sold as a slave to sin. I do not understand what I do. For what I want to do I do not do, but what I hate I do. And if I do what I do not want to do, I agree that the law is good. As it is, it is no longer I myself who do it, but it is sin living in me. For I know that good itself does not dwell in me, that is, in my sinful nature. For I have the desire to do what is good, but I cannot carry it out.

---

430 Shakespeare, William. (1623). *Macbeth*. Act 4, Scene 3.

For I do not do the good I want to do; but the evil I do not want to do—this I keep on doing. Now if I do what I do not want to do, it is no longer I who do it, but it is sin living in me that does it. So I find this law at work: although I want to do good, evil is right there with me. For in my inner being I delight in God's Law; but I see another law at work in me, waging war against the law of my mind and making me a prisoner of the law of sin at work within me. What a wretched man I am! Who will rescue me from this body that is subject to death? Thanks be to God, who delivers me through Jesus Christ our Lord!'

'Boundless intemperance in nature is a tyranny.' [431]

In all things, moderation is the key to a healthy and well-lived life. Indeed, temperance is a virtue, comparable to honesty, integrity, service, charity, kindness, sincerity, modesty, justice, courage, and patience. Overindulgence leads to disharmony and reckless conduct. In fact, too much of any one thing, is a bad thing, it does not matter if it is love, exercise, employment, reading, learning, financial capital, wealth accumulation, or private property. Anything that is pursued to excess, or extreme lengths, shall wreak havoc in a person's life. The exercise of self-restraint creates balance, peace, goodwill, and harmony in this world.

'But fear not yet to take upon you what is yours.' [432]

We must be bold to secure what is our birth right, inheritance, property right, estate, special endowment by will or prerogative, and much more. For the entire purpose of our life is to 'live', not simply to 'exist'. For many people, the presence and function of fear is a major inhibitor to the process of living a good and distinguished life. Therefore, the fear of fear itself must be wholly overcome,

---

431 Shakespeare, William. (1623). *Macbeth*. Act 4, Scene 3.
432 Shakespeare, William. (1623). *Macbeth*. Act 4, Scene 3.

if we are to truly achieve our highest potential and realise our God-given destiny.

'Such welcome and unwelcome things at once, it is hard to reconcile.' [433]

The course of life does not always proceed on the high moral principles of fairness, integrity, equality, honesty, loyalty, respect, compassion, equity, and justice. Therefore, we must make our peace with the 'favourable' and the 'unfavourable' aspects of our life. There is much uncertainty in the course of human affairs. At times, certain life events or personal experiences will be challenging and their presence be most undesired, however, this is an opportunity to develop our character and demonstrate our values. In the final analysis, we must be prepared to accept the presence of both 'good' and 'evil' in this world.

'What, man! Never pull your hat upon your brows. Give sorrow words: the grief that does not speak. Whispers the overfraught heart and bids it break.' [434]

It is not wise counsel to suppress and conceal our grief through life. For grief ought to be expressed and processed, in order to move forward through life. Internalising personal experiences with grief can lead to many psychological and physiological problems. Talking through grief allows us the opportunity to express how we feel and become better acquainted with our emotions, sensations, and feelings. The reality is that the human condition is not always guided by reason, logic, and good judgement. Therefore, we need to consciously navigate our complex emotions, feelings, and sensations, throughout the major stages of the human life cycle.

---

433 Shakespeare, William. (1623). *Macbeth.* Act 4, Scene 3.
434 Shakespeare, William. (1623). *Macbeth.* Act 4, Scene 3.

'Be this the whetstone of your sword. Let grief convert to anger. Blunt not the heart, enrage it.' [435]

The aforementioned statement is premised on an evil thought. This idea is the precursor to seeking revenge. If we convert grief to anger, we only serve to destroy our peace of mind. Not to mention, acts of retribution destroy, they do not develop, a person's character and conscience. Anger is an emotion, just like any another. For example, consider joy, happiness, sadness, surprise, fear, interest, grief, and disgust. Thus, it is entirely natural and normal to be annoyed or frustrated on occasion. However, we need to reflect on our anger and find more constructive methods to attend to it.

The ancient Greek philosopher, Aristotle, conveys considerable wisdom, when it comes to the management of anger. Aristotle states, 'Anyone can become angry—that is easy, but to be angry with the right person, and to the right degree, and at the right time, and for the right purpose, and in the right way, that is not within everyone's power, and that is not easy.' We need to be conscious of and regulate our expression of anger. It can be done. It is possible. Like with all things in life, practice makes perfect.

'Receive what cheer you may. The night is long that never finds the day.' [436]

A positive state of mind is of much comfort, during the times of distress, heartache, and grief. During challenging times, we all need to find passage through the dark and difficult periods of our life. While problems, difficulties, and issues are not always convenient to navigate, the pursuit of happiness and good company can render the journey of life more bearable. Of great importance, our perception matters. Having the right perspective shall make a world of difference to our beliefs, thoughts, speech, and action.

---

435 Shakespeare, William. (1623). *Macbeth.* Act 4, Scene 3.
436 Shakespeare, William. (1623). *Macbeth.* Act 4, Scene 3.

*'What need we fear who knows it, when none can call our power
to account?'* [437]

Shakespeare speaks volumes to the corrupt and evil nature of humanity. This demonstrates how the self-assured hubris among gentlemen and gentlewomen leads to a fictional sense of total control and limitless power. However, as modern history has shown, time and time again, politicians, of all stripes and colours, are all too human. Great leaders are susceptible to their ill-timed downfall in politics.

The English Catholic historian, politician, and writer, Lord Acton once stated on power, 'Power tends to corrupt, and absolute power corrupts absolutely.' Ultimately, a political leader never knows *when* and *how* their exercise of power shall be called to account. Therefore, it is prudent to always exercise power with the consent of the people, and only in the best interests of the people.

*'What, will these hands never be clean? All the perfumes of Arabia
will not sweeten this little hand.'* [438]

Actions have consequences. Figuratively speaking, it is not possible to cleanse one's hands of the stains of innocent blood that has been shed of another person. The effects of sin and ill deeds cannot be easily cleansed, as dirt is removed from soiled hands. Therefore, it is imperative that we carefully consider the consequences of our actions, before we execute them. Needless to say, the application of perfumes, potions, and antidotes are no remedy to the removal of a person's evil deeds. On the contrary, we must pray to God and seek forgiveness for our countless sins.

---

437 Shakespeare, William. (1623). *Macbeth.* Act 5, Scene 1.
438 Shakespeare, William. (1623). *Macbeth.* Act 5, Scene 1.

'What's done cannot be undone.' [439]

History is harsh. Good or evil alike, we cannot reverse the events of yesterday. However, the future is yet to be created. Therefore, the responsibility is upon us, to learn the enduring lessons of history, and enact positive change for a better world. We must strive to create a Modern World where there is peace, social justice, equality, prosperity, equity, and security for all people on Earth, regardless of a person's gender, sex, age, colour, faith, religion, ethnicity, country of birth, education, income, wealth, private property, political affiliation, marital status, race, disability, social class, or any other discriminatory factor.

> *'Foul whisperings are abroad, unnatural deeds do breed unnatural troubles. Infected minds to their deaf pillows will discharge their secrets. More needs she the Divine than a Physician. God, God forgive us all! Look after her, remove from her the means of all annoyance.'* [440]

Sooner or later, our ill deeds will adequately punish us. We shall secure the ripened fruit of our actions. Only God's Grace has the power to forgive all transgressions and misdeeds. No action is beyond the Redemptive Love of God to pardon. However, we must humble ourselves and earnestly pray to God for forgiveness. A physician employs the instrument of medicine, to better the human condition, treating the underlying symptoms of medical conditions, diseases, complaints, and ailments. However, God's Ways of healing humanity are through the unrivalled Power of the Spirit.

In all cases, God's Methods cannot be understood or ascertained by the finite limit of human reason. In the *Holy Bible*, within the *Book of Isaiah*, Chapter 55, Verses 8 and 9, we are told of how it is not always possible to understand God's Goodness towards us,

---

439 Shakespeare, William. (1623). *Macbeth*. Act 5, Scene 1.
440 Shakespeare, William. (1623). *Macbeth*. Act 5, Scene 1.

'For My Thoughts are not your thoughts, neither are your ways My Ways, declares the LORD. As the Heavens are higher than the Earth, so are My Ways higher than your ways and My Thoughts than your thoughts.'

'The mind I sway by and the heart I bear. Shall never sag with doubt nor shake with fear.' [441]

A resolved mind is the most powerful instrument within our power. For once we have fixed our mind to a course, we can then boldly proceed forward with total conviction and unreserved confidence. A mind banished of doubt is never subject to the problems of a double-mind. The heart, for its part, must be full of love and empty of fear, but for the fear of God. For love instils within us hope, faith, purpose, optimism, and passion.

'I have lived long enough. My way of life is fallen into the sere, the yellow leaf ... and that which should accompany old age, as honour, love, obedience, troops of friends, I must not look to have; but in their stead, curses not loud, but deep, mouth-honour, breath which the poor heart would fain deny and dare not.' [442]

Like all things in and of this Earth, our course of life must come to its inevitable end, to its fated conclusion. Therefore, the important questions concerning our Earthly existence are:

- What type of life do we want to live?
- How do we utilise our time?
- What do we want our legacy to be?
- How do we define a successful and accomplished life?
- Why do we do what we do?

---

441 Shakespeare, William. (1623). *Macbeth.* Act 5, Scene 3.
442 Shakespeare, William. (1623). *Macbeth.* Act 5, Scene 3.

- What are the values and beliefs that guide our thoughts and actions?
- Who do we want to spend our time with?

'Therein the Patient must minister to himself.' [443]

A Medical Doctor can provision all the good counsel to a Patient. However, it is within the agency and power of the Patient to act upon the sound advice of the Physician. This specific action the Physician cannot perform. Most importantly, without the conscious and concentrated action of the Patient, the Patient will never make a full recovery, nor treat the pathological basis of a medical disease or condition. The Greek physician, Hippocrates, has rightly asserted, 'If someone wishes for good health, one must first ask oneself, if they are ready to do away with the reasons for their illness. Only then is it possible to help them.'

> *'Let our just censures attend the true event, and put we on industrious soldiership. The time approaches that will with due decision make us know. What we shall say we have, and what we owe.'* [444]

It is a soldier's duty to be at the ready. The outcome of military battles shall determine the 'spoils of war' and the 'terms of peace'. It is upon us to perform to the best of our ability. To ensure that we secure success on the battlefield, such that those military victories shall turn into important gains at the negotiating table. Beyond the precision of preparation and organisation, it is essential to acknowledge that the outcome of a military campaign can be swayed by the indifferent forces of nature and circumstance. Indeed, advantage can be gained or lost, by forces beyond our immediate control.

---

443 Shakespeare, William. (1623). *Macbeth.* Act 5, Scene 3.
444 Shakespeare, William. (1623). *Macbeth.* Act 5, Scene 4.

'Life's but a walking shadow, a poor player. That struts and frets his hour upon the stage. And then is heard no more. It is a tale.' [445]

Life is bittersweet. Human life is short-lived. Each person has the opportunity to make their mark on the world stage, before the curtain closes on their life. Once we are gone, we are heard of no more. Thus, initiative must meet opportunity, for a person to leave their legacy on Earth. In the final analysis, positive thoughts coupled with productive actions, will witness us make the most of our precious lifetime.

'There is nor flying hence nor tarrying here. I begin to be aweary of the Sun, and wish the estate of the world were now undone. Ring the alarum-bell! Blow, wind! Come, wrack! At least we'll die with harness on our back.' [446]

Life is a series of battles. In some battles, we secure decisive victory. In others, we falter and lose ground. In the end, we must select our battles wisely. More importantly, we must be prepared to fight the Good Fight of Faith and advance God's Kingdom on Earth. In the course of our life, we cannot be assured the outcome of our actions. However, we must confront all adversities with courage, boldness, hope, conviction, strength of mind, unwavering belief, and total confidence in God's Goodness.

'But get thee back. My soul is too much charged with blood of thine already. I have no words. My voice is in my sword.' [447]

Since the committing of *Original Sin* and the *Fall of Man*, the continued perpetuation of sin has no end in this broken world. The vicious cycle of death and destruction, followed by revenge and retribution, shall never lead to a state of 'perpetual peace' on Earth.

---

445 Shakespeare, William. (1623). *Macbeth*. Act 5, Scene 5.
446 Shakespeare, William. (1623). *Macbeth*. Act 5, Scene 5.
447 Shakespeare, William. (1623). *Macbeth*. Act 5, Scene 8.

The human condition is such, that we are driven on by the powerful temptations of the flesh and the limitless desire for power, fame, influence, wealth, concupiscence, financial capital, private property, income, and material possessions. Unfortunately, the vast majority of humans are egocentric. For much of humanity perceives this material world through the narrow lens of the deceived ego.

'Your Son, My Lord, has paid a soldier's debt. Your cause of sorrow must not be measured by this worth, for then it hath no end.'[448]

To die a valiant death of a noble soldier is defined by outstanding gallantry. We cannot help but grieve over the loss of our own beloved family members. Even the outpouring of emotion and the intense expression of our grief can never do justice to the personal loss that we suffer in a beloved family member's death. During the difficult times, love, hope, prayer, and faith are the antidotes and remedies to manage the setbacks and losses that we experience in our life. While relationships and loved ones are irreplaceable, there is a season for grieving and a season for moving forward with our life. For our time here on Earth is not without limit or end.

---

448 Shakespeare, William. (1623). *Macbeth.* Act 5, Scene 8.

Chapter 20

MEASURE FOR MEASURE

*'There is scarce truth enough alive to make societies secure,
but security enough to make fellowships accurst. Much upon
this riddle runs the wisdom of the world.'*

SHAKESPEARE

Measure for Measure is a dark comedy. This play explores several intertwined themes, including justice, mercy, love, copulation, power, law, authority, forgiveness, and punishment. This play commences with Duke Vincentio appointing Lord Angelo in charge of Vienna. Lord Angelo is resolved on adopting a more 'black letter' law approach to public order in the city-state. Not to mention, Lord Angelo intends to employ law enforcement, to turnaround the deteriorating moral standards of the masses.

A gentleman by the name of Claudio impregnates his fiancée, Juliet. Claudio is condemned to death for his criminal offence against the city-state's law. Now Claudio appears to be in an all but helpless predicament. Claudio's sister, Isabella, has resolved on affirming religious vows, and she is about to enter into convent life. Upon receiving this most distressing news from Lucio, Isabella visits

Lord Angelo to plead her brother's case and seek mercy. While Lord Angelo is wholly resolved on his course of action, that is, to condemn Claudio to death, he is spell-bound by Isabella's natural beauty. Lord Angelo entertains the thought of further dialogue with Isabella.

Lord Angelo finally reveals his true motives and sinister intentions. Angelo offers to pardon Isabella's brother's life; if she sleeps with him and consents to the act of copulation. Isabella is disgusted with Lord Angelo. Isabella threatens to reveal Angelo's inferior character and immorality. However, Angelo is convinced that no reasonable person will believe Lady Isabella's word. Here we witness the dynamics of the 'power imbalance' between the sexes. We witness how Angelo improperly employs his position of power, for personal gain and the pursuit of pleasure.

Isabella is resolved to preserve her chastity at all costs. Isabella visits her brother in prison to inform him of the tragic news. Now Claudio values the preservation of his life, more than Isabella's vow to virginity. Claudio perceives this immoral exchange to be reasonable to preserve his precious life. Isabella is most disappointed in her brother, and she condemns him to death. Meanwhile, Duke Vincentio, who is in disguise as a friar, has overheard the exchange between Claudio and Isabella. Immediately thereafter, the friar offers to provide his invaluable assistance and support for Isabella's just cause, to save her brother's life.

The remainder of this play consists of twists and turns while Isabella and the friar seek to preserve the life of Claudio, and concurrently make novel arrangements for the fulfilment of Lord Angelo's sexual demands. At the end of this play, the disguised friar reveals his true identity as Duke Vincentio. Thereafter, Claudio's life is saved. Claudio is also permitted to wed Juliet. Now Lord Angelo repents for his misconduct. Angelo agrees to marry the gentlewoman he made love to (in the place of Isabella), namely, his ex-fiancée, Mariana. Last but not least, the honourable Duke

Vincentio makes a proposal for marriage to Lady Isabella. Isabella does not provide Vincentio with an answer to his modest overture.

'Spirits are not finely touched but to fine issues. Nor Nature never lends the smallest scruple of Her excellence. But, like a thrifty Goddess, she determines. Herself the glory of a creditor, both thanks and use.' [449]

In as much as we may attempt, we cannot escape the remarkable force of Nature. The institution of Nature determines the very existence and proper function of all species on Earth. Therefore, it is most advisable to live a life that is marked by harmony, peace, and balance. Live a life that accords to the Supreme Will of Nature.

'For terror, not to use, in time the rod becomes more mocked than feared; so our decrees, dead to infliction, to themselves are dead, and liberty plucks justice by the nose.' [450]

If not timely executed, the punishment for breaking the law loses it strong deterrent effect. Justice becomes an open travesty. The incentive to flout the law becomes greater. The Sovereign's subjects become increasingly aware that the 'Force of Law' can be circumvented. Eventually, a radical liberty ensues from such a condition of anarchy and lawlessness. As a consequence, justice is nowhere to be found in the civilised state.

'Our doubts are traitors and make us lose the good we oft might win by fearing to attempt.' [451]

We must not listen, nor provision any authority to the untrustworthy voice of doubt. For pondering on doubt only serves to make us hesitant in our great ambitions. Doubt functions to embed fear

---

449 Shakespeare, William. (1623). *Measure for Measure.* Act 1, Scene 1.
450 Shakespeare, William. (1623). *Measure for Measure.* Act 1, Scene 3.
451 Shakespeare, William. (1623). *Measure for Measure.* Act 1, Scene 5.

in our thoughts. To paralyse our motivation for action. Thus, we must transcend doubt with confidence. That is, confidence in our knowledge, abilities, experience, capacity, learning, and talents, to achieve our full potential. The outcome of our actions is always uncertain. However, without the earnest attempt, we are certain to never succeed in our endeavours.

> *'Well, Heaven forgive him! And forgive us all! Some rise by sin, and some by virtue fall.'* [452]

We are all sinners. As a result, we all require forgiveness. Importantly, none of us are beyond the Supreme Power of God to forgive our wrongs. In the natural course of things, we expect that virtuous people shall rise, and sinners shall fall. Yet the justice of this world is not always impartial and fair. Nevertheless, God watches over Creation, and all that is within it. Thus, no person shall escape the true and final Judgement of God's Sovereign Court.

> *'Mercy is not itself, that often looks so. Pardon is still the nurse of second woe.'* [453]

At times, a person is shown undeserving mercy by God's Grace. Indeed, the Redemptive Power of God to change the course of a person's life is truly inexplicable. We are shown undeserved mercy in unimaginable ways that are beyond human comprehension and understanding. Therefore, we must be grateful to God for such a profound blessing in our life.

Pardoning a perpetrator for an indictable offence is reflective of good intentions and provides an opportunity for one to seek rehabilitation in modern society. However, we must not discount or negate the real possibility, that pardoning a person may also lead to the act of re-offending. Therefore, in the case of pardoning

---

452 Shakespeare, William. (1623). *Measure for Measure.* Act 2, Scene 1.
453 Shakespeare, William. (1623). *Measure for Measure.* Act 2, Scene 1.

a convicted person, it is essential that they receive appropriate support and care, including access to education, counselling, medical care, housing, employment, child support, financial assistance, and access to other public services, in order to improve their chances of living a productive and good life in modern society.

'I have seen, when, after execution, judgement hath repented over his doom.' [454]

Human judgement contains much folly and error. It is entirely possible that we shall make mistakes in our reasoning, and therefore, apply an undue punishment upon an innocent person. The learned English jurist, Sir William Blackstone, makes a pertinent remark concerning law and justice, in his original work, *Commentaries on the Laws of England* (1765–1769), stating, 'It is better that ten guilty persons escape, than that one innocent suffer.'

The very real concept of a 'miscarriage of justice' is harsh. This error of law has profound legal, social, and economic consequences upon the innocent individual, who has suffered from such a misguided criminal sentence. While time served in jail for an innocent person can be addressed with monetary compensation. For an innocent person convicted of a crime which carries the death penalty, there is no 'second opportunity' at life. The profundity of human reasoning is imperfect and imprecise.

'Well, believe this, no ceremony that to great ones belongs, not the King's Crown, nor the Deputed Sword, the Marshal's Truncheon, nor the Judge's Robe, become them with one half so good a grace as mercy does.' [455]

Mercy surpasses all in this world. The Divine Power of Mercy transcends high or low birth, rank, personal wealth, education,

---

454 Shakespeare, William. (1623). *Measure for Measure.* Act 2, Scene 2.
455 Shakespeare, William. (1623). *Measure for Measure.* Act 2, Scene 2.

parentage, reputation, social status, income, position, influence, and private property. The presence of mercy and forgiveness allow for the most conducive conditions of peace, love, and justice on Earth. Indeed, it takes courage and wisdom to demonstrate mercy towards a person that has wronged us. Forgiveness is not for the weak-hearted. The noble expression of forgiveness requires the strength of character and a good conscience. Forgiveness requires that a person rise higher, and realise their full potential, in the pursuit of moral excellence.

> *'But man, proud man, dressed in a little brief authority, most ignorant of what he's assured, his glassy essence, like an angry ape, plays such fantastic tricks before High Heaven as makes the Angels weep; who, with our spleens, would all themselves laugh mortal.'* [456]

We all devise plots and plans. We scheme with the narrow perception of our ego, to further the pursuit of our self-interest in this world. The majority of humanity cannot foresee beyond the vices of greed, pride, ego, jealousy, concupiscence, envy, sloth, lust, covetousness, gluttony, profit, pecuniary gain, desire, and corruption. In the final analysis, we cannot escape the existential reality, that we are all mortal. We must be mindful, that we are responsible for our free moral actions, both the good and evil.

> *'Thieves for their robbery have authority, when Judges steal themselves.'* [457]

The unenlightened masses always look to the authority figures when it comes to what is defined as 'permissible' and 'impermissible' conduct in modern society. When the learned and honourable Chief Justice's speech and behaviour are questionable, then not

---

456 Shakespeare, William. (1623). *Measure for Measure.* Act 2, Scene 2.
457 Shakespeare, William. (1623). *Measure for Measure.* Act 2, Scene 2.

only does it serve to bring the entire legal profession into disrepute, however, such abysmal conduct also establishes a lower standard of expectation for the general public's behaviour. After all, rules are rules. We cannot expect from other people, what we do not perform ourselves.

> *'Most dangerous is that temptation that doth goad us on to sin in loving virtue, never could the strumpet with all her double vigour, art and nature, once stir my temper, but this virtuous maid. Subdues me quite.'* [458]

We are all prisoners of love. The seductive power of a gentlewoman's beauty is a force to be reckoned with. Not to mention, a gentlewoman's virtue, coupled with the captivating power of her beauty, only serves to diminish a gentleman's capacity to reason and employ the faculty of judgement. In matters of love, vice and virtue can become intertwined. Therefore, restraint and moderation are the keys to finding the appropriate balance that is required. For too much of love is poisonous. Whereas, too little of love is a life without colour, happiness, hope, feeling, pleasure, emotion, and fullness.

> *'I, now the voice of the recorded law, pronounce a sentence on your brother's life. Might there not be a charity in sin. To save this brother's life?'* [459]

A learned and noble person, in a position of authority, can employ or misemploy the law, to serve their peculiar ends. Here we witness the classic moral dilemma of 'means' and 'ends'. Shakespeare's aforementioned proposition proposes the philosophical and moral quandary: Is it permissible to subvert the proper means to achieve the desired end? In such a case, a person needs to consult their

---

458 Shakespeare, William. (1623). *Measure for Measure.* Act 2, Scene 2.
459 Shakespeare, William. (1623). *Measure for Measure.* Act 2, Scene 4.

values, beliefs, ideals, faith, and principles, to determine how best to proceed forward.

> *'Please you to do it, I'll take it as a peril to my soul, it is no sin at all, but charity … Pleased you to do it at peril of your soul, were equal poise of sin and charity. That I do beg his life, if it be sin, Heaven let me bear it!'* [460]

We are all sinners. Humans seek out profit, pleasure, passion, fame, power, gain, and self-interest in this world. The virtuous people are rare and honourable in this world. Evil-minded people shall tempt us to perform sin in order to secure their narrow and selfish objectives. At times, the most unfortunate force of circumstance is overpowering. As a result, we feel that we ought to compromise on our values, principles, and beliefs. However, we must persevere through adversity and always keep hope. For where there is love, hope, and faith, anything is possible.

> *'Fit thy consent to my sharp appetite. Lay by all nicely and prolixious blushes, that banish what they sue for. Redeem thy brother by yielding up thy body to my will, or else he shall not only die the death, but thy unkindness shall his death draw out to lingering sufferance. Answer me tomorrow, or by the affection that now guides me most, I'll prove a tyrant to him.'* [461]

Herein we witness how a learned and esteemed person, situated in a position of supreme authority, subverts the noble institution of law, for the pursuit of personal interest. Unfaithful and corrupt people abrogate the sound functioning of the Moral Law. All in order to fulfil personal desires, ambitions, and temptations. Such is the evil nature of humanity. The human condition is overwhelmingly

---

460 Shakespeare, William. (1623). *Measure for Measure.* Act 2, Scene 4.
461 Shakespeare, William. (1623). *Measure for Measure.* Act 2, Scene 4.

guided by the flesh. Evil intentions and impure motives rule the heart of the insincere and dishonourable person.

'As for you, say what you can, my false ... overweighs your true.' [462]

A person can improperly utilise their reputation, power, influence, high office, prestige, vocation, learning, education, knowledge, experience, and character to misconstrue the facts in such a manner that it is most beneficial to their interest and agenda. The Truth of an unlearned, illiterate, and poverty-ridden person may be afforded less value in matters concerning legal deliberation and judgement in this world. Such are the corrupt ways of this world. Unfortunately, all people have their biases, stereotypes, prejudices, and fallacies. Human thought, reason, judgement, and logic are not always precise.

'The miserable have no other medicine. But only hope. I have hope to live, and am prepared to die.' [463]

Hope is the greatest medicine of all. Hope has the unchecked capacity to transcend all the boundaries and the many limitations of the natural sciences. Therefore, we must place our high hope and total trust in God. God's Sovereign Power has no real, theoretical, or defined limits. Divine miracles can lead to a total turnaround in our fortunes and personal affairs.

While it is important that we are attentive to the external reality of our life, and that includes a conscious awareness of our own mortality, we must not doubt. We shall earnestly believe in God's goodness, grace, favour, and mercy, which are beyond any and all known limits of human reasoning. Indeed, God's Power is even beyond the faculty of the human imagination.

---

462 Shakespeare, William. (1623). *Measure for Measure.* Act 2, Scene 4.
463 Shakespeare, William. (1623). *Measure for Measure.* Act 3, Scene 1.

> *'Happy thou art not, for what thou hast not, still thou strivest to get, and what thou hast, forgettest.'* [464]

Shakespeare masterfully illustrates how contentment is beyond the reach of the vast majority of humankind. In pondering over what we have not accomplished, or what things are not within our possession, we often forget to consciously reflect upon what we have already achieved in our lifetime. We cannot have it all. Therefore, endless striving is representative of vanity. To be content with oneself is a profound blessing.

> *'The sense of death is most in apprehension, and the poor beetle, that we tread upon, in corporal sufferance finds a pang as great. As when a giant dies.'* [465]

Humans have the inherent capacity for thought, logic, judgement, and reason. These higher faculties can also cause us considerable psychological suffering, as we can endlessly entertain thoughts about death and our personal confrontation with mortality. We must be measured in the exercise of our faculties, so as not to let them get the better of us. Death is a fact of life that is indisputable. To constantly question and reason about death is not only unhelpful, but also irrational. A more productive and constructive dialogue is to entertain the thought of: 'How to Live a Good Life.'

> *'The weariest and most loathed worldly life that age, ache, penury, and imprisonment can lay on nature is a paradise to what we fear of death.'* [466]

Almost every person desires to live. Life is almost always preferable to death. No matter how inferior our conditions and circumstances are, we prefer life, over the dreaded date with our destiny of death.

---

464 Shakespeare, William. (1623). *Measure for Measure*. Act 3, Scene 1.
465 Shakespeare, William. (1623). *Measure for Measure*. Act 3, Scene 1.
466 Shakespeare, William. (1623). *Measure for Measure*. Act 3, Scene 1.

For it does not matter how undesirable our existence is. At least we know what existence is. That is to say, we are consciously aware of what existence feels, looks, smells, sounds, and tastes like. Whereas, we have no objective knowledge of non-existence after death. Thus, our fear truly resides in what we do not know—the unknown. We fear what is totally beyond the finite power of our faculties, and consequently, beyond human knowledge and personal experience to empirically ascertain. The human senses, which are subjective and deceptive, cannot know a reality beyond human life. What to humanity remains unknown, it shall fear.

'The goodness that is cheap in beauty makes beauty brief in goodness, but grace, being the soul of your complexion, shall keep the body of it ever fair.' [467]

All worldly beauty is superficial. It is not the luxurious Mulberry Silk Dress that makes the gentlewoman. Nor is it the finest two-fold Egyptian Cotton Shirt that makes the gentleman. It is a person's character, conscience, and moral principles that determine who they truly are. It is not the superficial outward form, the external appearance, but rather the inner essence, the eternal substance of a person, that makes them who they truly are. At the very core of a person's being, their soul is the determinant of who they are in this world. To receive unmerited grace from God is the highest goodness a person can receive in this lifetime. God's Divine Blessing shall sanctify a person with true and fair beauty.

'Virtue is bold, and goodness never fearful. No might nor greatness in mortality can censure escape.' [468]

Individuals who exemplify ideal standards of behaviour, including setting high moral standards are bold. The morally righteous people

---

467 Shakespeare, William. (1623). *Measure for Measure*. Act 3, Scene 1.
468 Shakespeare, William. (1623). *Measure for Measure*. Act 3, Scene 2.

distance themselves from the ignoble behaviour of unenlightened masses found in large public crowds within major cities. Rather, the virtuous people rise high above, like eagles soaring in the sky. Goodness has nothing to fear. For the power of goodness overcomes evil. Just as the overpowering and penetrating presence of light, overcomes the depths of despair, distress, and darkness.

'There is scarce truth enough alive to make societies secure, but security enough to make fellowships accurst. Much upon this riddle runs the wisdom of the world.' [469]

This world is not always full of trustworthy, honourable, and transparent people. The very modern realities of the pursuit of self-interest, profit, pecuniary gain, pleasure, income, liberty, private property, and personal wealth position brother against brother, and position sister against sister. There is no 'collective security' in this Modern World. For this is a Modern World founded upon greed, ego, lust, desire, discrimination, prejudice, bias, inequality, inequity, injustice, and pride. The 'common good' of all the people of this world is discarded, for the interests of the aristocratic, elite, learned, and affluent people of this world. Such a world can never be safe and secure.

'If his own life answer the straightness of his proceeding, it shall become him well. Wherein if he chance to fail, he hath sentenced himself.' [470]

We need to exercise utmost discretion in our speech. Thoughtful speech is immensely important when we take the stand in a court of law. When we are subject to cross-examination during testimony and evidence, we must be prudent. There is always the remote possibility that our speech can be used against us, and thus, we may

---

469 Shakespeare, William. (1623). *Measure for Measure*. Act 3, Scene 2.
470 Shakespeare, William. (1623). *Measure for Measure*. Act 3, Scene 2.

inadvertently self-incriminate ourselves. It is always wise to think twice and speak once. For once we have spoken, then we cannot retract our words.

'Put not yourself into amazement how these things should be. All difficulties are but easy when they are known.' [471]

We need not overly concern ourselves with why things are the way they are in this world. Overthinking can become a hindrance to our endeavours to proceed forward in life. Overthinking can stunt our ability to make good and timely decisions. The psychological concept of 'analysis paralysis' explains how irrational human behaviour aims to analyse every remote possibility or plausible outcome from a decision-making perspective. However, irrational behaviour creates additional fear, hesitation, confusion, and anxiety of making an error in our inexact determination.

'Alack, when once our grace we have forgot, nothing goes right.' [472]

We always need to remember that God is our one and only True Source in this world. God is our Provider. To forget God's Grace, is to forget the divine blessings we have freely been given. During both the good and the difficult times, we shall look to God and remember that God's Grace is always near at hand. We all too often forget the important message found within the *Holy Bible*, in the *Second Book of Corinthians*, Chapter 12, Verse 9, 'But He said to me, My Grace is sufficient for you, for My Power is made perfect in weakness.'

---

471 Shakespeare, William. (1623). *Measure for Measure*. Act 4, Scene 2.
472 Shakespeare, William. (1623). *Measure for Measure*. Act 4, Scene 4.

'Than this is all as true as it is strange. Nay, it is ten times true;
for truth is truth. To the end of reckoning.' [473]

The single and most important attribute of Truth is, that it is true in and of itself. The Truth shall remain true for all time. The Truth is never subject to modification, qualification, or variation, due to a change in season, period, or fashion. The Truth shall not be misappropriated or misrepresented. However, the Truth must be interpreted within the context and meaning of the age in which it is applied and utilised in. Each generation has different needs, and according to the time of each generation, the Eternal Truth serves to assist and guide that particular generation to live a prudent, productive, and purposeful life.

'That I am touched with madness! Make not impossible. That
which but seems unlike. It is not impossible.' [474]

Often the most significant endeavour that we aim to undertake can be misrepresented in our mind as an impossible undertaking. Perception is important. If something is unlikely, that does not necessarily mean that it is impossible. A person's mindset, attitude, thoughts, ideas, emotions, feelings, beliefs, and values exert overbearing influence on their ability to achieve significant endeavours. Successful people do not always have all the resources, tools, instruments, education, formal learning, knowledge, talent, ability, expertise, and financial capital at their disposal. However, successful people maximise the utility of what is in their possession.

---

473 Shakespeare, William. (1623). *Measure for Measure*. Act 5, Scene 1.
474 Shakespeare, William. (1623). *Measure for Measure*. Act 5, Scene 1.

*'O, My Dread Lord, I should be guiltier than my guiltiness, to think
I can be undiscernible, when I perceive your grace, like power
divine, hath looked upon my passes.'* [475]

With the constant passage of time, our self-interested plans and
egocentric intentions shall eventually come to light. We can conceal
our thoughts and actions with deception and false statements.
However, the fabric of falsehood is not durable. For the Truth
shall inevitably begin to disintegrate the very artificial seams of the
fabric of falsehood that we desperately attempt to hold together.
Thus, falsehood will ultimately be destroyed. Even if we escape
the justice of this world, God is the True and Final Arbitrator of all
people within Creation.

*'That life is better life, past fearing death, than that which lives
to fear.'* [476]

It is within all of us to transcend the irrational and undesired
emotion of fear. Fear functions to elicit doubt, depression,
confusion, anger, hesitation, anxiety, and a wide range of known
psychological conditions and psychiatric disorders in life. A person
that has transcended fear has overcome the psychological limitations
that define the theoretical boundaries of our worldly reality. On the
contrary, to live our life with fear is debilitating. For fear does
not allow us to realise our full potential or inherent capacities.

*'They say, best men are moulded out of faults, and, for the most,
become much more the better for being a little bad.'* [477]

No gentleman or gentlewoman is perfect. Every person is a work
in progress. Our faults are much a part of us, as the good intentions
that we harbour, and the good deeds that we perform. Sometimes

---

475 Shakespeare, William. (1623). *Measure for Measure.* Act 5, Scene 1.
476 Shakespeare, William. (1623). *Measure for Measure.* Act 5, Scene 1.
477 Shakespeare, William. (1623). *Measure for Measure.* Act 5, Scene 1.

we will make mistakes, and being wrong is part and parcel of the life-long journey of becoming a better person. Mistakes serve to develop our character, conscience, principles, and virtues. We must consciously reflect upon our mistakes. We have an obligation to learn from our personal experiences.

'Thoughts are no subjects, intents but merely thoughts.' [478]

In and of themselves, our thoughts do not manifest into action, into our conscious worldly reality, unless we intentionally act upon them. Therefore, we need to methodically analyse and consciously observe our thought patterns, to better understand the psychological processes that constitute the function of our cognition. When we accurately examine the intentions and discern the motivations underlying our thoughts, beliefs, emotions, ideas, and values, then we can better understand the Self that permeates our unique experience of being in this world.

---

478 Shakespeare, William. (1623). *Measure for Measure.* Act 5, Scene 1.

Chapter 21

THE MERCHANT OF VENICE

'Let him look to his bond. He was wont to call me usurer.
Let him look to his bond. He was wont to lend out money
for a Christian courtesy. Let him look to his bond.
Why, I am sure, if he forfeit, thou will not take his flesh.
What's that good for? To bait fish withal.
If it will feed nothing else, it will feed my revenge.'

SHAKESPEARE

The Merchant of Venice is a dramatic comedy. This play is characterised by overtones of racial prejudice, love, mercy, anti-Semitism, injustice, the rule of law, retribution, enforceable contracts, and the law of obligations. Unlike some of the other dark and tragic comedies written by Shakespeare, this comedy concludes with a memorable and jovial outcome. The narrative is set in the City of Venice. This play narrates the story of a gentleman named Bassanio, who has squandered his personal fortune. Bassanio now stands in dire need of financial capital to court a beautiful gentlelady named Portia of Belmont.

One of Bassanio's good friends, Antonio offers to assist Bassanio with a loan. Antonio's trouble is that his valuable merchandise is physically secured in commercial ships on the high seas. Therefore, Antonio and Bassanio negotiate a lawful contract with a Jewish moneylender, Shylock to arrange finance for Bassanio's lofty endeavour. Shylock agrees to lend Antonio three thousand ducats, for three months, without any interest charges.

However, Shylock's terms and conditions for the loan are guided by a long-held animosity between Antonio and himself. In the unfortunate event that the loan is not repaid, Shylock demands one pound of Antonio's flesh. While Bassanio finds the terms and conditions most unreasonable, Antonio appears all but certain, that his valuable merchandise, which is currently held up on ships will arrive ashore, in time for the loan's full repayment. Thus, the bond is freely sealed between the aforesaid consenting parties. As a result, the agreed contractual exchange is considered a legal and honourable undertaking in Venice.

Unfortunate news befalls Antonio. Sadly, the ships containing his treasured cargo are confirmed lost at sea. Now Antonio finds himself in the dreaded predicament that he is unable to discharge the loan granted by Shylock. As a result, Shylock takes the matter to a Venetian Court of Law for a formal hearing. Shylock demands to exact the bond, one pound of Antonio's flesh, as a condition for Antonio's inability to discharge the contractual agreement. The Duke, who is presiding over the Court, seeks legal counsel on the matter before him. The qualified and practising lawyer before the Court is Balthazar, who is actually Portia in disguise as a male lawyer.

Portia earnestly attempts to persuade Shylock to show mercy and accept the payment of monies owed to him by Antonio, in this case by the goodwill of a friend named Bassanio. Bassanio has offered to doubly repay the loan. Regrettably, Shylock is determined to exact his revenge, instead of accepting the proposed offer of monetary compensation. In Shylock's sinister intention to execute his evil deed he is undone. Shylock is not permitted to shed a single drop of Antonio's blood, to dissect the pound of flesh from his body.

Portia's brilliant legal discourse and captivating oratory skills save the day, and the limbs of Antonio. Shylock repents for his poor judgement and lack of good character. Shylock is punished by forfeiting his invaluable private property, and he renounces his Jewish Faith. Not to mention, Shylock is also subject to a forced conversion to Christianity.

Portia, disguised as a Doctor of Laws, in the company of her good friend, Nerissa, disguised as a Legal Clerk, both depart the Venetian Court and return home. The two gentlewomen have secured the rings of their lovers, Bassanio and Graziano, as payment of their legal fees. While Bassanio and Graziano steadfast refused to surrender their rings, Antonio demanded they give their rings as payment to the two lawyers, as sufficient recompense for saving his body from dismemberment.

Initially, the two gentlewomen, Portia and Nerissa, scold their lovers for offering up their sacred rings to other gentlewomen. The rings were a prized possession and truly symbolic of Portia and Nerissa's love for their lovers. Finally, Portia and Nerissa reveal themselves as the two male lawyers at the Venetian Court. The wise gentleladies return the precious rings to their true lovers. This play concludes with a beautiful and lovely celebration of marriage.

'In sooth, I know not why I am so sad.'[479]

Life is bittersweet. It is difficult, though not nigh impossible, to always be satisfied with one's achievements, possessions, and accomplishments. Often, we have what we require in life, from the basic requirements for survival and sustenance to the more grandeur possessions, such as higher education, private property,

---

479 Shakespeare, William. (1600). *The Merchant of Venice.* Act 1, Scene 1.

spouse, children, motor vehicle, private wealth, and much more. However, we never truly secure contentment with such 'material' aspects of living in the Modern World. What we lack is 'spiritual growth' and 'moral development'. Our connection with God is eroding in this post-Modern World. The New World is guided by the contemporary ideologies of individualism, capitalism, liberalism, hedonism, consumerism, secularism, and materialism.

> *'I hold the world but as the world, Gratiano. A stage where every man must play a part, and mine a sad one.'* [480]

Every person has an important and unique purpose to fulfil on Earth. We have all been endowed with skills, natural abilities, gifts, talents, and knowledge, to perform our mission on Earth. Some people will have an exceedingly grand purpose to perform in comparison to other people. However, each person's individual contribution allows the world to function in a systematic and calculated manner. Indeed, the whole world is greater than the sum of its parts. Synergy only comes about as a derivative of all people making their individual contribution to the world.

> *'I urge this childhood proof, because what follows is pure innocence. I owe you much, and, like a wilful youth, that which I owe is lost ... Thou knowest that all my fortunes are at sea. Neither have I money nor commodity to raise a present sum. Therefore, go forth, try what my credit can in Venice do.'* [481]

It is a sombre reality that life is full of mischance, luck, and fate. In fact, everything we have in our possession, including our life, we shall surely relinquish one day. No material being endures for eternity. No phenomenon is permanent, but for the existence of God. For God's Glory and God's Word, shall remain forever

---

480 Shakespeare, William. (1600). *The Merchant of Venice.* Act 1, Scene 1.
481 Shakespeare, William. (1600). *The Merchant of Venice.* Act 1, Scene 1.

and ever, even once this world is no more. God's Presence is not contingent upon God's Creation. Setting aside the complex theological and philosophical arguments, we have a legal and moral duty to fulfil our obligations to other people in modern society. We have a responsibility to discharge our obligations faithfully and truthfully. Righteous conduct ensures that our reputation, honour, integrity, conscience, and character, remain untainted and intact.

'If to do were as easy as to know what were good to do, Chapels had been Churches and Poor Men's Cottages Princes' Palaces.' [482]

There is a profound difference between action and knowledge. We can all effectuate action. Having said that, there is a significant distinction between good and evil action. The former produces merit and positively develops one's character. Whereas, the execution of the latter, leads to destruction and chaos in this world. Not to mention, the pursuit of knowledge takes considerable time, effort, critical thinking, rigorous study, and formal learning to master. On the other hand, action can be predicated without thought, judgement, or reason. Thus, it is never as convenient to know, as it is to perform action in the world. Indeed, action that is guided by knowledge is practical wisdom.

'Shylock, albeit, I neither lend nor borrow. By taking nor by giving of excess.' [483]

Being a lender or borrower has its difficulties. Both scenarios are likely to cause grief, worry, anxiety, and misery. In the specific case of a lender, one is always concerned about the repayment of the principal amount lent. On the other hand, a borrower is always concerned about the ability to make periodical payments as and when they fall due. It is most sound counsel for a person

---

482 Shakespeare, William. (1600). *The Merchant of Venice.* Act 1, Scene 2.
483 Shakespeare, William. (1600). *The Merchant of Venice.* Act 1, Scene 3.

to live within their financial means. Thus, one must not borrow to excess. For unfortunate circumstances can befall any person. As a consequence, making honouring a financial commitment most difficult.

'Mark you this, Bassanio, the Devil can cite Scripture for His purpose! An evil soul producing Holy Witness. Is like a villain with a smiling cheek, a goodly apple rotten at the heart.' [484]

We must be vigilant and exercise discretion in determining who to trust in society. Unfortunately, human nature is such, that people are selfish and egoistic. People can twist and turn the good for improper use to further evil in this world. Even the sworn disciple and one of the original *Twelve Apostles* of Jesus Christ, Judas Iscariot sinned against the *Messiah*. For it is written within the *Holy Bible*, in the *Book of Matthew*, Chapter 26, Verses 47 to 50, 'While he was still speaking, Judas, one of the Twelve, arrived. With him was a large crowd armed with swords and clubs, sent from the Chief Priests and the Elders of the people. Now the betrayer had arranged a signal with them: 'The one I kiss is the man; arrest him.' Going at once to Jesus, Judas said, 'Greetings, Rabbi! and kissed him. Jesus replied, 'Do what you came for, friend.' Then the men stepped forward, seized Jesus and arrested him.'

'You shall not seal to such a bond for me. I'd rather dwell in my necessity.' [485]

We need to exercise caution on the terms and conditions that we agree to when negotiating an agreement. For once our word is given to another person, we cannot retract it, without losing some credibility. To make a sworn statement, and then repudiate it, this is most detrimental to our character, conscience, and conduct. It is best

---

484 Shakespeare, William. (1600). *The Merchant of Venice*. Act 1, Scene 3.
485 Shakespeare, William. (1600). *The Merchant of Venice*. Act 1, Scene 3.

not to agree to an oath that we cannot keep, but rather endure the privations that we must. Living within our means ensures that we never become beholden to other people, for a promise, obligation, undertaking, or commitment, that we do not reasonably expect to discharge.

'All things that are, are with more spirit chased than enjoyed.' [486]

It is the very desire of obtaining an object or goal that gives us a superficial sense of satisfaction. However, once we have secured that desired object or goal, the sense of satisfaction and contentment is short-lived. The pursuit of an endeavour entertains exhilaration, a heart-stopping thrill, that only lasts until the pursuit is in action. Such is the reality of human nature. We can rarely, if ever, be content with the material objects or accomplishments within our possession. More significantly, the composition of our soul is of grand importance. Without the Presence of God, the human condition is incomplete.

'But love is blind, and lovers cannot see the pretty follies that themselves commit.' [487]

Love is an emotive and irrational force. Humans struggle to contain the limitless power of passion with the fragile rope of reason. Often lovers go out of their way, beyond their means, or to unprecedented heights or depths, to create a lasting impression, or to affirm their love for another person. In doing so, a person demonstrates much foolishness. Not to mention, we cannot accurately perceive our irrational behaviour, which makes us appear thoughtless and impolitic. The higher faculties of judgement, logic, and reason, not to mention, the incalculable value of personal experience, are

---

486 Shakespeare, William. (1600). *The Merchant of Venice.* Act 2, Scene 6.
487 Shakespeare, William. (1600). *The Merchant of Venice.* Act 2, Scene 6.

lacking in the youth of every generation. The youth are irrationally driven forward by the endless temptations of the flesh.

'All that glitters is not gold.' [488]

This is one of Shakespeare's most often quoted sayings. While it is a truism, it does contain much practical wisdom. There is much in this world, that portrays itself to be considerably more than it actually is, including people, corporations, institutions, associations, partnerships, and non-government organisations. The dismal reality is that the outward appearance of things does not always reconcile to their inner substance, or true worth. Therefore, it is essential that we conduct our due diligence in all things. In order to learn more about that, which we seek to interact or engage with. Never accept an object or person *prima facie* (on first impression).

'I think he only loves the world for him.' [489]

For each person the material world is an external representation of their will. Self love and egocentric behaviour are deep-rooted in each person's psychology. Every person perceives the world from a unique perspective. Each person is at the 'centre' of their world. If we cease to love the world for ourselves, in a conceptual and abstract sense, we cease to exist. For we become selfless in our very existence. We live for the betterment of other people. While this scenario is plausible in theory, it is incredibly difficult to effectuate in practice. That person who has wholly overcome their ego, has lived beyond the limited confines of the superficial Self.

---

488 Shakespeare, William. (1600). *The Merchant of Venice.* Act 2, Scene 7.
489 Shakespeare, William. (1600). *The Merchant of Venice.* Act 2, Scene 8.

'I will not choose what many men desire, because I will not jump with common spirits. And rank me with the barbarous multitudes.' [490]

It requires courage, confidence, and conviction to transcend the unenlightened and ignorant masses of this world. It is only the sheer power and imposing strength of a bold spirit, that dares to go beyond the ordinary, beyond the mundane. For such a rare spirit is only bound by the natural forces of conscience, righteousness, duty, justice, liberty, integrity, and morality. In no way is a rare spirit hindered by the worldly forces of tradition, custom, law, religious obligations, codes of conduct, conventions, or political consensus in society. Rare spirits desire liberty. Common spirits desire leadership.

'To offend and judge are distinct offices and of opposed natures.' [491]

To offend another person requires minimal reflection or quality of thought. Offence can be given, as easily as it can be received. Not to mention, in a modern society where the contemporary culture is increasingly defined by an unending quest for 'political correctness', offence is always near in sight and close at hand. On the contrary, the office of judgement requires critical thought, reason, reflection, and logic. If we are to determine a matter fairly and impartially, then we must carefully consider all the facts presented before us. Therefore, we must look to discern the merit in an argument, before granting it validity.

---

490 Shakespeare, William. (1600). *The Merchant of Venice.* Act 2, Scene 9.
491 Shakespeare, William. (1600). *The Merchant of Venice.* Act 2, Scene 9.

'Let him look to his bond. He was wont to call me usurer. Let him look to his bond. He was wont to lend out money for a Christian courtesy. Let him look to his bond. Why, I am sure, if he forfeit, thou will not take his flesh, What's that good for? To bait fish withal. If it will feed nothing else, it will feed my revenge.' [492]

Shakespeare vividly demonstrates the evil and ego-driven aspects of human nature. In an act of retribution, the victim's ego desires to seek revenge, and commit an evil deed against the perpetrator. Unfortunately, the vicious cycle of revenge never resolves an issue. Revenge only perpetuates the crisis. For both parties seek to right a wrong, with the application of another wrong. In every case and scenario, mercy triumphs revenge. However, this moral principle is incredibly difficult to effectuate in practice.

'I shall never see my gold again.' [493]

This is a sombre reality of life that each and every one of us have to accept. All worldly phenomena that we accumulate in this lifetime on Earth, including gold, silver, bronze, private property, financial capital, real assets, and any other forms of tangible or intangible wealth (i.e., shares, patents, copyright, or trademarks), we will inevitably have to relinquish at some point in the future. We shall renounce our possessions, either by the dire necessity of circumstance, the exigent demands of the present time, or finally, upon the irreversible and forthcoming stroke of death.

'So may the outward shows be least themselves. The world is still deceived with ornament.' [494]

It is the imperfection of human nature to judge by outward appearances. We all have biases and prejudices. However, external

---

492 Shakespeare, William. (1600). *The Merchant of Venice.* Act 3, Scene 1.
493 Shakespeare, William. (1600). *The Merchant of Venice.* Act 3, Scene 1.
494 Shakespeare, William. (1600). *The Merchant of Venice.* Act 3, Scene 2.

appearances never represent a person's character, integrity, conscience, morality, beliefs, principles, ideas, or values. We are all too often deceived by first impressions. We rarely demonstrate the depth required of a thoughtful conversation to appreciate the true substance, insight, and perspective of another person.

'But thou, thou meagre lead, which rather threatenest than dost promise aught. Thy plainness moves me more than eloquence. And here choose I. Joy be the consequence.' [495]

In all cases of unimpeachable honesty and total integrity, concise and pertinent speech that directly addresses the subject matter is almost always more persuasive than the employment of rhetoric and colourful language. In cases where we do employ a multitude of literary techniques in our speech, such as a metaphor, simile, symbolism, allegory, juxtaposition, alliteration, irony, euphemism, hyperbole, oxymoron, paradox, personification, satire, tautology, and motif, we are only deviating from the pressing issues at the centre of the discourse. There is little value in demonstrating much passion at the cost of prose.

'The Duke shall grant me justice. I will have no speaking. I will have my bond.' [496]

The Common Law must provision justice that is tempered with mercy. Even when we are in the right, if we adamantly insist on having our way, we ought to reflect on our grievances with reason, and seek to secure equity, for all the parties in a case. Indeed, rarely is one party wholly in the right, and the other party completely in the wrong. Sometimes, meeting our opposition on middle ground, with leniency, is the best method to forgive and move forward.

---

495 Shakespeare, William. (1600). *The Merchant of Venice.* Act 3, Scene 2.
496 Shakespeare, William. (1600). *The Merchant of Venice.* Act 3, Scene 3.

To plead a matter beyond its intrinsic worth, may lead to more self-destruction, than one stands to gain.

> *'These griefs and losses have so bated me, that I shall hardly spare a pound of flesh tomorrow to my bloody creditor. The pound of flesh, which I demand of him, is dearly bought. It is mine and I will have it. If you deny me, fie upon your law! There is no force in the decrees of Venice. I stand for judgement. Answer! Shall I have it?'* [497]

Humans can become irrational and emotive creatures. To exact revenge for nothing in return, but for the sake of revenge itself is futile. Shakespeare demonstrates the absurdity of human nature. Greed debases the morality and conscience found within humanity. There must be equity in law. Thus, all the circumstances and facts must be factored into consideration, when determining a credible judgement.

In this case, even if the wronged party seeks redress through the city's court of law for a favourable judgement, namely, 'a pound of flesh', this will not address the issue of non-payment of the principal debt. A more plausible and sensible alternative is a deferred payment date, or repayment of debt in instalments over an extended period of time. Beyond the sinister motives of the bond, 'a pound of flesh' is literally useless to the wronged party.

> *'I am a tainted wether of the flock, Meetest for death. The weakest kind of fruit. Drops earliest to the ground, and so let me.'* [498]

When we are wrong and guilty of an offence, we have limited options, but to seek pardon for our offence. However, no person is beyond the capacity of forgiveness. Forgiveness is an important principle that is universal in its application. While it is true, the

---

497 Shakespeare, William. (1600). *The Merchant of Venice.* Act 3, Scene 3.
498 Shakespeare, William. (1600). *The Merchant of Venice.* Act 4, Scene 1.

weakest people shall be the first to fall, this does not necessarily imply, that we shall let them fall. For it is within the capacity and power of the stronger, to assist the weaker. In upholding the principle of natural justice, we create a fairer and more equitable society for every person to realise their inherent potential.

'I stand here for law.' [499]

The Black Letter Law is the foundation stone of a well-established legal system. A well-governing and civilised sovereign nation-state must have a body of law which has codified statutes, rules, legislation, regulations, and case law in the appropriate and authorised law reports. Consistency in the application of the law allows a sovereign nation's citizens to appreciate how a court of law is likely to determine a case, based on previous legal cases with similar facts. Beyond the Doctrine of Precedent and the legal concept of *Stare Decisis* (to stand by things decided), it is also important to adhere to the higher principles of jurisprudence, morality, equality, human dignity, and natural law.

'Then must the Jew be merciful. On what compulsion must I? Tell me that.' [500]

This is a classic paradox. Morally, we must all be merciful to one another. However, there is no compulsion under law, to be merciful to anyone who has done us wrong. From a theological perspective, it is vital, it is absolutely necessary, that we forgive those who commit a wrong against us. So that we shall be forgiven for our sins. In this manner, we forgive others, in order that God may forgive us. No person is perfect, or free from error. Therefore, to demonstrate mercy, where it is not due, is the highest form of goodness that a person can exhibit in this world. Indeed, to demonstrate mercy,

---

499 Shakespeare, William. (1600). *The Merchant of Venice.* Act 4, Scene 1.
500 Shakespeare, William. (1600). *The Merchant of Venice.* Act 4, Scene 1.

is considerably more difficult than an act of charity, service, compassion, prayer, or love.

'The quality of mercy is not strained. It droppeth as the gentle rain from Heaven upon the place beneath. It is twice blest. It blesseth him that gives and him that takes. It is mightiest in the mightiest. But mercy is above this sceptred sway. It is enthroned in the hearts of Kings. It is an attribute to God Himself. And Earthly Power doth then show likest God's, when mercy seasons justice.' [501]

To demonstrate undeserved mercy towards a person that has done us wrong requires courage, confidence, and compassion. Yet mercy is the most constructive solution to an otherwise protracted state of conflict, and an endless state of war, in which both parties constantly seek to right the wrongs they have suffered. Mercy destroys the vicious cycle of sin. Mercy liberates a person from engaging in harmful conduct. Mercy emancipates both the victim and the perpetrator from sin. Mercy brings humanity closer to God.

'If this will not suffice, it must appear. That malice bears down truth. And I beseech you, wrest once the law to your authority. To do a great right, do a little wrong, and curb this cruel Devil of his will. It must not be. There is no power in Venice can alter a decree established. It will be recorded for a precedent, and many an error by the same example will rush into the State. It cannot be.' [502]

We must not allow learned people to employ the law as an instrument to inflict punishment on individuals, solely for the sake of administering pain and suffering to the perpetrator. A reasonable and balanced criminal sentence must be guided by the forces of reason, deterrence, rationality, logic, judgement, justice, and mercy.

---

501 Shakespeare, William. (1600). *The Merchant of Venice.* Act 4, Scene 1.
502 Shakespeare, William. (1600). *The Merchant of Venice.* Act 4, Scene 1.

The advancement of justice is simply one part of the purpose of Common Law in our modern society.

The law must also seek to uphold the State's Constitution, preserve individual liberties, enforce human rights, ensure public law and order in the State, protect every citizen's private property, and create a strong 'deterrent effect' that seeks to prevent citizen's from disobeying the law. An effective legal system operates to ensure that the law is much more than punishment for crimes and offences against the sovereign nation-state and its people.

'It doth appear you are a worthy Judge. You know the law. Your exposition hath been most sound. I charge you by the law, whereof you are a well-deserving pillar, proceed to judgement. By my soul, I swear, there is no power in the tongue of man to alter me. I stay here on my bond.'[503]

When a wronged party appears before the law courts, one has the reasonable expectation that the officers of the court, the sworn judges, the justices, the chief justice, accredited lawyers, learned barristers, and other members of the defendant's and plaintiff's legal counsel understand the 'body of law' pertaining to the dispute before the court's consideration. Having said that, the wronged party (i.e., the plaintiff) which is seeking a remedy (for example, monetary compensation from the defendant), must be prepared to accommodate a judgement that is fair and reasonable, with regard to the material facts of the case.

'Grieve not ... that I am fallen to this for you, for herein Fortune shows herself more kind than is her custom.'[504]

Sometimes it may be for good, other times for evil, however, the Office of Fortune has its way in every person's internal affairs.

---

503 Shakespeare, William. (1600). *The Merchant of Venice*. Act 4, Scene 1.
504 Shakespeare, William. (1600). *The Merchant of Venice*. Act 4, Scene 1.

We may entertain precise plans and cater to endless preparations on how we envisage our life trajectory to proceed. However, no person on Earth can make unconditional representations or guarantees with steadfast and complete certainty.

In any case, we all need to grieve our losses. Grief is a most natural part of life. It is equally important to remember that there is a better life waiting for us, beyond the present hurt, pain, suffering, and grief. Therefore, it is within us to seize the future and move forward. We must transcend what once was our reality, in exchange for what we can become. Yesterday is forever gone. Today is the here and now. Tomorrow is yet to come.

'Repent but you, that you shall lose your friend, and he repents not that he pays your debt. For if the Jew do cut but deep enough, I'll pay it instantly with all my heart.' [505]

We are under a legal obligation to repay our debts as and when they fall due. However, a person in hardship or confronting privation, must be shown mercy due to the dire circumstances that confront them. Inflicting injury or harm upon another person, as retribution for non-payment of a debt is an affront to the conscience of humanity. There are numerous other methods that can be utilised for non-payment of a principal debt. For example, consider forfeiture of real or personal property, the employment of labour, or the performance of community service.

---

505 Shakespeare, William. (1600). *The Merchant of Venice.* Act 4, Scene 1.

'We trifle time! I pray thee, pursue sentence. A pound of that same merchant's flesh is thine. The Court awards it, and the Law doth give it. Most rightful Judge. The Law allows it, and the Court awards it. Most learned Judge.' [506]

The law must be interpreted impartially and objectively with reference to the facts. The function of law is without regard or qualification as to how we may personally feel about a judgement. The citizens of a sovereign nation-state rightly expect the law to have consistency and reliability. Citizens rightly expect that the legislation that is passed through the institution of Federal Parliament, shall possess the 'Force of Law' within the jurisdiction of the sovereign nation-state's territory, in which they are domiciled.

Citizens, not-for-profit organisations, partnerships, associations, financial institutions, government agencies, and for-profit corporations require every 'confidence' in the law. This confidence allows for the execution of countless public and private transactions of a commercial and contractual nature in modern society.

If we do not have a reasonable understanding of what the law is, nor an expectation of how the law is applied or interpreted, the very basis of our modern society will fracture. A society that is disassociated from the function of law will lead to anarchy. No matter the countless imperfections that the law incorporates, civilised society cannot function without the 'Rule of Law'.

'For, as thou urgest justice, be assured thou shalt have justice— more than thou desirest ... Give me my principal, and let me go. I have it ready for thee. Here it is. He hath refused it in the Open Court. He shall have merely justice and his bond.' [507]

We must be careful what we wish for. We must be reasonable in our demands. More importantly, once an offer has been made to

---

506 Shakespeare, William. (1600). *The Merchant of Venice.* Act 4, Scene 1.
507 Shakespeare, William. (1600). *The Merchant of Venice.* Act 4, Scene 1.

us, and then if we reject it, subsequently, we should not entertain unfounded thoughts that we shall ever receive such an identical offer again. A second time offer may not be as lucrative as the first time offer. When a person becomes exceedingly greedy for pecuniary gain, they are more likely than not to lose considerably more, than had they accepted a reasonable sum as compensation, that was initially offered to them.

'That thou shall see the difference of our spirit. I pardon thee thy life before thou ask it; for half thy wealth, it is Antonio's. The other half comes to the General State.' [508]

An individual who demonstrates undeserved mercy and forgiveness towards a person who has committed a wrong has the greater spirit. We all have the inherent power within us to forgive another person, however, this is easier said than done. Forgiveness is an attribute of the courageous person. Forgiveness requires relinquishing the pain and suffering caused by another person, without harbouring the ill-thought of seeking revenge.

'How far that little candle throws his beams! So shines a good deed in a naughty world.' [509]

In a world that is full of evil, greed, profit, gain, self-interest, concupiscence, and corruption, good deeds done with a pure heart always stand out. Good deeds include acts of charity, selflessness, kindness, generosity, benevolence, compassion, community service, mercy, forgiveness, love, prayer, peace, or humanitarian aid. We must all make a determined and conscious effort, to fill the spiritual void of this world, with positive thought, speech, and action.

---

508 Shakespeare, William. (1600). *The Merchant of Venice.* Act 4, Scene 1.
509 Shakespeare, William. (1600). *The Merchant of Venice.* Act 5, Scene 1.

> *'When the Moon shone, we did not see the candle. So doth the greater glory dim the less. A substitute shines brightly as a King. Until a King be by, and then his state empties itself, as doth an inland brook into the main of waters.'*[510]

The character, merit, formal learning, knowledge, reputation, accomplishment, experience, and integrity of an honourable person casts a great shadow. In doing so, the highly accomplished person is almost always likely to transcend the positive attributes and desirable traits of a lesser accomplished person. Such is the dismal reality of this world. The 26th President of the United States, Theodore Roosevelt, famously remarked, 'Comparison is the thief of joy.' Regrettably, the temptation to make comparisons between ourselves and other accomplished people is omnipresent.

Therefore, it is extremely important that we never seek to compare ourselves and our achievements with other people. Comparison shall only lead to disappointment, discontent, and despair. There is always someone who has achieved far more than us. However, we must look to run our race, to the best of our ability. We must concentrate our thoughts and actions, to realise our highest potential. We must seek to become, the best version of ourselves.

---

510 Shakespeare, William. (1600). *The Merchant of Venice*. Act 5, Scene 1.

Chapter 22

THE MERRY WIVES OF WINDSOR

*'Good Mistress Page … for that I love your daughter
in such a righteous fashion as I do, perforce, against all checks,
rebukes, and manners. I must advance the colours of my love
and not retire. Let me have your good will.'*

SHAKESPEARE

The Merry Wives of Windsor is a romantic comedy. This play exhibits the themes of love, marriage, jealousy, private wealth, seduction, deception, and temptation. This play tells the story of a gentleman named Sir John Falstaff, who experiences great financial difficulties. With Falstaff out of luck, he seeks a desperate turnaround in his fortunes. In doing so, Falstaff looks to seduce the wives of two wealthy merchants, in the hope that he may benefit financially.

Falstaff pursues his ill-fated romantic endeavour by sending two identical love letters to Mistress Page and Mistress Ford. The two gentlewomen discover Falstaff's double-dealing. They resolve to proceed along with Falstaff's romantic scheme. However, the two gentlewomen are on a quest to outsmart Falstaff, and teach him a moral lesson that he will never forget. Mistress Page and Mistress

Ford beguile and seduce Falstaff. The two ladies take bittersweet revenge, by innocently misleading Falstaff. As this play progresses, it becomes self-evident that Page and Ford shall have the last laugh at Falstaff's expense.

This play categorically demonstrates the double-standards between the sexes in our modern society. We repeatedly witness how husbands do not trust their wives, nor give them the benefit of the doubt. Indeed, the theme of deception runs deep throughout the entirety of this play. The jealous Lord Frank Ford constantly mistrusts his noble wife, Mistress Ford. Lord Ford attempts to catch his wife in the intimate company of Falstaff, however, Lord Ford is unsuccessful in his countless attempts.

In vain, Falstaff continues his irrational pursuit of Mistress Ford. Mistress Ford most seductively lures Falstaff with unmatched persuasion and lovely charm. As a consequence, Falstaff finds himself subjected to all kinds of hilarious and entertaining acts, including being hidden in a laundry basket with dirty clothes, and being thrown out of the laundry basket into a muddy river bank. Not to mention, on one most unfortunate occasion, Falstaff hurriedly dresses and disguises himself as an elderly aunt to conceal his true identity. Now by sheer coincidence, Lord Ford hates the elderly aunt whom Falstaff is impersonating. Unfortunately, Falstaff is violently battered out of the Ford's family home.

In one final act of public embarrassment, Mistress Ford invites Falstaff to meet her at night time in Windsor Park. Interestingly, Mistress Ford convinces Falstaff to disguise himself as Herne the Hunter. Belatedly, Falstaff recognises that he has been deceived by Mistress Ford. Falstaff is caught in a comical act, with the butt of the joke being on him. Falstaff handles this hilarious event with much grace and remorse. Falstaff accepts his actions to pursue Mistress Ford were immoral and wrong. In the end, Falstaff makes his peace with Mistress Page and Mistress Ford, and their husbands. In addition, Lord Frank Ford is also reprimanded for mistrusting his impeccable and honest wife.

'Take heed, have open eye, for thieves do foot by night.'[511]

We must keep a watchful eye and remain vigilant when it comes to guarding our personal property, treasured possessions, and real property. It is a cliché, that thieves are more likely to engage in criminal activities under the cover of night, to provide them with a false sense of safety and security from being identified. For severe crimes also happen in broad daylight. Not to mention, with the latest advances and breakthroughs in information and communications technology, theft and fraud is becoming more sophisticated and elusive. The internet, mobile applications, personal computers, online banking, e-mail, and social media platforms are being utilised as instruments to commit identity theft and financial fraud.

'If he should intend this voyage towards my wife, I would turn her loose to him. And what he gets more of her than sharp words, let it lie on my head.'[512]

Herein the husband is entertaining the thought of punishing the individual who intends to court his wife, by allowing the offence to proceed. Infidelity is an issue of great concern in our modern society. We must always strive to be faithful to our spouse. We have a moral, social, and legal duty to be faithful to whom we have given our vows in marriage. Unfortunately, the nature of social relations between individuals is fast-changing in the contemporary world. Not to mention, there are several different types of relationships, beyond the traditional institution of marriage, that we can now enter. For example, consider *de facto* relationships, interracial relationships, long-distance relationships, polygamy relationships, casual relationships, same-sex relationships, and online relationships. The complexity and variation of relationships

---

511 Shakespeare, William. (1602). *The Merry Wives of Windsor.* Act 2, Scene 1.
512 Shakespeare, William. (1602). *The Merry Wives of Windsor.* Act 2, Scene 1.

in contemporary society, is testing the established principles, of everlasting commitment and personal responsibility.

'I will not lend thee a penny. Why, then the World's mine oyster. Which I with sword will open. I will retort the sum in a quippage. Not a penny! I have been content. Sir, you should lay my countenance to pawn.' [513]

Some people are wholly guided by legal principles, tradition, custom, faith, and moral values. To not lend financial capital is a free moral choice, much like an individual's decision to get married, have children, purchase real property, obtain a tertiary education, become a valued member of a distinguished profession or vocation, or adhere to a religion.

Most importantly, it does not matter what other people think about our moral choices. However, we must be content with our free moral choices. We must be content in such a manner, that we shall harbour no personal regrets for the decisions that we freely determine in life. Always remember, with the exercise of power comes personal responsibility. The employment of agency requires discretion.

'For it is not good that children should know any wickedness.' [514]

Children are astute observers of their surrounding environment. Children reflect upon the behaviour of people they witness in society. Children learn behaviours, ideas, thoughts, and actions from adults, both the good and evil. Thus, adults must be careful and conscious of the behaviour they exhibit around children. For exposure to wickedness will be of great consequence and most detrimental to a child's long-term development.

---

513 Shakespeare, William. (1602). *The Merry Wives of Windsor.* Act 2, Scene 2.
514 Shakespeare, William. (1602). *The Merry Wives of Windsor.* Act 2, Scene 2.

'Old folk, you know, have discretion, as they say, and know the World.'[515]

As we advance in age, the greater is our exposure to knowledge, education, formal learning, personal experiences, medical conditions, prejudice, debilitating diseases, inequality, economic crises, discrimination, world wars, humanitarian crises, financial crises, civil wars, and other life-changing events.

In our older years, we become better acquainted with the ways of this world. We are more conscious of the forces of self-interest, profit, pecuniary gain, and private property, which guide human behaviour. Indeed, much of the modern individual is guided by the endless desire for power, fame, private property, influence, prestige, territory, concupiscence, profit, luxury goods, personal wealth, financial capital, prohibited substances, and pharmaceutical drugs.

'For they do say, if money go before, all ways do lie open. Money is a good soldier, Sir, and will on. Troth, and I have a bag of money here that troubles me. If you will help to beat it, Sir John, take all, or half, for easing me of the carriage.'[516]

Financial capital is an economic instrument that is most necessary for individuals to further their pursuits in the Modern World. Regardless money be utilised to provide quality child care, a good school education, a first-rate university education, the pursuit of sporting endeavours, wedding celebrations, first home ownership, purchase a luxury motor vehicle, access medical care, purchase academic books, purchase prescription medicine, acquire a yacht, purchase a high-rise apartment, rent a helicopter, obtain legal advice, or travel the world. In all these cases, and many more, the necessity of money in the civilised world, is beyond question.

---

515 Shakespeare, William. (1602). *The Merry Wives of Windsor.* Act 2, Scene 2.
516 Shakespeare, William. (1602). *The Merry Wives of Windsor.* Act 2, Scene 2.

On the other hand, financial capital brings a myriad of issues and problems to the surface. For example, consider the cost of debt, repayment of principal, excessive interest charges, long-term mortgages, personal loans, car loans, credit card balances, and overdrafts. A person's world that is riddled with excessive debt, makes for a troubled mind and restless sleep.

'I shall discover a thing to you, wherein I must very much lay open mine own imperfections. But, Good Sir John, as you have one eye upon my follies, as you hear them unfolded, turn another into the register of your own, that I may pass with a reproof the easier. Sith you yourself know how easy it is to be such an offender.' [517]

We all have our faults and imperfections. Rather than examining the shortcomings of other people, we ought to strive to make ourselves better. We must seek to become the best version of ourselves. It is true wisdom for a person to know their strengths and limitations. A successful person works effectively within the parameters of their nature, personality, emotions, cognition, values, beliefs, and ideas, to create their external reality in this material world. The length of life is too short to focus on changing other people. Therefore, we must utilise our finite years wisely.

'Love like a shadow flies when substance love pursues. Pursuing that that flies, and flying what pursues.' [518]

Love is an elusive phenomenon. We all have a desire to pursue love. However, it is often difficult to secure that ideal love which brings the heart to total fulfilment. The highest love of God is often portrayed as an abstract and conceptual matter. A matter that is deeply enmeshed within complex and profound theological doctrines. However, God's Love is always near at hand.

---

517 Shakespeare, William. (1602). *The Merry Wives of Windsor.* Act 2, Scene 2.
518 Shakespeare, William. (1602). *The Merry Wives of Windsor.* Act 2, Scene 2.

On the other hand, love between a gentleman and gentlewoman is most uncertain. The expression and exchange of love between humans is kindled only to be dashed, full of hope and despair, brimming with happiness, and sometimes, filled with envy. Human love is also the inexact navigation of high expectations and low disappointments.

'I pray you, use your patience.' [519]

Patience is a virtue. Patience is also incredibly difficult to grasp and demonstrate during times of distress, despondency, and despair. We can all benefit from being more patient with ourselves and other people, however, this is easier said than done. Therefore, we must cultivate patience. Patience is developed with the passage of time, with a lifetime of adversity, personal experiences, tragedy, crises, privations, issues, difficulties, learning, knowledge, wisdom, and challenges. Patience develops within us, the capacity to better endure, what we must in this world.

'No, he shall not knit a knot in his fortunes with the finger of my substance. If he takes her, let him take her simply. The wealth I have waits on my consent, and my consent goes not that way.' [520]

As we proceed through our journey of life, we shall realise that there will be some people who are supportive of us, and some people who are against us. This is an indisputable fact of life. A black-and-white reality that we must come to accept. Nonetheless, we cannot afford to place our faith and trust in other people, in order for us to accomplish our grand endeavours, personal goals, and God-given destiny. We must create and utilise our agency, resources, abilities, endowments, talents, knowledge, learning, experience, and skill to create our desired reality.

---

519 Shakespeare, William. (1602). *The Merry Wives of Windsor.* Act 3, Scene 1.
520 Shakespeare, William. (1602). *The Merry Wives of Windsor.* Act 3, Scene 2.

'Why, now let me die, for I have lived long enough. This is the period of my ambition. O this blessed hour!' [521]

The human condition is complex, irrational, and dynamic. Often, we can become disillusioned with reality, and ambivalent in our thoughts. To keep an even mind through heartache, pain, suffering, loss, privation, and grief, this is one of the hardest things to do. We must have the courage, confidence, and conviction, that we will overcome the heartache. We will transcend the tallest mountains. We will secure total victory in our endeavours!

'Now, be not amazed. Call all your senses to you. Defend your reputation, or bid farewell to your good life for ever.' [522]

Honour, morality, reputation, conscience, character, integrity, steadfastness, righteousness, and trustworthiness. These are the most noble ideals and virtues, that have the potential to positively define our life and legacy. We must always be prepared to defend these golden virtues with our life. For a life without moral excellence is not the same. We must not let the difficulties of the time, nor the overwhelming force of circumstance, define, nor dictate, our free moral actions. Our highest purpose on Earth is to realise our God-given destiny.

'Good Mistress Page ... for that I love your daughter in such a righteous fashion as I do, perforce, against all checks, rebukes, and manners. I must advance the colours of my love and not retire. Let me have your good will.' [523]

Love knows no bounds. We are all prepared to go the additional step to court the love of our life. The employment of beautiful and lovely words is nothing more than symbolism. It is the actions

---

521 Shakespeare, William. (1602). *The Merry Wives of Windsor.* Act 3, Scene 3.
522 Shakespeare, William. (1602). *The Merry Wives of Windsor.* Act 3, Scene 3.
523 Shakespeare, William. (1602). *The Merry Wives of Windsor.* Act 3, Scene 4.

that we undertake which truly demonstrate our commitment, dedication, loyalty, and passion for another person. Love at first sight is special in its own right. However, beyond fancy first impressions, only the passage of time and the endless confrontation with tribulations, will determine if love is more than surface level chemistry. After all, a spark can ignite a fire, however, the spark cannot sustain the fire.

'Be not as extreme in submission as in offence.' [524]

We must never let another person take advantage of our vulnerabilities or distressing circumstances. We shall always be vigilant in the information that we share with other people. Our personal information can be used against us, against our best interests. In times of submission, we ought to utilise our cognition and agency, to preserve our dignity, honour, and self-respect. For every person has God-given human dignity that makes them important, regardless of one's accomplishments, social status, wealth, education, gender, sex, marital status, colour, private property, income, religion, country of origin, disability, ethnicity, or any other discriminatory factor. By the universal virtue of humanity, we are all equal.

'Well, if I had wind enough to say my prayers, I would repent.' [525]

It is always best to offer our sincere prayers to God in the present moment. To seek forgiveness. Also, to perform penance today. For no person knows the future. Therefore, no person knows how long they have remaining in this lifetime. We must not sow the seeds for despair, regret, and sadness in our life. Delay never resolves anything. Delay only defers the resolution of significant problems in our life.

---

524 Shakespeare, William. (1602). *The Merry Wives of Windsor.* Act 4, Scene 4.
525 Shakespeare, William. (1602). *The Merry Wives of Windsor.* Act 4, Scene 5.

'Master Fenton, talk not to me. My mind is heavy. I have had a great loss. I will give over all.' [526]

During times of grief, we may prefer solitude over good company. This is entirely reasonable. No person can truly understand how we feel. However, isolation never resolves the serious life issues that we confront. Isolation rarely improves our well-being. It is essential that we have the right conversation, with the right person, at the right time. This approach shall provide us with an opportunity to express our thoughts, feelings, sensations, and emotions, and navigate them more successfully. Most importantly, there is a season for everything. This includes an opportune season to grieve, and a season to move forward. Always remember, no lifetime has an infinite number of years within it.

'In love, the Heavens themselves do guide the State. Money buys lands, but wives are sold by fate.' [527]

This is an archaic expression. One that is most reflective of the time in which Shakespeare wrote it. Money still purchases private property in the twenty-first century. However, gentlewomen have the inherent freedom, dignity, and legal right to determine whom to marry. Regrettably, still in some countries today, gentlewomen are subject to forced marriage.

It is important to acknowledge that not all marriages are based on 'love at first sight'. There may be a consensual 'marriage of convenience', or marriages may be based on religious tradition, cultural practices, family, custom, friendships, corporate associations, business arrangements, or the joining of private wealth and property between family groups. Some differences in expectations and arrangements pertaining to marriage shall be

---

526 Shakespeare, William. (1602). *The Merry Wives of Windsor.* Act 4, Scene 6.
527 Shakespeare, William. (1602). *The Merry Wives of Windsor.* Act 5, Scene 5.

tolerated and permitted, due to distinct cultural, ethnic, racial, legal, and religious practices. However, no gentlewoman shall be married to another gentleman against her will, period.

'What cannot be eschewed must be embraced.' [528]

This is a platitude that we all have to learn to accept. Destiny and fate may lead us, where we do not want to proceed. However, come what may on our journey of life, it is necessary that we wholly and truly embrace it. We must have total confidence that God has given us the grace to navigate the Path that is before us. For our part, we must demonstrate the courage to fulfil our mission on Earth. When all is said and done, we shall be able to say, the sacred words within the *Holy Bible*, in the *Second Book of Timothy*, Chapter 4, Verse 7, 'I have fought the Good Fight. I have finished the Race. I have kept the Faith.'

---

528 Shakespeare, William. (1602). *The Merry Wives of Windsor.* Act 5, Scene 5.

Chapter 23

A MIDSUMMER NIGHT'S DREAM

'I mean that my heart unto yours is knit, so that one heart we can make of it. Two bosoms interchained with an oath, so then two bosoms and a single troth. Then by your side no bed-room me deny; For lying so, Hermia, I do not lie.'

SHAKESPEARE

A Midsummer Night's Dream is a story of romance, jealousy, true love, and marriage. This play narrates the story of Egeus, an honourable gentleman in the Court of Athens, bringing his defiant daughter Hermia before the Duke of Athens, Theseus. Egeus is insistent that Hermia marry Demetrius. However, Hermia abruptly refuses the marriage proposal. Hermia is deeply in love with Lysander, although her endless pleas and reasoning to her father falls on deaf ears. The Duke orders Hermia to obey the will of her father. Alternatively, Hermia is to be put to death, or she may determine to enter into a convent life.

Hermia is not content with any of the three options before her, i.e., marriage proposal to Demetrius, the death penalty, or a convent life. Thus, Hermia determines to escape with her lover,

Lysander. Together, the two lovers disappear into the depths of the forest in the cover of night. Hermia has informed her close friend, Helena, who is secretly in love with Demetrius, of her plans to escape with Lysander. As a result, Helena and Demetrius also follow suit. Now these four lovers proceed on an adventure in the open wilderness of the forest.

This play demonstrates Helena's endless pursuit of Demetrius, to win his love and affection. The plot is intertwined with beautiful fairies, magic spells, and enchanted potions, to confuse the lovers. This environment creates a sense of chaos and disorder amongst the characters. Towards the end of this play, Helena's determination and resolve witnesses Demetrius confess his profound love for her. The closing of this play is marked by marriage on the basis of true love. With Lysander wedding Hermia, and Demetrius wedding Helena.

'I would my Father looked but with my eyes. Your eyes must with his judgement look.' [529]

Shakespeare very eloquently captures the necessity of tradition and custom. For a gentlewoman seeks that love be understood from her perspective, from the point of view of whom her heart truly desires to seek union with. Yet, in the *Early Modern Period*, the subordinate position of gentlewomen, kept them confined to the traditional capacity of housewife, mother, daughter, sister, nun, or abbess.

However, the dire necessity of this period in history meant that a gentlewoman must obey her father's wishes and desires in the grand question of marriage. Regrettably, during the *Early Modern Period*, the gentlewoman was expected to subordinate herself to the gentleman in the household. Furthermore, once upon a time, gender roles and sexism explicitly defined the higher purpose of gentlewomen in society. For the most part of the History of

---

529 Shakespeare, William. (1600). *A Midsummer Night's Dream.* Act 1, Scene 1.

Medieval England (1066–1485), a gentlewoman's purpose was restricted to sexual reproduction, raising of children, and the performance of household duties.

'Ay me! For aught that I could ever read, could ever hear by tale or history. The course of true love never did run smooth.' [530]

True love is full of heightened emotions, endless passions, speechless sensations, and phenomenal feelings. In reality, true love is anything, but smooth. True love is comparable to navigating a rudderless steamship on the high seas, with fierce winds, amongst the backdrop of heavy rain, and the echo of endless thunderstorms. However, true love endures with great hope. Indeed, one day, the Sun will shine bright. Also, the rough sea waves will calm down. Rarely is true love as picturesque as it seems on the surface.

'O Hell! To choose love by another's eyes.' [531]

Every person has the desire and the right to love and to be loved. The exercise of free choice is a must in the most profound matters of the heart. We cannot consign ourselves to a fate, where love is involuntarily forced upon us. Love must always be advanced by mutual consent between two parties. To experience love is the most beautiful and complete expression of humanity. The presence of love makes the human condition bearable. Not to mention, love also advances the desirable conditions for peace, mercy, social justice, forgiveness, equality, and the high hope of Heaven on Earth.

---

530 Shakespeare, William. (1600). *A Midsummer Night's Dream*. Act 1, Scene 1.
531 Shakespeare, William. (1600). *A Midsummer Night's Dream*. Act 1, Scene 1.

> *'If then true lovers have been ever crossed, it stands as an edict in destiny. Then let us teach our trial patience, because it is a customary cross, as due to love as thoughts and dreams and sighs, wishes and tears, poor fancy's followers.'* [532]

True love is rare. Love is often fraught with challenges and difficulties. Unfortunately, love is not always smooth sailing. Nor is love wholly representative of the idiomatic expression—'happily ever after'. More importantly, we must look to support our spouse through the ebbs and flows of marriage, navigate the highs and lows, and work through the satisfying and disappointing times in life.

> *'His folly, Helena, is no fault of mine. None, but your beauty, O would that fault were mine.'* [533]

The beauty of this world is deceptive and illusive. Often beauty is the guiding force of love at first sight. We must not endlessly strive in vain to be made in another person's image. Instead, we must accept ourselves, for who we are. Comparison destroys the basis for contentment. We are all made in God's Image. Therefore, we are all made perfect in the Image of God. We shall not wish to have another person's personality, character, gender, sex, genetics, genotypes, or phenotypes. We must learn to truly embrace ourselves. Therein resides the secret to our confidence, accomplishments, and success.

> *'Things base and vile, holding no quantity, love can transpose to form and dignity.'* [534]

Love has a truly transformative power. Love can change our perception towards another person, animate object, or inanimate object. While love can be subjective, as in the sense that, 'Beauty is

---

532 Shakespeare, William. (1600). *A Midsummer Night's Dream*. Act 1, Scene 1.
533 Shakespeare, William. (1600). *A Midsummer Night's Dream*. Act 1, Scene 1.
534 Shakespeare, William. (1600). *A Midsummer Night's Dream*. Act 1, Scene 1.

in the eye of the beholder', love is also universal. For love transcends all boundaries, both real and superficial, such as race, gender, sex, colour, ethnicity, faith, religion, age, profession, education, wealth, private property, disability, income, social status, culture, language, and heritage.

> *'For that it is not night when I do see your face. Therefore, I think I am not in the night. Nor doth this wood lack worlds of company. For you, in my respect, are all the world. Then how can it be said I am alone, when all the world is here to look on me?'* [535]

When we find true love in one person, our world is complete. The bond of love transcends all the ills of the Modern World. Love makes life worth living. Love is the sustainer of hope, faith, and family. Meaning and purpose in this world is derived from the presence of love. We can be in the association of several hundred people, and still feel the presence of loneliness. On the other hand, we can be in the vicinity of the one person, whom we truly admire and love, and feel content. Love is not about quantity. Love is about quality. Love overcomes the depths of despair and despondency.

> *'Your wrongs do set a scandal on my sex. We cannot fight for love as men may do; we were not made to woo. I'll run from thee. And leave thee to the mercy of wild beasts! I'll follow thee, and make a Heaven of Hell. To die upon the hand, I love so well.'* [536]

Shakespeare illustrates the distinctions between the male and female sex. Distinctions in gender roles that were all too apparent, fixed, and rigid in the *Early Modern Period*. Society's historical expectations, in conjunction with the customs and traditions of the time, meant that a gentleman almost always courted a gentlewoman. Therefore, the gentlewoman had to wait upon the bold advances of her 'Knight

---

535 Shakespeare, William. (1600). *A Midsummer Night's Dream*. Act 2, Scene 1.
536 Shakespeare, William. (1600). *A Midsummer Night's Dream*. Act 2, Scene 1.

in shining armour'. In the contemporary world, the social trends between the sexes are rapidly changing. In addition, we witness variations in relationships, beyond the traditional institution of marriage.

> *'I mean that my heart unto yours is knit, so that one heart we can make of it. Two bosoms interchained with an oath, so then two bosoms and a single troth. Then by your side no bed-room me deny; For lying so, Hermia, I do not lie.'* [537]

When two lovers unite in marriage, their heart and soul become one. Marriage is a divine union in the Image of God. Marriage allows for each spouse to enjoy their lover's exclusive company, time, and association. Marriage is the foundation upon which the husband and wife build their lives, raise children, embrace the family life, and live a good and whole life in the midst of society and state.

> *'But, gentle friend, for love and courtesy lie further off, in human modesty.'* [538]

Modesty is an admirable and virtuous quality. To be modest in one's esteem, opinion, or estimation of oneself is to have one's ego under restraint and in check. A quiet confidence in one's abilities, coupled with determination, resolve, love for God, patience, prayer, and petition to God, and a strong work ethic, are all the requisite elements that a person requires to succeed in life. The greater the modesty a person has within themselves, the greater such a person is able to love and demonstrate courtesy towards other people.

---

537 Shakespeare, William. (1600). *A Midsummer Night's Dream*. Act 2, Scene 2.
538 Shakespeare, William. (1600). *A Midsummer Night's Dream*. Act 2, Scene 2.

'The will of man is by his reason swayed, and reason says you are the worthier maid.' [539]

While there is a place for emotion, passion, sensation, and feeling in matters of true love, the heart alone must not guide a person's determination to seek a spouse. The exercise of reason must establish mutual compatibility, and also consider important factors, such as the expectation of the lovers, communication styles, personal goals and life endeavours, profession or vocation, lifestyle choices, desire to have children, faith, beliefs, values, and personality type. In the final analysis, measured reasoning through the fire of passion, is more likely than not to determine if the likelihood of a long-term relationship is genuinely viable. The compatibility and suitability of lovers is both art and science.

'Things growing are not ripe until their season. So, I, being young, till now ripe not to reason; and touching now the point of human skill, reason becomes the marshal to my will, and leads me to your eyes.' [540]

There is a season for all things in life. We must wait for the opportune time, to reap a harvest for what we have sowed. All things take place according to God's Timing, and God's Plan for our life. The formal learning and knowledge of this world requires considerable time and effort to accomplish. The longer we have lived life, and the more personal experiences that we have encountered, collectively serve to aid our reasoning, thought, judgement, and logic. To master a skill, profession, or vocation requires a lifetime of learning, dedication, commitment, and practice.

---

539 Shakespeare, William. (1600). *A Midsummer Night's Dream*. Act 2, Scene 2.
540 Shakespeare, William. (1600). *A Midsummer Night's Dream*. Act 2, Scene 2.

*'O weary night, O long and tedious night, Abate thy hours! …
And sleep, that sometimes shuts up sorrow's eye. Steal me awhile
from my own company.'* [541]

This is a broken world. This is a world that is full of trouble, tragedy, turmoil, trial, and tribulation. Sleep brings temporary relief to our worries and sorrows; however, it is not the durable solution. Sleep provides the respite and rest that we require to recuperate and re-energise our mind, spirit, and body. Thus, we shall be better prepared to address and resolve life's many challenges. To transcend the myriad of issues that we confront on our life journey.

*'The best are but shadows, and the worst are no worst if
imagination amend them.'* [542]

The best of this world is often not as grand and imposing as it is made out to appear. On the contrary, the worst-case scenario is usually a fabrication of our thoughts, that more often than not, tend to exaggerate worldly reality and play on our fears, anxiety, doubt, and worries. In all things, we must place our complete confidence and total trust in God. For God's goodness, mercy, favour, and grace are perfect.

'In courtesy, in all reason, we must stay the time.' [543]

Depending on the event, issue, circumstance, or experience, that we confront, enduring the necessity of time can be extremely difficult. We must be patient in all things, and allow God's Grace to work and yield positive results in our lives. Employing the instrument of reason over emotion is not always an effortless endeavour. However, earnest prayer and petition to God shall always assist our cause.

---

541 Shakespeare, William. (1600). *A Midsummer Night's Dream*. Act 3, Scene 2.
542 Shakespeare, William. (1600). *A Midsummer Night's Dream*. Act 5, Scene 1.
543 Shakespeare, William. (1600). *A Midsummer Night's Dream*. Act 5, Scene 1.

Chapter 24

MUCH ADO ABOUT NOTHING

'Friendship is constant in all other things. Save in the office and affairs of love. Therefore, all hearts in love use their own tongues. Let every eye negotiate for itself and trust no agent. For beauty is a witch against whose charms faith melteth into blood.'

SHAKESPEARE

Much Ado About Nothing is a comedy centred around the themes of courtship, love, marriage, romance, and friendship. Shakespeare narrates the interesting plot of two separate love stories. First, we witness, Hero and Claudio fall in love with each other, only to be subject to the evil intentions and sinister motives of Don John who is intent on destroying their relationship. Second, Sir Benedick, a courageous soldier, and Lady Beatrice, the niece of Messina's Governor (Leonato), have an open hostility against one another. Benedick has resolved on remaining a bachelor for life. Not to mention, Beatrice has vowed never to marry a gentleman. However, Duke Don Pedro schemes to play Cupid. Don Pedro brings Benedick and Beatrice into an irresistible longing for each other.

In Don Pedro's high endeavours to bring Benedick and Beatrice into the orbit of love, he is aided by Claudio and Hero. For Claudio and Hero engage in a series of intimate conversations within earshot of Benedick and Beatrice, to unassumingly convince them that the two individuals are truly and deeply in love with each other. Benedick and Beatrice take the bait. Slowly, but surely, they express attention, affection, and admiration for one another.

Regrettably, Claudio falls for Don John's evil plot to frame Hero before their wedding day. On the day of Claudio and Hero's wedding, Claudio accuses Hero of infidelity. Hero is taken aback by this most false claim against her integrity, chastity, and character. Claudio renounces his bride before the High Priest, and he rescinds the proposal to marry Hero. The High Priest is not convinced that Hero has been unfaithful to Claudio. Thus, with the assistance of the High Priest, Beatrice, Leonato, and Benedick, Hero is portrayed as dead. Until the opportune time has arrived, to clear Hero's name of the false charges levied against her.

As the play progresses, Don John's treachery is discovered. The truth is now out in the open. Claudio sincerely repents for his mistaken impression of Hero. In Hero's place, Claudio accepts the proposal to marry Leonato's niece. This play concludes with Hero returning to the scene, and having proved her innocence, she is reunited with her beloved Claudio. Thereafter, Claudio and Hero are married, along with the marriage of Sir Benedick and Lady Beatrice.

'A victory is twice itself when the achiever brings home full numbers.' [544]

There is a difference between a close victory and a total victory. The former is a win by a small margin, in which the final outcome could have ventured either way. Whereas, the latter is a definitive win.

---

544 Shakespeare, William. (1600). *Much Ado About Nothing.* Act 1, Scene 1.

A total victory provides no opportunity for the opposing belligerent to have won, regardless of the battlefield tactics, the uncertainty of the weather, the disruption to supply lines, the quantity of conventional weapons, or the battlefield casualties.

> *'He hath borne himself beyond the promise of his age. Doing in the figure of a lamb the feats of a lion.'* [545]

Age is no barrier to a person's success or accomplishment. As long as an individual displays resilience, drive, determination, ambition, perseverance, ingenuity, righteousness, steadfastness, and aptitude in a chosen field, area of study, or sport, then such a person can strive to achieve greatness in that specific endeavour they wholly and truly commit to. The key to our success, is a single-minded determination to achieve our desired endeavour. Thus, there is no place for doubt, fear, hesitation, confusion, anxiety, or uncertainty in the pursuit of our objective.

> *'He wears his faith but as the fashion of his hat; it ever changes with the next block.'* [546]

Shakespeare showcases how human nature is self-centred, egocentric, and full of self-love. Humans are rarely committed to their faith with a selfless desire to please God and advance God's Kingdom on Earth. The reality is that where there is more of faith, there is less of ego. Unfortunately, selflessness is against the very disposition of human nature. For the flesh seeks out the corruptness of sin. While each person has the right to freely determine their faith, values, thoughts, ideas, and beliefs, it is essential that a person live to their creed.

---

545 Shakespeare, William. (1600). *Much Ado About Nothing.* Act 1, Scene 1.
546 Shakespeare, William. (1600). *Much Ado About Nothing.* Act 1, Scene 1.

> *'Can the World buy such a jewel? In mine eye she is the sweetest Lady that ever I looked on. Well, I can see yet without spectacles and I see no such matter.'* [547]

Beauty is always in the eye of the beholder. What one person considers lovely and beautiful, another person may find of no such merit or value. Beauty is subjectively measured. For each person considers for themselves, what is aesthetically pleasing to the senses. In the final analysis, every gentlewoman is beautiful in her own right and capacity. A gentlewoman must never look upon another gentlewoman for comparison or validation. Each and every gentlewoman must find her sense of self-worth within her and from God's Love.

> *'But all women shall pardon me. Because I will not do them the wrong to mistrust any. I will do myself the right to trust none. And the fine is, for the which I may go the finer, I will live a bachelor.'* [548]

The highs and lows of married life are not for every person. In the Modern World, individuals are increasingly deferring marriage and having children much later in life. Not to mention, divorce rates are on the rise across much of the Developed First World. In the early twenty-first century, we are witnessing an unprecedented economic, legal, political, and cultural transformation in social relations amongst the human population. Having said that, harmony and balance resides in gentlemen and gentlewomen co-existing alongside one another. The traditional idea of marriage may not be every person's default preference, however, there are alternative options (for example, consider *de facto* relationships).

---

547 Shakespeare, William. (1600). *Much Ado About Nothing.* Act 1, Scene 1.
548 Shakespeare, William. (1600). *Much Ado About Nothing.* Act 1, Scene 1.

'Why are you thus out of measure sad? There is no measure in the occasion that breeds. Therefore, the sadness is without limit. You should here reason.' [549]

Humans are an emotive, irrational, and unpredictable species. While we are capable of demonstrating reason, thought, judgement, and logic, humans are also subject to passions, desires, sensations, emotions, and feelings. In order to live the Good Life, we must strive to strike a balance between the two extremes of emotion and reason. This is easier said than done. Not to mention, the necessity of time and the force of circumstance can weigh heavily upon the heart. Yet, in all things, we must always keep the Faith.

'I cannot hide what I am. I must be sad. When I have cause and smile at no man's jests. Eat when I have stomach and wait for no man's leisure. Sleep when I am drowsy and tend on no man's business. Laugh when I am merry and claw no man in his humour.' [550]

Fundamentally, we are who we are. We are the essence of our being. Every person is unique in that they are a representation and summation of their chemistry, genetics, perspective, parentage, cognition, formal learning, knowledge, emotions, feelings, and personal experiences. Not to mention, we are all subject to the physiological forces of the human body, the biological realities of human mortality, and the psychological forces that make lasting impressions on the human brain. In the final analysis, we must unconditionally embrace who we are.

---

549 Shakespeare, William. (1600). *Much Ado About Nothing*. Act 1, Scene 3.
550 Shakespeare, William. (1600). *Much Ado About Nothing*. Act 1, Scene 3.

> *'If I had my liberty, I would do my liking. In the meantime, let me be that I am and seek not to alter me.'* [551]

In the Modern World, our ancient liberty is constrained by the function and institution of law. The law governs what human conduct is lawful, and opposingly, what conduct is considered unlawful. Beyond the domain of law, morality, religion, faith, and our conscience also function to determine the parameters of permissible human behaviour in civilised society. We all wish to fully express who we are in this world, whether that be through our vocation, profession, ministry, life experience, knowledge, education, formal learning, sporting prowess, ingenuity, or natural talent.

> *'Friendship is constant in all other things. Save in the office and affairs of love. Therefore, all hearts in love use their own tongues. Let every eye negotiate for itself and trust no agent. For beauty is a witch against whose charms faith melteth into blood.'* [552]

Where matters of self-interest are strongest, that is to say, love, private property, money, influence, and power, we can rarely place our trust in another person, to further our best interest. Therefore, we must utilise our own intuition, judgement, logic, agency, and reason to navigate the best course forward for our life. It is best counsel not to entrust other people with critical decisions about our life trajectory. Shakespeare cautions us not to capitulate to the seduction of beauty. For the charm of beauty is powerful. Beauty has the capacity to inhibit the proper function of reason.

---

551 Shakespeare, William. (1600). *Much Ado About Nothing.* Act 1, Scene 3.
552 Shakespeare, William. (1600). *Much Ado About Nothing.* Act 2, Scene 1.

'By my troth, My Lord, I cannot tell what to think of it, but that she loves him with an enraged affection. It is past the infinite of thought.' [553]

Love knows no bounds. The power of passion triumphs recourse to reason. Love can make a person irrational and vulnerable in their thoughts and actions. Not to mention, one may proceed to extreme lengths to court the individual whom they truly and deeply love. Like all things in life, passion must be tempered and restrained. Otherwise, the expression of emotions, feelings, and sensations can become overpowering and chaotic.

'But doth not the appetite alter? A man loves the meat in his youth that he cannot endure in his age.' [554]

The reality of early adult life is that both the inexperienced and unlearned gentleman and gentlewoman are guided by the forces of lust and desire for the opposite sex. In early adulthood, both sexes are driven forward by carnal feelings and sensual desires. However, this type of passionate love is fleeting, short-lived, and superficial. For erotic and passionate love only expresses the physical dimension of love. There is no profound spiritual, emotional, and psychological connection between the lovers.

Outward beauty is most captivating to the inexperienced eyes of the youth. However, beauty alone fails to illustrate the wholeness of a person, who they truly are. Love found solely on the basis of sexual attraction, shall struggle to endure against the test of time. The tell-tale tragedy of travesty awaits young lovers.

---

553 Shakespeare, William. (1600). *Much Ado About Nothing.* Act 2, Scene 3.
554 Shakespeare, William. (1600). *Much Ado About Nothing.* Act 2, Scene 3.

*'When I said I would die a bachelor, I did not think I should live
till I were married.'* [555]

People change over the course of time. Throughout the course of our life, we are exposed to new ideas, experiences, doctrines, knowledge, and ideologies. In addition, we may learn more about a particular faith or religion, explore career changes, embark on new relationships, reorient our belief and value system, or change our place of domicile. Not to mention, with advances in our age, our life priorities and expectations also require adjustment and re-adjustment. What we once thought was 'set' and 'fixed' is not entirely the case. Indeed, much of human life and thought is malleable.

'Well, every one can master a grief, but he that has it.' [556]

This is an expression that will remain true for all time. We can all give advice to a person that is experiencing grief; however, we are not in their position. It is incredibly difficult to process grief. Thus, every person needs their time and space to navigate the unfolding emotions, feelings, and sensations. To come to a place of peace, with the way things are in this world. Acceptance does not mean defeat. Acceptance means 'letting go' of the things that are beyond our control. Things that we cannot change. Rather, we must concentrate our finite time, energy, and resources on the things that are within our control. The very things that we have the power to change.

*'God has blessed you with a good name. To be a well-favoured man
is a gift of Fortune, but to write and read comes by Nature.'* [557]

God's Blessing is a prerequisite to our success in any endeavour that we wish to undertake, be it marriage, friendship, tertiary education,

---

555 Shakespeare, William. (1600). *Much Ado About Nothing.* Act 2, Scene 3.
556 Shakespeare, William. (1600). *Much Ado About Nothing.* Act 3, Scene 2.
557 Shakespeare, William. (1600). *Much Ado About Nothing.* Act 3, Scene 3.

having children, purchasing real property, beginning a newfound career, travelling around the world, or creating our personal wealth. God's Favour cannot be earned through the performance of good works. God's Favour is a gift, freely given by God, to those individuals that God Predestines. It is within every person's capacity to become learned and honourable. However, it is not within every person's agency to acquire God's Favour.

'As they say, when the age is in, the wit is out.' [558]

This statement is an undeniable reality of ageing. As we advance in age, we lose the once quick-witted precision of our memory, judgement, reasoning, logic, and intelligence. We also become more reliant on other people, to assist us with our daily living activities. In addition, there are the countless number of medical conditions, that eventuate, and become progressively worse, with advanced age. For example, consider Alzheimer's Disease, Parkinson's Disease, Osteoarthritis, Chronic Obstructive Pulmonary Disease, Atherosclerosis, Cellulitis, and Chronic Kidney Disease.

'For it so falls out. That what we have we prize not to the worth. Whiles we enjoy it, but being lacked and lost. Why, then we rack the value, then we find the virtue that possession would not show us whiles it was ours.' [559]

This is the dismal reality of human nature. We often tend to overlook the value and worth of something that is already within our possession. Then, once we have lost what was once ours, we express remorse or regret, and come to cherish what we once had. To truly appreciate the value of an important person, animate object, or inanimate object, we have to relinquish it. We have to come to experience our life, without what we value.

---

558 Shakespeare, William. (1600). *Much Ado About Nothing.* Act 3, Scene 5.
559 Shakespeare, William. (1600). *Much Ado About Nothing.* Act 4, Scene 1.

'Come, Lady, die to live. This wedding day perhaps is but prolonged. Have patience and endure.' [560]

All our hopes and desires do not come to pass as we envisage. Nevertheless, we must keep our faith in God's Word. We must pray to God with a sincere heart. We must keep hope, that our requests will be granted in God's Timing. It can be extremely difficult to demonstrate patience, when our expected plans do not proceed as we had anticipated. In all things, we must endure the test of time. We shall keep hope that a turnaround is always possible. Be it in our relationships, finances, education, marriage, income, career, wealth, employment, health, or family. Where there is hope, there is the ability to endure any tragic event, or profound crisis.

'But there is no such man. For brother, men can counsel and speak comfort to that grief which they themselves not feel, but tasting it, their counsel turns to passion, which before would give preceptial medicine to rage, fetter strong madness in a silken thread, charm ache with air and agony with words.' [561]

Grief is a highly personal experience. The emotion of grief is often difficult to adequately express through verbal communication. We can attempt to relate with other people in relation to our grief. However, no two people comprehend or perceive the same event in exactly the same manner. Lived experience is personal. Grief requires the passage of time, thought, prayer, reflection, quality relationships, social support, and finally, coming to terms with our worldly reality, in order to 'move forward' with our life.

---

560 Shakespeare, William. (1600). *Much Ado About Nothing.* Act 4, Scene 1.
561 Shakespeare, William. (1600). *Much Ado About Nothing.* Act 5, Scene 1.

'No, no, it is all men's office to speak patience. To those that wring under the load of sorrow. But no man's virtue nor sufficiency to be so moral, when he shall endure the like himself.' [562]

It is convenient to give other people counsel on how they can better manage an issue or problem that is confronting them. Yet, the self-love, evil, and egocentric nature of humankind, prevents witness to the true and honourable brotherly and sisterly love. Whereby, a person endures the suffering and pain of another person. This type of compassion is extremely rare in this world.

'In a false quarrel there is no true valour.' [563]

There must be reason in disagreement between parties. If two or more people are arguing over a subject matter, their argument must be of some importance, and it must concern a dispute about which party's position is true and correct. If the disagreement is founded on a false premise, then the conclusion that follows it must also necessarily be false. Therefore, no courage is to be found in provisioning thought, time, and effort to engage in a worthless disagreement.

562 Shakespeare, William. (1600). *Much Ado About Nothing.* Act 5, Scene 1.
563 Shakespeare, William. (1600). *Much Ado About Nothing.* Act 5, Scene 1.

Chapter 25

OTHELLO

'Now, whether he kill Cassio, or Cassio him,
or each do kill the other, every way makes my gain.'

SHAKESPEARE

Othello is a tragedy concerning sexual jealousy. *Othello* explores the themes of marriage, love, jealousy, pride, self-interest, power, trust, betrayal, corruption, and evil. This play narrates the dramatic story of Iago being furious and jealous at his General, Othello. Now Othello has overlooked Iago for a senior promotion to a Lieutenant position, at the gain of Michael Cassio. As a consequence, Iago is discontent with holding the inferior rank of Ensign. Now Iago seeks to cause trouble, for the pursuit of personal gain.

In the background, Roderigo has been in pursuit of a Venetian gentlelady, Desdemona. However, Othello has secretly married Desdemona. Now this news is of much grief to Roderigo's heart. Through spreading rumours, fabricating evidence, and making ill-founded accusations, Iago manipulates and convinces the Moorish General, Othello that his beloved wife, Desdemona is unfaithful towards him. Unfortunately, Othello increasingly comes to rely upon the misguided counsel of Iago. As a consequence, Othello becomes consumed with anger, jealousy, rage, and hysteria.

Towards the close of this play, Othello murders his wife, Desdemona, as punishment for her presumed adultery. During Desdemona's murder, she helplessly pleads her innocence to Othello. However, Othello is now beyond all hope of reason. Othello is totally consumed by the irrationality of rage. Shortly thereafter, the Truth is out in the open. Iago is the sinister person behind the widespread evil consuming this close-knit community.

Othello is genuinely remorseful for causing the violent death of his beloved wife. As a result, Othello determines not to confront his trial. Instead, Othello makes a short speech, speaking his conscience, and then he commits suicide. As for Iago, he is detained and taken into custody. Iago is to be tortured in the depths of the dungeons for his corrupt and evil schemes. This play concludes with Cassio being reinstated as the legitimate Governor of Cyprus.

'We cannot all be Masters, nor all Masters cannot be truly followed.' [564]

Some people are leaders by the irrevocable call of destiny. While other people are naturally inclined to follow. Authentic leadership requires an individual to demonstrate the possession of inherent traits, such as personal responsibility, confidence, initiative, diligence, humility, steadfastness, ingenuity, righteousness, selflessness, inquisitiveness, courage, honour, conscientious, discipline, and trustworthiness. While it is possible to cultivate our virtues and strengthen our positive traits through experience, knowledge, formal learning, and education, some people naturally excel in the demonstration of select traits and desired behaviours that make them ideal leaders.

---

564 Shakespeare, William. (1622). *Othello.* Act 1, Scene 1.

'Heaven is my Judge. Not I for love or duty, but seeming so, for my peculiar end. For when my outward action doth demonstrate the native act and figure of my heart in complement extern. It is not long after I shall wear my heart on my sleeve for daws to peck at. I am not what I am.' [565]

We are all responsible for our actions in this world. Humans have 'free moral choice' in their determinations. We are capable of exercising the higher faculties of reason, logic, thought, discernment, and good judgement. Therefore, we must factor into consideration the known consequences of our actions. As a result, we consciously determine to perform good or evil actions in this world. In the final analysis, no person can escape the True Justice of God. While our outward speech and external actions can be misconstrued, to conceal our true intentions and motivations, the ultimate reality is that, sooner or later, the Truth shall come to light.

'Take hold on me. For my particular grief. Is of so flood-gate and overbearing nature. That it engluts and swallows other sorrows. And it is still itself.' [566]

Grief is a complex and traumatic emotion. Grief can render life extremely difficult. At times, grief makes life almost unbearable. Often the worst pain and suffering we experience is psychological in nature. In most, though not all cases, the physical signs of our bodily damage heal much sooner than the mental suffering from trauma that we experience in our mind. It is important to position life in perspective. Not to mention, nothing lasts forever in this world. Every person's life consists of some challenges, issues, difficulties, and privations. Unfortunately, this is not a perfect world, rather a broken world defined by sin. However, we must look to

---

565 Shakespeare, William. (1622). *Othello.* Act 1, Scene 1.
566 Shakespeare, William. (1622). *Othello.* Act 1, Scene 3.

life's challenges as newfound opportunities to develop our virtues, conscience, and character in this lifetime.

'If remedies are past, the griefs are ended by seeing the worst which late on hopes depended.'[567]

No matter what calamity, crisis, or catastrophe befalls upon us, we must keep the Faith. Through our unwavering belief in God's goodness, mercy, forgiveness, grace, and favour, all things are possible. Therefore, we must strive to move forward in our life with hope, love, and the power of prayer. A better future is always on the horizon. It is within us, to overcome the multitude of difficulties, that shall confront us on our life journey.

'To mourn a mischief that is past and gone is the next way to draw new mischief on. What cannot be preserved when fortune takes patience her injury a mockery makes.'[568]

We must beseech God for forgiveness, for our countless sins and transgressions. We must consciously seek to better ourselves in our thought, speech, and action. The pursuit of moral excellence is a lifelong endeavour. We shall utilise our finite time on Earth to create a better future for all people. We must fill this world with love, hope, opportunity, and faith in God's Goodness. The battle between Good and Evil. The battle between the Flesh and the Spirit. The battle between Righteousness and Wickedness. These are all the protracted conflicts, that shall define our body, mind, and soul.

The second half of the aforementioned statement illustrates that it is difficult to keep an even mind during the tragic time of a grave crisis. We must diligently persevere in our worldly suffering

---

567 Shakespeare, William. (1622). *Othello*. Act 1, Scene 3.
568 Shakespeare, William. (1622). *Othello*. Act 1, Scene 3.

like a valiant soldier, with faith, humility, diligence, and honour. We must not turn away from our true and final mission. To further God's Kingdom on Earth.

'I have but an hour of love, of worldly matter and direction, to spend with thee. We must obey the time.' [569]

This is a transient world. Our existential reality on this Earth is limited. The Earth is not our permanent abode. Sooner or later, we must leave the Earth. A person who truly understands and comprehends how short their lifetime is to make a positive impact. To define the contours of modern society. To make a unique contribution to this world. To reflect on God's Word and Glory. Such a person exhibits the hallmarks of an enlightened individual. At some point in our life, in particular as we advance in our years, we will come to the realisation, that few things matter in life. The most important of those things, is our especial relationship with God.

'Ah, it's silliness to live, when to live is torment, and then have we a prescription to die, when death is our physician.' [570]

This assertion captures the tragedy of life. Indeed, this statement by Shakespeare demonstrates the very misfortune of the human condition. Life is pain and suffering. Life is a challenge. Life is difficult. Thus, the most meaningful existential and philosophical questions that ought to concern our conscience include:

- How to create a meaningful and purposeful life?
- What to make of our finite time on Earth?
- Where can we make the greatest positive impact?
- How do we enhance our relationship with God?

---

569 Shakespeare, William. (1622). *Othello.* Act 1, Scene 3.
570 Shakespeare, William. (1622). *Othello.* Act 1, Scene 3.

'It is in ourselves that we are thus or thus. Our bodies are our gardens, to the which our wills are gardeners … why, the power and corrigible authority of this lies in our wills.' [571]

We possess free will and personal agency to determine our speech and actions in this world. Our beliefs, thoughts, values, faith, personal experience, knowledge, childhood, parentage, formal learning, and relationships, all perform a critical role in how we relate to the external world. However, we are ultimately responsible for our state of being. For our Self, that perceives the external world.

The German philosopher, poet, and philologist, Friedrich Nietzsche, in his work, *The Will to Power* (1901), describes this abstract and conceptual phenomenon of the 'Will to Power' as the primary motivating force that governs human action in the world. Indeed, our very ability to accomplish our destiny resides within the inherent capacity of our will.

'If the balance of our lives had not one scale of reason to poise another of sensuality … the blood and baseness of our natures would conduct us to most preposterous conclusions. But we have reason to cool our raging motions, our carnal stings, our unbitted lusts.' [572]

The human condition consists of a combination of the higher faculties, such as reason, logic, discernment, thought, and judgement. However, the human condition also exhibits the more base instincts, such as emotion, sensuality, passion, feeling, and sensation. The wise person seeks the path of the 'Middle Way' in creating a balanced and harmonious life.

We must employ the higher faculties in our everyday life, to create the best reality that we can envisage for ourselves. Having

---

571 Shakespeare, William. (1622). *Othello.* Act 1, Scene 3.
572 Shakespeare, William. (1622). *Othello.* Act 1, Scene 3.

said that, we cannot wholly deny the existence and function of our base instincts. For we are all too human. From a psychological perspective, our thoughts must be constructive and balanced, if we are to create a productive and good life.

> '*The Moor, how be it that I endure him not, is of a constant, loving, noble nature. And dare I think he'll prove to Desdemona a most dear husband. Now, I do love her too, not out of absolute lust, though peradventure I stand accountant for as great a sin, but partly led to diet my revenge, for that I do suspect the lustful Moor hath leaped into my seat, the thought whereof doth like a poisonous mineral gnaw my inwards. And nothing can or shall content my soul till I am even with him, wife for wife. Or failing so, yet that I put the Moor at least into a jealousy so strong that judgement cannot cure.*' [573]

Shakespeare creatively illustrates the worst of humanity. It is within the bounds of human nature to seek revenge and retribution. Each person is constantly in a life-long struggle between the Flesh and the Spirit. Indeed, the Flesh seeks to bring each person down to their base human condition, governed by instinct, sensation, and the many vices. Whereas, the Spirit seeks to raise a person beyond their worldly desires and trivial concerns.

Through God's mercy, favour, goodness, grace, and blessing, the individual who seeks the Spirit, shall create a higher, purposeful, and meaningful life. An honourable life that is defined by compassion, charity, forgiveness, honesty, kindness, integrity, and community service. On the other hand, the unenlightened person shall desire the temptation of revenge. The morally reprehensible person falls deeper into the depths of sinful conduct.

---

573 Shakespeare, William. (1622). *Othello.* Act 2, Scene 1.

'Knavery's plain face is never seen till used.' [574]

We can never truly know another person's intentions, thoughts, or motivations. Until their actions reveal them. A person may undertake extreme measures to conceal their plans and thoughts. Until the time is most opportune, for them to act and bring their heart's desires to fruition. Action affirms witness to the Truth. Action reveals any falsehood in a person's character, integrity, ethics, principles, values, ideas, morals, or conscience.

'If consequence do but approve my dream, my boat sails freely,
both wind and stream.' [575]

The fate of fortune cannot be escaped. The consequences, both intended and unintended, are the fruits of our free moral actions. When fortune favours us, then we secure unmerited gains in areas of our life where we hoped for success. For example, consider finances, health and well-being, relationships, marriage, education, children, private property, income, wealth, and business. On the contrary, if the consequences, both anticipated and unanticipated, of our actions are negative, then we suffer losses. Such negative consequences, all but reverse (or frustrate) our efforts to realise our greatest ambitions in life.

'Well, God's above all, and there be souls must be saved, and there
be souls must not be saved.' [576]

God is the True and Final Arbitrator of our deeds. This world is full of good and evil. Now some people determine to be a force for good in this world. Whereas, other people are equally determined to be a force for evil. The former group shall be saved for their just

---

574 Shakespeare, William. (1622). *Othello*. Act 2, Scene 1.
575 Shakespeare, William. (1622). *Othello*. Act 2, Scene 3.
576 Shakespeare, William. (1622). *Othello*. Act 2, Scene 3.

cause in advancing the Kingdom of God on Earth. Whereas, the latter group shall be punished for the injustice they have caused on Earth. In the final analysis, no person is beyond good and evil.

'You see this fellow who is gone before. He is a soldier fit to stand by Caesar and give direction. And do but see his vice. It is to his virtue a just equinox. The one as long as the other. It is pity of him.' [577]

Every person has their virtues and vices. No individual is completely perfect in all respects. Unfortunately, a person's vices can equalise their virtues. Such a condition only serves to diminish the praise and worth of a person, in the opinion of the people. We must strive to cultivate our virtues. While we seek to eliminate our vices. A person's character takes a lifetime to perfect. The pursuit of moral excellence is no overnight endeavour. Each and every difficulty that we confront is a test. A moral test, that shall define our character, conduct, and conscience.

'Worthy Othello, I am hurt to danger. Nor know I aught by me that's said or done amiss this night. Unless self-charity be sometimes a vice, and to defend ourselves it be a sin when violence assails us.' [578]

We may employ our speech to deceive and mislead other people. To create fabrications and misconceptions concerning our intentions, objectives, and aims. More importantly, we cannot deceive God. Thus, we shall be held accountable for our actions during our time on Earth. It is too often the case, that honesty, valour, courage, integrity, justice, honour, dignity, character, and faith are sacrificed for trivial and inconsequential gains. Advantages that are as fleeting, as our finite years on Earth.

---

577 Shakespeare, William. (1622). *Othello.* Act 2, Scene 3.
578 Shakespeare, William. (1622). *Othello.* Act 2, Scene 3.

'What are you hurt, Lieutenant? Ay ... past all surgery. Marry, God forbid. Reputation. Reputation. I have lost my reputation. I have lost the immortal part of me, and what remains is bestial. My reputation, Iago. My reputation.' [579]

Our reputation outlives our finite time on the Earth. Therefore, it is essential that we carefully consider how we act. We must factor into consideration the lasting consequences of our actions. In the life-long endeavour of creating our enduring reputation, we need to carefully reflect upon the following questions:

- What type of life do we wish to create?
- How best to utilise our time on Earth?
- What shall be our lasting legacy?

'I am desperate of my fortunes, if they check me here.' [580]

Often times, through no fault of our own, we can find ourselves in desperate circumstances. Where it appears, that we have very limited, if any options, to make a decision that is in our best interest. It is extremely difficult to maintain one's composure and positive thinking through testing times. However, we always have a free moral choice, on how to respond to forces outside of our control. For example, consider financial crises, humanitarian crises, civil wars, economic shocks, world wars, internal displacement, and other unfortunate external events that we find ourselves situated in.

The Austrian Psychiatrist, Viktor Emil Frankl, renowned author of *Man's Search for Meaning* (1946), shared a remarkable insight into human behaviour, 'Everything can be taken from a person, but one thing. The last of the human freedoms—to choose one's attitude in any given set of circumstances. To choose one's own way.' In the final analysis, we always have a free moral choice. That is to say, we

---

579 Shakespeare, William. (1622). *Othello*. Act 2, Scene 3.
580 Shakespeare, William. (1622). *Othello*. Act 2, Scene 3.

are not merely helpless victims of our external environment. Even though all the events, situations, experiences, and circumstances during our lifetime are not within our immediate control. We are conscious agents, embedded with personal agency.

> *'How poor are they that have not patience! What wound did ever heal, but by degrees? Thou knowest we work by wit and not by witchcraft, and wit depends on dilatory time.'*[581]

Patience is a virtue. However, it is not within every person's inherent capacity to demonstrate the requisite patience to transcend their privations. It takes considerable time and effort to accomplish a grand endeavour. To adequately heal from a loss or heartbreak. To recover from a life-threatening illness or traumatic event. To learn a foreign language. To master a reputable profession.

Individuals that demonstrate patience are in a superior position. Not only to visualise their future, but also to realise their desired future in their lifetime. As the *Holy Bible* states within the *Book of Ecclesiastes*, Chapter 3, Verse 1, 'There is a time for everything, and a season for every activity under the Heavens.' Thus, we need to trust in God's Timing. We need to continue forward in our quest to realise our destiny.

> *'Though other things grow fair against the Sun, yet fruits that blossom first will first be ripe. Content thyself awhile.'*[582]

There is a natural process to the fullness and fruition of all things in this world. We cannot artificially expedite a natural process, and consequently expect the terminal outcome that we truly desire. It is essential that we allow change and progress to take place at a rate which is sustainable over a given period of time. In all our work, we need to ensure that our rate of productivity is reflective

---

581 Shakespeare, William. (1622). *Othello*. Act 2, Scene 3.
582 Shakespeare, William. (1622). *Othello*. Act 2, Scene 3.

of a rate which accomplishes durable quality in the output of our labour, with respect to the time that we have expended.

'Pleasure and action make the hours seem short.' [583]

Action is the basis of all life on Earth. Without the performance of action, we are unable to create a life on Earth that is full of meaning, purpose, and value. On the other hand, pleasure makes us forget our worries, anxieties, stresses, concerns, and responsibilities. Indeed, the pursuit of pleasure is a diversion mechanism to escape from the tribulations and troubles of everyday reality.

In the final analysis, we must strive to strike a harmony and balance in our life. Some action and pleasure are good. However, some rest and recovery from work, conscious reflection on our accomplishments, and moderation in our desires is also good. There is much wisdom in pausing and reflecting on what we have accomplished in life. In addition, we must be thankful to God for how far we have come in life. If anything, we stand to gain from the state of contentment.

'For such things in a false disloyal knave are tricks of custom; but in a man that's just they're close dilations, working from the heart, That passion cannot rule.' [584]

It is a person's character, integrity, values, principles, motives, and reputation, that determine the true intention behind their free moral actions. If a person is untrustworthy and dishonest, then they will make it a habit to engage in immoral and unlawful activities, in order to make dishonourable gains. However, at times, even the most righteous and learned person, can capitulate to the forces of temptation and desire. Such is the overwhelming power of passion.

---

583 Shakespeare, William. (1622). *Othello.* Act 2, Scene 3.
584 Shakespeare, William. (1622). *Othello.* Act 3, Scene 3.

'Good name in man and woman ... Dear My Lord, is the immediate jewel of their souls. Who steals my purse steals trash: it is something, nothing. It was mine, it is his, and has been slave to thousands. But he that filches from me my good name ... robs me of that which not enriches him and makes me poor indeed.' [585]

Shakespeare makes the important point that our financial capital, prized possessions, and personal property are not the most important things in our life. For these material items can be bought, sold, exchanged, lost, transferred, destroyed, or bartered. Therefore, such material possessions, which are of this world, are not ours forever. Our material possessions are only ours for a brief period of time. The ownership of material possessions is always uncertain.

More importantly, our name is attached to us from birth until death. Following our inevitable encounter with death, the long memory of history shall remember our name, and the reputation, and accomplishments that are attached to it. Therefore, we must not only protect and preserve our good name. However, we shall further our good name's standing and reputation in this world.

'O curse of marriage. That we can call these delicate creatures ours, and not their appetites.' [586]

The institution of marriage is not always happiness, prosperity, and joy. By law and moral right, each spouse has the exclusive right to the warm affection, good company, pleasant conversation, and heartfelt intimacy with their beloved partner. At times, there are difficulties and challenges to navigate in a marriage. This can be due to changes in one's circumstances, fortune, loss, grief, employment, housing, life-changing experiences, finances, tertiary education, child raising, death of a loved family member, and many

---

585 Shakespeare, William. (1622). *Othello.* Act 3, Scene 3.
586 Shakespeare, William. (1622). *Othello.* Act 3, Scene 3.

other equally important and consequential factors. It is incumbent upon us, that we seek to address these genuine concerns, with consideration, warmth, and sensitivity for both spouses.

'It is destiny unshunnable, like death.' [587]

We must confront our destiny with bravery and courage. We have to become, who we were meant to be. To realise our highest purpose here on Earth. To transcend the ordinary challenges of life. To reach new heights. To not only aspire to an accomplished life, but to truly achieve it. Fear not, and resolutely proceed forward in life. For our destiny determines who we truly are. When we are no more on this Earth, it shall be our legacy that endures for all time.

'Trifles light as air are to the jealous, confirmations strong as Proofs of Holy Writ.' [588]

Individuals who are jealous shall always confront the temptation of becoming envious at another person's gain. No matter how trivial or inconsequential the quantum of gain. However, the strong fire of jealousy only serves to consume the person experiencing it. Jealousy destroys a person's character, integrity, honour, reputation, and good name. We must seek to completely destroy the powerful vices that tempt us to commit evil acts. Of great importance, we shall strive to perfect our virtues that make us better individuals in this world.

---

587 Shakespeare, William. (1622). *Othello.* Act 3, Scene 3.
588 Shakespeare, William. (1622). *Othello.* Act 3, Scene 3.

'Dangerous conceits are, in their natures, poisons. That at the first are scarce found to distaste ... but with a little act upon the blood, burn like the mines of sulphur.' [589]

We must be conscious and self-aware of the many dangers and countless pitfalls of excessive pride in the Self. A reasonable pride and healthy ego in the Self is necessary and indicative of confidence. A moderate and self-regulated ego, can assist us to accomplish and create a meaningful life. However, pride and ego, taken to fundamental extremes and radical excess, can destroy a person. We are no better than any other person, and no other person is better than us. Thus, we shall treat every person, how we would like to be treated.

In the final analysis, every person has God-given human dignity. No matter a person's age, private property, income, wealth, sex, gender, race, religion, ethnicity, country of origin, faith, or colour. It is solely by the virtue of being human, that each person is automatically afforded human dignity. Not to mention, how we treat other people is a reflection of our character, integrity, values, beliefs, moral principles, and ethics.

'O wretched fool, that livest to make thine honesty a vice. O monstrous world! Take note, take note. O world, to be direct and honest is not safe. I thank you for this profit, and from hence I'll love no friend since love breeds such offence. Nay, stay; thou shouldst be honest. I should be wise, for honesty's a fool, and loses that it works for.' [590]

The paradox with being too transparent, frank, candid, and honest, is that individuals in modern society can take advantage of the personal information that we share with them, and use it against us. While honesty is, and always will be a virtue, however, not

---

589 Shakespeare, William. (1622). *Othello.* Act 3, Scene 3.
590 Shakespeare, William. (1622). *Othello.* Act 3, Scene 3.

everyone is honest. Corrupt people in the Modern World stand to make a gain or profit from the confidential information that we disclose to them. The best counsel herein is also provided by William Shakespeare in his majestic play, *All's Well That Ends Well* (1623), 'Love all. Trust a few. Do wrong to none.'

> *'Make her amends, she weeps. O Devil, Devil! If that the Earth could teem with woman's tears, each drop she falls would prove a crocodile. Out of my sight!'* [591]

It is the reality of human nature, that we are all impacted by the personal experience of tragedy, grief, heartache, and loss in this broken world. The psychology of emotions, feelings, and sensations is a part and parcel of our human existence. Having said that, we must not be too strongly swayed by the powerful currents of passion. The ferocious winds of emotions. Nor the unchecked tides of sensation. It is within us, and for our greater good, that we allow the function of reason, judgement, and logic to guide our thought, speech, and action.

> *'Unkindness may do much. And his unkindness may defeat my life, but never taint my love.'* [592]

Love is the highest good in this world. Love can overcome all difficulties, privations, challenges, and troubles in this world. We shall never let our love for humanity be defeated by the dark forces of evil and vice in this world. We must transcend evil with good. Defeat hate with love. Conquer jealousy with contentment. Extinguish doubt with confidence. Also, vanquish fear with faith. Then, we have surpassed the baseness of this world. Indeed, in performing the above righteous actions, we have made remarkable progress in the perfection of our character.

---

591 Shakespeare, William. (1622). *Othello.* Act 4, Scene 1.
592 Shakespeare, William. (1622). *Othello.* Act 4, Scene 2.

'It makes us, or it mars us. Think on that, and fix most firm thy resolution.' [593]

We must never permit doubt, hesitation, confusion, uncertainty, or fear to hinder our intentions or ambitions in life. It is only when we are truly and wholly resolved to achieve an endeavour, with a single-minded determination, that we provision ourselves with the highest opportunity to attain success. If we permit uncertainty to enter and entertain our thoughts, then we become unfirm in our endeavours. We must not begin to doubt what is possible. In all cases, belief is the critical ingredient to our success.

'Now, whether he kill Cassio, or Cassio him, or each do kill the other, every way makes my gain.' [594]

Shakespeare, quite blatantly and literally, demonstrates the naked and callous nature of humanity. Each person seeks to further their self-interest, gain, influence, power, or profit in this world. Such is the selfish and evil nature of humankind. In particular, when we examine the contemporary world, we witness a Modern World constructed upon the ideologies of secularism, individualism, consumerism, liberalism, materialism, capitalism, and hedonism.

Humanity has very quickly lost sight of ancient wisdom found in morality, ethical conduct, religious education, conscience, and the love of God. In the final analysis, a life that is lived in pursuit of self-interest is a meaningless life. Such a life is totally devoid of a higher purpose. Conversely, a meaningful life is forged on the principles of selfless service, compassion, honesty, integrity, duty, righteousness, and moral excellence.

---

593 Shakespeare, William. (1622). *Othello.* Act 5, Scene 1.
594 Shakespeare, William. (1622). *Othello.* Act 5, Scene 1.

'I pray you, in your letters, when you shall these unlucky deeds relate, Speak of me as I am.'[595]

When we are no longer on this Earth, we shall wish to be remembered for who we truly were. That is to say, our actions, accomplishments, ambitions, dreams, hopes, beliefs, values, principles, character, integrity, and achievements. Therefore, in the present time, we have an obligation and duty to conduct ourselves, as we would like the enduring memory of history to remember us. The future is always created in the present moment. Not to mention, the present time comes to determine the past. This is the fixed trajectory of action that concerns every person's lifetime. It cannot be otherwise.

---

595 Shakespeare, William. (1622). *Othello*. Act 5, Scene 2.

Chapter 26

PERICLES PRINCE OF TYRE

'Alas, the Sea hath cast me on the rocks, washed me from shore to shore, and left me breath nothing to think on but ensuing death. Let it suffice the greatness of your powers to have bereft a Prince of all his fortunes. And having thrown him from your watery grave, here to have death in peace is all he'll crave.'

SHAKESPEARE

Shakespeare's *Pericles Prince of Tyre* is a story of lost and found. This play commences with a poet named Gower narrating the story of King Antiochus' seemingly unsolvable riddle. King Antiochus is protecting a most incestuous and immoral relationship with his beautiful daughter. The King has made an offer for his daughter's hand in marriage, to any gentleman that can resolve his riddle. However, if the suitor is unsuccessful, he shall be sentenced to death. Many handsome gentlemen make bold and brave attempts to solve King Antiochus' riddle, however, none are successful.

The youthful Prince Pericles of Tyre is knowledgeable of the correct answer to the King's riddle. Prince Pericles does not directly reveal the immoral relationship between the King and his beloved daughter. However, Pericles answers the King's riddle in such a manner, that it is obvious that Pericles is aware of the King's vice and dishonourable conduct with his beautiful daughter. While Prince Pericles has all too correctly solved the riddle, King Antiochus is left ashamed and embarrassed, that the Truth concerning his immorality has come to light. Therefore, King Antiochus intends that Prince Pericles be put to death.

As a result, Prince Pericles flees to Tyre for his safety and life. King Antiochus informs his servant, Thaliart to murder Pericles. The following scenes of the play narrate the story of Pericles constantly travelling from one city to another, in an attempt to escape his unjust pursuers. During the course of Prince Pericles' journey, the Prince wins the favour of King Simonides. Shortly thereafter, Pericles marries the King's daughter, Thaisa.

Before long, news comes to Prince Pericles that King Antiochus has passed away. As a result, Pericles sets course for the journey by sea, to return to Tyre and reclaim his right to the Throne, with his beloved wife, Thaisa. On the journey, Thaisa gives birth to a baby daughter, however, Thaisa sadly passes away. This unwelcome force of circumstance results in Pericles landing at Tarsus, where he entrusts the care of his infant daughter, Marina to the Governor Cleon and his wife, Dionyza.

Mysteriously, Thaisa's coffin safely and securely arrives at Ephesus, where the kindness and generosity of Doctor Cerimon's efforts result in Thaisa's miraculous revival back to life. Thereafter, Thaisa resolves to enter the Temple of Diana as a nun. Meanwhile, with the passage of time, Marina has matured to become a beautiful young gentlewoman. Now Marina's stepmother, Dionyza is exceedingly jealous of Marina's beauty. Dionyza seeks to destroy the favour upon Marina's life. Dionyza arranges for Marina's brutal murder, however, Marina is haphazardly captured by pirates. Thereafter, Marina is sold to a brothel in Mytilene. Marina vows to uphold her chastity. While Marina is confined within the brothel, she entertains a chance encounter with Governor Lysimachus.

Prince Pericles is full of sorrow. By the winds of fortune, Pericles arrives in Mytilene, where he is visited by Governor Lysimachus on board his ship. It is during this time that Marina is finally reunited with her father. In amazement and wonder, Prince Pericles is shaken free from his long-held grief. Once again, Pericles is filled with joy, laughter, and happiness. In the closing scenes of this play, the Goddess Diana instructs Pericles to offer a sacrifice at her Temple in Ephesus. Thus, Pericles and Marina set sail to fulfil this noble mission.

'For death remembered should be like a mirror, who tells us life's but breath, to trust it error.' [596]

We all have to confront the undeniable fact that we are mortal. We stare at death every day. One day, we shall come face to face with death. For all living species on Earth, including the human civilisation, life is transient, uncertain, and impermanent. Therefore, we make a grave error to place our trust in life. For we are certain to confront life's demise. Trust in God's Kingdom. For God's Kingdom is destined to reign forever and ever. For all eternity. God's Majestic Glory is without beginning or end.

'Thus, ready for the way of life or death. I want the sharpest blow, Antiochus.' [597]

Sooner or later, we must confront our demise in this world. Death may come at us in a multitude of forms, such as the Ebola virus, infantile paralysis, systemic lupus erythematosus, Creutzfeldt–Jakob disease, diabetes mellitus, acquired immunodeficiency syndrome, extreme neonatal conditions, breast cancer, cardiovascular disease, tuberculosis, malaria, Parkinson's disease, Alzheimer's disease, lung cancer, prostatic carcinoma, or cervical cancer. However, we must

---

596 Shakespeare, William. (1609). *Pericles Prince of Tyre.* Act 1, Scene 1.
597 Shakespeare, William. (1609). *Pericles Prince of Tyre.* Act 1, Scene 1.

confront our death with courage, conviction, dignity, strength, faith, honour, and total trust in God's Mercy.

'Great King, few love to hear the sins they love to act.' [598]

We often find it unbearable to listen to the evil, wicked, and cruel deeds, that we are all too willing to execute. Human nature is despicable. We witness the worst of it, when we engage in sinful conduct. The sinful nature of humanity is such, that we are full of greed, jealousy, envy, pride, lust, hate, sexual desire, and anger. The moral responsibility is on the individual to overcome one's sinful nature. To turn one's heart towards God. To perfect one's virtues. To destroy one's vices. With God's Mercy and Goodness, we shall become the best version of ourselves. The Righteous Path towards moral excellence is never a convenient endeavour.

'For vice repeated is like the wandering wind. Blows dust in other's eyes, to spread itself, and yet the end of all is bought thus dear. The breath is gone and the sore eyes see clear.' [599]

It is the nature of vice to destroy a person's character. Regardless of the type of vice we experience or demonstrate in this lifetime. Vice mistakenly leads us on into temptation. Vice lures us further into the depths of evil. When we are in the advanced years of our life. When we approach the very end of our lifetime. Then we perceive, all too clearly, how we wasted away the precious years of our lifetime in vain, in the irrational pursuit of pride, anger, sexual desire, lust, arrogance, profit, power, pecuniary gain, and private property. Regrettably, the vanity of self-interest is exposed, at the exact time of our death. After a lifetime of sinful conduct.

---

598 Shakespeare, William. (1609). *Pericles Prince of Tyre.* Act 1, Scene 1.
599 Shakespeare, William. (1609). *Pericles Prince of Tyre.* Act 1, Scene 1.

'Kings are Earth's Gods, in vice their law's their will. And if Jove stray, who dares say Jove doth ill?' [600]

Kings and Queens are the True Sovereigns on Earth. Kings and Queens rule nation-states with their decrees, representing their rightful and privileged Royal Prerogative. By the virtue of unchecked power, position, and authority, the law of the land comes to represent the King's or Queen's unquestionable will. Regrettably, unchecked and unquestioned power leads to the improper exercise of political authority. Unfortunately, the majority of subjects do not consider to question the Sovereign of their nation-state. This unquestioning obedience of the masses, arises from the fear of losing the one thing, that all of humanity love the most. That is, one's precious and cherished life.

'For wisdom sees, those men blush not in actions blacker than the night, Will shun no course to keep them from the light.' [601]

We are all sinners. Some people greater than others. A person who commits a crime or evil deed, is more likely than not to evade the Truth. To conceal their actions from scrutiny and investigation. In a desperate attempt to pervert the course of justice, an individual may fabricate evidence, destroy evidence, present a false witness, provide a false written declaration or verbal testimony. However, God is Omnipresent. God Perceives all things within the world. Indeed, God is the Searcher of hearts and Knower of souls.

---

600 Shakespeare, William. (1609). *Pericles Prince of Tyre*. Act 1, Scene 1.
601 Shakespeare, William. (1609). *Pericles Prince of Tyre*. Act 1, Scene 1.

> *'Murder's as near to lust as flame to smoke. Poison and treason are the Hands of Sin, and the targets to put off the shame. As thou will live, fly after, and ... like an arrow shot from a well-experienced archer hits the mark his eye doth level at. So thou never return unless thou say, Prince Pericles is dead.'* [602]

We must be vigilant in our thought, speech, and conduct. There are numerous temptations in this world. To seek revenge is just one of them. Regardless of the worldly gain that we stand to inherit in exchange for sinful conduct, we must exercise care and caution. We must not fall for the temptations of the Devil. Carefully reflect on the following question: What is the true worth of gaining this world, if we lose our soul? This is a most meritless exchange. An exchange in which we shall find no everlasting peace or genuine happiness.

> *'What wouldst thou have me do? To bear with patience such griefs as you do lay upon yourself. Thou speakest like a Physician that ministers a potion unto me that thou wouldst tremble to receive thyself.'* [603]

During our time in grief, we must seek the counsel of a trusted advisor. A person who has our best interests at heart. Grief is an incredibly difficult emotion to process. Grief requires considerable time, much patience, good conversation, and emotionally-intelligent company to navigate. It is always more convenient for an individual, who is not directly experiencing or impacted by grief, to converse about it. However, it is the person in the midst of grief, who truly struggles, to express their feelings, emotions, and sensations through coherent speech.

---

602 Shakespeare, William. (1609). *Pericles Prince of Tyre*. Act 1, Scene 2.
603 Shakespeare, William. (1609). *Pericles Prince of Tyre*. Act 1, Scene 2.

*'The care I had and have of subjects' good on thee I lay whose
wisdom's strength can bear it. I'll take thy word for faith, not ask
for oath. Who shuns not to break one, will sure crack both.'* [604]

Trust is a condition upon which all honourable relationships are founded. Without trust, there can be no commitment and honour between two or more parties. For example, consider the relationship between a nation-state's sovereign and a loyal subject. There exists a 'social contract', with both parties expected to perform their duties and faithfully discharge their obligations.

In an ideal social contract, the Sovereign is expected to provide security for the subject. Protection of the subject's private property. Ensure the subject has equal protection under the law. Guarantee that the subject's liberty is preserved, unless the subject has committed a criminal offence against the nation-state. In which case, a finite deprivation of liberty may be a necessary punishment. On the other hand, the subject is expected to positively contribute to society. Discharge tax obligations. Comply with the nation-state's laws. Above all, be a loyal subject of the Sovereign.

*'My Dionyza, shall we rest us here, and by relating tales of others'
griefs, see if it will teach us to forget our own? That were to blow
at fire in hope to quench it, for who digs hills because they do
aspire throws down one mountain to cast up a higher.'* [605]

Revisiting the grief and sorrow of another person, will rarely, if ever, resolve our problems. Too often, we are the masters of other people's grief. We are good advisors, on how others can resolve their life challenges. However, we have not yet resolved, let alone mastered our own difficulties. We ought to utilise our limited time, energy, resources, and efforts, to address our problems. So that we can create the life, that we truly envisage.

---

604 Shakespeare, William. (1609). *Pericles Prince of Tyre*. Act 1, Scene 2.
605 Shakespeare, William. (1609). *Pericles Prince of Tyre*. Act 1, Scene 4.

'Thou speakest like him's untutored to repeat. Who makes the fairest show means most deceit.' [606]

People are not always who they appear to be. A person may demonstrate the employment of kind and sincere words. A person may exhibit admirable conduct, however, such an individual may be concealing sinister intentions and impure motives. Usually, the individual who is keen to construct the most favourable impression, upon other members of an association, community, or institution, is the one most likely to harbour deception in their heart.

'Yet cease your ire, you angry Stars of Heaven! Wind, Rain, and Thunder, remember, Earthly man is but a substance that must yield to you. And I, as fits my nature, do obey you.' [607]

Humans are subject to the destructive power of the natural elements. We cannot escape the wrath of the elements. Therefore, we must seek to best protect ourselves, from their destructive damage. Nature determines the course of every life. Thus, we have no agency, but to act in accordance with the determination of Nature. Indeed, Nature's Will is supreme in matters of birth and death. The natural instinct for sexual reproduction. Ageing. The human desire to seek adequate nourishment and hydration. Self-preservation. Also, the involuntary function of the physiological systems of the human body. No person is beyond the natural and scientific laws of Biology. To live our life as proximate to the intention and design of Nature. Therein resides practical wisdom.

---

606 Shakespeare, William. (1609). *Pericles Prince of Tyre.* Act 1, Scene 4.
607 Shakespeare, William. (1609). *Pericles Prince of Tyre.* Act 2, Scene 1.

'Alas, the Sea hath cast me on the rocks, washed me from shore to shore, and left me breath nothing to think on but ensuing death. Let it suffice the greatness of your powers to have bereft a Prince of all his fortunes. And having thrown him from your watery grave, here to have death in peace is all he'll crave.' [608]

It is an unquestionable reality that we shall confront many struggles and challenges throughout our lifetime. No matter if a person is a king, queen, prime minister, president, wealthy merchant, malnourished beggar, distraught widow, or illiterate labourer, we shall all have our destined date with death. Regardless of a person's wealth, position, status, class, private property, education, influence, prestige, income, or power, the fortune of this world shall pass us by. Fortune is as fleeting and transient as life itself. A peaceful and comfortable death of natural causes is a blessing. On the other hand, the accumulation of incalculable worldly treasure, cannot grant us peace, even for a single day.

'Opinion is but a fool, that makes us scan the outward habit for the inward man.' [609]

We must not take any assurance or comfort in the opinion of other people. For the opinions and judgements of the masses are as changing as the fashion trends of a season. Public opinion is unpredictable, impulsive, and spontaneous. We must be mindful not to form an uneducated opinion about another person on the basis of their external behaviour or speech. We must remember, that our narrow powers of observation, rarely ascertain the true character, values, beliefs, principles, ideas, or thoughts of a person.

---

608 Shakespeare, William. (1609). *Pericles Prince of Tyre*. Act 2, Scene 1.
609 Shakespeare, William. (1609). *Pericles Prince of Tyre*. Act 2, Scene 2.

'Be quiet then as men should be till, he hath passed necessity.
I'll show you those in troubles reign, losing a mite, a mountain
gain.' [610]

We shall all confront challenges and troubles in this world; however, they can be transcended. Sometimes, it is the case, that patience, coupled with inaction, is the best remedy to our difficulties. To act with haste, does not always accomplish good outcomes. Therefore, we must exercise judgement, restraint, and forbearance in our conduct. From a theological perspective, when we place our unconditional trust in God. When we pray to God. Also, when we seek God's Mercy and Goodness. Then we must keep the Faith, that God shall defeat the enemies, that we confront in our life.

Within the *Holy Bible*, there are many references to God's Grace, Favour, and Mercy in action. For example, consider the *Book of Deuteronomy*, Chapter 9, Verse 3, 'But be assured today that the LORD your God is the one who goes across ahead of you like a devouring fire. He will destroy them. He will subdue them before you. And you will drive them out and annihilate them quickly, as the LORD has promised you.' In addition, consider the following passage in the *Book of Isaiah*, Chapter 43, Verse 2, 'When you pass through the waters, I will be with you; and when you pass through the rivers, they will not sweep over you. When you walk through the fire, you will not be burned; the flames will not set you ablaze.'

'But you, my Knight and guest, to whom this wreath of victory
I give, and Crown you King of this day's happiness. It is more
by fortune, Lady, than my merit. Call it by what you will, the day
is yours.' [611]

Often, we expend considerable effort, time, resources, and energy in successfully accomplishing our most noble endeavours. However,

---

610 Shakespeare, William. (1609). *Pericles Prince of Tyre*. Act 2, Scene 2.
611 Shakespeare, William. (1609). *Pericles Prince of Tyre*. Act 2, Scene 3.

sometimes it is the case, that we gain a decisive victory, not by our personal efforts, but by the operation of chance, fate, luck, or destiny.

Most importantly, a victory shall never result, unless we have faith for the beginning, faith for the middle, and faith for the end. We need to believe the impossible is possible. We need to believe that the mountain before us can be transcended. We need to believe that we can accomplish all things that we set our mind to. Where there is belief, all things are possible. Indeed, a person's beliefs will determine their potential in life.

'Whereby I see that Time's the King of Men. He's both their parent, and he is their grave, and gives them what he will, not what they crave.' [612]

We are all beholden to the function and value of time. No person in the flesh is beyond the constraint, compulsion, and capacity of time. In order to maximise the value of our life, we must act, perform, and accomplish our desires and ambitions within the parameters of our time on Earth. Living a life with passion, purpose, and productivity, allows us to reflect on our life in our advanced years, and have no basis for regret or remorse. Indeed, at the finality of our lifetime, we must be prepared to assert, 'That was a life well-lived', for this is an honourable accomplishment.

'Then you love us, we you. And we'll clasp hands. When Peers thus knit, a Kingdom ever stands.' [613]

There is strength and synergy in unity. On the contrary, a house divided against itself cannot stand. There is considerable unrealised force in the agreement of two or more parties. Everyone has their distinctions, differences, and dissimilarities. In the end, the people

---

612 Shakespeare, William. (1609). *Pericles Prince of Tyre*. Act 2, Scene 3.
613 Shakespeare, William. (1609). *Pericles Prince of Tyre*. Act 2, Scene 4.

who set aside their differences, and promote consensus on common ground, they will create union in their relationships. They will promote harmony in the community.

'My actions are as noble as my thoughts. That never relished of a base descent.' [614]

Actions always speak louder than words. Through affirming witness to a person's actions, we can ascertain the nobleness or baseness of an individual's thoughts. The imperative is upon us to critically question and reflect upon our thoughts. By closely examining our thoughts, we can better inform our speech and action. In the final analysis, our thoughts determine our actions. Thus, our actions determine our worldly reality. Therefore, the formation of our living reality, commences with, and in our thoughts. Hence, we must provision due consideration to our thoughts.

'Your strokes of fortune, though they hurt you mortally, yet glance full woundingly on us. O your Sweet Queen! That the strict fates had pleased you had brought her hither, to have blessed mine eyes with her. We cannot but obey the Powers above us. Could I rage and roar, as doth the Sea she lies in. Yet the end must be as it is.' [615]

Humans are subject to limitations in their capacities and abilities. Above all, humans are only mortal. Humans can become disillusioned with their reality, with the turns, tides, and twists of fortune. However, we must accept the world, and all that is in it. The world is comprised of the good, and unfortunately, the undeniable presence of evil. Each person's time on Earth is limited. We must find harmony, balance, and peace in our existence. In the final analysis, the demise of every person's life is inevitable. Each life

---

614 Shakespeare, William. (1609). *Pericles Prince of Tyre.* Act 2, Scene 5.
615 Shakespeare, William. (1609). *Pericles Prince of Tyre.* Act 3, Scene 3.

has a beginning. Thus, it is by the force of necessity, each life shall also have an end.

'Thou canst not do a thing in the world so soon to yield thee so much profit.' [616]

Human behaviour is all too driven by the quest for self-interest, fame, profit, power, influence, concupiscence, and pecuniary gain. It is not only despicable, but also deplorable, to witness humanity diminish itself for the desire of personal wealth, pecuniary gain, private property, and personal income.

In the contemporary world, the modern individual has been conditioned to act in a rational, economic, self-interested, and profit-maximising manner. This small-minded behaviour of individuals and corporations is in accordance with the prevailing ideas and contemporary principles of Neoclassical Economics. In concise terms, the 'market forces' of 'demand' and 'supply' are responsible for global economic activity, such as the production, consumption, and pricing of goods and services. This globalised, commoditised, and commercialised world, now assigns an economic value on all things, including human life.

The New World is founded upon the novel ideas, theories, thoughts, principles, and concepts of the English economist, John Maynard Keynes. Keynes' economic views, commonly known as 'Keynesian Economics', globally inform national government's economic policy concerning inflation, taxation, interest rates, unemployment, government spending, and investment.

In more recent times, the American economist, Milton Friedman, has pioneered a more fundamental approach to free-market capitalism and libertarian economics. Friedman's Monetarism promotes a greater emphasis of the Scottish

---

616 Shakespeare, William. (1609). *Pericles Prince of Tyre.* Act 4, Scene 1.

economist and philosopher, Adam Smith's ideas, such as the free and independent action of individuals, which aim to enhance the utility of resources, maximise output, and create personal wealth.

'How have I offended, wherein my death might yield her any profit, or my life imply her any danger? My commission is not to reason of the deed, but do it. You will not do it for all the world, I hope.' [617]

Our guilt or innocence is not established through words, but through our actions. We may have been assigned an immoral duty to discharge; however, we must always remember that we are personally responsible for our actions. Our soul shall be held accountable for our free moral actions. Therefore, above all, we must let our conscience, moral principles, and morality guide our better judgement. Lest we become tainted, with the consequential effects of sin.

'I think thou saidest thou hadst been tossed from wrong to injury, and that thou thoughtest thy griefs might equal mine, if both were opened.' [618]

We all have our fair share of problems, challenges, grief, loss, trauma, and troubles in this broken world. Sometimes the sheer agony and psychological distress of our suffering is overwhelming. However, we must always take comfort in the knowledge, that we are not alone in our pain and suffering. Indeed, the existential reality of pain and suffering is a reality that is a common attribute to all of humanity. In the final analysis, humans shall experience differences in the degrees and types of suffering during their lifetime. However, in substance, our suffering is all too similar. The universality of human suffering is impossible to deny.

---

617 Shakespeare, William. (1609). *Pericles Prince of Tyre.* Act 4, Scene 1.
618 Shakespeare, William. (1609). *Pericles Prince of Tyre.* Act 5, Scene 1.

'Your present kindness makes my past miseries sports.'[619]

A friendly smile. A thoughtful gesture of thanks. Sincere speech containing considerate words. Lending a non-judgemental ear. Giving a meal and beverage to a person in dire need. A kind act of love. These actions bring much cheer and comfort to a distressed heart or a troubled mind. Good deeds of kindness shall momentarily make us forget the countless troubles that we confront in this world. More importantly, the presence of goodness reminds us, that there is much to live for in this world. The presence of goodness brings hope to humanity. It is hope, that we can make this world a better place for all people, that makes life worth living.

---

619 Shakespeare, William. (1609). *Pericles Prince of Tyre.* Act 5, Scene 3.

Chapter 27

RICHARD II

'O, but they say the tongues of dying men enforce attention like deep harmony. When words are scarce, they are seldom spent in vain. For they breathe truth, that breathe their words in pain.'

SHAKESPEARE

This historical play narrates the life and death of His Majesty King Richard II. The story commences in King Richard's Royal Court, where Henry Bolingbroke vehemently accuses Thomas Mowbray (the Duke of Norfolk) of defrauding the Crown of its financial capital, and also plotting the death of his uncle, the Duke of Gloucester. In response, Thomas protests his innocence in the presence of King Richard II. Furthermore, Thomas calls into question the character and integrity of Henry.

Henry Bolingbroke and Thomas Mowbray prepare for a duel to settle their dispute. However, King Richard II intervenes and stops the two gentlemen from resorting to armed conflict. King Richard II exiles Henry for a period of ten years, which is subsequently reduced to six years. On the other hand, Thomas is exiled for the remainder of his natural life. Neither party is satisfied with the judgement of King Richard II. However, both Henry and Thomas accept the King's Royal Decree.

Meanwhile, John of Gaunt (the Duke of Lancaster), who has a fractured relationship with King Richard II, confronts his death. Upon John's death, King Richard II seizes John's private property, and thereby, denies Henry Bolingbroke his legitimate inheritance. Thereafter, King Richard II sets course for Ireland. The departure of King Richard II sets the scene for Henry Bolingbroke's return to England. This development presents Henry with the opportune time to plot a rebellion against King Richard II's rule.

Henry Bolingbroke convinces his uncle York, that his return to England is not aimed at initiating a rebellion against the English Crown. Henry seeks to reclaim his rightful inheritance and return to his native English homeland. Following the *Irish War*, King Richard II returns to England. King Richard II learns that the Welsh troops have betrayed him. Not to mention, York has sided with Henry. Now the common folk of England are turning against King Richard II's rule as Sovereign.

The scene is ready for diplomacy. King Richard II and Henry Bolingbroke enter into formal negotiations on how to resolve their protracted quarrel. Henry offers to surrender his armaments in exchange for King Richard II reversing the Decree on his banishment from England, and restoring his inheritance. In an interesting turn of events, King Richard II's cousin, the Duke of Aumerle has been accused of murdering the Duke of Gloucester. As a result, Henry arrests the suspected parties who were involved in the murder of the Duke of Gloucester. Thereafter, King Richard II abdicates the English Throne. This presents the momentous opportunity for Henry Bolingbroke to announce his coronation as His Majesty King Henry IV.

King Henry IV is not safe as the newly established Sovereign of England. There is a plot against the newly enthroned King's life. While King Henry IV has imprisoned Richard II in Pontefract Castle, some of the Nobles, loyal to the cause of Richard II, seek to restore him to the English Throne. The Nobles are undone in their illegitimate cause, as York discloses this plot to King Henry

IV. While York's son, Aumerle, was involved in the plot to restore Richard II to the English Throne, Aumerle confesses before King Henry IV, and the King pardons him for this offence.

King Henry IV is now more conscious of the threats against his position as Sovereign of England. King Henry IV instructs Exton to eradicate 'all threats' against his rule as the Sovereign of England. Exton understands this communication to implicitly imply the murder of Richard II. Without delay, Exton has performed the evil deed of murdering Richard II. Upon bringing Richard II's deceased body to London, King Henry IV accuses Exton of a 'misunderstanding' of his true intentions. This play concludes with King Henry IV banishing Exton from England, ordering a funeral for the late Richard II, and King Henry IV undertaking a pilgrimage to the Holy Land (Jerusalem), to repent for his sins.

'I take it up, and by the sword, I swear which gently laid my Knighthood on my shoulder, I'll answer thee in any fair degree, or chivalrous design of knightly trial. And when I mount, alive may I not light if I be traitor or unjustly fight!' [620]

We must live up to our motto, creed, commitment, duty, and obligation. If we are sworn to our rank or position in public office, or to our sovereign nation's armed forces, then it is our duty to remain loyal and true to our affirmations. Our speech and conduct shall determine our reputation and character. We must not let the temptation or desire, for pecuniary gain or profit, obstruct the discharge of our oath. For when we are no more on this Earth, the countless pages of history shall remember our name, and the reputation attributed to it.

---

620 Shakespeare, William. (1597). *Richard II*. Act 1, Scene 1.

'In haste whereof, most heartily I pray Your Highness to assign our trial day. Wrath-kindled gentlemen, be ruled by me. Let's purge this choler without letting blood. This we prescribe, though no Physician. Deep malice makes too deep incision. Forget, forgive, conclude, and be agreed. Our Doctors say, this is no month to bleed.' [621]

To forgive and demonstrate mercy is a most noble act that demonstrates true courage and valour. We must strive to make peace, where the opportunities seem plentiful to declare war. We cannot always obtain everything that we truly desire. The delicate process of negotiation shall inevitably consist of some 'give' and 'take'. However, if all parties are genuinely interested in the creation of a durable peace, then compromises and concessions are necessary. This negotiation strategy shall create the conditions for an equitable peace.

'My Dear, Dear Lord, the purest treasure mortal times afford is spotless reputation. That away, men are but gilded loam or painted clay.' [622]

Our reputation is all that we truly have in our possession. A person's reputation is their most prized possession. A person's reputation is timeless. It shall outlast the person's finite lifetime. Furthermore, beyond reputation, consider the following question: What is a person? Nothing more than the physical, biological, chemical, electrical, mechanical, and physiological construct of the human body. Combined with the intelligence of the human brain, the power of emotions, the expression of genetics, and the accumulation of lived experience. For the secrets of the Soul, are beyond empirical examination. Spirituality is an inner secret, one that can only be discovered by the Self.

---

621 Shakespeare, William. (1597). *Richard II*. Act 1, Scene 1.
622 Shakespeare, William. (1597). *Richard II*. Act 1, Scene 1.

'Mine honour is my life; both grow in one. Take honour from me, and my life is done. Then, dear my liege, mine honour let my try. In that I live, and for that will I die.' [623]

In the Ancient World, a person lived and died by honour. For honour came to determine a person's self-worth, reputation, standing in society, credibility, integrity, and character. Without the presence of honour, life was not worth living. While we prize honour less rigorously in the Modern World, an honourable person keeps their word to other people, is reliable, and dependable. Most importantly, an honourable person understands the legality and morality of functioning as a respectable citizen in modern society.

'Grief boundeth where it falls, not with the empty hollowness, but weight. I take my leave before I have begun, for sorrow ends not when it seemeth done.' [624]

Grief makes the heart heavy. Psychologically speaking, grief burdens us with many unpleasant thoughts. The presence of grief can become a major impediment to our progress. Grief has the potential to damage a person's self-esteem or confidence. Therefore, it is best that a person acknowledges the grief they are experiencing, and subsequently, addresses it. We must be conscious of the remote possibility, that our sorrow can endure, far beyond the events that caused it to occur.

'Thy grief is but thy absence for a time. Joy absent, grief is present for that time. What is six winters? They are quickly gone. To men in joy, but grief makes one hour ten.' [625]

All of life oscillates between grief and joy. While time is a constant factor in life, we experience time subjectively. When we are happy

623 Shakespeare, William. (1597). *Richard II.* Act 1, Scene 1.
624 Shakespeare, William. (1597). *Richard II.* Act 1, Scene 2.
625 Shakespeare, William. (1597). *Richard II.* Act 1, Scene 3.

and overfilled with joy, the hours quickly pass us by. To the contrary, when we are sad and full of grief, the hours seem like days, if not months. In all cases, we must exercise restraint. We must not allow our emotions to overwhelm us. Life is an experience of all sorts of emotions, the positive and the negative. It is irrational to expect that life will always consist of memorable moments and ecstatic experiences. This is simply not the case.

'Teach thy necessity to reason thus. There is no virtue like necessity.' [626]

Unfortunately, we must suffer the hardships and privations that the time of necessity presents us with. It can be incredibly difficult to demonstrate the requisite patience that is required during our pain and suffering. However, at times, we have no choice, but to acquiesce to the dismal reality that is before us. As we learn to endure the time of necessity in relation to the difficult events or challenging circumstances that we confront, we also experience personal growth and moral development through our countless struggles.

'O, but they say the tongues of dying men enforce attention like deep harmony. When words are scarce, they are seldom spent in vain. For they breathe truth, that breathe their words in pain.' [627]

When a person is about to confront their death, energy and time are most limited. Therefore, such a person, who is in their last moments of life, is likely to expend their remaining time and energy carefully. In doing so, the person nearest to death is more likely than not to speak words of value and importance. Beyond death, even when we are alive and well, any precious commodity that is scarce in quantity, we must utilise with utmost care and concern.

---

626 Shakespeare, William. (1597). *Richard II*. Act 1, Scene 3.
627 Shakespeare, William. (1597). *Richard II*. Act 2, Scene 1.

*'He that not more must say is listened more. Than they whom
youth and ease have taught to glose.'* [628]

Shakespeare's enigma here is that we provision greater attention
to a person who speaks less. Whereas, a person who is talkative,
we listen to, with less attention. While both the talkative and quiet
person may equally have important information or knowledge to
share, the distinction herein is one of human nature. A person who
has spoken less, we have less speech to listen to, and therefore, we
are more likely than not, to spend some time reflecting on their
words and discourse. On the other hand, an individual who has
much to speak, we are more likely than not, to lose attention and
interest, with the increasing passage of time.

*'Pardon me, if you please. If not, I, pleased not to be pardoned,
am content withal.'* [629]

It is truly powerful when we can assert that we are content with
our lot in life. We can secure contentment, regardless of the
circumstances that befall upon us. The twists and turns of fate. The
many privations that we confront in everyday life. It is essential to
remember, that contentment is a state of satisfaction, that is not
contingent on how much, or how little we have accomplished,
accumulated, or attained in life. Contentment is being at peace with
'who' we are. Being satisfied with 'what' we have in life.

*'Farewell. If heart's presages be not vain. We three here part,
that never shall meet again.'* [630]

Every person is on their unique journey in life. At times, select
people will cross paths with us. Some people, we shall meet and
connect with, and we will form a long-lasting relationship with

---

628 Shakespeare, William. (1597). *Richard II*. Act 2, Scene 1.
629 Shakespeare, William. (1597). *Richard II*. Act 2, Scene 1.
630 Shakespeare, William. (1597). *Richard II*. Act 2, Scene 2.

them. In contrast, other people, may only cross our path and enter our life for a short period of time. In any case, at some point or another, we must all part ways. For we are all destined to depart this Earth.

'And hope to joy is little less in joy. Than hope enjoyed.'[631]

God, hope, love, faith, work, and family. These are all central pillars of a meaningful and purpose-filled life. At times, circumstances can be difficult, and we feel like our hope in life is being tested. However, we must keep our privations in perspective. They are temporary. Thus, we shall transcend them. It may not always be the case that our hope is realised. However, we must remember, that God has given us grace, that is sufficient for our journey.

'Things past redress, are now with me past care.'[632]

Shakespeare demonstrates remarkable wisdom in this considerably concise statement. We must not worry about things that are in the past. For we have no power to change the past in the present time. Nor in the foreseeable future. What is past redress, meaning what is past change or remedy, is now a waste of our precious present time to contemplate, or afford serious attention. Thus, we must not attend our concern with affairs or events that we cannot change. This manner of thought allows us to move forward. We must commit our time, energy, resources, and knowledge to more productive endeavours.

---

631 Shakespeare, William. (1597). *Richard II*. Act 2, Scene 3.
632 Shakespeare, William. (1597). *Richard II*. Act 2, Scene 3.

'This and much more, much more than twice all this, condemns you to the death. See them delivered over to execution and the hand of death. More welcome is the stroke of death to me than Bolingbroke to England! Lords, farewell! My comfort is that Heaven will take our souls, and plague injustice with the pains of Hell!' [633]

The exercise of absolute power is corruptible and intertwined with injustice. In politics, the sovereign is more likely than not to have several enemies. Thus, execution is often the most convenient and certain method to purge one's enemies. Alternative options to contend with one's enemies, include house arrest, imprisonment, banishment, forced labour camps, or exile to a foreign country. There is much exercise of arbitrary power in politics. As a consequence, injustice is the inevitable outcome of all false dealing.

'The worst is death, and death will have his day.' [634]

The worst tragedy that can befall us is to confront our death. For death serves to ensure that we do not have another chance. Another opportunity. Another moment to make a positive impact. To regain lost territory. To take action. To make this world a better place. Nor to complete the things, that matter most to us. Regardless of our age, health, gender, ethnicity, sex, colour, race, income, private property, education, circumstances, vocation, and fortune, we will all meet our destined date with death. The occurrence of our death is not a matter of if, it is only a matter of when. Therefore, our death is only a matter of time. Peace be with you.

---

633 Shakespeare, William. (1597). *Richard II*. Act 3, Scene 1.
634 Shakespeare, William. (1597). *Richard II*. Act 3, Scene 2.

'Cover your heads, and mock not flesh and blood with solemn reverence. Throw away respect, tradition, form, and ceremonious duty, for you have but mistook me all this while. I live with bread like you, feel want, taste grief, need friends. Subjected thus, how can you say to me, I am a King?' [635]

We are all human. No matter our social status, rank, influence, ability, income, gender, sex, colour, race, ethnicity, wealth, age, education, private property, country of origin, vocation, or any other discriminatory factor, we are all equal members of the human civilisation. Even Kings and Queens must confront death. Even Kings and Queens are subject to sadness, happiness, joy, grief, loss, anger, and many more emotions. Even Kings and Queens have physiological needs pertaining to the human body. In the final analysis, no person is above the human condition.

'My Lord, wise men never sit and wail their woes, but presently prevent the ways to wail. To fear the foe, since fear oppresseth strength, gives in your weakness, strength unto your foe, and so your follies fight against yourself.' [636]

What is past and lost is no more. Thus, there is little purpose in grieving over what cannot be changed. The exercise of rationality and intelligence resides in transcending one's losses. Wisdom resides in not letting one's losses consume a person's thoughts. Often times, we do not consciously realise that we become our greatest enemy. This reality arises due to our self-limiting beliefs about what we can accomplish or achieve in our lifetime. We must not give into fear, confusion, anger, uncertainty, or doubt. Rather, we shall create unity in our positive thoughts. We shall proceed forward, to boldly and resolutely conquer the aims and objectives that are before us.

---

635 Shakespeare, William. (1597). *Richard II.* Act 3, Scene 2.
636 Shakespeare, William. (1597). *Richard II.* Act 3, Scene 2.

'Fear and be slain. No worse can come to fight, and fight and die is death destroying death. Where fearing dying pays death servile breath.' [637]

Sooner or later, we shall all confront our existential demise. Death can come in a multitude of forms. However, we must resolve our hearts and minds to confront death with courage in adversity. We must not fear the inevitable occurrence of death. Rather, we must be firm in our conviction. That we can confront death with boldness and confidence. A person who does not fear death, has taken away the power of the Devil to torment their life.

'Let's fight with gentle words. Till time lend friends, and friends their helpful swords.' [638]

At times, we shall find ourselves standing in dire need of assistance and the provision of aid. We must acknowledge the real challenges that circumstance, fortune, or necessity present before us. We must act accordingly. It is essential that we do not act out of haste. However, we must bide our time. Until a more opportune moment arrives. When we are able to fulfil our important mission, with success and victory.

'In God's Name, let it go. I'll give my jewels for a set of beads ... my gorgeous palace for a hermitage ... my gay apparel for an almsman's gown ... my figured goblets for a dish of wood ... my sceptre for a palmer's walking-staff ... my subjects for a pair of carved Saints, and my large Kingdom for a little grave. A little, little grave. An obscure grave.' [639]

One day, we shall all depart this world. What we crave most is peace, security, justice, love, and harmony. Desire prohibits the

---

637 Shakespeare, William. (1597). *Richard II.* Act 3, Scene 2.
638 Shakespeare, William. (1597). *Richard II.* Act 3, Scene 3.
639 Shakespeare, William. (1597). *Richard II.* Act 3, Scene 3.

heart's content. The will remains unsatisfied with our state of being in this world. That person who can relinquish this world. That is to say, not remain beholden to the things of this world. The desires. The wants. The hopes. The fame. The profit. The private property. Also, the numerous worldly objects of high esteem and great value. Such a person can secure liberation from bondage.

'Up, cousin, up. Your heart is up, I know, thus high, at least, although your knee be low.' [640]

We must not always judge a person by their outward demeanour. A person may mislead us, by deceptive actions and behaviour. While in their heart, there may be lust, greed, envy, pride, jealousy, hate, sloth, and anger. It is within our capacity to utilise our judgement appropriately, to determine a person's true intentions and motives. It takes considerable time, effort, thought, observation, and social interaction, to ascertain the true measure of a person.

'They well deserve to have. That know the strongest and surest way to get.' [641]

It is upon us to utilise our knowledge, skills, abilities, judgement, logic, reason, experience, and resources, to create our desired reality on Earth. Every person shall encounter obstacles, challenges, difficulties, and issues along their life journey. Resistance is inevitable. However, it is the person who overcomes the resistance, that strives, and surpasses resistance, with unwavering resolve, such an individual is likely to fulfil their grand ambition. To attain their noble undertaking with total success.

---

640 Shakespeare, William. (1597). *Richard II*. Act 3, Scene 3.
641 Shakespeare, William. (1597). *Richard II*. Act 3, Scene 3.

'Tears show their loves, but want their remedies.' [642]

The person or object that we shed tears for, is what we value most in life. This might be a most meaningful relationship, or a prized possession to us. When we attach or assign a significant value to who or what we love, our heart becomes heavy for their pain, suffering, or loss. On the other hand, what we desire, we seek at all costs. Not to mention, our countless worldly wants are only satisfied by attaining what our heart desires.

'Here, cousin, seize the Crown. Here, cousin. On this side, my hand, and on that side, thine. Now is this Golden Crown like a deep well that owes two buckets, filling one another. The emptier, ever dancing in the air. The other, down, unseen, and full of water. That bucket down and full of tears am I, drinking my griefs, whilst you mount up on high. I thought you had been willing to resign. My Crown I am, but still my griefs are mine. You may my glories and my State depose, but not my griefs. Still am I King of those. Part of your cares you give me with your Crown. Your cares set up, do not pluck my cares down. My care is loss of care, by old care done. Your care is gain of care, by new care won. The cares I give I have, though, given away, they tend the Crown, yet still with me they stay.' [643]

We can surrender our most invaluable worldly possessions. However, our feelings, sensations, thoughts, ideas, values, beliefs, and emotions are our own. The many treasures of this world are our temporary possessions. We can lose all of them at a moment's notice. In contrast, a person's grief, cares, worries, and thoughts are their own possessions for a lifetime. We can share our personal concerns with other people, however, for someone to truly and wholly understand them is another matter altogether. In the final

---

642 Shakespeare, William. (1597). *Richard II.* Act 3, Scene 3.
643 Shakespeare, William. (1597). *Richard II.* Act 4, Scene 1.

analysis, the one and only Timeless Treasure is God. We can always rely and depend upon God for counsel, care, and compassion.

> *'My grief lies all within. And these external manners of lament*
> *are merely shadows to the unseen grief … that swells with silence*
> *in the tortured soul. There lies the substance.'* [644]

People can bury their grief deep within themselves. Negative memories and traumatic experiences can remain with us for a lifetime. This cumbersome psychological burden can consume a person's life. The psychology of a person impacts every part of their well-being, including physiology, cell physiology, immunobiology, microbiology, histology, molecular biology, kinesiology, and neurology. In the grand scheme of things, communication, counsel, consolation, and confession are the most appropriate remedies for a heavy heart and restless soul. It is not only our physical body, but also our spirit, which requires nourishment.

> *'The love of wicked men converts to fear, That fear to hate, and*
> *hate turns one or both. To worthy danger and deserved death.'* [645]

We must exercise care and discretion in our personal relationships and professional associations. If we engage and relate with people who are of questionable character, poor integrity, and dishonourable in their dealings, then such a social engagement will never flourish into a constructive relationship. We must keep the following principle in our mind: What we sow, sets the foundation, for what we shall reap.

---

644 Shakespeare, William. (1597). *Richard II*. Act 4, Scene 1.
645 Shakespeare, William. (1597). *Richard II*. Act 5, Scene 1.

'So shall my virtue be his vice's bawd! And he shall spend mine honour with his shame, as thriftless Sons their scraping Fathers' gold. Mine honour lives when his dishonour dies, or my shamed life in his dishonour lies. Thou killest me in his life, giving him breath. The traitor lives. The true man's put to death.' [646]

We must exercise prudence and rational judgement in our thinking. It is a matter of convenience to become angry and assign blame to another party. However, no person on Earth is without fault, imperfection, or defect. Therefore, rather than proposing a mutually exclusive outcome, we must seek common ground to preserve the peace. After all, there is no higher aspirational cause than social justice for all the people on Earth.

'But whatever I be, nor I, nor any man that but man is ... with nothing shall be pleased. Till he be eased with being nothing.' [647]

We must seek contentment with who we are, without attachment to material possessions, private property, wealth, education, income, spouse, family, children, profit, capital gains, interest, pecuniary gain, or personal assets. A person who can accept and be content with just themselves, shall find a genuine sense of satisfaction with their life. On the other hand, a person who gains all the pleasures, desires, and prized objects of this world, is never assured equanimity of mind, nor a peaceful life.

---

646 Shakespeare, William. (1597). *Richard II*. Act 5, Scene 3.
647 Shakespeare, William. (1597). *Richard II*. Act 5, Scene 5.

'So proud that Bolingbroke was on his back! That jade hath eat bread from my Royal hand. This hand hath made him proud with clapping him. Would he not stumble? Would he not fall down, since pride must have a fall and break the neck of that proud man that did usurp his back?' [648]

Pride must eventually meet its downfall. A person can marvel at their victories. Revel in their accomplishments. Not to mention, one can boast about their remarkable gains. However, everything gained in this world is subject to loss and destruction. All things in and of this world are temporary. It is best to be content with what one has achieved. It is best to be humble before God's goodness, favour, grace, and mercy. Indeed, without God's Grace, we are not able to achieve even a tenth of what we have accomplished.

---

648 Shakespeare, William. (1597). *Richard II.* Act 5, Scene 5.

RICHARD III

Shakespeare's *Richard III* is a play is about the protracted struggle for absolute power. Richard of Gloucester, the brother of His Majesty King Edward IV, is resolved on securing the English Crown for himself. Richard expands his power and influence through a number of avenues, most notably by courting Lady Anne Neville. Even though Anne is aware that Richard murdered her first husband, she agrees to the marriage proposal. Subsequently, Lady Anne becomes the Duchess of Gloucester. Richard creates the circumstances for the imprisonment of his elder brother, Clarence. While Clarence is confined to the Tower of London, Richard plots and plans for his assassination.

The progression of this play witnesses King Edward IV subject to ill health. As a result, Richard begins to govern in the King's name. In this unsuspecting endeavour, Richard is counselled by the Duke of Buckingham and Lord Hastings. Now Richard engages in the ancient art of *realpolitik*. Richard begins to weaken and destroy his enemies, who present a threat, between him and the English Throne. First, Richard confines his nephews, the Prince of Wales, and his brother, George, the Duke of Clarence, to the Tower of London. Second, Richard has Lord Chamberlain and Lord Hastings executed for a plot to murder him. Third, Richard captures and executes Lord Buckingham.

Richard becomes tyrannical in his exercise of power. Now Richard demands the total security of absolute power. This most unreasonable desire for certainty drives Richard towards insanity. Now Richard is intent on courting the noblewoman Elizabeth of York, Edward IV's daughter. Richard is seeking Elizabeth's hand in marriage, in order to secure his reign as King of England. To further his political cause, Richard has his current wife, Lady Anne Neville murdered.

Richard III's meteoric rise to power, a rise built on assassinations, imprisonments, and executions, is now beginning to disintegrate. Richard's despotic rule in England cannot endure. Thus, plans are in motion, to end Richard's despotic regime. Henry Tudor, the Earl of Richmond, actively recruits an army in France to overthrow Richard III. Henry and Richard's armed forces meet at Bosworth in Leicestershire. On the eve of military battle, several ghosts appear in harrowing visions to Richard III. The ghosts are the deceased victims of Richard's merciless murders. The ghosts curse Richard III and wish him an ill-fated outcome in the military battle. On the other hand, the same ghosts bless the Earl of Richmond for the upcoming military campaign.

As the Sun rises, and the day of fighting dawns upon the two opposing sides, Richard III persuasively rallies his armed forces to military battle. Despite the formidable odds, Richard III demonstrates remarkable courage, absolute bravery, and perfect discipline in battle. At the close of play, the Earl of Richmond kills Richard III at Bosworth Field. Thereafter, the Earl of Richmond is proclaimed King Henry VII of England. King Henry VII plans to wed Elizabeth of York. As a consequence, through the bonds of marriage, unite the House of Lancaster and the House of York. This Royal Marriage ushers in a new period of peace, prosperity, and power for the Kingdom of England.

'Foul Devil, for God's Sake, hence and trouble us not. For thou hast made the happy Earth thy Hell, filled it with cursing cries and deep exclaims.' [649]

We must be vigilant against the endless temptations and countless desires that the Devil places along our path. We will be tempted during our time on Earth. The Flesh and the Spirit are in a battle for supremacy. With each competing for the control of our destiny. Thus, we must pray and make our earnest petitions to God for God's mercy, goodness, favour, and grace. It is not through our power, reason, free will, agency, choice, judgement, or intellect that we conquer evil in this world. However, it is through God's Goodness towards us.

'Your beauty was the cause of that effect. Your beauty that did haunt me in my sleep. To undertake the death of all the world, So I might live one hour in your sweet bosom.' [650]

A gentlewoman's captivating beauty can lead a gentleman to perform irrational, illogical, and ill-conceived actions. Love is a blind and emotive force. Love pulls the heart strings, far beyond the shallow capacity of reason. It is fascinating, as much as it is interesting, to witness the immeasurable length that a gentleman is prepared to journey. In order to secure a tender-hearted, trivial, and transient moment of a gentlewoman's love and affection.

---

649 Shakespeare, William. (1597). *Richard III*. Act 1, Scene 2.
650 Shakespeare, William. (1597). *Richard III*. Act 1, Scene 2.

'But, now thy beauty is proposed my fee. My proud heart sues, and prompts my tongue to speak. Teach not thy lip such scorn; for it was made for kissing, Lady, not for such contempt. If thy revengeful heart cannot forgive, Lo here I lend thee this sharp-pointed sword; Which if thou please to hide in this true breast, And lay the soul forth that adoreth thee, I lay it naked to the deadly stroke, And humbly beg the death upon my knee.' [651]

The beauty and love of this world leads us into countless temptations. We intend to secure what we most desire in this world. When we cannot live without what we desire, we become enslaved to that very thing. For it takes away our happiness, liberty, conscience, reasoning, freedom of choice, agency, logical thinking, and rationality. In the end, we become obliged, to what we cannot secure. Indeed, when we reach such an inferior position, then life itself becomes unbearable.

'I had rather be a country servant-maid than a Great Queen with this condition, to be so baited, scorned, and stormed at small joy have I in being England's Queen.' [652]

No matter the superior or inferior position that we occupy in modern society, the underlying reality is that contentment is considerably difficult to obtain in this world. Joy and happiness are never sourced from external events, objects, or accomplishments, such as the ownership of private property, exorbitant private wealth, high social rank, income, education, fame, influence, power, prestige, formal learning, or superior social class. In fact, quite the opposite is true. Joy and happiness are found within us. These positive emotions are reflective of our inner state of being. A superior metaphysical reality is founded upon a state of being, that is not dependent or contingent upon our external environment.

---

651 Shakespeare, William. (1597). *Richard III*. Act 1, Scene 2.
652 Shakespeare, William. (1597). *Richard III*. Act 1, Scene 3.

'God pardon them that are the cause thereof! A virtuous and a Christian-like conclusion. To pray for them that have done scathe to us!' [653]

To pray for those that have done us wrong is indicative of true mercy and forgiveness in action. Such an action is only possible through God's Grace. It is beyond the selfish and egocentric nature of the Flesh to transcend sin, greed, desire, and corruptness. It is the nature of the Flesh to seek revenge and retribution in this world. On the other hand, the Spirit desires to rise above the worldly and petty quarrels of this world. The Spirit seeks union with God. Individuals who act in accordance with the Spirit, shall find lasting peace in this troubled world.

'Princes have but their titles for their glories. An outward honour for an inward toil, and for unfelt imaginations, they often feel a world of restless cares, so that between their titles and low name there's nothing differs, but the outward fame.' [654]

This world is all pomp, fanfare, desire, and illustrious ceremony. This world is driven forward by the human's limitless pursuit of copulation, fame, personal wealth, pecuniary gain, power, influence, income, profit, and private property. A high-ranking title or royal position never establishes a person's character, conscience, principles, or integrity. Rather, status, fame, and power test the traits and qualities of a person.

What we purport to be to the outside world is not a true representation of our inner state of being. Furthermore, personal status, prestigious titles, powerful positions, well-remunerated professions, financial capital, private property, and many more worldly things, are pursuits of the ego. The ego knows no ends in its desire to seek. The ego is without limit or restraint. The ego

---

653 Shakespeare, William. (1597). *Richard III*. Act 1, Scene 3.
654 Shakespeare, William. (1597). *Richard III*. Act 1, Scene 4.

acts irrationally out of threat, fear, and doubt, to prove its fictitious sense of existence and importance in this world. In reality, the ego's unfounded and ignorant actions only conceal the spiritual poverty of the soul, which desires union with God.

> *'Why, he shall never wake until the Great Judgement Day. Why then he'll say we stabbed him sleeping. The urging of that word judgement hath bred a kind of remorse in me. What, art thou afraid? Not to kill him, having a warrant; but to be damned for killing him, from the which no warrant can defend me.'* [655]

We are all personally responsible for our actions during our time on Earth. Our duty shall be to King and Country; however, we are responsible for our soul. Actions have consequences. Thus, we must carefully consider how to act in this world. For when our time on Earth has come to its conclusion, and we leave this world behind, we shall take an account of our actions and character with us. In the end, we shall stand before the Highest Court of God, to be held accountable for our conduct. Yes, we do possess free will. However, with the right to free moral choice, comes the undeniable personal responsibility for its consequences.

> *'Edward, My Lord, thy Son, our King, is dead. Why grow the branches when the root is gone? Why wither not the leaves that want their sap? If you will live, lament; if die, be brief.'* [656]

Loss is painful and difficult to come to terms with. However, we must all depart this world one day. Regardless, if one is a wealthy Prince, or a destitute beggar, death does not discriminate against any person. While loss is inevitable in this broken world, we have a free moral choice to preserve faith, love, and hope. These three

---

655 Shakespeare, William. (1597). *Richard III*. Act 1, Scene 4.
656 Shakespeare, William. (1597). *Richard III*. Act 2, Scene 2.

timeless treasures, we must never surrender. For the fullness of our life depends upon them. We must not let fortune, circumstance, necessity, or chance create a deviation in our God-given destiny.

> *'What stay had I but Edward? And he's gone. What stay had we but Clarence? And he's gone. What stay had I but they? And they are gone. Was never Widow had so dear a loss. Were never Orphans had so dear a loss. Was never Mother had so dear a loss. Alas ... I am the Mother of these griefs! Their woes are parcelled, mine is general.'* [657]

This is a broken world. Therefore, we must come to terms with the heartache, pain, suffering, grief, and sorrow that we experience on Earth. Everything that we have in this world, we must relinquish at some point in time. No person is without grief in this world. Each person has their fair share of challenges and difficulties to confront. We can only position our security in God. For God's Word is where we shall place our unconditional trust.

> *'Comfort, Dear Mother, God is much displeased. That you take with unthankfulness His doing. In common worldly things it is called ungrateful. With dull unwillingness to repay a debt. Which with a bounteous hand was kindly lent; much more to be thus opposite with Heaven, for it requires the Royal debt it lent you.'* [658]

We must be content that all of Creation is subject to God's Sovereign Will. At times, we may not understand why certain undesirable situations, traumatic events, personal crises, or terrible tragedies have befallen upon us. However, rest assured, everything is subject to God's Supreme Will. Therefore, we must act with the remembrance of God in our hearts. We must seek to advance God's Kingdom at all costs.

---

657 Shakespeare, William. (1597). *Richard III*. Act 2, Scene 2.
658 Shakespeare, William. (1597). *Richard III*. Act 2, Scene 2.

If we seek our happiness, pleasure, and the imposition of our will upon the world, we shall not only act in vain, but also be frustrated with our inability to create the world in our image. Within the *Holy Bible*, in the *Gospel of Luke*, Chapter 22, Verse 42, we ascertain the true words of wisdom of the *Messiah*, 'Father, if You are willing, take this cup from me; yet not my will, but Yours be done.'

'Drown desperate sorrow in dead Edward's grave, and plant your joys in living Edward's Throne. Sister, have comfort. All of us have cause. To wail the dimming of our shining star. But none can help our harms by wailing them.' [659]

All of human life oscillates between joy and grief. Between sadness and happiness. Earth is not Heaven. Thus, we shall confront losses, grief, tragedy, and crises in this broken world. Most importantly, we all have cause for comfort in God's Word. We must remember that rarely, if ever at all, does sorrow or anger, achieve anything productive. We shall strive forward, seek to transcend our heartache, in the hope that the future is brighter and better. In the final analysis, all of life is a matter of perspective. For example, consider the well-known phrase, 'The optimist perceives the glass as half-full.' Whereas, 'The pessimist perceives the glass as half-empty.' Both empirical observations are correct. However, the former observation is superior. For it accurately ascertains the value of what we already have. In addition to how much more we can secure.

---

659 Shakespeare, William. (1597). *Richard III*. Act 2, Scene 2.

'I fear, I fear it will prove a giddy world. Doth the news hold of Good King Edward's death? Ay, Sir, it is too true. God help the while! Then, Masters, look to see a troublous world. No, no; by God's Good Grace, his Son shall reign. Woe to that land that's governed by a child. In him there is a hope of Government. Which, in his nonage, Council under him, and, in his full and ripened years, himself, no doubt, shall then, and till then, govern well.' [660]

There is much uncertainty in this world. We must accept this undeniable fact and function within the parameters of conventional reality. Holding on to political power is uncertain. Life is uncertain. Personal wealth is uncertain. Even our very own health is uncertain. All the leadership succession planning in the world can never bring about certainty in government. In all cases, a learned and honourable Sovereign, who has the fear of God in their heart, is most fit to rule a nation-state. Such a righteous leader must secure the hearts and minds of the common people. Indeed, a charismatic leader, that wins over the ordinary people, has secured the confidence and mandate to govern the people.

'Come, come, we fear the worst. All will be well. When clouds are seen, wise men put on their cloaks. When great leaves fall, then winter is at hand; When the Sun sets, who doth not look for night? Untimely storms makes men expect a dearth. All may be well; but if God sort it so, it is more than we deserve or I expect. Truly, the hearts of men are full of fear. You cannot reason almost with a man that looks not heavily and full of dread.' [661]

In most cases, the human imagination constructs worst-case scenarios of unforeseen events and future expectations. We must instruct the mind to employ the faculties of reason, logic, and good

---

660 Shakespeare, William. (1597). *Richard III*. Act 2, Scene 3.
661 Shakespeare, William. (1597). *Richard III*. Act 2, Scene 3.

judgement more often in our endeavours. A wise person takes notice of their surrounding environment, and acts accordingly.

In all things, we must place our high hope and total trust in God. God is the only True Redeemer and Saviour of humanity. From infancy, humans are psychologically conditioned to avoid the presence of fear-inducing events and experiences. However, too many people become full of fear and doubt. Unfortunately, this negative cycle of emotions obstruct individuals from performing constructive actions and creating a better life for themselves. Fear obstructs a person's rational thought. Fear also inhibits a person's rational judgement. Last but not least, fear obstructs an individual's use of logic in resolving life's many surmountable challenges.

'Ay me! I see the ruin of my House. The tiger now hath seized the gentle hind. Insulting tyranny begins to jut upon the innocent and aweless Throne. Welcome, destruction, blood, and massacre! I see, as in a map, the end of all.' [662]

We have no assurance of security and certainty in this world. Nature is indifferent to the suffering of any individual member of the human species. Nature is only concerned with the survival of the human species on Earth. The strong members of the human species shall dominate the weaker members of the human species.

The reality of this world is accurately discerned by the Athenian historian and general, Thucydides, in his grand work, *History of the Peloponnesian War*, 'The strong do what they can, and the weak suffer what they must.' Justice is not always the ruling instrument which prevails in the civilised world. On the other hand, military power, the use of force, political clout, and economic might. These factors, they all collectively function to determine the contemporary world order.

---

662 Shakespeare, William. (1597). *Richard III*. Act 2, Scene 4.

'The benefit thereof is always granted to those whose dealings have deserved the place, and those who have the wit to claim the place.' [663]

Only in part, do our social interactions with other learned and honourable constituents in the Modern World determine our place, reputation, influence, power, and standing in civilised society. We may 'deserve' our place through many means, such as the privilege of noble birth, high parentage, private wealth, inheritance, intelligence, beauty, strength, courage, or natural ability. However, in all cases, what is attained can be lost. Unless we demonstrate the proper judgement, exercise of rationality, and the use of reason to tactfully secure, and subsequently utilise, what rightfully belongs to us.

'But say, My Lord, it were not registered, methinks the truth should live from age to age. As it were retailed to all prosperity, even to the general all-ending day.' [664]

The Truth was true in the beginning, before the world came into existence. The Truth remains true even in the midst of the falsehood of this broken world. The Truth shall endure long after this material world has ceased to exist. The Truth is eternal and beyond this world. The existence and function of the Truth is not contingent, nor is it dependent upon, this impermanent world. To know the Truth is to find peace in this world. Yet, to practice the Truth is to transcend this world.

---

663 Shakespeare, William. (1597). *Richard III*. Act 3, Scene 1.
664 Shakespeare, William. (1597). *Richard III*. Act 3, Scene 1.

'O momentary grace of mortal man. Which we more hunt for than the Grace of God! Who builds his hope in air of your good looks. Lives like a drunken Sailor on a mast; Ready, with every nod, to tumble down into the fatal bowels of the deep.' [665]

We must never position our most sacred trust in God into the hands of any other person. The Source of all Grace is God. Individuals are only a resource. If we shall position our hopes, dreams, ideas, ambitions, and endeavours in the trust of another person, we will inevitably realise disappointment. Human nature is sinful, evil, selfish, and egocentric. Therefore, we must turn our hearts and minds towards God. With the power of earnest prayer and petition, we must seek from God the ability, drive, ambition, and courage to advance God's Kingdom on Earth.

'Yet, who so bold but says he sees it not? Bad is the world, and all will come to naught. When such ill dealing must be seen in thought.' [666]

The ways of this world are full of corruption, sin, evil, self-interest, fame, income, pecuniary gain, pleasure, profit, and the endless pursuit of the pleasures of the flesh. The ignorant human desires all the things of this material world. In the pursuit of materialism, the individual expends considerable time, effort, energy, and resources, to obtain fleeting desires and momentary pleasures. Only to relinquish such trivial gains in the future, or upon one's inevitable encounter with death. We must utilise the higher faculties, such as reason, logic, thought, and good judgement, to ascertain the true nature of this material world.

---

665 Shakespeare, William. (1597). *Richard III*. Act 3, Scene 4.
666 Shakespeare, William. (1597). *Richard III*. Act 3, Scene 6.

> *'First, if all obstacles were cut away, and that my path were even to the Crown. As the ripe revenue and due of birth, yet so much is my poverty of Spirit, so mighty and so many my defects, That I would rather hide me from my greatness.'* [667]

First, no person has a straight path in life. While we all have personal goals, endeavours, ambitions, drives, and desires to succeed at something, or become accomplished in our chosen field, there shall always be setbacks, losses, distressing experiences, and unfortunate events along our life journey. Second, the poverty of our Spirit is a universal attribute of the human condition. This inner poverty, this void of the soul, can only be fulfilled by our mystical union with God.

> *'I must be married to my Brother's Daughter, or else my Kingdom stands on brittle glass. Murder her Brothers, and then marry her! Uncertain way of gain! But I am in, so far in blood that sin will pluck on sin.'* [668]

We all further the pursuit of our desires and personal affairs in this world. Not realising, that we commit much sin and immorality in the process. A person who is covetous, rarely finds satisfaction or contentment in life. In imposing our will upon this world, we suffer untold consequences. We lose our peace of mind. We are drawn further away from God's Word. Therefore, we must forsake our ego and pride. Repent for our sins. Also, turn our heart towards God. We ought to live our life based on God's Word. We ought to position God's Divine Instructions into practice. Only then shall we live a blessed and honourable life.

---

667 Shakespeare, William. (1597). *Richard III*. Act 3, Scene 7.
668 Shakespeare, William. (1597). *Richard III*. Act 4, Scene 2.

'Wrong not her birth, she is a Royal Princess. To save her life, I'll say she is not so. Her life is safest only in her birth. And only in that safety died her Brothers. Lo, at their births good stars were opposite. No, to their lives ill friends were contrary. All unavoided is the doom of destiny. True, when avoided grace makes destiny. My babes were destined to a fairer death. If grace had blessed thee with a fairer life.' [669]

There is no surety in life. Surety is only found in our confrontation with death. The sombre reality of living is that opposition, setbacks, loss, challenges, injustice, and difficulties shall come upon our life journey. However, regardless of the concerns and issues that trouble us, we must have unconditional confidence and total trust in God's Plan for our life. God decides each person's destiny. In all things, God has the Final Say.

'All for our vantage. Then, in God's Name, march. True hope is swift and flies with swallow's wings; Kings it makes Gods, and meaner creatures Kings.' [670]

Advantage not seized is advantage lost. When we have the opportunity, we must act to seize the advantage. Otherwise the favourable moment shall pass us by. Nothing lasts forever, except for God's Glory and God's Word. We must remain in hope. We must keep our thoughts and prayers with God. We must move forward to accomplish our endeavours with belief, confidence, and faith. For a person who believes, all things are possible.

---

669 Shakespeare, William. (1597). *Richard III*. Act 4, Scene 4.
670 Shakespeare, William. (1597). *Richard III*. Act 5, Scene 2.

'I shall despair. There is no creature loves me. And if I die, no soul will pity me: And wherefore should they, since that I myself. Find in myself, no pity to myself?' [671]

Our beliefs and thoughts determine how we perceive the external world. We must have a positive belief in ourselves. A strong belief in our ability, capacity, talent, and determination, to create the life that we desire. The psychology of 'self-talk', the inner narrative that we constantly indoctrinate ourselves with, comes to define us, both in a positive and negative manner. A constant association with pity is harmful to the development of the Self. There is an appropriate time for despair and agony. However, there is also an opportune time to move forward. A time filled with hope, grace, mercy, and goodness. Do not relinquish the invaluable present moment, for the unchangeable past.

'Let not our babbling dreams affright our souls. Conscience is but a word that cowards use. Devised at first to keep the strong in awe. Our strong arms be our conscience, swords our law.' [672]

We must not permit fear, apprehension, confusion, uncertainty, and doubt, to govern our thoughts, ideas, and beliefs. We must not let fear, apprehension, confusion, uncertainty, and doubt destroy our inherent capacity for reason. Conscience is a double-edged sword. However, in all things, we must be guided by a sense of duty, purpose, and conviction of what is morally right and what is morally wrong.

Unfortunately, for the overwhelming majority of human history, humanity has been guided by power, might, and force. Rather than the forces of practical reason, good judgement, and sound logic. Therefore, the ultimate quest for 'universal peace' remains beyond the reach of human civilisation.

---

671 Shakespeare, William. (1597). *Richard III*. Act 5, Scene 3.
672 Shakespeare, William. (1597). *Richard III*. Act 5, Scene 3.

Chapter 29

ROMEO AND JULIET

'A glooming peace this morning with it brings.
The Sun for sorrow will not show his head. Go hence, to
have more talk of these sad things. Some shall be pardoned,
and some punished. For never was a story of more woe.
Than this of Juliet and her Romeo.'

SHAKESPEARE

Romeo and Juliet is a romantic tragedy. This play narrates the timeless story of two young Italian lovers, namely, Romeo and Juliet. The handsome Romeo is a Montague. This young gentleman, Romeo, is deeply in love with the beautiful Juliet, who is a Capulet. The burden of history is against the two lovers. There is a long-standing feud between the Montagues and the Capulets. However, Romeo and Juliet bravely defy the odds. The young and passionate duo, seek the affection and good company of each other.

This play captures the riveting story of love at first sight. Romeo and Juliet determine to get married and start a life together. However, fortune and fate has other plans for them. While Juliet's father seeks to arrange the marriage of his daughter to County Paris, he is unable to convince Juliet of this marriage proposal.

Disagreement on marriage causes a rupture in the relationship between father and daughter.

Meanwhile, the tide of fortune and force of circumstance spell trouble for Romeo. The chance encounter with a foe leads to a street fight. Juliet's cousin, Tybalt sent a challenge for a duel to Romeo. Now Romeo declined the fight. This decision angered Romeo's close friend, Mercutio, who then bravely engages in a street battle with swords against Tybalt. While Romeo attempts to end the fight, his actions witness Tybalt take full advantage of the situation. Tybalt forcefully strikes down Mercutio. The wounds Mercutio receives are fatal and bloody, which lead to his death. During Mercutio's last moments of his life, he rains down curses on both the House of Montague and the House of Capulet.

Romeo is understandably angered and enraged by the death of his close friend, Mercutio. Romeo perceives he has become 'soft-hearted' after 'falling in love' with Juliet. Thus, in a moment of pure madness and total rage, Romeo draws his sword and fights Tybalt. This duel witnesses the death of Tybalt. Romeo flees the scene in fear of his safety, only later to be officially banished.

Friar Laurence makes the necessary arrangements for the secret marriage of Romeo and Juliet. Friar Laurance provides Juliet with a potion to put her to sleep for several days, which will make her appear dead to her family. This potion serves to abrogate the arranged marriage proposal between Juliet and County Paris. A messenger is arranged to send word to Romeo. That Juliet shall be in a state of rest for several days. However, this critical piece of news never reaches Romeo in time.

Unfortunately, Romeo mistakenly learns that Juliet is dead. The destiny of tragedy now begins to unfold. Romeo acquires poison to end his life. Romeo then visits the tomb, where Juliet is resting. A chance encounter witnesses a sword fight between Romeo and Paris. Now Paris is slain. Romeo consumes the poison in the vicinity of Juliet. Shortly thereafter, Romeo succumbs to his death. Juliet regains consciousness, and she finds her beloved Romeo dead by her side. Friar Laurence attempts to reason with Juliet; however, the stronghold of passion destroys any hope of her yielding to reason. As a consequence, Juliet commits suicide, and she dies besides Romeo. The tragic deaths of Romeo and Juliet, witness the Montagues and the Capulets make a lasting peace. The two families make a promise to build a monument in the everlasting memory of Romeo and Juliet.

> *'Love is a smoke raised with the fume of sighs; being purged, a fire sparkling in lovers' eyes.'* [673]

Worldly love is driven on by desire, attachment, physicality, lust, sensuality, and emotion. It is difficult to obtain a lasting happiness in Earthly love. For true satisfaction is always beyond our reach. The love of this world is fleeting, momentary, and impermanent. In contrast, the purest form of love is the Love of God. For the Love of God is unconditional, comforting, merciful, non-judgemental, and universal in its reach.

> *'Did my heart love till now? Forswear it, sight! For I never saw true beauty till this night.'* [674]

The inner will is moved by the beauty of this world. In particular, by the beauty of the opposite sex. Too often, worldly love is based on surface-level beauty, facial appearance, the spark of chemistry, and an attractive physique. Unfortunately, our eyes are unable to pierce the character, personality, integrity, morality, conscience, parentage, faith, beliefs, values, education, accomplishments, and etiquette of our lover. These finer characteristics, in our preferred partner, require much time and effort to become wholly acquainted with. It is only through repeated social interactions and personal

---

673 Shakespeare, William. (1597). *Romeo and Juliet*. Act 1, Scene 1.
674 Shakespeare, William. (1597). *Romeo and Juliet*. Act 1, Scene 5.

exchanges with our desired partner, that we become more familiar with who they truly are.

> '*Being held a foe, he may not have access to use these vows as lovers use to swear, and she as much in love, her means much less. To meet her new beloved anywhere; but passion lends them power, time means to meet, tempering extremities with extreme sweet.*'[675]

Love finds a way. In life, we often confront what appear to be insurmountable obstacles and tall barriers to courting the person we truly love. There are cultural, lingual, racial, ethnic, personal wealth, education, social class, income, nobility, status, parentage, and private property divides, that create disparities between members of our modern society. Most importantly, we must remember that we are all common and equal members of the human civilisation. The concept of a foe is a figment of our imagination. In the final analysis, love conquers all.

> '*The orchard walls are high and hard to climb, and the place death, considering who thou art, if any of my kinsmen find thee here. With love's light wings did I overperch these walls. For stony limits cannot hold love out, and what love can do, that dares love attempt.*'[676]

No barriers are too high to keep love out. True love will overcome the tallest of mountains. The highest tree tops. The darkness of a lonely light. The despair of agony and torment. Also, the grief of loss. Love has no limits. Love makes life bearable. Love makes life worth living. For without the presence of love, this world shall be a cold, dark, gloomy, and dull place. Love brings hope, light, warmth, intimacy, good company, and affection to this world.

---

675 Shakespeare, William. (1597). *Romeo and Juliet*. Act 2, Prologue.
676 Shakespeare, William. (1597). *Romeo and Juliet*. Act 2, Scene 2.

'My bounty is as boundless as the Sea, my love as deep. The more I give to thee, the more I have, for both are infinite.' [677]

The expression of true love knows no real limits. When we go out of our way for a loved one, it is not even perceived as a minor inconvenience. True love is unconditional and selfless. True love is much more concerned with giving than receiving. Within the *Holy Bible*, in the *Book of Corinthians*, Chapter 13, Verses 4 and 5, we are told of the attributes of love, 'Love is patient. Love is kind. It does not envy. It does not boast. It is not proud. It does not dishonour others. It is not self-seeking. It is not easily angered. It keeps no record of wrongs.'

'By holy marriage: when, and where, and how we met, we wooed and made exchange of vow, I'll tell thee as we pass; but this I pray, that thou consent to marry us today. Holy Saint Francis, what a change is here! Is Rosaline, whom thou didst love so dear, so soon forsaken? Young men's love then lies, not truly in their hearts, but in their eyes.' [678]

The winds of love are subject to change. The lustful desire for beauty is the driving force behind our sexual attraction. More importantly, true beauty resides in the soul, not in mere appearances. We must not rely upon, nor be deceived by, the senses. Rather, we must carefully employ the powers of observation, in order to ascertain the traits, qualities, values, and characteristics of the person, that we truly desire to spend our lifetime with. Marriage is a life-long commitment. Marriage ought to endure, far beyond the immediate temptation of physical attraction.

---

677 Shakespeare, William. (1597). *Romeo and Juliet*. Act 2, Scene 2.
678 Shakespeare, William. (1597). *Romeo and Juliet*. Act 2, Scene 3.

'There's no trust, no faith, no honesty, in men; all perjured, all forsworn, all naught, all dissemblers.' [679]

Trust is a rare and precious commodity in this world. We must exercise discretion in whom we place our trust. Trusting other people creates the opportunity for being betrayed. Regrettably, the people of this Modern World, are all too concerned with pecuniary gain, profit maximisation, and private property. The narrow-minded, rational, and self-interested person is conditioned by the ideologies of consumerism, materialism, secularism, capitalism, neoliberalism, individualism, and hedonism.

'These woes, these griefs, these sorrows make me old.' [680]

As we reach maturity in life, adulthood presents us with many obligations, laws, and duties. We also experience heartache, tragedy, pain, suffering, and trauma, from unpleasant events during the course of our lifetime. These difficult times tend to weigh us down, and can psychologically, make us feel considerably older than our biological age.

The key to our success is a resilient mindset. Combined with positive thinking, and learning to 'let go' of our pain and suffering. People who concentrate on the select things that are within their control, are the individuals who make progress in life. Whereas, people who become distracted with what they cannot change or control, become undone and are unable to move forward in their life. Our destiny is realised through the control of our beliefs, thoughts, and actions.

---

679 Shakespeare, William. (1597). *Romeo and Juliet.* Act 3, Scene 2.
680 Shakespeare, William. (1597). *Romeo and Juliet.* Act 3, Scene 2.

'O shut the door! And when thou hast done so, come weep with me—past hope, past cure, past help! Ah, Juliet, I already know thy grief. It strains me past the compass of my wits.' [681]

Grief can totally absorb our thought and life. However, no matter how painful and tormenting the onset of grief is, we are never past hope, cure, or help. During times of tragedy, we shall be tested. Indeed, our faith shall be tested. When we are in the midst of sorrows, there is limited motivation for the exercise of practical reason, rational judgement, positive thought, or sound logic. The unrestrained sway of emotions, feelings, and sensations tend to guide our behaviour during times of distress. However, we must exert control over our mind. We must strive to bring the power of reason to rule our thoughts. To direct our speech. Also, to guide our actions.

'Death is my Son-in-Law. Death is my Heir. My Daughter he hath wedded. I will die and leave him all. Life, living, all is death's.' [682]

No person shall escape the noose of death that hangs above each person's head. We must confront our mortality. Such is the inescapable reality of the human condition. Therefore, we ought to concentrate our finite time, energy, resources, expertise, talent, and abilities on the here and now. We must envision and execute the idea to create the life, that we truly desire. So, when all is said and done. When we reflect on our life in old age. We can say, we have no regrets. That we have lived a purposeful and meaningful life.

---

681 Shakespeare, William. (1597). *Romeo and Juliet*. Act 4, Scene 1.
682 Shakespeare, William. (1597). *Romeo and Juliet*. Act 4, Scene 5.

> *'My soul, but not my child! Dead art thou! Alack, my child is dead, and with my child my joys are buried! Peace, ho, for shame! Confusion's cure lives not in these confusions. Heaven and yourself had part in this fair maid! Now Heaven hath all, and all the better is it for the maid.'* [683]

The grief of losing a loved one, not to mention, a young child is truly unimaginable. The torment, anguish, sadness, heartache, and psychological agony of such a traumatic experience is beyond the descriptive capacity of words to illustrate. The bereaved parent is likely to experience an overwhelming surge in emotions and feelings, such as anger, denial, guilt, sadness, fear, confusion, frustration, doubt, and hopelessness. To describe such a devastating event as 'heart-breaking' is an understatement.

> *'The world is not thy friend. Not the world's law; the world affords no law to make thee rich. Then be not poor, but break it and take this. My poverty, but not my will, consents. I pay thy poverty and not thy will.'* [684]

The curse of circumstances and sheer moments of desperation can induce us to extreme and irrational conduct in our behaviour. We must never let our thoughts stray towards ill intentions, self-harm, suicide, rape, assault, murder, or a range of other criminal and immoral activities. We must transcend the poverty of the soul and the weakness of the human condition, through the power of prayer, penance, and petition.

---

683 Shakespeare, William. (1597). *Romeo and Juliet.* Act 4, Scene 5.
684 Shakespeare, William. (1597). *Romeo and Juliet.* Act 5, Scene 1.

'There is thy gold, worse poison to men's souls. Doing more murder in this loathsome world, than these poor compounds that thou mayst not sell. I sell thee poison, thou hast sold me none.' [685]

People's endless desire for gold and money has perpetuated much evil in this world. There is goodness in the world, however, we witness less of it, in comparison to the proliferation of hate, injustice, discrimination, prejudice, and evil. This world is plagued with incessant warfare, pandemics, epidemics, humanitarian crises, economic crises, financial crises, civil wars, environmental disasters, terrorism, world wars, political violence, genocide, massacres, ethnic cleansing, crimes against humanity, sexual discrimination, religious discrimination, and racial discrimination. It is only by God's grace, mercy, favour, and goodness, that we transcend the baseness of this world, and advance God's Kingdom on Earth.

---

685 Shakespeare, William. (1597). *Romeo and Juliet*. Act 5, Scene 1.

Chapter 30

THE TAMING OF THE SHREW

'For it is the mind that makes the body rich.
And as the Sun breaks through the darkest clouds,
so honour peereth in the meanest habit.'

SHAKESPEARE

The Taming of the Shrew is a romantic comedy. This play narrates the story of a student named Lucentio who travels to Padua to engage in formal study. Lucentio learns that a merchant by the name of Baptista Minola has two unmarried daughters. The younger daughter is named Bianca, and the older daughter is named Katherina. Bianca is a beautiful gentlelady. Bianca already has two suitors, Gremio and Hortensio. On the other hand, Bianca's older sister, Katherina, is a fiercely independent and strong-willed gentlewoman.

The three gentlemen, Gremio, Hortensio, and Lucentio all make quite the effort to court Bianca. The two daughter's father, Baptista insists that the older daughter, Katherina, must be married first, before he will consent to Bianca's hand in marriage. Meanwhile, a young gentleman named Petruccio arrives from Verona to visit his close friend, Hortensio. The noble bachelor, Petruccio, takes a romantic interest in Katherina, and he is determined to court her for marriage. Initially, Katherina is opposed to Petruccio's advances, however, Petruccio is not about to waver in his courtship of her.

Petruccio determines a wedding date for his marriage to Katherina. Following the wedding ceremony, Petruccio sets course for Verona, with his newly wedded wife. Once home, Petruccio intentionally mistreats his wife. For example, consider that Petruccio denies his wife, food and rest. With the passage of time, Katherina submits to her husband's demands. Thereafter, Katherina is granted permission from her husband to visit her father in Padua.

Now that Katherina is married to Petruccio, the marriage of Bianca is only a matter of time. The gentleman Hortensio is rejected by Bianca. Thereafter, Hortensio resolves to marry a wealthy widow. On the other hand, Lucentio has finally become successful in his unwavering efforts to court Bianca. With both daughters now married, Baptista finds his inner peace. In the spirit of celebration, Baptista hosts a wedding feast for both Katherina and Bianca.

Towards the end of this play, Petruccio devises a clever scheme to affirm who has the most 'obedient' wife. All three married gentlemen, Hortensio, Lucentio, and Petruccio, call for their wife to attend upon them, however, only Katherina arrives at the request of Petruccio. Beyond reasonable doubt, Petruccio has been the most successful gentleman, in making his wife compliant to his request.

'No profit grows where is no pleasure taken. In brief, Sir, study what you most affect.' [686]

We ought to pursue the endeavours that we are most passionate about in our lifetime. The pursuit of profit and pecuniary gain are

---

686 Shakespeare, William. (1623). *The Taming of the Shrew.* Act 1, Scene 1.

secondary and inferior schemes. Profit shall arise as a consequential result of our time, effort, energy, resources, and abilities being directed in the primary pursuit of our most passionate endeavours. Furthermore, our motivation, enthusiasm, commitment, and ambition shall be greatest in the pursuit of activities that we find most pleasing. Within the *Holy Bible*, in the *Gospel of Matthew*, Chapter 6, Verse 21, we are taught an Eternal Truth about the human condition, namely, 'For where your treasure is, there your heart will be also.'

'He that runs fastest gets the ring.' [687]

Life is defined by initiative, grit, hope, faith, resolve, determination, love, work, boldness, and courage. People who take initiative in life are likely to accomplish their dreams and endeavours. Shakespeare's quote is comparable to the well-known proverb, 'The early bird catches the worm.' We cannot wait for life, to present us with the opportunities and circumstances that are most favourable to our mission. Rather, we must act with a sense of urgency and importance. We must transform our dreams into a living reality.

'Content you, gentlemen. I will compound this strife. It is deeds must win the prize.' [688]

We can employ persuasive and colourful language that is full of rhetoric and prosody. However, it is our actions which determine our accomplishments. Our actions shall form our character, merit, achievements, and success in life. In the pursuit of righteous and noble deeds, we shall encounter opposition, setbacks, obstacles, disappointment, resistance, challenges, and issues. However, individuals that strive and stay the course on their mission, shall gain the prize of their labour.

---

687 Shakespeare, William. (1623). *The Taming of the Shrew.* Act 1, Scene 1.
688 Shakespeare, William. (1623). *The Taming of the Shrew.* Act 2, Scene 1.

'And when in music we have spent an hour, your lecture shall have leisure for as much. Preposterous ass, that never read so far to know the cause why music was ordained! Was it not to refresh the mind of man after his studies or his usual pain? Then give me leave to read philosophy, and while I pause, serve in your harmony.' [689]

The sound of pleasant music is entertaining and relaxing to the intellectually exhausted Scholar. Prolonged study is a laborious and strenuous endeavour. Study requires intermittent rest and respite, in order to appropriately recover. Listening to music is just one of the many methods that a person can utilise to de-stress. For example, consider the classical music of Ludwig van Beethoven and Wolfgang Amadeus Mozart. Both of these gifted gentlemen were great Musicians of their time.

'A knack, a toy, a trick, a baby's cap. Away with it! Come, let me have a bigger. I'll have no bigger. This doth fit the time, and gentlewomen wear such caps as these. When you are gentle, you shall have one too, and not till then. That will not be in haste. Why, Sir, I trust I may have leave to speak, and speak I will. I am no child, no babe. Your betters have endured me say my mind, and if you cannot, best you stop your ears. My tongue will tell the anger of my heart, or else my heart concealing it, will break. And rather than it shall, I will be free even to the uttermost, as I please, in words! Why, thou sayest true. It is a paltry cap. A custard-coffin, a bauble, a silken pie. I love thee well in that thou likest is not. Love me, or love me not, I like the cap. And it I will have, or I will have none.' [690]

Shakespeare draws out the endless quarrels between husband and wife. Indeed, marriage, and married life has its fair share of challenges. At times, each spouse will have different expectations

---

689 Shakespeare, William. (1623). *The Taming of the Shrew.* Act 3, Scene 1.
690 Shakespeare, William. (1623). *The Taming of the Shrew.* Act 4, Scene 3.

and standards of their partner. Sometimes, the husband or wife shall fall short of their partner's expectations. Such is the imperfect condition of our human nature. No person in this world is perfect. More importantly, being calm and reasonable, coupled with open lines of communication is the advisable strategy to navigate spousal conflict.

> *'For it is the mind that makes the body rich. And as the Sun breaks through the darkest clouds, so honour peereth in the meanest habit.'* [691]

Our thoughts and beliefs determine our external reality. The manner in which the mind thinks and perceives the material world, either serves to make us poor or rich in our life. Our personal experience of life starts with our thoughts. Our thoughts create the psychological basis for our actions. As a direct and immediate consequence, our actions create our worldly reality. Therefore, it is of great importance and considerable consequence, that we consciously analyse our thoughts. Why do we think, the way we think?

> *'Where, then, do you know best. We be affied, and such assurance taken as shall with either part's agreement stand? Not in my house, Lucentio, for you know pitchers have ears, and I have many servants.'* [692]

We must be vigilant and diligent, when we discuss our private affairs and confidential information amongst other people. It is always possible that people, who have naught to do with the contents of our conversation, may be within earshot of our speech. When we accidentally expose sensitive information to other people, we

---

691 Shakespeare, William. (1623). *The Taming of the Shrew.* Act 4, Scene 3.
692 Shakespeare, William. (1623). *The Taming of the Shrew.* Act 4, Scene 4.

inadvertently create risk, that such information can be used against us for personal gain, or to the contrary of our best interests.

> *'Thy Husband is thy Lord, thy Life, thy Keeper, thy Head, thy Sovereign; one that cares for thee, and for thy maintenance commits his body to painful labour both by sea and land, to watch the night in storms, the day in cold, whilst thou liest warm at home, secure and safe. But craves no other tribute from thy hands but love, fair looks, and true obedience. Too little payment for so great a debt. Such duty as the subject owes the Prince, even such a woman oweth to her husband. And when she is froward, peevish, sullen, sour, and not obedient to his honest will, what is she but a foul contending rebel and graceless traitor to her loving Lord?'* [693]

Shakespeare enunciates the traditional gender roles of a husband and wife in Early Modern Society. Historically speaking, the husband was deemed the Head of the household. The sole Provider. Also, the Guarantor for family safety. The husband engaged in the public sphere of society. The husband would gain employment, and therefore, be the primary economic and financial provider for the family. The role of the traditional housewife and mother was mostly confined to the private sphere of the household. The wife and mother were primarily engaged in the performance of domestic duties, such as cleaning, washing, cooking, and parenting of the young children.

Shakespeare's writing highlights the inequality in social mobility between the male and female sex. In the late 16th century English society, gentlewomen had very limited rights, liberties, and freedoms. Often, the wife, being in a subordinate and dependent position vis-à-vis her husband, had limited or no agency in the

---

693 Shakespeare, William. (1623). *The Taming of the Shrew.* Act 5, Scene 2.

marriage. It was expected of a wife, to be obedient and act in accordance with her husband's will. Otherwise, the wife was considered unfaithful.

Chapter 31

THE TEMPEST

*'And my ending is despair. Unless I be relieved by prayer,
which pierces so that it assaults mercy itself, and
frees all faults. As you from crimes would pardoned be.
Let your indulgence set me free.'*

SHAKESPEARE

The Tempest is part comedy and part tragedy. This play commences with a devastating storm near the coast of a Mediterranean island. A ship on the high seas is situated in the eye of the storm. The ship is carrying King Alonso of Naples, the King's son, Ferdinand, and the King's brother, Sebastian. The three noble gentlemen were on their journey home from Tunis to Italy, however, this brutal storm has destroyed their ship. The three shipwrecked gentlemen are accompanied by the courtier, Gonzalo and also the Duke of Milan, Antonio.

Already situated on the island, Prospero, the former Duke of Milan, witnesses the passage of the devastating storm and its aftermath. Most notably, Prospero witnesses the shipwreck and its distraught crew disembark onto the remote island. Prospero is accompanied by his beautiful daughter, Miranda. While on the island, Prospero enslaves a native islander by the name of Caliban.

In addition, Prospero also has frequent contact with a spirit named Ariel. During the course of this play, Prospero reveals a significant personal experience from his past. Prospero retells Miranda, how over a decade ago, his brother, Antonio, had removed him from power in a coup.

There are scenes of romance scattered throughout this play. The King's son, Ferdinand is helplessly in love with Prospero's daughter, Miranda. In return, Miranda is most welcoming of Ferdinand's advances, and she also falls in love with him. Meanwhile, the spirit, Ariel strikes a deal with Prospero for his liberation. Ariel proves a wise and loyal spirit. Ariel uncovers a plot by Antonio and Sebastian, to kill the King while he is asleep. Regrettably, there is much more mischief waiting around the corner.

At Caliban's insistence, Stephano and Trinculo collectively agree for the trio to murder Prospero. In Prospero's place, the trio agree to install Stephano as the new Lord of the island. Ariel is privy to their evil plot. Ariel immediately informs his Master, Prospero. With respect to more pure matters of the heart, Prospero finally agrees to Ferdinand and Miranda's marriage, however, the joy and celebration is short-lived. For Prospero must attend to Caliban's wicked plot to overthrow him.

Ariel and Prospero establish a novel trap to capture Caliban, Stephano, and Trinculo in the execution of their sinister scheme. As a result, Caliban, Stephano, and Trinculo become distracted by quirky and absurd clothes. The trio fail to carry out their wicked mission. Once the trio are totally engrossed by the fancy pieces of clothing, they are caught and chased away by several spirits.

The final scene of this play witnesses Prospero revealing his true identity to the several constituents on the island. Rather than seek revenge for his overthrow as the former Duke of Milan, Prospero forgives those who did him wrong. Prospero accepts the return of his Dukedom as recompense. Prospero fulfils his promise to emancipate Ariel, who is now finally free after years of servitude. Not to mention, Caliban and his ill-minded servants are reprimanded for their mischievous plot. Ironically, the play concludes with Prospero asking the audience to set him free.

> *'You are a Counsellor; if you can command these elements to silence, and work the peace of the present, we will not hand a rope more. Use your authority. If you cannot, give thanks you have lived so long, and make yourself ready in your cabin for the mischance of the hour, if it so hap.'* [694]

While humans demonstrate free will and agency, not every situation or event is within a person's immediate control. For one, the natural elements, namely, the weather is wholly beyond our control. Whether it rain, hail, or thunderstorm, we cannot dictate, nor impose, its occurrence or non-occurrence. True wisdom resides in focusing one's awareness and concentration, on matters that are within the individual's power to change.

> *'I thus neglecting worldly ends, all dedicated to closeness and the bettering of my mind in my false brother awaked an evil nature; and my trust, like a good parent, did beget of him a falsehood, in its contrary as great as my trust was; which had indeed no limit, A confidence sans bound.'* [695]

We must exercise proper care and due diligence in whom we position our profound trust. Human nature is not all benevolent, charitable, and generous in its aims and objectives. Indeed, humans act out of conceit, self-interest, pride, haste, evil, prejudice, the pursuit of profit, and an unfettered desire for pecuniary gain. When we position our confidence in another person, we knowingly assume the inherent risk, that it may amount to our undoing.

---

694 Shakespeare, William. (1623). *The Tempest.* Act 1, Scene 1.
695 Shakespeare, William. (1623). *The Tempest.* Act 1, Scene 2.

'Hell is empty, and all the Devils are here.' [696]

We must appreciate, that in the present moment, this is where our pain and suffering truly reside. The concept of 'Hell' is but a figment of our infinite imagination. We are tormented in the present lifetime. A disturbed mind and heavy heart is the cause of much worldly suffering and trouble. It is within our agency and free will to either create 'Heaven' or 'Hell' on Earth. In the final analysis, what we sow is what we shall reap. Therefore, we must concentrate our energy, time, and resources on cultivating good intentions, and performing honourable actions, in order that we find peace on Earth.

'Is there more toil? Since thou dost give me pains, let me remember thee what thou hast promised, which is not yet performed me. How now, moody? What is it thou canst demand? My liberty.' [697]

We all cherish our highly prized freedom. It is ideal and wishful thinking to desire freedom from social, political, legal, religious, and economic institutions, rules, procedures, laws, duties, responsibilities, obligations, commitments, and state taxes. The pursuit and attainment of freedom resides in finding a balance. A 'middle ground' in state and society. Being a responsible, diligent, progressive, thoughtful, and mature citizen. This is how our practical freedom is secured. There is no freedom, without personal responsibility.

---

696 Shakespeare, William. (1623). *The Tempest.* Act 1, Scene 2.
697 Shakespeare, William. (1623). *The Tempest.* Act 1, Scene 2.

'I have no hope that he's undrowned. O, out of that 'no hope' what great hope have you! No hope that way is another way so high a hope, that even ambition cannot pierce a wink beyond, but doubt discovery there.' [698]

No matter what struggles, privations, hardships, traumatic experiences, major issues, significant challenges, or difficulties that we confront in the course of life, we must always hold on to hope, faith, and love. The enduring presence of hope is a powerful mechanism to address grief and sorrow in life. While there is no absolute surety in hope, it is the expectation for a brighter and better future, which guides us forward to surmount seemingly insurmountable obstacles. It is the power of hope that destroys the incapacity of doubt.

'Hear my soul speak. The very instant that I saw you, did my heart fly to your service. There resides to make me slave to it; and for your sake am I this patient log-man. Do you love me? O, Heaven, O, Earth, bear witness to the sound, and crown what I profess with kind event, if I speak true! If hollowly, invert what best is boded me to mischief! I, beyond all limit of what else in the world, do love, prize, honour you.' [699]

Love is the highest good on Earth. We must all strive to treat every individual with love, kindness, respect, dignity, and courtesy. There is no discrepancy or discrimination in matters of love. For love transcends the distinctions of language, race, colour, faith, ethnicity, age, gender, sex, political affiliation, country of origin, disability, wealth, income, education, private property, social class, reputation, and status. In addition, a life of Worship to God and service to humanity is a life well-lived. A life that incorporates the Presence of God is a meaningful and purposeful life.

---

698 Shakespeare, William. (1623). *The Tempest.* Act 2, Scene 1.
699 Shakespeare, William. (1623). *The Tempest.* Act 3, Scene 1.

'By our Ladykin, I can go no further, Sir. My old bones ache. By your patience, I needs must rest me. Old Lord, I cannot blame thee, who am myself attached with weariness to the dulling of my spirits. Sit down and rest.' [700]

We are only human. We all have physical, physiological, biological, reproductive, chemical, mechanical, electrical, intellectual, and emotional limitations to our capacities. The human body has a finite life span. As we progressively confront old age, we become more familiar and better acquainted with our inherent limitations. A sagacious person is consciously aware of their strengths and weaknesses. An insightful person functions within the boundaries and parameters of what is possible to create a harmonious and good life.

'Then, as my gift, and thine own acquisition … worthily purchased … take my daughter. But if thou dost break her virgin-knot before all sanctimonious ceremonies may with full and holy rite be ministered, no sweet aspersion shall the Heavens let fall to this contract grow; but barren hate, sour-eyed disdain and discord, shall bestrew the union of your bed with weeds so loathly that you shall hate it both. Therefore, take heed, as flymen's lamp shall light you. As I hope for quiet days, fair issue, and long life, with such love as it is now, the murkiest den, the most opportune place, the strongest suggestion our worser genius can, shall never melt mine honour into lust, to take away the edge of that day's celebration. When I shall think, or Phoebus' steeds are foundered, or night kept chained below.' [701]

Shakespeare's writing reflects the era of his time. A period in English History, when tradition, duty, custom, and the institution of marriage were instrumental and foundational concepts of

---

700 Shakespeare, William. (1623). *The Tempest.* Act 3, Scene 3.
701 Shakespeare, William. (1623). *The Tempest.* Act 4, Scene 1.

a good and orderly life in society. An honourable and learned gentleman, who intended to court a gentlelady for marriage, did so with the premise, that he shall abide by, and respect the honour and reputation of his future wife. Indeed, the function of religion, and religious rules and beliefs, determined the manner in which a gentleman courted a gentlewoman.

In the contemporary world, we witness a period of time guided by the philosophy of secularism, individualism, liberalism, materialism, hedonism, and consumerism. In addition, the nature and character of relationships is ever-changing, with commitment and expectations no longer being fixed and static. For example, consider the presence of *de facto* relationships, long distance relationships, inter-racial relationships, polyamorous relationships, casual relationships, and open relationships.

In the early twenty-first century, relationships are becoming increasingly dynamic, fluid, and malleable. Furthermore, historically speaking, fixed and assumed gender roles and the long-held 'husband' and 'wife' expectations are now being questioned and overturned. For example, consider in the 1620s, in English society, gentlewomen were accustomed to a future in which they were a housewife, mother, widow, religious sister, nun, or abbess.

'O Peer! O Worthy Stephano! Look what a wardrobe here is for thee! Let it alone, thou fool, it is but trash. The dropsy drown this fool! What do you mean to dote thus on such luggage? Let it alone, and do the murder first. If he awake, from toe to crown he'll fill our skins with pinches; make us strange stuff. I will have none of it! We shall lose our time, and all be turned to barnacles, or to apes with foreheads villainous low.' [702]

When we are led into temptation and the endless pursuit of the many desires of this world, we relinquish the opportunity to fulfil

---

702 Shakespeare, William. (1623). *The Tempest.* Act 4, Scene 1.

our mission in a timely manner. An opportunity missed never arises again. The key to success in any endeavour or mission is the single-minded determination and unflinching resolve to make progress. We must not become distracted by the news of worldly events, or the occurrence of trivial affairs, in the grand quest to secure our destiny.

'The rarer action is in virtue than in vengeance.'[703]

A person who can forgive and forget has overcome this world. It is the innate desire of the flesh to seek retribution and pursue revenge. Whereas, the spirit seeks more lofty endeavours defined by righteousness, love, and purity. In the grand pursuit of one's moral development, conscience, and character, an individual must aspire to rise above the endless temptations and misconceived intentions of the flesh. The expression of virtue in our thought, speech, and behaviour, not only makes us better people, however, virtue also creates a better world.

'How sharp the point of this remembrance is. My Dear Son, Ferdinand. I am woe for it, Sir. Irreparable is the loss; and patience says it is past her cure. I rather think you have not sought her help, of whose soft grace for the like loss. I have her sovereign aid, and rest myself content. You ... the like loss? As great to me as late ... for I have lost my Daughter.'[704]

A loss is a loss. No matter how we justify our loss, or psychologically come to terms with it. Unfortunately, remembrance serves to make the loss feel greater. In our finite lifetime, we shall confront loss, heartache, tragedy, trials, tribulations, troubles, pain, sorrow, and sadness. However, we must always strive to move forward and

---

703 Shakespeare, William. (1623). *The Tempest*. Act 5, Scene 1.
704 Shakespeare, William. (1623). *The Tempest*. Act 5, Scene 1.

upward. In all things, there is a time to grieve, and there is a time to move forward.

Most importantly, we must not allow our life narrative to be completely defined by the issues and problems that we confront. It is within us to transcend these challenges and rise higher. To create a life full of achievement, attainment, and accomplishment. We must always remember, there is an expensive 'opportunity cost' to pay, if we discard the present time, to live in the memory of the fixed past.

'And my ending is despair. Unless I be relieved by prayer, which pierces so that it assaults mercy itself, and frees all faults. As you from crimes would pardoned be. Let your indulgence set me free.'[705]

When we near the end of our lifetime, what we truly desire is freedom, faith, and forgiveness. We will make mistakes during our lifetime on Earth. Not to mention, we shall experience much pain, sorrow, and grief in this world. Indeed, pain, sorrow, and grief are much a part and parcel of the experience of our life, as the involuntary physiological processes of life itself.

As we seek forgiveness for our sins, thus, we must forgive those people that have sinned against us. In the final analysis, we can always turn our heart towards God. We have a free moral choice in this respect. No matter the circumstances, necessity, or fortune that we confront, we can always pray to God for mercy, grace, favour, love, and goodness.

---

705 Shakespeare, William. (1623). *The Tempest*. Act 5, Epilogue.

Chapter 32

TIMON OF ATHENS

'My Loved Lord, though you hear now, too late, yet now's a time.
The greatest of your having lacks a half to pay your present debts.
Let all my lands be sold. It is all engaged, some forfeited and gone,
and what remains will hardly stop the mouth of present dues.'

SHAKESPEARE

Timon of Athens is a play that demonstrates the real limits of private property and personal wealth, the impermanence of political influence, and it reveals the fragile bonds of true friendship. This play commences with Timon, an exorbitantly wealthy and extremely popular figure in Athens, entertaining his aristocratic friends. Timon is generous. Timon flaunts his personal wealth, lavishing expensive gifts on his friends. Timon entertains fine banquets for his many affluent guests. Timon bestows unprecedented favours upon the aristocrats of Athens. Despite Timon's innocence, unquestioning trust, and insouciance, his good fortune is not destined to last.

Timon kindly offers to repay the mounting debts of his friend, Ventidius, who is situated in a debtors' prison. Timon's kind-hearted generosity extends beyond class, status, or rank. For Timon also makes the necessary financial arrangements for the marriage of his loyal servant. One of Timon's sincere friends, Apemantus provides him invaluable counsel on how to preserve his personal wealth and live more modestly. However, Timon rejects Apemantus' well-intended advice. In addition, Flavius, Timon's faithful steward, attempts to reason with his Master, that his finances are in dire trouble. Regrettably, Timon also ignores Flavius.

Now circumstances, fortune, and necessity combine to confront Timon. Unfortunately, Timon is unable to repay his personal debts as and when they fall due. Timon sends his honourable servant, to request his friends to provide him with much needed financial assistance. Timon finds that, despite his extravagant and considerable expenditure of private wealth, to entertain and advance his friends personal interests, none of his friends offer to assist him in his hour of need.

In a hostile act of open retribution, Timon hosts one final feast for his affluent friends. This banquet is to demonstrate his disgust and anger at his friends insincerity, lack of financial support, and betrayal of him. Timon recklessly serves his honourable guests a meal consisting of stones and cold water. Timon violently curses his friends. Timon also speaks curses over the City of Athens, and its people, before abruptly leaving the great city.

Timon is now left to fend for himself. Timon is exposed to the harshness of the natural elements. Timon sources food, to ensure his survival. To Timon's surprise and amazement, he finds gold. In the wilderness, the loyal Flavius makes a noble effort to search for his honourable Master, Timon. Thereafter, a General named Alcibiades finds Timon and offers to engage in friendship. Formerly, Timon had hosted Alcibiades at one of his extravagant banquets. Alcibiades reveals his intention to destroy the City of Athens. Timon immediately offers Alcibiades a portion of the gold that he had found in the wilderness, to further Alcibiades' most destructive ambition.

While remaining in the open wilderness, Timon has a chance encounter with Apemantus. The two gentlemen criticise the shallowness and insincerity of their former Athenian friends.

Apemantus and Timon now perceive this world for what it truly is. That is to say, this broken world consists of countless unenlightened people, who embody an insatiable love of riches, wealth, private property, fame, power, pleasure, profit, and pecuniary gain.

In the closing scenes of this play, two honourable and learned Senators attempt to persuade Timon to return to Athens, in order to prevent Alcibiades' imminent attack. Timon rejects their proposal. Thereafter, Timon's gravestone is discovered by one of Alcibiades' soldiers. Alcibiades' negotiates an arrangement with the Senators for a new peace. When tragic news reaches Alcibiades on the death of Timon, Alcibiades proclaims peace in Athens and he honours Timon's life, love, and legacy.

> *'Well, I am not of that feather to shake off my friend when he must needs me. I do know him a gentleman that well deserves a help, which he shall have. I'll pay the debt, and free him. Your Lordship ever binds him. Commend me to him. I will send his ransom. And being enfranchised, bid him come to me. It is not enough to help the feeble up, but to support him after.'* [706]

The aforementioned statement is the representation of true and unconditional generosity. Such an honourable friendship is a rare commodity in the contemporary world. Here we witness the definition of true brotherhood and sisterhood in action. A sense of selflessness defines this friendship. By helping another person in their time of need, we witness the overcoming of self-interest, ego, pride, conceit, and selfishness. Indeed, it is only the pomp and vanity of this world, which keeps us from the performance of community service, charity, and social justice.

---

706 Shakespeare, William. (1623). *Timon of Athens.* Act 1, Scene 1.

'How dost thou like this jewel, Apemantus? Not so well as plain dealing, which will not cost a man a doit.'[707]

Plain dealing and the majestic riches of this world are more often than not incompatible. Plain dealing is characterised by honour, righteousness, integrity, and honesty. However, it is the endless and irrational pursuit of pleasures, personal wealth, sensual desires, profit, pecuniary gain, and private property, which furthers the selfish and egocentric person's corrupt ways and narrow agenda. In the final analysis, honourable dealing preserves our character and reputation. Whereas, corrupt practices in pursuing personal wealth, profit, gain, power, influence, and private property, cost us our peace of mind.

'And as in grateful virtue I am bound. To your free heart, I do return those talents, doubled with thanks and service, from whose help I derived liberty. O, by no means, honest Ventidius, you mistake my love. I gave it freely ever, and there's none can truly say he gives, if he receives. If our betters play at that game, we must not dare to imitate them. Faults that are rich are fair. A Noble Spirit!'[708]

Humility, love, and gratefulness are worthy traits for the betterment of a person's character and moral development. When we do good in the world, we make it a better and brighter place. It is only the powerful light of good deeds that eradicate the depths of darkness and presence of evil in this world. To assist another person in their time of need is a meritorious act.

Indeed, within the *Holy Bible*, in the *Book of Hebrews*, Chapter 13, Verse 2, we are informed of the importance of demonstrating kindness, to every person we meet on our journey of life, 'Do not forget to show hospitality to strangers, for by so doing some people have shown hospitality to Angels without knowing it.'

---

707 Shakespeare, William. (1623). *Timon of Athens*. Act 1, Scene 1.
708 Shakespeare, William. (1623). *Timon of Athens*. Act 1, Scene 2.

'Nay, My Lord, ceremony was but devised at first to set a gloss on faint deeds, hollow welcomes, recanting goodness, sorry ere it is shown. But where there is true friendship, there needs none.'[709]

The mark of true friendship is that it does not require fanfare, pomp, illustrious welcome ceremonies, or any other form of extravagance. These vain displays of influence, power, prestige, and pride only attract friendship, so long as the material riches are present. For when personal wealth, private property, power, influence, income, and prestige are no more, then self-interested friendships disappear. Quite like a ghost, that vanishes in the darkness of night.

'I wonder men dare trust themselves with men. Methinks they should invite them without knives, good for their meat, and safer for their lives. There's much example for it. The fellow that sits next to him, now parts bread with him, pledges the breath of him in a divided draught, is the readiest man to kill him.'[710]

We must exercise discretion and diligence in whom we position our trust. For once we share personal information with other people, we assume the inherent risk, that it may be utilised in a detrimental manner against our best interests. Similarly, the presence of unfavourable conditions, or external threats, can create an environment, which also serves to our overall disadvantage. For example, consider the weather. The clouds can unexpectedly cover the Sun, and thunderstorms begin to bring a heavy downpour of rain. Alternatively, the tides on the sea may suddenly change, and create rough conditions for sailing. Last but not least, the atmospheric pressure at high altitudes can result in turbulence during an aeroplane flight. No matter our efforts, certain conditions and events are beyond our control.

---

709 Shakespeare, William. (1623). *Timon of Athens*. Act 1, Scene 2.
710 Shakespeare, William. (1623). *Timon of Athens*. Act 1, Scene 2.

> *'I should fear that those that dance before me, now would one day stamp upon me. It has been done. Men shut their doors against a setting Sun.'* [711]

It is a sombre reality that we shall be betrayed by those people that are closest to us. Unfortunately, it is the principle of self-interest and the unrelenting desire for profit that drives and dictates much of human behaviour in the modern society. We need to ensure that we do not structure our life, in such a vulnerable manner, that another individual has the unfettered opportunity to exploit our life, labour, leisure, love, land, and liberty.

> *'What will this come to? He commands us to provide, and give great gifts, and all out of an empty coffer. Nor will he know his purse, or yield me this, to show him what a beggar his heart is, being of no power to make his wishes good. His promises fly so beyond his state that what he speaks is all in debt, he owes for every word. He is so kind that he now pays interest for it. His lands put to their books.'* [712]

Generosity and charity are admirable traits. However, we need to ensure that our giving is sustainable. So that we can maintain our financial affairs in good order. We are personally responsible for our debts and taxes in society. Thus, we must have provision to meet our obligations. Having said that, when we can give to the less fortunate people, we must do so. Philanthropy is much greater than any one person. Philanthropy is about a just cause that promotes goodness, equality, opportunity, and inclusion for all people of the modern world.

---

711 Shakespeare, William. (1623). *Timon of Athens.* Act 1, Scene 2.
712 Shakespeare, William. (1623). *Timon of Athens.* Act 1, Scene 2.

'Alcibiades, thou art a solider, therefore, seldom rich. It comes in charity to thee. For all thy living is amongst the dead, and all the lands thou hast lie in a pitched field.' [713]

A state of contentment, good health, and peace of mind are the greatest gains in this world. Everything else that we possess, be it private property, personal wealth, family, friends, luxury vehicles, income, prized yachts, in summary, all the things of this world, are but temporary, transient, trivial, and trifling objects or personal relations. Possessions that one day we shall relinquish.

'Get on your cloak, and haste you to Lord Timon. Importune him for my moneys. Be not ceased by slight denial, nor then silenced when ... "Commend me to your Master" and the cap plays in the right hand, thus. But tell him, my uses cry to me, I must serve my turn out mine own. His days and times are past and my reliance on his fracted dates have smit my credit. I love and honour him, but I must not break my back to heal his finger. Immediate are my needs, and my relief must not be tossed and turned to me in words, but find supply immediate.' [714]

The majority of people in the Modern World endeavour to further their personal interest, private property portfolio, personal wealth, income, procure profit, and pecuniary gain. Indeed, it is when we stand in need, that friendships and loyalties are tested. During our times of trouble, tribulation, and torment, we shall bear witness to who is a faithful friend, and who is a timely traitor.

---

713 Shakespeare, William. (1623). *Timon of Athens.* Act 1, Scene 2.
714 Shakespeare, William. (1623). *Timon of Athens.* Act 2, Scene 1.

'Come hither, I pray you. I beseech you, how goes the world, that I am thus encountered with clamorous demands of debt, broken bonds, and the detention of long-since-due debts, against mine honour? My Loved Lord, though you hear now, too late, yet now's a time. The greatest of your having lacks a half to pay your present debts. Let all my lands be sold. It is all engaged, some forfeited and gone, and what remains will hardly stop the mouth of present dues.' [715]

The contemporary economic world is all about global financial markets, private assets, treasury bonds, loans, and personal debts. How much debt we can acquire, and then utilise to create productive assets, which shall yield a positive rate of return on our investments. This is the grand objective of individuals, that desire 'financial success' in the modern world.

However, it must not exceed the parameters of our finite reason, that personal bankruptcy and financial ruin are also real possibilities that we may confront, in our quest for financial freedom. Insofar as it concerns the sound management of financial capital, pragmatic stewardship is a non-negotiable requirement. In all cases, it is good financial advice to live within one's means. Excessive debt can be our downfall.

'The future comes apace, what shall defend the interim? And at length how goes our reckoning? To Lacedaemon did my land extend! O My Good Lord, the world is but a word. Were it all yours to give it in a breath, how quickly were it gone!' [716]

We are fooled into believing that the things of this world are permanently our own. Regardless of the precision in a person's planning, the future is always uncertain and unpredictable. No matter the unprecedented heights of our worldly success in life, be

---

715 Shakespeare, William. (1623). *Timon of Athens.* Act 2, Scene 2.
716 Shakespeare, William. (1623). *Timon of Athens.* Act 2, Scene 2.

it in private property, personal wealth creation, tertiary education, intimate relationships, quality friendships, marriage, finances, employment, or health, in the finality of our life, upon the surety of our death, we have to relinquish it all.

> *'Flaminius, I have noted thee always wise. I have observed thee always for a towardly prompt spirit, give thee thy due, and one that knows what belongs to reason, and canst use the time well, if the time use thee well. Good parts in thee. Draw nearer, honest Flaminius. Thy Lord's a bountiful gentleman, but thou art wise, and thou knowest well enough, although thou comest to me, that this is no time to lend money, especially upon bare friendship, without security.'* [717]

Shakespeare shows us the dark reality of naked self-interest in operation within the Modern World. Each person is seeking to advance their self-interest. Even at the expense of providing assistance to a true friend, who stands most in need. Each person seeks surety in their personal dealings and private transactions with other individuals in civilised society. This can be by way of a bond, promissory note, real property security, secondary guarantor, alternatively, some other legal or financial mechanism to ensure performance of a lawful contract. Without the presence of a surety, it is simply not possible to lend money, for genuine concern that the principal lent, is subject to a high risk of forfeiture.

---

717 Shakespeare, William. (1623). *Timon of Athens.* Act 3, Scene 1.

'Is it possible the world should so much differ, and we alive that lived? Fly, damned baseness, to him that worships thee! Let moulten coin be thy damnation, thou disease of a friend, and not himself! Has friendship such a faint and milky heart, it turns in less than two nights? O you Gods, I feel my Master's passion! This slave, unto his honour, has My Lord's meat in him. Why should it thrive and turn to nutriment, when he is turned to poison? O, may diseases only work upon it! And, when he's sick to death, let not that part of nature which My Lord paid for, be of any power to expel sickness, but prolong his hour!' [718]

Betrayal and deception are part and parcel of human nature. Often, people will entertain a relationship where there is cause for 'mutual interest' or 'personal gain'. However, when such an opportunity for pecuniary gain, influence, power, profit, income, fame, or prestige is no more, then the self-centred individual will discard the relationship. Unfortunately, the contemporary world consists of individuals, who are all too concerned with the exploitation of people, for their selfish needs and personal ends. It is a most rare exception to the primary rule of self-interest, that friendships are founded exclusively on the moral principle of altruism.

'Nothing emboldens sin so much as mercy.' [719]

Demonstrating mercy towards those individuals that have done us wrong is incredibly humble and takes enormous courage. However, the Prerogative of Mercy can be used against us. For when we forgive other people, it also affords them the opportunity to continue their offence unabated, or become encouraged, in the negative sense of the term, that their actions have no profound consequences. Therefore, we must exercise caution, to whom we extend forgiveness. So that our mercy is not misappropriated.

---

718 Shakespeare, William. (1623). *Timon of Athens.* Act 3, Scene 1.
719 Shakespeare, William. (1623). *Timon of Athens.* Act 3, Scene 5.

'He's truly valiant that can wisely suffer the worst that man can breathe, and make his wrongs his outsides, to wear them like his raiment, carelessly. And never prefer his injuries to his heart, to bring it into danger. If wrongs be evils and enforce us kill, what folly it is to hazard life for ill!' [720]

It is not within the finite power of every individual, to preserve their patience and rely upon natural reason, during times of acute distress. The majority of unenlightened people will let 'animality' override 'rationality' during challenging times. While sensibility is within the reach of every person, it is rarely employed as often as it is merited. However, that individual, who can preserve reason and patience, shall find peace of mind, and not be swayed by the endless troubles of this world. Most importantly, peace is the highest accolade that a person can secure in this world.

'Who cannot condemn rashness in cold blood? To kill, I grant, is sin's extremest gust, but, in defence, by mercy, it is most just.' [721]

The aforementioned statement constitutes a classic moral dilemma. It is wrong, morally, ethically, and legally to murder another person, period. However, the important question before us is one of self-defence. In the moment of life and death, is it acceptable to take the precious life of another person, in order to save our own life? While the extenuating circumstance of self-defence may appear to extend some credibility to answer this question in the affirmative, a wrong is a wrong. A wrong does not constitute a right.

In theory, the taking of another human's life is not a rational course to resolving one's own problems or concerns. In practice, it is essential that sacred moral principles guide the course of our life. Our free moral actions must be subject to certain fundamental

---

720 Shakespeare, William. (1623). *Timon of Athens.* Act 3, Scene 5.
721 Shakespeare, William. (1623). *Timon of Athens.* Act 3, Scene 5.

principles. Foremost of them being, the preservation of all human life. The sanctity of human life is beyond question.

> *'Let's shake our heads, and say, as it were a knell unto our Master's fortunes, we have seen better days. Let each take some. Nay, put out all your hands. Not one word more. Thus, part we rich in sorrow, parting poor. O, the fierce wretchedness that glory brings us! Who would not wish to be from wealth exempt, since riches point to misery and contempt?'* [722]

The pursuit of personal wealth and private property only leads to the accumulation of incalculable worries, despair, gloom, anxiety, and distress. We are all subject to the twists and turns of fate. Not to mention, the total loss of private property and personal wealth during our lifetime, is always a real possibility. Thus, we only endlessly strive to accumulate private property, personal wealth, and financial capital in vain.

First, we are primarily concerned with how we shall 'accumulate' our wealth portfolio. Second, we are overly concerned with how to 'safeguard' our wealth from loss of value, or outright theft. Third, we are excessively concerned with 'inter-generational wealth transfer'. That is to say, the preservation and protection of our wealth for our children and grandchildren. Thus, our entire lifetime is indirectly dedicated to the 'servitude' of wealth.

> *'Willing misery. Outlives incertain pomp, is crowned before. The one is filling still, never complete, the other, at high wish.'* [723]

We are all but assured the presence of misery in our lives. Whereas, pomp, fame, wealth, private property, influence, income, and power are momentary and fleeting possessions. What is in our power is the ability to be content with what we have achieved and

---

722　Shakespeare, William. (1623). *Timon of Athens.* Act 4, Scene 2.
723　Shakespeare, William. (1623). *Timon of Athens.* Act 4, Scene 3.

accomplished. It is within our power to be satisfied with who we are. For the psychological state of contentment is not contingent upon how much or how little we have accomplished, but consciously affirming that we are human.

Always remember, that it is by the virtue of being human, and not by personal wealth, private property, income, social class, education, gender, sex, age, colour, race, ethnicity, political affiliation, country of birth, or any other distinguishing factor, characteristic, trait, or attribute, that we are all afforded human dignity. In the final analysis, only contentment can transcend misery.

'The middle of humanity thou never knewest, but the extremity of both ends.'[724]

It is only by treading the 'Middle Way', by seeking the middle ground in all things, that we shall obtain an incommunicable inner peace within ourselves. On the other hand, extremity is the cause of much grief, pain, suffering, and sorrow in the Modern World. For when we have too much, or too little of an object, substance, entity, individual, or any other desirable material or immaterial phenomenon, then we establish the formal grounds for our dissatisfaction.

The ancient Greek philosopher, Aristotle describes in his masterpiece work titled *Nicomachean Ethics*, the novel idea of a 'Golden Mean'. In all things, there is a 'Golden Mean'. Thus, we ought to exercise our good judgement and ability to reason. To live with a reasonable quantity of our material possessions. We shall strive to be content with moderation in all things in our life, including in the gratification of our desires.

---

724 Shakespeare, William. (1623). *Timon of Athens.* Act 4, Scene 3.

'What things in the world canst thou nearest compare to thy flatterers? Women nearest, but men, men are the things themselves.' [725]

Gentlewomen are masters in the art of persuasion. Gentlewomen possess both the talent and wit to navigate their circumstances, events, environment, and affairs, with considerable tact and diplomacy. On the contrary, gentlemen can often treat every person they associate with in a similar fashion, or comparable manner. That is to say, without considerable regard for finesse in the management of interpersonal communication within their relationships.

'The Commonwealth of Athens is become a forest of beasts.' [726]

Moral decadence in the body politic is inevitable. Even in the most advanced sovereign nation-state, the forces of war and conflict are real threats. History has shown, that civilisations, societies, empires, and kingdoms are subject to destruction and disintegration. The dismal reality is that human nature is static and fixed. Human civilisation is plagued by the vices of jealousy, hate, envy, greed, lust, sloth, and pride. The majority of humans struggle to transcend their base nature, which is guided by the deceived ego and the deceptive senses.

The institution of Common Law functions to constrain and regulate human behaviour in the sovereign nation-state. While the existence of the law is a prerequisite foundation to the advancement of modern society, the law is imperfect. From time to time, the citizens will transgress the law. In the furtherance of their self-interest or personal agenda, individuals circumvent the law. In the end, we are all but guaranteed a condition of anarchy in the nation-state.

---

725 Shakespeare, William. (1623). *Timon of Athens.* Act 4, Scene 3.
726 Shakespeare, William. (1623). *Timon of Athens.* Act 4, Scene 3.

'I am sick of this false world, and will love nought but even the mere necessities upon it.' [727]

This world, and all that is in it, is full of much falsehood and wretchedness. We will be deceived, betrayed, and abandoned by someone, at some point in our lives. True wisdom resides in placing our total trust and complete confidence in God. We can only rely upon God for our Salvation and Redemption. A person who places the possibility of the fulfilment of their hopes, dreams, and ambitions in humans is naive.

'The laws, your curb and whip, in their rough power have unchecked theft.' [728]

Laws are imperfect and imprecise. Regardless of the good intentions that learned senators and honourable members of the Federal Parliament intend for their sovereign nation-state. Laws do not always function as envisaged. It is for this reason, among several others, that amendments and revisions to statutes become all too necessary in the body politic. Not to mention, the legislators of a body politic are always susceptible to bribery, corruption, self-interest, financial incentives, and other forms of personal gain, in the cumbersome process of enacting laws in Parliament.

---

727 Shakespeare, William. (1623). *Timon of Athens.* Act 4, Scene 3.
728 Shakespeare, William. (1623). *Timon of Athens.* Act 4, Scene 3.

Chapter 33

TITUS ANDRONICUS

'And look you eat no more than will preserve just so much strength in us as will revenge these bitter woes of ours. Marcus, unknit that sorrow-wreathen knot. Thy niece and I, poor creatures, want our hands and cannot passionate our tenfold grief with folded arms. This poor right hand of mine is left to tyrannise upon my breast, who, when my heart, all mad with misery, beats in this hollow prison of my flesh, then this I thump it down.'

SHAKESPEARE

Titus Andronicus is a play defined by tragedy, horror, revenge, power, retribution, and justice. It narrates the story of General Titus who returns from war, with five prisoners, namely, Tamora, the Queen of the Goths, her three beloved sons, and Aaron the Moor. The valiant Titus makes a sacrifice of Tamora's eldest son, despite Tamora's countless pleadings which fall on Titus' deaf ears. This brutal act of murder, which Titus performs as part of a burial ritual for his deceased sons, ignites the fury and rage of Tamora. As Tamora is forced to helplessly watch the death of her beloved son, she vows to seek revenge against Titus and his family.

Titus is offered the rare opportunity to be enthroned Emperor. However, Titus rejects this majestic proposal, due to his advanced age. In Titus' place, the honourable Saturninus is proclaimed the new Emperor of Rome. There is some inter-family rivalry and conflict between Titus and his sons. As a result, Titus kills one of his sons named Mutius. Emperor Saturninus initially claims Titus' daughter, Lavinia as his wife. Shortly thereafter, Saturninus seeks Tamora to be his Empress, and Tamora whole-heartedly agrees. Later on, Tamora shall exploit this Royal Appointment. Empress Tamora shall create the perfect opportunity, for her to further the evil endeavour of destroying Titus and his family.

Tamora's two sons murder Bassianus. They dispose of his body in an unmarked grave. Subsequently, Tamora's two sons rape Lavinia and then disfigure her body, mutilating her tongue and dismembering her hand. Following this tragic incident, Lavinia is unable to orally narrate her harrowing rape ordeal. Emperor Saturninus mistakenly concludes that Titus' sons are responsible for the murder of Bassianus in exchange for gold.

The tribune, Marcus Andronicus finds his niece, Lavinia distraught and in extreme distress. Regrettably, Lavinia is unable to speak to Marcus and share her tragic story with him. Titus' two sons, wrongly accused of murdering Bassianus, are condemned to death. Titus' remaining son, Lucius is banished from Rome. Aaron the Moor takes outright advantage of Titus' desperate situation. Aaron offers Titus the opportunity to salvage his two son's lives, in exchange for a severed hand from a member of Titus' family. Titus willingly sacrifices his own hand and gives this offering to Aaron the Moor, to be presented to the Roman Emperor as a ransom. In exchange, Titus receives the severed heads of his beloved sons, along with his severed hand, returned to him.

Titus finally discovers the true perpetrators who raped his beloved daughter, Lavinia. Meanwhile, Aaron the Moor has impregnated Tamora. Tamora now desires the newborn infant be killed. As the baby boy's black skin colour will expose to Emperor Saturninus, that her newborn baby is not His Royal Birth-child. Aaron the Moor does not permit the murder of his first-born son.

Rather, Aaron murders the nursemaid and he escapes with his infant son.

Titus seeks to secure justice with his own might and strength. Titus masterfully plays out his innocence of the knowledge of the rape of his daughter, and the death of his sons in front of Tamora's eyes. Unfortunately, Tamora's lapse of judgement witnesses her leave her two sons in Titus' vicinity. Now Titus and Lavinia seize the opportunity to kill Tamora's sons.

Thereafter, Titus calls for a Royal Banquet, where he entertains Emperor Saturninus and Empress Tamora as honourable guests. Titus serves a cooked pie containing the body parts of Tamora's sons. Now while Emperor Saturninus and Empress Tamora are feasting, Titus reveals the Truth. Titus then murders his daughter, Lavinia. As this is the only honourable end for her. Thereafter, Titus murders Empress Tamora, and consequently, Emperor Saturninus kills Titus. In the end, Titus' last remaining son, Lucius kills Emperor Saturninus.

In the midst of total chaos, Marcus Andronicus implores the Roman people to peace, good judgement, and reason. Lucius explains his actions before the Roman people. Lucius is crowned the next Emperor of Rome. Titus and Lavinia are afforded the courtesy of a Royal Burial. On the other hand, Tamora's body is dishonourably discarded. Tamora's body is left exposed to the natural elements, as food for the vultures, ravens, and other wild animals.

'Sweet mercy is nobility's true badge.'[729]

A person who is merciful towards other people, overcomes the Self. Demonstrating mercy means 'letting go' of the ill desire for retribution. Mercy is the attribute of a noble, wise, and honourable person. The weak-willed person shall always seek the temptations

---

729 Shakespeare, William. (1594). *Titus Andronicus.* Act 1, Scene 1.

of the flesh. That is to secure retribution and inflict some form of punishment upon the perpetrator as revenge. However, the strong-willed person shall be guided by the Spirit. The noble person will transcend hate, envy, and bitterness.

> *'In peace and honour, rest you here, my Sons. Rome's Readiest Champions, repose you here in rest, secure from worldly chances and mishaps. Here lurks no treason. Here no envy swells. Here grow no damned grudges. Here are no storms, no noise, but silence … and eternal sleep.'* [730]

After our destined date with death, we are safe from the troubles, tortures, tragedies, tribulations, terrors, and traumas of this world. For after death, no person, entity, institution, association, or company can harm us. Some people shall find peace in the thought of death. Death can be described as an unending period of rest. To never again embody the flesh. Death is inevitable. We are all mortal. Therefore, we shall all confront our destined demise.

> *'Noble Patricians, Patrons of my right, defend the justice of my cause with arms and, Countrymen, my loving followers, plead my successive title with your swords.'* [731]

We must be resolved to make a defiant stand for justice, integrity, equality, and honour. The 'Good Fight' for justice is not always a linear path. However, justice is a meritorious cause, and therefore, one that we ought to persevere in, and defend with all our strength. There is no guarantee of justice in this world. Having said that, we ought to be on the right side of history. We must also be mindful to create history, for all the right reasons.

---

730 Shakespeare, William. (1594). *Titus Andronicus.* Act 1, Scene 1.
731 Shakespeare, William. (1594). *Titus Andronicus.* Act 1, Scene 1.

'I am his first-born Son. That was the last that wear the Imperial Diadem of Rome. Then let my father's honours live in me, nor wrong mine age with this indignity.' [732]

Throughout the course of ancient and modern history, there has been a special status afforded to the first-born son of a family. The first-born son held social, political, economic, and legal influence, that went far beyond the remaining sons, and the daughters of a household. In the contemporary world, with changing conceptions of gender roles, and the proliferation of universal human rights, the privilege of the first-born son has diminished. However, these newfound human rights in gender, sex, and racial equality are not representative of how every human is treated across all the cultures, continents, and countries in the Modern World.

'Romans, friends, followers, favourers of my right, if ever Bassianus, Caesar's Son, were gracious in the eyes of Royal Rome, Keep then this passage to the Capitol and suffer not dishonour to approach the Imperial Seat. To virtue consecrate. To justice continence and nobility; But let desert in pure election shine, and Romans, fight for freedom in your choice.' [733]

Above all things, we desire love, understanding, belonging, justice, and freedom in this world. Loyalties and allegiances are not guaranteed in the world. Not to mention, political alliances are temporary in nature. The prized fight for freedom is always uncertain. For example, consider in the twenty-first century, the freedom of movement and political communication are implied legal rights in most developed Western nation-states. However, these fundamental liberties and cherished human rights are not guaranteed to endure indefinitely. Common Law rights are always subject to the remote possibility of subversion by statute.

---

732 Shakespeare, William. (1594). *Titus Andronicus.* Act 1, Scene 1.
733 Shakespeare, William. (1594). *Titus Andronicus.* Act 1, Scene 1.

'I have been thy Soldier forty years and led my Country's strength successfully. And buried one and twenty valiant sons, knighted in field, slain manfully in arms, in right and service of their noble Country. Give me a staff of honour for mine age.'[734]

To serve one's country is an honourable undertaking. Now those people who have discharged this duty well, have brought honour and pride to their sovereign nation-state. Acknowledgements, awards, and accolades for one's commendable military service, serve as due recognition for such an officer's valiant sacrifices in the course of military duty. We must pay our respects to those gentlemen and gentlewomen in uniform. For it is due to their service and sacrifice, that we entertain a peaceful, productive, and purposeful civilian life.

'My Lord, be ruled by me, be won at last. Dissemble all your griefs and discontents. You are but newly planted in your Throne. Lest, then, the People and Patricians, too, upon a just survey, take Titus' part, and so supplant you for ingratitude, which Rome reputes to be a heinous sin. Yield at entreats. And then let me alone. I'll find a day to massacre them all and raze their faction and their family, the cruel Father and his traitorous Sons, to whom I sued for my Dear Son's life, and make them know what it is to let a Queen kneel in the streets and beg for grace in vain.'[735]

We must not take another person's kind words at face value. An influential person may tirelessly work to gain our trust in the foreground, while seeking to plot turmoil, disorder, chaos, and retribution in the background. Deception is a dismal reality in this world. For example, consider that the *Messiah* was betrayed by one of the *Twelve Apostles*. It is the very dark essence of human nature to be evil, egoistic, and equivocate.

---

734 Shakespeare, William. (1594). *Titus Andronicus.* Act 1, Scene 1.
735 Shakespeare, William. (1594). *Titus Andronicus.* Act 1, Scene 1.

'O Noble Father, you lament in vain. The Tribunes hear you not. No man is by and you recount your sorrows to a stone. Ah, Lucius, for thy Brothers let me plead. Grave Tribunes, once more I entreat of you … My Gracious Lord, no Tribune hears you speak. Why, it is no matter, man. If they did hear, they would not mark me, or if they did mark, they would not pity me, yet plead I must and bootless unto them. Therefore, I tell my sorrows to the stones; who, though they cannot answer my distress, yet in some sort they are better than the Tribunes, for that they will not intercept my tale. When I do weep, they humbly at my feet receive my tears and seem to weep with me. And, were they but attired in grave weeds, Rome could afford no Tribunes like to these. A stone is soft as wax. Tribunes more hard than stones. A stone is silent and offendeth not, and Tribunes … with their tongues doom men to death.' [736]

We shall all experience grief, sorrow, distress, tragedy, loss, heartbreak, lament, pain, suffering, and misery in this broken world. Protesting to higher authority figures, does not always achieve the outcome, or resolution that we desire. However, we must not place our faith in tribunes, senators, politicians, officers, magistrates, justices, or the chief justice. Rather, we must totally and unconditionally position our trust in God. The Path of Faith is not for the weak-hearted. However, those blessed individuals who have kept the Faith, they can find peace and security amidst a sea of troubles.

---

736 Shakespeare, William. (1594). *Titus Andronicus*. Act 3, Scene 1.

'O Brother, speak with possibility and do not break into these deep extremes. Are not my sorrows deep, having no limit? Be then my passions limitless with them. But yet let reason govern thy lament! If there were reason for these miseries, then into limits could I bind my woes. When Heaven doth weep, doth not the Earth overflow? If the winds rage, doth not the sea wax mad, threatening the welkin with his big-swollen face? And wilt thou have a reason for this coil?' [737]

The human condition is betwixt the extremes of reason and emotion. Happiness and sadness. Joy and grief. Animality and rationality. Also, indecision and judgement. The best counsel that can be proffered herein is to find a balance. A harmony. A state of homeostasis in this world. That individual who secures a calmness amidst the endless storm and chaotic rage of this broken world, has indeed found a Lasting Peace. An Eternal Peace that transcends all possibility of realisation with the finite power of human reason, thought, judgement, discernment, and logic.

'Now let hot Etna cool in Sicily and be my heart an ever-burning Hell. These miseries are more than may be borne. To weep with them that weep doth ease some deal, but sorrow flouted at is double death. Ah! That this sight should make so deep a wound and yet detested life not shrink there at. That ever death should let life bear his name, where life hath no more interest, but to breathe. Alas, poor heart, that kiss is comfortless as frozen water to a starved snake. When will this fearful slumber have an end?' [738]

The powerful presence of sorrow and grief can endure without end in this world. It is all too possible that our sorrow and grief turn into a life-long ordeal with darkness and misery. However, we must transcend the boundaries and perceived limitations of the human

---

737 Shakespeare, William. (1594). *Titus Andronicus.* Act 3, Scene 1.
738 Shakespeare, William. (1594). *Titus Andronicus.* Act 3, Scene 1.

condition. It is within the capacity of our thinking to do so. A life consumed by sorrows is difficult to tolerate. We must rise above and beyond worldly pain and suffering, to create a life, that when we are near death, we can assert, it was a meaningful life.

'Ah, now no more will I control thy griefs. This is a time to storm! Why art thou still? Why dost thou laugh? It fits not with this hour. Why? I have not another tear to shed. Besides ... this sorrow is an enemy. And would usurp upon my watery eyes and make them blind with tributary tears. Then which way shall I find revenge's cave?'[739]

Grief can further an individual towards irrationality, evil thoughts, and the performance of sin. While we shall all have our personal encounters with grief, we must not let grief consume us, nor destroy our character, faith, moral principles, integrity, and conscience. The dark temptation of revenge entices us to tread the ill-fated Path of Evil. We must not solely rely upon our will power and good judgement, however, we ought to seek guidance and strength from God, to overcome evil with good.

In the final analysis, the entire story of our life is a battle between the Spirit and the Flesh. We must conquer the Flesh, if we are to abide by the high moral standards of the Spirit. Our time on Earth is a battleground between the Flesh and the Spirit. This life is an opportunity to define and refine our character. To overcome the Flesh. To become one with the Spirit. We must strive to seek union with God. Indeed, this is the Epic Battle of our lifetime.

---

739 Shakespeare, William. (1594). *Titus Andronicus.* Act 3, Scene 1.

> *'And look you eat no more than will preserve just so much strength in us as will revenge these bitter woes of ours. Marcus, unknit that sorrow-wreathen knot. Thy niece and I, poor creatures, want our hands and cannot passionate our tenfold grief with folded arms. This poor right hand of mine is left to tyrannise upon my breast, who, when my heart, all mad with misery, beats in this hollow prison of my flesh, then thus I thump it down.'* [740]

We must not live to seek revenge. For this is a most shallow and meaningless endeavour. The motivation to live, the will to live, must not be established upon the evil desire to further the presence of vice. Those individuals who let their pain and sorrow consume them, will fall for the Devil's schemes. On the contrary, our motivation to live our life must be to advance God's Kingdom on Earth. The highest cause, indeed the greatest cause, that we can commit to, in order to further our virtue and character, is to ensure the fulfilment of God's Sovereign Will in all matters.

> *'Then cheer thy Spirit, for know, thou Emperor, I will enchant the old Andronicus with words more sweet and yet more dangerous, than baits to fish or honey-stalks to sheep, when as the one is wounded with the bait, the other rotted with delicious feed. But he will not entreat his son for us. If Tamora entreat him, then he will. For I can smooth and fill his aged ears with golden promises, that, were his heart almost impregnable, his old ears deaf, yet should both ear and heart obey my tongue.'* [741]

Words can be employed in a deceptive, manipulative, and persuasive manner. We must never underestimate the strength of speech, to secure significant aims and consequential objectives. Words can masterfully misconstrue intentions, desires, thoughts, and motivations. Actions reveal the true intent of their moral agents.

---

740 Shakespeare, William. (1594). *Titus Andronicus.* Act 3, Scene 2.
741 Shakespeare, William. (1594). *Titus Andronicus.* Act 4, Scene 4.

As we accumulate worldly experience, formal learning, and practical knowledge in our lifetime, we must become more conscious of how the employment of words are subject to rhetorical devices. We must exercise reason, discernment, prudence, logic, and good judgement, to better ascertain the real meaning underlying an individual's employment of select words.

> *'Lucius, save the child, and bear it from me to the Empress. If thou do this, I'll show thee wondrous things, that highly may advantage thee to hear. If thou wilt not, befall what may befall, I'll speak no more but vengeance rot you all! Say on, and if it please me which thou speakest, thy child shall live, and I will see it nourished.'* [742]

Desperate times force us towards desperate measures. During times of desperation, people utilise any and all information, resources, financial capital, ability, natural endowment, formal learning, skill, personal wealth, knowledge, income, education, or private property they possess, in order to secure their personal safety, cherished liberty, or protect a loved one. The art of negotiation and barter are as old as human civilisation itself.

> *'My Lord, the Emperor, resolve me this. Was it well done of rash Virginius to slay his daughter with his own right hand, because she was enforced, stained, and deflowered? It was, Andronicus. Your reason, mighty Lord? Because the girl should not survive her shame and, by her presence, still renew his sorrows. A reason mighty, strong, and effectual.'* [743]

Honour is important. However, honour is not the all-encompassing and sole virtue in the world. Liberty, intelligence, learning, beauty, temperance, knowledge, honesty, kindness, charity, and justice. These are all equally important traits and significant virtues in

---

742 Shakespeare, William. (1594). *Titus Andronicus.* Act 5, Scene 1.
743 Shakespeare, William. (1594). *Titus Andronicus.* Act 5, Scene 3.

their own capacity. We must not let self-evident limitations in our capacity for reason, coupled with the ancient bonds of tradition, custom, and culture, define our thought and behaviour in modern society. All of human life is honourable. Human life must be preserved.

'As for that ravenous tiger, Tamora … no funeral rite, nor man in mourning weed … no mournful bell shall ring her burial, but throw her forth to beasts and birds to prey. Her life was beastly and devoid of pity. And, being dead, let birds on her take pity.' [744]

What we sow, is what we shall reap. We must not be deceived or fooled into thinking that we can circumvent God's Righteousness and Perfect Justice. If we perform evil on Earth, what hope do we have of obtaining God's favour, blessing, and goodness? While no person is beyond God's Sovereign Power for mercy and forgiveness, we must never act to misappropriate God's Love and special gift of Salvation.

---

744 Shakespeare, William. (1594). *Titus Andronicus.* Act 5, Scene 3.

Chapter 34

TROILUS AND CRESSIDA

'Women are Angels, wooing. Things won are done. Joy's soul lies in the doing. That she beloved knows nought that knows not this. Men prize the thing ungained more than it is. That she was never yet that ever knew love got so sweet as when desire did sue. Therefore, this maxim out of love I teach. Achievement is command, ungained, beseech. Then though my heart's content firm love doth bear, nothing of that shall from mine eyes appear.'

SHAKESPEARE

Troilus and Cressida is a play characterised by the themes of love, tragedy, and war. This play is situated in the time of the *Trojan War*. King Agamemnon, along with his brother, Menelaus are resident at a Greek cantonment. The two honourable gentlemen are accompanied by wise counsellors, Nestor and Ulysses. Meanwhile, the famed soldier, Achilles is disinterested in combat. Achilles spends his time in association with his friend, Patroclus.

In the City of Troy, King Priam is entertaining an argument with his noble sons, Hector and Paris. Now Paris is guilty of seducing Menelaus' beautiful wife, Helen. Paris' immoral actions, which transpired several years ago, sparked the outbreak of the *Trojan War*. The content of King Priam and his two sons argument is concerned with whether Paris ought to return Helen to her rightful husband. However, the trio determine to continue the *Trojan War*.

The endless social affairs of affluent gentlemen and gentle-women continue in the background of this play. The Prince's sister, Cassandra makes an unfavourable prophesy, foretelling doom and destruction for all the belligerents in the *Trojan War*. A young gentleman named Troilus has fallen in love with Cressida. In an interesting, but not unexpected turn of events, the legendary Trojan warrior, Hector has openly challenged Greece, to send forth its best warrior, for a one-on-one duel.

The favour of Cressida's uncle, Pandarus is upon the two lovers. Pandarus assists Troilus and Cressida to consummate their union. Now Cressida's father makes an arrangement to exchange his daughter for a Trojan prisoner. Cressida leaves the company of Troilus and her father; she makes an oath of loyalty to Troilus. The flames of war shall test the bonds of true love. For now, Troilus is left heartbroken by the sudden departure of Cressida.

Greece responds to Hector's challenge for a duel by sending Ajax, rather than the famed Achilles. The Greek Commanders hoped, in vain, that by answering Hector's call for a duel with Ajax, this act will strain Achilles' most cherished pride, and tempt him to fight Hector. The plan spectacularly fails. Mighty Hector refuses to engage in the fight, because Ajax is related to his family line.

While Cressida is confined to the Greek camps, a Prince named Diomedes befriends her. Initially, Cressida is hesitant and somewhat resistant to Diomedes' advances and desires for a romantic union. However, Cressida finally agrees to entertain a friendship with the Prince. Unbeknown to Cressida, Troilus has left Troy to seek his beloved gentlelady. However, Troilus, in the company of Ulysses, has overheard the encounter between Cressida and Diomedes. To say the least, Troilus is whole-heartedly disappointed and totally ashamed of Cressida. Nonetheless, Troilus contains his rage and fury at Cressida.

The closing of this play is marked by Hector killing Patroclus. This event awakens Achilles from his slumber, and finally motivates him to engage in combat. Initially, it appears that Hector has the advantage, however, Achilles successfully traps Hector, and disarms him. Hector is finally slaughtered by Achilles' soldiers. Troilus vows revenge for his beloved brother's death, and for the loss of Cressida. The final scene of this play concludes with Pandarus asserting there is no hope for this world. Given the selfish nature of the human condition and the dishonourable art of *Realpolitik*.

> *'Have you any discretion? Have you any eyes? Do you know what a man is? Is not birth, beauty, good shape, manhood, discourse, learning, gentleness, virtue, youth, liberality, and the like, the spice and salt that season a man?'*[745]

Attractive qualities and favourable traits can further a person's character, conscience, and integrity. While no individual has all the gifts of nature in their possession, we must strive to work within our limitations, to create the exemplary life. Our life shall be guided by virtue, righteousness, faith, moral excellence, reason, logic, good judgement, honesty, and temperance. In the pursuit of wisdom, we must acknowledge, that we have imperfections. Also, more importantly, that we are a 'work in progress'. It takes an entire lifetime to become truly accomplished.

---

745 Shakespeare, William. (1609). *Troilus and Cressida.* Act 1, Scene 2.

> *'Princes, what grief hath set the jaundice on your cheeks?*
> *The ample proposition that hope makes in all designs begun on*
> *Earth below fails in the promised largeness. Checks and disasters*
> *grow in the veins of actions highest reared as knots, by the conflux*
> *of meeting sap, infects the sound pine and diverts his grain.*
> *Tortive and errant, from his course of growth.'* [746]

We must persevere in hope. It is through hope, that all things are possible. Hope sustains life. Most notably, during difficult and testing ordeals, hope provides us with comfort and optimism for a brighter future. At times, our many hopes may not realise or manifest as we had intended. Such is the dismal nature of worldly reality. We must remember that not all aspects of existence are within our personal agency. In fact, losses, setbacks, heartaches, sorrows, grief, and misery are part and parcel of life. Having said that, the wise person seeks to surpass and transcend the mundane issues of life. The astute individual creates a good and fulfilling life.

> *'Why should a man be proud? How doth pride grow? I know not*
> *what pride is. Your mind is the fairer, Ajax, and your virtues the*
> *clearer. He that is proud eats up himself. Pride is his own glass,*
> *his own trumpet, his own chronicle. And whatever praises itself*
> *but in the deed, devours the deed in the praise.'* [747]

Excessive pride in oneself inevitably leads to an individual's downfall. A person who is overly consumed by their pride, ego, and sense of self-importance possesses a narrow field of vision. Such an individual cannot perceive beyond the Self. Regrettably, the conventional reality of this world is such, that the majority of the unenlightened people cannot perceive of a world that is beyond self-interest. Insofar as it concerns human affairs in modern society, vanity is omnipresent.

---

746 Shakespeare, William. (1609). *Troilus and Cressida.* Act 1, Scene 3.
747 Shakespeare, William. (1609). *Troilus and Cressida.* Act 2, Scene 3.

In this world, each person looks to secure their advantage, profit, gain, income, and interest, without an iota of consideration for the welfare of the most vulnerable and disadvantaged people in our modern society. This is what the contemporary world, defined by the ideologies of secularism, consumerism, materialism, individualism, liberalism, and capitalism, collectively reflects and represents in the early twenty-first century.

On the contrary, it is the distinguished mark of a selfless person to perceive the pain and suffering of other people in the world. The compassionate person provisions much needed goodness, love, faith, hope, charity, community service, and benevolence. The selfless person shall provision concern for the welfare and well-being of the destitute people, who stand most in need for assistance, be it in the form of food, water, housing, electricity, clothing, education, or personal safety.

'In love, in faith, to the tip of the nose. He eats nothing but doves, love, and that breeds hot blood, and hot blood begets hot thoughts, and hot thoughts beget hot deeds, and hot deeds is love.' [748]

Love is many things. However, above and beyond all, love is passion, emotion, feeling, and sensation. Love contains much irrationality and desire. Love limits the function of sound logic, rationality, reason, and good judgement. Yet, love is the prerequisite for life on Earth. Without love, there is no hope, final cause, power, or faith for a better life. A brighter future for humanity, and a better world, is to be established on the unmatched power of love.

Within the *Holy Bible*, in the *Book of First Corinthians*, Chapter 13, Verse 13, Paul the Apostle reminds us of the profound importance of love, 'And now these three remain: faith, hope, and love. But the greatest of these is love.' It is the power of love that makes our life worth living. Love transforms people, societies, cultures,

---

748 Shakespeare, William. (1609). *Troilus and Cressida*. Act 3, Scene 1.

continents, countries, and the world. Without the presence of love, this world, and our human experience, would not be the same.

> *'I'll fetch her. It is the prettiest villain. She fetches her breath as short as a new taken sparrow. Even such a passion doth embrace my bosom. My heart beats thicker than a feverous pulse, and all my powers do their bestowing lose, like vassalage at unawares encountering the eye of majesty.'* [749]

Beauty is immeasurable. Beauty captives the soul and transfixes the mind beyond reason. Attempt as we may, to exercise the higher faculties of judgement, logic, and discernment. They are powerless in the face of inestimable beauty. Nothing moves the soul, like love and beauty. Unconsciously, we are attracted to beauty. Very similar to how the force of gravity, naturally attracts all material objects towards the Earth's centre.

> *'What too curious dreg espies My Sweet Lady in the fountain of our love? More dregs than water if my fears have eyes. Fears make Devils of Cherubims. They never see truly. Blind fear, that seeing reason leads, oft finds safer footing than blind reason stumbling without fear. To fear the worst-off cures the worse. O, let mine Lady apprehend no fear.'* [750]

Fear is an irrational and illogical hindrance to our steady progress in life. The presence of fear does not resolve a problem, concern, or issue. Fear only serves to magnify life's challenges. Fear paralyses us from taking decisive action. Fear is best portrayed as an artificial hologram. The surreal illusion of fear appears most real. However, courage, conviction, and confidence can shatter the hologram. In the end, fear is revealed to be nothing more than a fictitious fabrication of the doubtful mind.

---

749 Shakespeare, William. (1609). *Troilus and Cressida*. Act 3, Scene 2.
750 Shakespeare, William. (1609). *Troilus and Cressida*. Act 3, Scene 2.

> *'This is the monstrosity in love, Lady; that the will is infinite and the execution confined, that the desire is boundless, and the act a slave to limit. They say all lovers swear more performance than they are able and yet reserve an ability that they never perform, vowing more than the perfection of ten and discharging less than the tenth part of one.'*[751]

In seeking a spouse, we often overestimate our ability, talent, and capacity to provision love, affection, attention, and good company in marriage. In reality, marriage is the doubling of one's personal responsibilities, and the halving of one's enforceable rights vis-à-vis one's spouse. A successful marriage is defined by transparent communication between spouses. The management of numerous expectations. The adjustment and re-adjustment of individual priorities. Not to mention, a willingness to overlook the faults and imperfections of one's spouse.

In marriage, we need to effectively navigate endless change. Change throughout life's major milestones and consequential experiences. For example, consider childbirth, relocation of principal place of residence, raising children, changes in employment, management of family finances, management of medical conditions, organising travel commitments, and the pursuit of further tertiary education.

> *'Pray you, content you. What offends you, Lady? Sir, mine own company. You cannot shun yourself. Let me go and try. I have a kind of Self resides with you; but an unkind Self, that itself will leave to be another's fool. I would be gone.'*[752]

We must accept ourselves for who we truly are. Authenticity is the starting point of all progress in this world. We cannot escape from ourselves. Make no illusion or fabrication. We are within our

---

751 Shakespeare, William. (1609). *Troilus and Cressida*. Act 3, Scene 2.
752 Shakespeare, William. (1609). *Troilus and Cressida*. Act 3, Scene 2.

immediate (and inescapable) vicinity from birth to death. Therefore, rationality and wisdom shall witness a sensible person come to terms with their personal identity, faith, beliefs, culture, religion, age, country of birth, sex, gender, colour, values, strengths, moral principles, weaknesses, dreams, hopes, and ambitions. If we can accept ourselves, perfections and imperfections alike, we shall find peace within ourselves. We do not have to be perfect. We have to be authentic.

'It is certain, greatness, once fallen out with fortune, must fall out with men too. What the declined is he shall as soon read in the eyes of others as feel in his own fall.' [753]

The history of human civilisation has demonstrated, time and time again, the rise and fall of great gentlemen and gentlewomen. This is the essence of human nature, it contains imperfections, frailties, weaknesses, limitations, and countless errors of judgement. Wisdom resides in our ability to examine the invaluable lessons from history. We must learn from the mistakes of previous generations. However, all too often, succeeding generations of the human civilisation, repeat the grave mistakes of their preceding generations. For example, consider the continuity of war and conflict throughout the long course of human history.

'My mind is troubled like a fountain stirred, and I myself see not the bottom of it.' [754]

Sometimes the straight path in life is lost. For life does contain twists, turns, tests, tragedies, tribulations, and trials that assess our faith and will to live. During challenging and troubling times, one should strive to maintain an equanimity of mind. The best counsel herein is to demonstrate non-attachment to material objects,

---

753 Shakespeare, William. (1609). *Troilus and Cressida*. Act 3, Scene 3.
754 Shakespeare, William. (1609). *Troilus and Cressida*. Act 3, Scene 3.

people, thoughts, and worldly phenomena. For everything in and of this world is transient and temporary.

Thus, by fixating, or attempting to fixate a state of permanency in this world, this shall become a cause for our considerable misery and grief. For we are attempting to hold on to worldly phenomena, which by definition, is fleeting and momentary. When everything, including our very life is temporary, why then are we troubled with the presence of flux in an impermanent and ever-changing reality?

'I will go meet with them. And My Lord, Aeneas, we met by chance. You did not find me here. Good, Good, My Lord. The Secrets of Nature have not more gift in taciturnity.' [755]

When we carefully reflect upon our life, some of our present reality and personal experiences have been defined by circumstance. Being in the right place, at the right time, can provision an unmerited opportunity to advance our life. An unmerited advancement, where effort, dexterity, or labour will make no adequate substitute. In all the things of this world, fortune, necessity, and fate have their impact. However, we cannot let the course of our life be defined by favourable or unfavourable events.

'O, you Gods Divine. Make Cressid's Name the very Crown of Falsehood, if ever she leave Troilus! Time, force, and death, do to this body what extremes you can, but the strong base and building of my love is as the very centre of the Earth, drawing all things to it.' [756]

Unfortunately, the vows of marriage and the oaths of true love, will be tested, and, at times, irreversibly broken. We must be psychologically prepared for the uncertain course of tribulations that will befall upon our life. Most importantly, we must preserve

---

755 Shakespeare, William. (1609). *Troilus and Cressida.* Act 4, Scene 2.
756 Shakespeare, William. (1609). *Troilus and Cressida.* Act 4, Scene 2.

our inner peace. For this priceless treasure of peace is too valuable to relinquish in our confrontation with the many external afflictions that shall attempt to torment and trouble us in this broken world.

> *'Now, Hector, I have fed mine eyes on thee. I have with exact view perused thee, Hector, and quoted joint by joint. Is this Achilles? I am Achilles. Stand fair, I prithee, let me look on thee. Behold thy fill. Nay, I have done already. Thou art too brief. I will a second time, as I would buy thee, view thee limb by limb. O, like a book of sport, thou shalt read me over. But there's more in me than thou understand'st.'* [757]

It takes a lifetime to understand the human condition. To come to terms with life. Let alone master our mind, body, spirit, and emotions. We can study a person from different vantage points and perspectives. However, to truly and wholly understand a person, we have to examine every aspect of their being, including medical, physical, emotional, spiritual, psychological, religious, intellectual, metaphysical, and social. There is always more to every person than what we know, or perceive through the method of empirical observation.

> *'Here is a letter from Queen Hecuba. A token from Her Daughter, my fair love. Both taxing me and gaging me to keep an oath that I have sworn. I will not break it. Fall Greeks, fail fame, honour, or go or stay; my major vow lies here, this I'll obey. Come, come, Thersites, help to trim my tent. This night in banqueting must all be spent. Away, Patroclus!'* [758]

Our character, integrity, and honour reside in keeping our sworn oaths and performing our obligations. History shall be our judge. In so far as we are true to ourselves, and to those people to whom

---

757 Shakespeare, William. (1609). *Troilus and Cressida*. Act 4, Scene 5.
758 Shakespeare, William. (1609). *Troilus and Cressida*. Act 5, Scene 1.

we have a duty or obligation, we shall possess a transcendental peace, that surpasses the shallow depth of natural reason. If we cannot be trusted to keep our word, we shall lose our honourable and esteemed reputation, good standing in society, credit-worthiness, and invaluable trust. The aforesaid treasures, once lost, are incredibly difficult to regain.

> *'It is as lawful, for we would give much to use violent thefts, and rob in the behalf of charity. It is the purpose that makes strong the vow, and vows to every purpose must not hold. Unarm, Sweet Hector. Hold you still, I say. Mine honour holds the weather of my fate. Life every man holds dear. But the dear man holds honour far more precious-dear than life.'*[759]

Our purposes and ends determine if we have the requisite motivation to secure the realisation of our vows. Vows made for any and every purpose are not sufficient cause for their performance and preservation. In all matters, we must value human life. For without life, we shall confront the end of our existence on Earth, being the final and irreversible reality of death.

More important than life itself is honour. For our present lifetime is fixed, however, the countless pages of history shall record our life for the endless ages to come. It is for this reason, that a noble gentleman or gentlewoman is prepared to sacrifice this life, where the security of one's prized honour stands in jeopardy. Our lifetime on Earth is very limited, however, our legacy shall endure for centuries to come.

---

759 Shakespeare, William. (1609). *Troilus and Cressida.* Act 5, Scene 3.

Chapter 35

TWELFTH NIGHT

'Alas, it is the baseness of thy fear that makes thee strangle thy propriety. Fear not, Cesario, take thy fortunes up. Be that thou knowest thou art, and then thou art as great as that thou fearest.'

SHAKESPEARE

Twelfth Night is an entertaining comedy concerning mistaken identity. This play narrates the story of Orsino, the Duke of Illyria, who is in utter despair that he is rejected by the Countess Olivia. Meanwhile, a group of thoughtful sailors have rescued a young gentlelady named Viola from an unexpected violent storm at sea. Viola is in total sorrow over the loss of her twin brother, Sebastian, who is presumed dead in the shipwreck. Viola is without economic, social, and political support. Therefore, Viola resolves to cross-dress as a gentleman, to gain employment as a Page to Duke Orsino.

Duke Orsino instructs Cesario, who is Viola, with her newly assumed identity as an honourable gentleman, to court Olivia on his behalf. To further complicate matters, Cesario is in love with Duke Orsino. Now while Olivia continues to reject Duke Orsino, Olivia is in love with Cesario.

This play is not without inter-family rivalry and the politics of society. Members of Olivia's own household, namely, Olivia's uncle, Sir Toby Belch, Olivia's servant, Maria, and Toby's good friend, Sir Andrew Aguecheek, are conspiring to act against the steward, Malvolio. Not to mention, Sir Andrew is also courting the Countess Olivia. Thus, Sir Andrew has a personal interest in plotting against Malvolio.

As this play progresses, it is revealed that Viola's twin brother, Sebastian has survived the shipwreck. Sebastian safely arrives in Illyria. Meanwhile Andrew's unconditional love for Olivia makes him envy Cesario. The remainder of this play illustrates endless quarrels, duels, misunderstandings, and even injustice levied against Malvolio. Not to mention, Malvolio is falsely imprisoned for a brief duration. This play concludes with Servant Maria being wedded to Toby. A union between Olivia and Sebastian. Last but not least, Orsino seeks to marry Viola.

> *'Will you stay no longer. Nor will you not that I go with you? By your patience, no. My stars shine darkly over me. The malignancy of my fate might, perhaps, distemper yours. Therefore, I shall crave of you your leave that I may bear my evils alone. It were a bad recompense for your love, to lay any of them on you.'* [760]

We cannot always be with those individual's that desire our warm affection and good company. Our lifetime is not of infinite measure. Indeed, the length of life is short. Therefore, it is entirely appropriate and warranted, that we make conscious decisions, concerning who we spend our lifetime with. As a matter of principle, we ought to be loving and kind to all people. However, we shall exercise proper discretion in whom we position our trust. We must also employ our good judgement in whom we determine to associate with.

---

760 Shakespeare, William. (1623). *Twelfth Night.* Act 2, Scene 1.

*'I am bound to the Count Orsino's Court. Farewell. The gentleness
of all the Gods go with thee. I have many enemies in Orsino's
Court, else would I very shortly see thee there. But come what may,
I do adore thee so that danger shall seem sport, and I will go.'*[761]

Based on our rank, status, title, or position in modern society, we all have contractual obligations that we must fulfil. This reality is part and parcel of life. We shall encounter many people on our life journey. In sincerity, we ought to wish everyone well. We must not forget that every person has their own struggles and personal challenges in life.

As for our life, we shall have the boldness, the conviction, and the fearless determination to confront our darkest enemies. With confidence, we must tread the Path that is before us. Always remember, that without risk, chance, and uncertainty, nothing great is ever accomplished.

*'For the Love of God, Peace! My Masters, are you mad? Or what
are you? Have you no wit, manners, nor honesty, but to gabble
like tinkers at this time of night? Do ye make an ale-house of My
Lady's House, that ye squeak out your coziers' catches without
any mitigation or remorse of voice? Is there no respect of place,
persons, nor time, in you?'*[762]

Morality is fast diminishing in the contemporary world. We inhabit a Modern World where custom, moderation, restraint, tradition, culture, religion, faith, honour, and the belief in God are all progressively on the decline. The secular, self-interested, superficial, and soulless society is embracing liberty without virtue. Rights without responsibilities. Freedoms without obligations. Expectations without duties. As a consequence, moral decadence is inevitable in this day and age.

---

761 Shakespeare, William. (1623). *Twelfth Night*. Act 2, Scene 1.
762 Shakespeare, William. (1623). *Twelfth Night*. Act 2, Scene 3.

> *'In delay there lies no plenty. Then come kiss me, sweet-and-twenty, youth's a stuff will not endure.'* [763]

In all things, timing is of the essence. We must not be under any illusion of the very finite quantity of time in our life. Indeed, the present moment is constantly passing us by. The illusion of human life is that it appears certain and permanent. However, all of life is change and impermanence. This much is certain, our very life is characterised by mortality. We must make the most of our youth when we have it on our possession. For one day, the time of youth will be no more.

> *'Once more, Cesario, get thee to yond same sovereign cruelty. Tell her my love, more noble than the world, prizes not quantity of dirty lands. The parts that Fortune hath bestowed upon her, tell her, I hold as giddily as Fortune, but it is that miracle and Queen of Gems that Nature pranks her in attracts my soul.'* [764]

Beauty is in the eye of the beholder. Natural beauty is esteemed and prized. It is the mark of good fortune to be endowed with the gift of natural beauty. However, beauty does not make a gentleman or gentlewoman complete in all respects. For beauty is but one desirable attribute. Among other admirable virtues and qualities, a person ought to possess intellect, strength, character, conscience, morality, charity, etiquette, confidence, courage, respect, faith, love for God, and service to humanity.

---

763 Shakespeare, William. (1623). *Twelfth Night*. Act 2, Scene 3.
764 Shakespeare, William. (1623). *Twelfth Night*. Act 2, Scene 4.

'Say that some Lady, as perhaps there is, hath for your love as great a pang of heart as you have for Olivia. You cannot love her. You tell her so. Must she not then be answered? There is no woman's sides can bide the beating of so strong a passion as love doth give my heart. No woman's heart so big to hold so much; they lack retention.' [765]

Love is desirable. However, the heart's desire to secure everlasting love is a far-fetched reality for most people. Indeed, sexual attraction, passion, emotion, and chemistry create the basis for love. Yet, these properties are not the prerequisites to a long-lasting relationship. Much more is required than the power of attraction, to create a fulfilling relationship. This includes trust, honesty, commitment, respect, integrity, faithfulness, loyalty, and perseverance. Most importantly, none of the aforesaid immaterial attributes are found in a person's romantic courtship endeavours, initial feeling of chemistry, physique, or facial appearance.

'In my stars I am above thee, but be not afraid of greatness. Some are born great, some achieve greatness, and some have greatness thrust upon them.' [766]

Our beliefs determine our limits. We must not preconceive or impose any artificial limits upon our cognition. For this will limit our inherent capacity to realise our full potential. Every person has God-given potential and dignity. Regardless of sex, gender, colour, race, creed, age, private wealth, private property, country of origin, ethnicity, faith, religion, social class, economic status, personal income, or any other distinguishing factor, every human possesses the inherent capacity and innate ability to achieve their highest potential. The collective responsibility is upon the human

---

765 Shakespeare, William. (1623). *Twelfth Night*. Act 2, Scene 4.
766 Shakespeare, William. (1623). *Twelfth Night*. Act 2, Scene 5.

civilisation to create a more equal, fair, just, and tolerant world. A world whereby each person can flourish, and thereby, create a life which reflects the fullness of the Human Spirit.

> '*O, what a deal of scorn looks beautiful in the contempt and anger of his lip. A murderous guilt shows not itself more soon than love that would seem hid. Love's night is noon. Cesario, by the roses of the spring, by maidhood honour, truth, and everything, I love thee so that, maugre all thy pride, nor wit, nor reason can my passion hide.*' [767]

Love pulls the strings of the heart in many conflicting directions. This reality makes it difficult to correctly reason and exercise good judgement. A person whom we truly love, even in their moment of rage and anger, we may subjectively perceive their beauty to be more pleasing to the eye, than reason shall afford cause for their ill-advised speech. It is not as difficult for a guilty person to conceal their corrupt conscience. As opposed to a lover's inability to hide their true feelings of affection and fondness for their beloved partner or spouse.

> '*Do not extort thy reason from this clause, for, that I woo, thou therefore hast no cause. But rather reason thus with reason fetter. Love sought is good, but given unsought is better. By innocence I swear, and by my youth, I have one heart, one bosom, and one truth, and that no woman has, nor never none shall mistress be of it, save I alone.*' [768]

To love another person, we need not reason, but the universal nature of love itself is the true and sufficient cause for this noble endeavour. The presence of love makes the world a better place. A world of goodness, grace, and gentleness. The Highest Truth in

---

767 Shakespeare, William. (1623). *Twelfth Night*. Act 3, Scene 1.
768 Shakespeare, William. (1623). *Twelfth Night*. Act 3, Scene 1.

this world is that of love. An individual who unconditionally loves God and demonstrates genuine love for humanity, has overcome the Self. For that person has shattered the very egoistic nature of being. A person who transcends the self-limiting concept of 'I', can perceive the very likeness of all the human civilisation. A universal likeness that surpasses the political, economic, racial, ethnic, biological, financial, legal, and social distinctions found amongst humanity.

> *'My kind Antonio, I can no other answer make but thanks, and thanks, and ever thanks. And oft good turns are shuffled off with such uncurrent pay, but were my worth, as is my conscience, firm, you should find better dealing.'* [769]

Being grateful for another person's assistance is an admirable quality. Often times the ability of words to truly express our gratitude is overestimated. In reality, it is the thought of kindness, and the kind gesture of sincere thanks that counts. While financial capital has its economic value in modern society, money alone is never a satisfactory commodity in exchange for a person's most honourable deeds.

> *'Nothing, that can be, can come between me and the true prospect of my hopes.'* [770]

Shakespeare's wise maxim is worth committing to memory. Self-determination requires conviction and boldness. We must possess an unmatched unity in our beliefs, thoughts, speech, and action, that what we hope for, shall come to pass during our lifetime. This is not to infer that difficulties, challenges, problems, and issues will be non-existent during our lifetime. Rather, we must believe that we have the ability, drive, and motivation to overcome any and all

---

769 Shakespeare, William. (1623). *Twelfth Night.* Act 3, Scene 3.
770 Shakespeare, William. (1623). *Twelfth Night.* Act 3, Scene 4.

challenges. Most limitations that we perceive in the external world, actually begin in our cognition. Our way of thinking determines the true prospects for our success.

'I prithee, gentle friend, let thy fair wisdom, not thy passion, sway in the uncivil and unjust extent against thy peace.' [771]

The human condition is fixed betwixt reason and emotion. It is not always possible to have our speech and action guided by the instrument of reason alone. For passion, emotion, feeling, and sensation perform a critical role in human thought, speech, and behaviour. However, it is within our agency, to defer to the higher powers of natural reason and good judgement. It is incumbent upon us to ensure that we do not permit purposeless passions and dark desires unchecked reign in our life.

'Alas, it is the baseness of thy fear that makes thee strangle thy propriety. Fear not, Cesario, take thy fortunes up. Be that thou knowest thou art, and then thou art as great as that thou fearest.' [772]

Fear inhibits our thought, action, and speech. Fear stunts progress. Fear diminishes our inherent capacity to realise the fullness of the human potential. Fear must be transcended. Nothing in this world is as base as the psychology of fear. It is only by directly confronting fear, by the conscious power of reasoning, and the execution of action, that we mount our mighty crusade against fear. To obliterate fear. Thereafter, we must strive forward, to realise our inherent potential, which is wholly within our grasp.

---

771 Shakespeare, William. (1623). *Twelfth Night.* Act 4, Scene 1.
772 Shakespeare, William. (1623). *Twelfth Night.* Act 5, Scene 1.

Chapter 36

THE TWO GENTLEMEN OF VERONA

'She is fair. So is Julia that I love. That I did love, for now my love is thawed, which, like a waxen image against a fire, bears no impression of the thing it was. Methinks my zeal to Valentine is cold, and that I love him not as I was wont. O, but I love his Lady too, too much, and that's the reason I love him so little.'

SHAKESPEARE

The Two Gentlemen of Verona is a romantic comedy which explores the themes and ideas of betrayal, disguise, jealousy, love, youth, travel, maturity, desire, friendship, passion, forgiveness, and reconciliation. This play commences with two young gentlemen and close friends, Proteus and Valentine saying goodbye to each other. Valentine has determined to leave his home town of Verona in order to travel abroad to Milan.

On the other hand, Proteus decides to remain in Verona, for he is deeply in love with Julia. As the play progresses, we realise, through the exchange of letters, that Julia also loves Proteus. The honeymoon period between the two lovers is short-lived. For Proteus' father, Antonio, sends Proteus to the Duke's Court.

However, Proteus and Julia exchange rings and vows as a symbol of their true love, before Proteus hurriedly departs Verona.

In Milan, Proteus becomes aware that Valentine is in love with the Duke's daughter, Silvia. To Valentine's favour, Silvia returns the affection. Silvia also has a great fondness for the young Valentine. Now Proteus is also attracted to Silvia, and he seeks to court her, despite his solemn vows and seemingly faithful exchange of rings with Julia. This love story only gets more complicated. Not to mention, the Duke is planning to arrange Thurio's marriage to his beautiful daughter, Silvia. In response, Valentine intends to speedily elope with Silvia. Valentine innocently discloses his plan to Proteus. The envious Proteus immediately informs the Noble Duke of the young Valentine's plot. As a consequence, the Duke banishes Valentine from his Court.

In Valentine's absence, Proteus attempts to court Silvia, however, she is not interested in him. Meanwhile, Julia has disguised herself as a pageboy, and she assumes the name Sebastian. Julia arrives in Milan, where she finds Proteus. On the other hand, Silvia remains truly and deeply committed to her lover, Valentine. It appears that Proteus is unrelenting in his mad pursuit of Silvia. In an act of sheer desperation, Proteus attempts to force himself upon Silvia. At this most opportune moment, Valentine's perfect-timing return is set into motion. Valentine forcibly removes Proteus from Silvia's immediate vicinity.

At the conclusion of this play, Julia faints, before uncovering her pageboy disguise. Finally, Proteus realises his true love resides with Julia. Now Thurio relinquishes his romantic interest in Silvia. This news leaves Valentine and Silvia the opportunity to seek marriage. The Duke finally approves of Valentine, and now the Duke has no qualms about Valentine marrying his beloved daughter. After the expression of sincere remorse and much regret, both Proteus and Valentine are reconciled in their great friendship. In celebration, the two pair of lovers, namely, Proteus and Julia, as well as Valentine and Silvia, all agree to hold their wedding ceremony on the same day.

'Home-keeping youth have ever homely wits, were it not affection chains thy tender days to the sweet glances of thy honoured love, I rather would entreat thy company to see the wonders of the world abroad. Than, living dully sluggardised at home, wear out thy youth with shapeless idleness. But since thou lovest, love still and thrive therein, even as I would when I to love begin.' [773]

Life is an adventure. Literally, life is a 'once-in-a-lifetime' experience. The thrill and exhilaration of life is not felt peacefully residing at home. We have to leave behind the comfortable, the familiar, and the well-known environment of the family home, in order to go further in life. To seek new relationships. To explore new opportunities. To learn a foreign language. To experience a distinct culture. To meet different people. To traverse a foreign continent. To pursue a new endeavour. Nothing is gained, from wasting away the precious years of our life, by remaining idle and stagnant, in all too familiar territory.

'Thou, Julia, thou hast metamorphosed me, made me neglect my studies, lose my time, war with good counsel, set the world at nought, made wit with musing weak, heart sick with thought.' [774]

Love is a powerful, blind, emotive, and irrational force. When we pursue true love, we do so with the inherent risk that we shall labour over the pursuit of an individual, with much loss of time, resources, energy, effort, and even against the function of our better judgement. Everything in our life must be pursued with moderation. Love represents no modification or qualification to this sound advice.

---

773 Shakespeare, William. (1623). *The Two Gentlemen of Verona*. Act 1, Scene 1.
774 Shakespeare, William. (1623). *The Two Gentlemen of Verona*. Act 1, Scene 1.

'I have considered well his loss of time and how he cannot be a perfect man, not being tried and tutored in the world. Experience is by industry achieved and perfected by the swift course of time.' [775]

As we advance in age, we become better acquainted with the true reality of our imperfections. We all have imperfections, gentlemen and gentlewomen alike. There are no perfect people on the Earth. Any attempt to find the perfect gentleman or gentlewoman, is likely to be a cause for considerable heartache. Over time, through the accumulation of worldly knowledge, formal learning, and the power of personal experience, we must come to the inevitable conclusion, that it is only within our power to recalibrate our thoughts and adjust our expectations of the important people in our life. In all things, we must be reasonable in our demands.

'Have patience, gentle Julia. I must, where is no remedy. When possibly I can, I will return. If you turn not, you will return the sooner. Keep this remembrance for thy Julia's sake. Why then, we'll make an exchange, here, take you this. And seal the bargain with a holy kiss. Here is my hand for my true constancy. And when that hour overslips me in the day wherein I sigh not, Julia, for thy sake, the next ensuing hour, some foul mischance torment me for my love's forgetfulness.' [776]

The necessity of time. The force of circumstance. The twists and turns of fate. These unforeseeable situations can create a reality, in which it is difficult to endure life. Patience is a virtue not always conveniently secured. In intimate matters of the heart, patience can be most difficult to obtain. In any case, we must preserve faith, sustain belief, and hold on to hope. The future is brighter, better, and beneficial. No matter the odds, we must remain optimistic in our unavoidable encounter with adversity.

---

775 Shakespeare, William. (1623). *The Two Gentlemen of Verona.* Act 1, Scene 3.
776 Shakespeare, William. (1623). *The Two Gentlemen of Verona.* Act 2, Scene 2.

'O gentle Proteus, Love's a Mighty Lord, and hath so humbled me, as, I confess, there is no woe for his correction, nor to his service no such joy on Earth. Now, no discourse, except it be of love. Now can I break my fast, dine, sup, and sleep, upon the very naked name of love!' [777]

The very feeling of love is difficult to comprehensively capture and concisely convey in words. The experience of love is private, personal, and paradoxical. Love consists of pleasure and pain. Yet, despite the many difficulties and flaws of human love, it is the presence of love that makes life worth living. Love is the highest good in this world. Love is the greatest universal expression of humanity's power. Indeed, the pursuit and possession of love makes life worth living.

'I reckon this always. A man is never undone till he be hanged, nor is he welcome till some certain shot be paid and the hostess say: Welcome.' [778]

During the course of our life, unfortunate circumstances befall upon us. As a result, we suffer tragedy, loss, grief, sorrow, and heartache. However, we can overcome these unwelcome challenges. In life, the presence of resilience, hope, belief, faith, love, confidence, and perseverance are the Golden Keys to transcending the countless challenges that are before us. It is always within our power to turn a mountain into a molehill. It is our internal mindset, not our external circumstances, that determine who we become, our very date with destiny.

---

777 Shakespeare, William. (1623). *The Two Gentlemen of Verona*. Act 2, Scene 4.
778 Shakespeare, William. (1623). *The Two Gentlemen of Verona*. Act 2, Scene 5.

*'To lesson me and tell me some good mean, how, with my honour,
I may undertake a journey to my loving Proteus. Alas, the way
is wearisome and long! A true-devoted Pilgrim is not weary
to measure Kingdoms with his feeble steps, much less shall she
that hath love's wings to fly, and when that flight is made to
one so dear, of such divine perfection, as Sir Proteus.'* [779]

No matter the challenges and difficulties that we confront in life,
we must always hold on to hope, love, belief, and faith, along our
special journey of life. Favourable results may not eventuate as
quickly as we would like. Having said that, we must remember
that tests and tribulations are part and parcel of our life journey. In
fact, challenges assist us to develop our golden virtues. Challenges
also shape the contours of our character and demonstrate our
conscience in action. To achieve the perfection of our character
is an endless pursuit, one which requires a lifetime's dedication to
moral excellence. In the long term, the road less travelled is always
more rewarding and fulfilling, than the path of least resistance.

*'O, knowest thou not his looks are my soul's food? Pity the dearth
that I have pined in, by longing for that food so long a time. Didst
thou but know the inly touch of love, thou wouldst as soon go
kindle fire with snow as seek to quench the fire of love with words.
I do not seek to quench your love's hot fire, but qualify the fire's
extreme rage, lest it should burn above the bounds of reason.
The more thou dammest it up, the more it burns.'* [780]

Love can totally consume the body, mind, and spirit. It is difficult
to quench the rage and storm of passion, with the sensibilities of
reason, logic, discernment, and judgement. We desire what we love
more than anything in this world. However, much of worldly pain
and suffering arise from the undesirable extremities of attachment

---

779 Shakespeare, William. (1623). *The Two Gentlemen of Verona.* Act 2, Scene 7.
780 Shakespeare, William. (1623). *The Two Gentlemen of Verona.* Act 2, Scene 7.

and aversion. In all things, we must seek moderation. We must demonstrate the ability to self-regulate our thought, speech, and action. Otherwise, we inadvertently risk becoming inhospitable in society and the world.

> *'But tell me, wench, how will the world repute me for undertaking so unstaid a journey? I fear me, it will make me scandalised. If you think so, then stay at home and go not. Nay, that I will not. Then never dream on infamy, but go.'* [781]

Though the final outcome is most uncertain, we must undertake the journey. For the length of life is too short. Thus, the possibility of multiple opportunities almost inconceivable. Our worst enemies are doubt, confusion, hesitation, anger, uncertainty, and fear. These enemies seek to destroy the basis for a firm belief in our dreams and hopes. All things are possible, for those that dare to believe. It is true beyond question, the practical wisdom contained within the writings of the English poet, Geoffrey Chaucer, author of *The Canterbury Tales* (1392). Geoffrey's *The Reeve's Tale*, states, 'I will arise and take a chance, too, by my faith! Nothing ventured, nothing gained.' In the final analysis, always remember that double-mindedness never accomplished anything great.

---

781 Shakespeare, William. (1623). *The Two Gentlemen of Verona*. Act 2, Scene 7.

'And why not death rather than living torment? To die is to be banished from myself, and Silvia is myself. Banished from her is self from self. A deadly banishment. What light is light, if Silvia be not seen? What joy is joy, if Silvia be not by? Unless it be to think that she is by and feed upon the shadow of perfection. Except I be by Silvia in the night, there is no music in the nightingale. Unless I look on Silvia in the day, there is no day for me to look upon. She is my essence, and I leave to be, If I be not by her fair influence fostered, illumined, cherished, kept alive. I fly not death, to fly his deadly doom. Tarry I here, I but attend on death. But, fly I hence, I fly away from life.' [782]

Given our encounter with difficult circumstances, the allure to confront death by suicide can present itself as a tempting option, to end one's worldly misery and existential suffering. The unsound logic of suicide holds, for where our worldly existence ceases to be, where there is no more being, a destruction of the Self, therein the possibility of agony and torment is no more. In reality, the act of suicide is a logical fallacy. The entire purpose of life is to be. To exist. To experience. To realise our inherent potential. We must always remember that suicide is not the resolution to our challenges. There are a number of possibilities to navigate the complexities and challenges of life, suicide is not one of them, period.

'Cease to lament for that which thou canst not help, and study help for that which thou lamentest. Time is the nurse and breeder of all good. Here if thou stayest, thou canst not see thy love. Besides, thy staying will abridge thy life. Hope is a lover's staff. Walk hence with that and manage it against despairing thoughts.' [783]

It is irrational to focus our time, energy, resources, and effort towards matters that we have no control over. To the contrary, we

---

782 Shakespeare, William. (1623). *The Two Gentlemen of Verona.* Act 3, Scene 1.
783 Shakespeare, William. (1623). *The Two Gentlemen of Verona.* Act 3, Scene 1.

ought to concentrate our time, energy, resources, and effort upon matters that we can exercise agency over. We must not remain trapped in past events or experiences. For we only stand to lose the present time, and gain naught, by the introspective method of constant reflection. A good and whole life is built upon love, hope, faith, study, work, charity, community service, and prayer. With these invaluable instruments at hand, we can surpass any and all difficulties in our life.

'Why do I pity him that with his very heart despiseth me? Because he loves her, he despiseth me. Because I love him, I must pity him. This ring I gave him when he parted from me, to bind him to remember by good will. And now am I, unhappy messenger, to plead for that which I would not obtain, to carry that which I would have refused, to praise his faith which I would have dispraised. I am my Master's true-confirmed love, but cannot be true servant to my Master, unless I prove false traitor to myself. Yet will I woo for him, but yet so coldly. As, Heaven it knows, I would not have him speed.' [784]

The extremes of 'love' and 'hate' create the grounds for jealousy, envy, insecurity, resentment, and anxiety. In matters of the heart, it is often difficult to exercise reason and secure clarity in our thoughts. Unfortunately, given the unchanging reality of human nature, we can find ourselves in toxic relationships, where there is deception, mistrust, infidelity, or falsehood.

Come what may, we must firmly resolve to guard our sanctuary of peace. We must not permit the heart to be troubled by another person's actions and speech. This advisable course of action is extremely difficult to put into practice, not to mention, almost impossible to contemplate actioning, if it is our spouse who is mistreating us. The reality is that we have no control, nor

---

784 Shakespeare, William. (1623). *The Two Gentlemen of Verona.* Act 4, Scene 4.

are we responsible for, the speech or action of another person. Furthermore, we are not responsible for the happiness of other people.

> *'Thou hast no faith left now, unless thou wouldst two, and that's far worse than none. Better have none than plural faith which is too much by one, thou counterfeit to thy true friend!'* [785]

It is best to resolve upon the selection and adherence to one faith. This singular approach to faith creates clarity in thought, belief, body, mind, and spirit. A person with multiple faiths is likely to possess competing beliefs, incompatible ideologies, and loyalties will be tested and strained. In the final analysis, a person's belief in several faiths is likely to cause psychological and theological distress, rather than the provision of additional spiritual value. In that case, it is best to be secular in one's world view, rather than to tread such a complex and ambiguous religious path.

> *'Thou common friend, that's without faith or love, for such is a friend now, treacherous man. Thou hast beguiled my hopes. Nought but mine eye could have persuaded me. Now I dare not say I have one friend alive. Thou wouldst disprove me. Who should be trusted, when one's own right hand is perjured to the bosom? Proteus, I am sorry I must never trust thee more, but count the world a stranger for thy sake. The private wound is deepest. O time, most accurst, amongst all foes, that a friend should be the worst.'* [786]

It is a heartbreaking tragedy; however, we will be betrayed and abandoned by our most loyal and trusted companions in this world. The unrelenting desire for profit, pecuniary gain, political power,

---

785 Shakespeare, William. (1623). *The Two Gentlemen of Verona*. Act 5, Scene 4.
786 Shakespeare, William. (1623). *The Two Gentlemen of Verona*. Act 5, Scene 4.

pleasure, private property, and personal interest dictate the actions and agenda of gentlemen and gentlewomen in modern society.

Regrettably, in matters concerning personal gain and self-interest, we all too often witness the baseness of the human condition, where friendships and families are fractured, all for the individual's narrow perception of the Modern World. A world defined by, 'Me, Myself, and I.' We witness an invaluable loss, for a trivial gain. Such an inferior exchange defines the irrationality and absurdity of human behaviour.

Chapter 37

THE WINTER'S TALE

'Apprehend nothing but jollity. The Gods themselves, humbling their deities to love, have taken the shapes of beasts upon them. Jupiter became a Bull, and bellowed the Green Neptune a Ram, and bleated, and the fire-robed God, Golden Apollo, a poor humble Swain, As I seem now. Their transformations were never for a piece of beauty rarer, nor in a way so chaste, since my desires run not before mine honour, nor my lusts burn hotter than my faith.'

SHAKESPEARE

The Winter's Tale is characterised by suffering, jealousy, irrationality, suspicion, hate, and tyranny. All of which finally give way to reason, compassion, forgiveness, redemption, trust, and love. Most importantly, this play dramatises how romance has its pitfalls. The play commences with Leontes, the King of Sicilia, who hosts his honourable friend, Polixenes, the King of Bohemia. While the Royal Kings exchange pleasantries and things appear cordial between the two powerful gentlemen, Leontes becomes immensely jealous of Polixenes.

Now Leontes' wife, Hermione, performs the role of Peacemaker, and she persuades Polixenes to overlook the offence. Rather than accept the olive branch, Leontes, becomes enraged with his wife, and suspects her of being unfaithful. His Majesty King Leontes moves further towards the edge of madness and insanity. Leontes instructs his Cupbearer, Camillo to poison Polixenes. Camillo refuses to follow through on this immoral instruction. Instead Camillo discreetly warns Polixenes. As a result, Camillo and Polixenes determine to hurriedly depart King Leontes' company. This leaves Hermione, and her young son, to confront the agitated and irrational King Leontes.

In giving way to irrationality, King Leontes imprisons his wife, Hermione. While Hermione is subject to incarceration, she gives birth to a baby girl. King Leontes refuses to accept the beautiful baby girl as his own child. Instead, King Leontes orders that the baby girl be sent into exile. King Leontes subjects his wife, Hermione to a mock trial. While a divine message from the Oracle of Delphi supports Hermione's innocence, King Leontes remains suspicious of his wife. Towards the end of this mock trial, Hermione faints and thereafter, she is taken away by her close friend, Paulina. Thereafter, Paulina returns and announces Hermione's death. King Leontes repents and weeps in remorse for his most treasured loss, his beautiful and sincere wife.

Hermione's baby girl is blessed, and her personal safety is secure, while she is left alone and exposed to the unforgiving natural elements. For this infant is found by a shepherd and his son, who willingly take the baby girl home, and also nurture her. Now the constant passage of time shows its face, and some sixteen years have passed. Despite the wisdom, wit, and wondrous intellect of his learned and honourable advisors, King Leontes remains in a saddened state of prolonged grief.

It appears there is only one thing that can awaken Leontes out of his slumber, bringing the long-lost memory of Hermione back to life. The play concludes with a miracle. Paulina unveils a beautiful Statue of Hermione. In the illustration of a paradox, the Statue looks exactly like a real-life figure of Hermione. The Statue leaves King Leontes, and his companions in total wonder and utter amazement. Upon Paulina's command, the Statue of Hermione begins to move. In a surreal manner, we witness Hermione return to the fullness of life. In the closing of this play, King Leontes and Queen Hermione embrace each other. As though it was for their very first time.

'Would they else be content to die? Yes, if there were no other excuse why they should desire to live. If the King had no Son, they would desire to live on crutches till he had one.' [787]

Our desire to live must be to advance God's Kingdom on Earth. This is our sole purpose, and our life mission on Earth. In doing so, we must advance the cause of social justice, peace, prosperity, liberty, equality, and moral righteousness in the world. Furthermore, we must strive to create a world that is without poverty, illiteracy, preventable diseases, thirst, and hunger for all people. Any person on Earth who purports to live for themselves, for the furtherance of their ego and pride, shall find no lasting peace for their remaining days on Earth.

'Time as much, again, my Brother, would be filled up with our thanks. And yet we should, for perpetuity, go hence in debt.' [788]

A debt of thanks is considerably difficult to repay. Often times, we accumulate debts of gratitude, that we cannot make amends for. A large part of being grateful, is to pass on the favour, the blessing, the mercy, and the kindness to other people, who are less fortunate, and stand in need of assistance. We may not adequately be able to thank those people that helped us. However, we can help countless other people in society, with our time, financial capital, resources, knowledge, abilities, formal learning, and personal experience.

---

787 Shakespeare, William. (1623). *The Winter's Tale*. Act 1, Scene 1.
788 Shakespeare, William. (1623). *The Winter's Tale*. Act 1, Scene 2.

'I have trusted thee, Camillo, with all the nearest things to my heart, as well my chamber councils, wherein, Priest-like, thou hast cleansed my bosom I from thee departed thy penitent reformed. But we have been deceived in thy integrity, deceived in that which seems so. Be it forbid, My Lord! To bide upon it, thou art not honest, or if thou inclinest that way, thou art a coward, which hoxes honesty behind, restraining from course required. Or else you must be counted a servant grafted in my serious trust, and therein negligent. Or else a fool that sees the game played home, the rich stake drawn, and takest it all for jest. My Gracious Lord, I may be negligent, foolish, and fearful. In every one of these, no man is free.' [789]

We are all human. We ought to exercise care and caution in whom we position our trust. For deception and betrayal are always possible outcomes. The virtues and noble qualities of honesty and courage are admirable. These positive traits form the basis of integrity and good conduct. We can never wholly negate self-interest as the prime motivator for another person's thought, speech, and action. Not to mention, it is the pursuit of self-interest, which almost always leads to the breach of trust between two or more parties. In the final analysis, we are all imperfect. We all have our flaws. No gentleman or gentlewoman is different in this respect.

---

789 Shakespeare, William. (1623). *The Winter's Tale*. Act 1, Scene 2.

'Is whispering nothing? Is leaning cheek to cheek? Is meeting noses? Kissing with inside lip? Stopping the career of laughter with a sigh?—a note infallible of breaking honesty—horsing foot on foot? Skulking in corners? Wishing clocks more swift? Hours, minutes, noon, midnight? And all eyes blind with the pin and web but theirs, theirs only. That would unseen be wicked? Is this nothing? Why, then, the world and all that's in it is nothing. The covering sky is nothing. Bohemia's nothing. My Wife is nothing. Nor nothing have these nothings, if this be nothing.' [790]

Physical expressions of love are important in our most significant relationship with our spouse. However, signs of love must accompany meaningful action, coupled with trust, commitment, faithfulness, kindness, and honesty. This world is nothing, without love. Love is the eternal substance that keeps life together. Love is the binding force that brings humanity together.

Love helps to bridge the many differences and distinctions between people from all around the world. Love transcends gender, religion, colour, sex, age, race, ethnicity, occupation, social class, education, tradition, custom, income, faith, personal wealth, private property, language, culture, and countless other points of differentiation. Every person in the world is receptive to the unmatched power of love. There is nothing comparable to love.

'This jealousy is for a precious creature. As she's rare, must it be great, and as his person's mighty, must it be violent, and as he does conceive, he is dishonoured by a man which ever did profess to him. Why, his revenge must in that be made more bitter.' [791]

Jealousy, anger, and hatred achieve nothing productive. These negative emotions only serve to destroy the peace of the person harbouring them. We must not concern ourselves with the charm,

---

790 Shakespeare, William. (1623). *The Winter's Tale*. Act 1, Scene 2.
791 Shakespeare, William. (1623). *The Winter's Tale*. Act 1, Scene 2.

wit, beauty, intelligence, education, knowledge, prosperity, and learning, that is upon another person's life. However, we ought to turn our heart towards God. We shall ask God for what we require. God has plenty of provision for all of God's Creation. Why then become bitter and narrow-minded at the success and favour upon another person?

> *'There is a plot against my life, my Crown. All's true that is mistrusted. That false villain whom I employed was pre-employed by him. He hath discovered my design, and I remain a pinched thing; yea, a very trick for them to play at will.'* [792]

We will be deceived in life, by those people we trust most of all. This unfortunate scenario should not come as a complete surprise to us. The evil forces of jealousy, envy, hate, desire, greed, pride, self-interest, pecuniary gain, and profit, turn brother against brother, and sister against sister. Therefore, it is upon us to utilise our good judgement, logic, and reason, coupled with the power of discernment, to carefully consider whom we share our grand designs, aims, and objectives with.

> *'No. I'll not rear another's issue.'* [793]

There is much wisdom in this simple and concise statement. We must not look to become involved in the personal affairs of other people. Successful people establish boundaries. Productive people prioritise the use of their precious time. Wise individuals do not create the capacity to entertain the countless concerns and worldly worries of other people within modern society. We have limited resources, time, energy, learning, and knowledge. We ought to help

---

792 Shakespeare, William. (1623). *The Winter's Tale*. Act 2, Scene 1.
793 Shakespeare, William. (1623). *The Winter's Tale*. Act 2, Scene 3.

other people, however, we ought not to diminish our life in the pursuit of another person's issues. We shall endeavour to live our life to the best of our ability.

'For life, I prize it. As I weigh grief, which I would spare. For honour, it is a derivative from me to mine, and only that I stand for.' [794]

A life without the personal experience of pain, sorrow, heartache, suffering, and loss is not a life truly lived. Life is valuable and precious; however, it comes with its fair share of challenges. The events and environment which surround us, are not always within our immediate control. Yet, more importantly, our attitude, beliefs, and thoughts, collectively determine our response to them. While it is by no means convenient, we can always self-determine our reaction to any given situation, event, or environment. The former Roman Emperor and philosopher, Marcus Aurelius, provisions humanity with considerable wisdom in his Stoic philosophy contained within *The Meditations*, 'You have power over your mind —not outside events. Realise this, and you will find strength.'

'What's gone and what's past help. Should be past grief.' [795]

We must not constantly dwell upon our mistakes, losses, tragic events, traumatic experiences, and failures in life. The past is forever past. Wisdom resides in reflecting and learning from such personal experiences. Emotional Intelligence is seeking to develop from life's good and not so good experiences. The present moment is fleeting and constantly diminishing. There is no time to remain stagnant in the memory of the past. In all things, there is a time for grief, and a time to move forward.

---

794 Shakespeare, William. (1623). *The Winter's Tale*. Act 3, Scene 2.
795 Shakespeare, William. (1623). *The Winter's Tale*. Act 3, Scene 2.

'Thou Dearest Perdita, with these forced thoughts, I prithee, darken not the mirth o' the feast. Or I'll be thine, my fair, or not my Father's. For I cannot be mine own, nor anything to any, if I be not thine. To this I am most constant, though destiny say no.' [796]

When we attempt to impose our will upon the world, it is a source and strategy for much regret and grief. It is important that we develop a sense of personal agency, individuality, and independence in our speech, thoughts, ideas, actions, beliefs, values, and behaviour. However, we must not attempt to force all that is within our environment to our heart's content. Such an irrational expectation is likely to position us for immense pain and avoidable sorrow.

'What a fool Honesty is! And Trust, his sworn brother, a very simple gentleman.' [797]

It is an unfortunate reality, that while honesty and trust are most admirable virtues, the reality of this world dictates that honesty and trust, can and will be misappropriated. There are ill-intended individuals, who will seek personal advantage from the information and knowledge within their possession, in the pursuit of personal gain and profit maximisation. Therefore, we must be careful who we trust, for we may be betrayed.

'I see this is the time the unjust man doth thrive. O, what an exchange had this been without boot! What a boot is here with this exchange!' [798]

Honourable and fair dealing is not guaranteed in the contemporary world. The majority of people are seeking to advance their self-interest, maximise pecuniary gain, and accumulate an exorbitant

796 Shakespeare, William. (1623). *The Winter's Tale.* Act 4, Scene 4.
797 Shakespeare, William. (1623). *The Winter's Tale.* Act 4, Scene 4.
798 Shakespeare, William. (1623). *The Winter's Tale.* Act 4, Scene 4.

profit. While this most narrow and superficial thinking does further the illegitimate and unchecked aims of the ego, pause for a moment, and reflect on the following question: What good does it do us, to unfairly gain the riches of this world, and in exchange, relinquish our priceless soul?

> *'The King is not at the Palace. He is gone aboard a new ship to purge melancholy and air himself. For, if thou beest capable of things serious, thou must know the King is full of grief.'* [799]

No person is past the powerful grip of grief. No matter the personal wealth, private property, income, education, gender, sex, colour, race, ethnicity, faith, religion, age, learning, knowledge, language, culture, or any other distinguishing factor. Every person on this Earth will experience and be subject to grief. While being subject to grief is not within our control, we can self-determine how we respond to our personal experience of grief. Within a person's unique response to grief, therein resides a person's true power to overcome the negative experiences, traumatic events, unfortunate circumstances, and the many undesirable environments of this broken world.

> *'Sir, you have done enough, and have performed a Saint-like sorrow. No fault could you make, which you have not redeemed. Indeed, paid down more penitence than done trespass. At the last, do as the Heavens have done, forget your evil. With them forgive yourself.'* [800]

We all make mistakes. Sometimes, we fall short. We will demonstrate errors in our judgement. Such is the true and unfortunate state of humanity in this broken world marred by sin. The human condition is not without its faults and imperfections. The resolution resides

---

799 Shakespeare, William. (1623). *The Winter's Tale*. Act 4, Scene 4.
800 Shakespeare, William. (1623). *The Winter's Tale*. Act 5, Scene 1.

in learning how to forgive and forget. Life is incredibly short to endlessly ponder on our sins. Therefore, we must repent and move forward with our life. That individual who forgives themselves, has mastered the art of life. Such a person has liberated themselves from the negative power of guilt, fear, shame, indignity, anger, confusion, indecision, and doubt.

> 'My Lord, your sorrow was too sore laid on, which sixteen winters cannot blow away, So many summers dry. Scarce any joy did ever so long live, no sorrow but killed itself much sooner.' [801]

All of human life oscillates between pleasure and pain. Between joy and grief. Between good and evil. This is the eternal and unchanging nature of the human condition on Earth. The personal responsibility is upon us to secure a balance between the many extreme ends found in this world. It is upon us, to create a peaceful and blessed life. A life which acknowledges that suffering, pain, and sorrow will come, but not be overwhelmed by their temporary presence. Our worldly reality commences in our ideas, beliefs, and thoughts. It is within our unique perception, that the external world of being is formed and transformed. Our life does not necessarily have to be defined by fate. For our life can be refined by fate.

---

801 Shakespeare, William. (1623). *The Winter's Tale.* Act 5, Scene 3.

CONCLUSION

This Commentary has examined each of the thirty-seven majestic plays of the English playwright, poet, and actor, William Shakespeare. Through analysing the remarkable plays of this inquisitive and insightful gentleman, this book has explored the themes of ambition, power, corruption, intimacy, mortality, love, hate, destiny, faith, greed, deception, morality, betrayal, war, good, evil, human nature, fate, cruelty, marriage, guilt, religion, romance, and many more. Shakespeare's plays are a repository of knowledge, for any individual wanting to learn more about English Literature.

The study and formal learning of literature is extremely important for a number of reasons. Most notably, studying literature allows a person to gain an awareness and appreciation for a nation's culture, language, history, people, traditions, customs, and heritage. Shakespeare's plays, such as *Antony and Cleopatra, The Comedy of Errors, Hamlet, King Lear, Romeo and Juliet, Macbeth, Love's Labour's Lost, A Midsummer Night's Dream,* and *The Merry Wives of Windsor* are a timeless masterpiece of Western Literature. Shakespeare's plays will continue to educate and entertain people from all around the world.

This Commentary has expounded upon the many ideas, themes, values, and concepts found throughout Shakespeare's memorable plays. This Commentary shines a new light on Shakespeare's writing. This Commentary provides a unique textual analysis, with references to psychology, theology, sociology, anthropology, political science, economics, history, law, and philosophy. The newfound perspective of this Commentary has elucidated Shakespeare's brilliant plays, for the benefit of countless future generations.

Bibliography

Abraham, H. J. (1998). *The Judicial Process.* Seventh Edition. Oxford: Oxford University Press.

Abrams, D., and Hogg, M. A. (Eds.) (1999). *Social Identity and Social Cognition.* Oxford: Blackwell Publishers.

Allan, TRS. (1993). *Law, Liberty, and Justice: The Legal Foundations of British Constitutionalism.* Oxford: Oxford University Press.

Allport, G. (1954). *The Nature of Prejudice.* Cambridge: Addison-Wesley Publishing Company.

Aquinas, T. (Fathers of the English Dominican Province, Trans.) (1981). *Summa Theologica.* Volumes I–V. Indiana: Christian Classics.

Aquinas, T. (1998). *Selected Writings.* London: Penguin Classics.

Aristotle. (W. K. C. Guthrie, Trans.) (1939). *Aristotle: On the Heavens.* (Loeb Classical Library). Cambridge, Massachusetts: Harvard University Press.

Aristotle. (1952). *Aristotle: Meteorologica.* (Loeb Classical Library). Cambridge, Massachusetts: Harvard University Press.

Aristotle. (H. Tredennick, Trans.) (1960). *Posterior Analytics.* Cambridge, Massachusetts: Harvard University Press.

Aristotle. (J. L. Ackrill and L. Judson, Eds.) (J. L. Ackrill, Trans.) (1975). *Aristotle: Categories and De Interpretatione.* New York: Oxford University Press.

Aristotle. (J. Barnes, Ed.) (1984). *The Complete Works of Aristotle.* Volume I. Princeton; New Jersey: Princeton University Press.

Aristotle. (J. Barnes, Ed.) (1984). *The Complete Works of Aristotle.* Volume II. Princeton; New Jersey: Princeton University Press.

Aristotle. (R. Smith, Trans.) (1989). *Prior Analytics.* Indianapolis: Hackett Publishing Company.

Aristotle. (H. Lawson-Tancred, Ed. and Trans.) (1992). *The Art of Rhetoric.* London: Penguin Books.

Aristotle. (R. F. Stalley, Ed.) (E. Barker, Trans.) (1995). *Politics.* New York: Oxford University Press.

Aristotle. (H. Lawson-Tancred, Trans.) (1999). *The Metaphysics.* London: Penguin Books.

Aristotle. (D. Bostock, Ed.) (R. Waterfield, Trans.) (2008). *Physics*. New York: Oxford University Press.

Aristotle. (2010). *On Sense and the Sensible*. Montana: Kessinger Publishing, LLC.

Aristotle. (2010). *On Sophistical Refutations*. Montana: Kessinger Publishing, LLC.

Aristotle. (R. C. Bartlett, and S. D. Collins Trans.) (2012). *Aristotle's Nicomachean Ethics*. London: University of Chicago Press.

Aristotle. (E. M. Edghill, Trans.) (2014). *The Categories*. California: CreateSpace Independent Publishers.

Aristotle. (2015). *Topics*. London: Aeterna Press.

Aristotle. (F. D. Miller Jr. Trans.) (2018). *On the Soul: and Other Psychological Works*. New York: Oxford University Press.

Aristotle. (2018). *On Generation and Corruption*. Knutsford: A & D Publishing.

Augustine, S. (R. S. Pine-Coffin, Trans.) (1961). *Confessions*. London: Penguin Classics.

Augustine, S. (H. Bettenson, Trans.) (G. R. Evans, Ed.) (2003). *City of God*. London: Penguin Classics.

Augustine, S. (P. Schaff, Ed.) (2017). *On Grace and Free Will*. New York: GLH Publishing.

Aurelius, M. (1997). *Meditations*. London: Dover Publications.

Ayer, A. J. (1949). *Language, Truth, and Logic*. London: Victor Gollancz Ltd.

Ayer, A. J. (1963). *The Concept of a Person and Other Essays*. New York: St. Martin's Press.

Ayer, A. J. (1965). *Philosophical Essays*. London: Macmillan & Co Ltd.

Ayer, A. J. (1968). *The Origins of Pragmatism*. Toronto: Macmillan Company.

Ayer, A. J. (1968). *The Humanist Outlook*. London: Pemberton, Barrie & Rockliff.

Ayer, A. J. (1971). *Russell and Moore: The Analytical Heritage*. Cambridge, Massachusetts: Harvard University Press.

Ayer, A. J. (1972). *Probability and Evidence*. New York: Columbia University Press.

Ayer, A. J. (1974). *The Central Questions of Philosophy*. New York: Holt, Rinehart, and Winston.

Ayer, A. J. (1979). *Perception and Identity*. London: Macmillan.

Ayer, A. J. (1982). *Philosophy in the Twentieth Century*. New York: Vintage Books.

Ayer, A. J. (1984). *Freedom and Morality and other Essays*. Oxford: Oxford University Press.

Ayer, A. J. (1988). *Essays on Moral Realism*. New York: Cornell University Press.

Ayer, A. J. (1988). *The Meaning of Life*. London: Orion Publishing Co.

Ayer, A. J. (1990). *The Problem of Knowledge*. New York: Penguin Books.

baron de Montesquieu, C. (D. W. Carrithers, Ed.) (1977). *The Spirit of the Laws: A Compendium of the First English Edition*. Berkeley: University of California Press.

Baweja, P. (2021). *A Philosophical Treatise of Reality*. Volume I. Melbourne: Paul Baweja.

Baweja, P. (2021). *A Philosophical Treatise of Reality*. Volume II. Melbourne: Paul Baweja.

Baweja, P. (2021). *A Philosophical Treatise of Reality*. Volume III. Melbourne: Paul Baweja.

Baweja, P. (2021). *A Philosophical Treatise of Reality*. Volume IV. Melbourne: Paul Baweja.

Bennett, R. (Director). (1980). *Hamlet*. (Film). The BBC Shakespeare Collection. London: The British Broadcasting Corporation.

Bentham, J. (R. Harrison, Ed.) (1988). *Bentham: A Fragment on Government*. Cambridge: Cambridge University Press.

Berryman, J. (1999). *Berryman's Shakespeare*. New York: Farrar, Straus, and Giroux.

Billington, K. (Director). (1979). *Henry VIII*. (Film). The BBC Shakespeare Collection. London: The British Broadcasting Corporation.

Blackstone, W. (W. Prest, Ed.) (2016). *The Oxford Edition of Blackstone: Commentaries on the Laws of England: Book I: Of the Rights of Persons*. Oxford: Oxford University Press.

Blackstone, W. (W. Prest, Ed.) (2016). *The Oxford Edition of Blackstone: Commentaries on the Laws of England: Book II: Of the Rights of Things*. Oxford: Oxford University Press.

Blackstone, W. (W. Prest, Ed.) (2016). *The Oxford Edition of Blackstone: Commentaries on the Laws of England: Book III: Of Private Wrongs*. Oxford: Oxford University Press.

Blackstone, W. (W. Prest, Ed.) (2016). *The Oxford Edition of Blackstone: Commentaries on the Laws of England: Book IV: Of Public Wrongs*. Oxford: Oxford University Press.

Bourdieu, P. (1987). The Force of Law: Towards a Sociology of the Juridical Field. *Hastings Law Journal*. Volume 38. No. 5, pp. 814–853.

Bowling, A. (2005). *Ageing Well: Quality of Life in Old Age*. New York: Open University Press.

Bradley, H., and Scott, M. (2017). *Talking Shakespeare: Shakespeare into the Millennium*. London: Bloomsbury Publishing.

Bulman, J. C. (2017). *The Oxford Handbook of Shakespeare and Performance*. Oxford: Oxford University Press.

Burge, S. (Director). (1984). *Much Ado About Nothing*. (Film). The BBC Shakespeare Collection. London: The British Broadcasting Corporation.

Burr, V. (2015). *Social Constructionism*. Third Edition. London: Routledge.

Chan, W., (Trans.). (1969). *A Source Book in Chinese Philosophy.* Princeton, New Jersey: Princeton University Press.

Cicero, M. T. (W. A. Falconer, Ed.) (1923). *On Old Age. On Friendship. On Divination.* Cambridge, Massachusetts: Harvard University Press.

Cicero, M. T. (M. Hadas, Ed.) (1951). *The Basic Works of Cicero.* New York: Modern Library.

Cicero, M. T. (H. Rackham, Ed.) (1972). *De Natura Deorum; Academica.* Cambridge, Massachusetts: Harvard University Press.

Cicero, M. T. (M. Grant, Trans.) (1980). *On the Good Life.* London: Penguin Classics.

Cicero, M. T. (J. G. F. Powell, Ed.) (1988). *Cicero: Cato Maior de Senectute.* Cambridge: Cambridge University Press.

Cicero, M. T. (H. E. Gould, and J. L. Whiteley, Eds.) (2013). *De Amicitia.* London: Bloomsbury Publication.

Coke, E. (S. Sheppard, Ed.) (2005). *The Selected Writings of Sir Edward Coke. Volumes I–III.* Indiana: Liberty Fund, Inc.

Coleman, B. (Director). (1978). *As You Like It.* (Film). The BBC Shakespeare Collection. London: The British Broadcasting Corporation.

Comyns, J. (S. Rose, Ed.) (1800). *A Digest of the Laws of England.* Fourth Edition. London: A Strahan.

Cooley, C. H. (1902). *Human Nature and the Social Order.* New York: Charles Scribner's Sons.

Davis, D. (Director). (1979). *Measure for Measure.* (Film). The BBC Shakespeare Collection. London: The British Broadcasting Corporation.

Dewey, J. (1894). *The Study of Ethics: A Syllabus.* Ann Arbor, Michigan: G. Wahr.

Dewey, J. (1899). *The School and Society: Being Three Lectures.* Chicago: University of Chicago Press.

Dewey, J., and Tufts, J. H. (1906). *Ethics.* New York: Henry Holt & Company.

Dewey, J. (1909). *Moral Principles in Education.* New York: Houghton Mifflin Company.

Dewey, J. (1913). *Interest and Effort in Education.* Boston: Houghton Mifflin Co.

Dewey, J. (1922). *Human Nature and Conduct.* New York: Henry Holt & Company.

Dewey, J. (1925). *Experience and Nature.* LaSalle, Illinois: Open Court Press.

Dewey, J. (1926). *Reconstruction in Philosophy.* New York: Henry Holt & Company.

Dewey, J. (1929). *The Sources of a Science of Education.* New York: Horace Liveright.

Dewey, J. (1930). *Individualism Old and New.* New York: Milton Balch & Company.

Dewey, J. (1934). *A Common Faith.* New Haven: Yale University Press.

Dewey, J. (1935). *Liberalism and Social Action.* New York: G. P. Putnam's Sons.

Dewey, J. (1938). *Experience and Education.* New York: Macmillan Co.

Dewey, J. (1938). *Logic: The Theory of Inquiry.* New York: Henry Holt & Company.

Dewey, J. (1939). *Freedom and Culture.* New York: G. P. Putnam's Sons.

Dewey, J. (J. A. Boydston., and F. Bowers., Eds.) (1969). *John Dewey: Essays and Outlines of a Critical Theory of Ethics.* Carbondale: Southern Illinois University Press.

Dewey, J. (1997). *How We Think.* New York: Dover Publications.

Dewey, J. (2004). *Reconstruction in Philosophy.* New York: Dover Publications.

Dicey, A. V. (Allison, J. W. F., Ed.) (2013). *The Law of the Constitution.* Oxford: Oxford University Press.

Durant, W. (2001). *Heroes of History: A Brief History of Civilisation from Ancient Times to the Dawn of the Modern Age.* New York: Simon & Schuster.

Durant, W. (Little, J., Ed.) (2002). *The Greatest Minds and Ideas of All Time.* New York: Simon & Schuster.

Durant, W. (2005). *The Story of Philosophy.* New York: Simon & Schuster.

Durant, W., and Durant, A. (2010). *The Lessons of History.* New York: Simon & Schuster.

Dworkin, R. (1986). *Law's Empire.* Massachusetts: Belknap Press.

Edwardes, M. (1971). *Nehru: A Political Biography.* London: Allen Lane.

Eklund, H. (2019). Shakespeare's Littoral and the Dramas of Loss and Store. *Studies in English Literature, 1500–1900.* Volume 59, No. 2, pp. 349–365.

Eklund, H., and Hyman, W. B. (2019). *Teaching Social Justice Through Shakespeare: Why Renaissance Literature Matters.* Edinburgh: Edinburgh University Press.

Frankl, V. E. (2006). *Man's Search for Meaning.* Boston: Beacon Press.

Friedman, M. (1962). *Capitalism and Freedom.* Chicago: University of Chicago Press.

Gandhi, M. K. (1993). *An Autobiography: The Story of My Experiments with Truth.* Boston: Beacon Press.

Gibbon, E. (H. Trevor-Roper, Introduction) (2010). *The Decline and Fall of the Roman Empire.* Volume I–VI. New York: Knopf Doubleday Publishing Group.

Giles, D. (Director). (1979). *Henry IV: Part One.* (Film). The BBC Shakespeare Collection. London: The British Broadcasting Corporation.

Giles, D. (Director). (1979). *Henry IV: Part Two.* (Film). The BBC Shakespeare Collection. London: The British Broadcasting Corporation.

Giles, D. (Director). (1979). *Henry V.* (Film). The BBC Shakespeare Collection. London: The British Broadcasting Corporation.

Giles, D. (Director). (1984). *The Life and Death of King John.* (Film). The BBC Shakespeare Collection. London: The British Broadcasting Corporation.

Gold, J. (Director). (1980). *The Merchant of Venice.* (Film). The BBC Shakespeare Collection. London: The British Broadcasting Corporation.

Gold, J. (Director). (1983). *Macbeth.* (Film). The BBC Shakespeare Collection. London: The British Broadcasting Corporation.

Goldsworthy, J. (1999). *The Sovereignty of Parliament: History and Philosophy.* Oxford: Clarendon Press.

Goleman, D. (1995). *Emotional Intelligence: Why It Can Matter More Than IQ.* New York: Bantam Books.

Gorrie, J. (Director). (1980). *The Tempest.* (Film). The BBC Shakespeare Collection. London: The British Broadcasting Corporation.

Gorrie, J. (Director). (1980). *Twelfth Night.* (Film). The BBC Shakespeare Collection. London: The British Broadcasting Corporation.

Gray, J. (1995). *Liberalism.* Second Edition. Buckingham: Open University Press.

Gray, P. (2018). *Shakespeare and the Fall of the Roman Republic: Selfhood, Stoicism, and Civil War.* Edinburgh: Edinburgh University Press.

Grotius, H. (R. Tuck, and K. Haakonssen, Eds.) (2005). *The Rights of War and Peace.* Indianapolis: Liberty Fund.

Grotius, H. (S. C. Neff, Ed.) (2012). *Hugo Grotius: On the Law of War and Peace.* Cambridge: Cambridge University Press.

Hackworth, R. (1945). *Plato's Examination of Pleasure.* Cambridge: Cambridge University Press.

Hadfield, A. (2005). *Shakespeare and Republicanism.* Cambridge: Cambridge University Press.

Hale, M. (2014). *The History and Analysis of the Common Law of England.* New Jersey: The Lawbook Exchange.

Hale, M. (G. J. Postema, Ed.) (2017). *Matthew Hale: On the Law of Nature, Reason, and Common Law. Selected Jurisprudential Writings.* Oxford: Oxford University Press.

Hamilton, A., Madison, J., and Jay, J. (B. F. Wright, Ed.) (1961). *The Federalist.* Cambridge: Harvard University Press.

Harper, R. F. (2010). *The Code of Hammurabi: King of Babylon.* New Jersey: The Lawbook Exchange.

Hart, H. L. A. (1959). *Causation in the Law.* Oxford: The Clarendon Press.

Hart, H. L. A. (1961). *The Concept of Law.* Oxford: The Clarendon Press.

Hart, H. L. A. (1963). *Law, Liberty, and Morality.* Stanford: Stanford University Press.

Hart, H. L. A. (1968). *Punishment and Responsibility.* Oxford: The Clarendon Press.

Hart, H. L. A. (1982). *Essays on Bentham.* Oxford: The Clarendon Press.

Hart, H. L. A. (1983). *Essays in Jurisprudence and Philosophy.* Oxford: The Clarendon Press.

Harter, S. (1999). *The Construction of the Self: A Developmental Perspective.* New York: Guilford Press.

Harvey, D. (1989). *The Condition of Postmodernity. An Enquiry into the Origins of Cultural Change.* Oxford: Basil Blackwell.

Harvey, D. (2006). *A Brief History of Neoliberalism*. Oxford: Oxford University Press.

Harvey, P. (1990). *An Introduction to Buddhism: Teachings, History, and Practices*. Cambridge: Cambridge University Press.

Heider, F. (1958). *The Psychology of Interpersonal Relations*. New York: John Wiley.

Henkin, L. (1990). *The Age of Rights*. New York: Columbia University Press.

Hobbes, T. (E. Curley, Ed.) (1994). *Leviathan: With Selected Variants from the Latin Edition of 1668*. Indiana: Hackett Publishing Company.

Hodge, C. (1960). *Systematic Theology*. Volumes I–III. Michigan: William B. Eerdmans Publication Co.

Howell, J. (Director). (1981). *The Winter's Tale*. (Film). The BBC Shakespeare Collection. London: The British Broadcasting Corporation.

Howell, J. (Director). (1983). *Henry VI: Part One*. (Film). The BBC Shakespeare Collection. London: The British Broadcasting Corporation.

Howell, J. (Director). (1983). *Henry VI: Part Two*. (Film). The BBC Shakespeare Collection. London: The British Broadcasting Corporation.

Howell, J. (Director). (1983). *Henry VI: Part Three*. (Film). The BBC Shakespeare Collection. London: The British Broadcasting Corporation.

Howell, J. (Director). (1983). *Richard II*. (Film). The BBC Shakespeare Collection. London: The British Broadcasting Corporation.

Howell, J. (Director). (1983). *The Tragedy of Richard III*. (Film). The BBC Shakespeare Collection. London: The British Broadcasting Corporation.

Howell, J. (Director). (1985). *Titus Andronicus*. (Film). The BBC Shakespeare Collection. London: The British Broadcasting Corporation.

Hume, D. (1875). *Essays Moral, Political, and Liberty*. London: Longmans, Green, and Co.

Hume, D. (J. Y. T. Greig, Ed.) (1932). *The Letters of David Hume*. Volume I. New York: Oxford University Press.

Hume, D. (J. Y. T. Greig, Ed.) (1932). *The Letters of David Hume*. Volume II. New York: Oxford University Press.

Hume, D. (R. Klibansky, and E. C. Mossner, Eds.) (1954). *New Letters of David Hume*. Oxford: Clarendon Press.

Hume, D. (L.A. Selby, Ed.) (Revised by P. H. Nidditch) (1975). *A Treatise on Human Nature*. Second Edition. Oxford: Clarendon Press.

Hume, D. (R. H. Popkin, Ed.) (1980). *Dialogues Concerning Natural Religion. Of the Immortality of the Soul, of Suicide, and of Miracles*. Cambridge: Hackett Publishing Company.

Hume, D. (W. B. Todd, Ed.) (1983). *The History of England*. Indianapolis: Liberty Classics.

Hume, D. (1985). *The History of England*. Volumes I–VI. Indianapolis: Liberty Fund.

Hume, D. (E. F. Miller, Ed.) (1985). *Essays: Moral, Political, and Literary*. Indianapolis: Liberty Classics.

Hume, D. (1998). *An Enquiry Concerning the Principles of Morals*. Oxford: Oxford University Press.

Hume, D. (K. Haakonssen, Ed.) (1994). *Hume: Political Essays*. Cambridge: Cambridge University Press.

Hume, D. (2000). *A Treatise of Human Nature*. Oxford: Oxford University Press.

Hume, D. (T. L. Beauchamp, Ed.) (2007). *A Dissertation on the Passions and the Natural History of Religion*. Oxford: Clarendon Press.

Hume, D. (D. Coleman, Ed.) (2007). *Dialogues Concerning Natural Religion*. Cambridge: Cambridge University Press.

Hume, D. (2008). *An Enquiry Concerning Human Understanding*. Oxford: Oxford University Press.

Hutson, L. (2017). *The Oxford Handbook of English Law and Literature, 1500–1700*. Oxford: Oxford University Press.

Jeffrey, R. (1965). *The Logic of Decision*. Chicago: University of Chicago Press.

Jeffrey, R. (2004). *Subjective Probability: The Real Thing*. Cambridge: Cambridge University Press.

Jenkins, R. (2001). *Churchill: A Biography*. New York: Penguin Books.

Jennings, R. E. (1994). *The Genealogy of Disjunction*. Oxford: Oxford University Press.

Jones, D. H. (Director). (1982). *The Merry Wives of Windsor*. (Film). The BBC Shakespeare Collection. London: The British Broadcasting Corporation.

Jones, D. H. (Director). (1984). *Pericles: Prince of Tyre*. (Film). The BBC Shakespeare Collection. London: The British Broadcasting Corporation.

Jones, J. C. (Director). (1983). *The Comedy of Errors*. (Film). The BBC Shakespeare Collection. London: The British Broadcasting Corporation.

Jung, C. G. (W. Dell, and C. Baynes, Trans.) (1933). *Modern Man in Search of a Soul*. New York: A Harvest Book.

Jung, C. G. (1980). *Psychology and Alchemy*. Princeton, New Jersey: Princeton University Press.

Jung, C. G. (2014). *Dream Interpretation Ancient and Modern*. Princeton, New Jersey: Princeton University Press.

Kane, R. (Ed.) (2011). *The Oxford Handbook of Free Will*. New York: Oxford University Press.

Kant, I. (T. M. Greene, and H. H. Hudson, Trans.) (1960). *Religion within the Limits of Reason Alone*. New York: Harper and Row.

Kant, I. (1987). *Critique of Judgment*. Cambridge: Hackett Publishing Company.

Kant, I. (J. M. Young, Ed.) (1992). *Lectures on Logic*. Cambridge: Cambridge University Press.

Kant, I. (1995). *Opus Postumum*. New York: Cambridge University Press.

Kant, I. (P. Guyer, and A. W. Wood, Eds. and Trans.) (1999). *Critique of Pure Reason*. New York: Cambridge University Press.

Kant, I. (M. J. Gregor, Trans.) (1999). *Practical Philosophy*. New York: Cambridge University Press.

Kant, I. (P. Guyer, and E. Matthews, Trans.) (2001). *Critique of the Power of Judgement*. New York: Cambridge University Press.

Kant, I. (2001). *Lectures on Metaphysics*. New York: Cambridge University Press.

Kant, I. (A. W. Wood, and G. di Giovanni, Eds. and Trans.) (2001). *Religion and Rational Theology*. New York: Cambridge University Press.

Kant, I. (2002). *Critique of Practical Reason*. Cambridge: Hackett Publishing Company.

Kant, I. (D. Walford, and R. Meerbote, Eds.) (2003). *Theoretical Philosophy, 1755–1770*. New York: Cambridge University Press.

Kant, I. (A. Zweig, Ed.) (2007). *Correspondence*. Cambridge: Cambridge University Press.

Kant, I. (2007). *Critique of Pure Reason*. London: Penguin Classics.

Kant, I. (P. Heath, and J.B. Schneewind, Eds.) (2010). *Lectures on Ethics*. New York: Cambridge University Press.

Kant, I. (R. B. Louden, and G. Zoller, Eds. and Trans.) (2011). *Anthropology, History, and Education*. Cambridge: Cambridge University Press.

Kant, I. (E. Watkins, Ed.) (M. Schonfeld, J. B. Edwards, O. Reinhardt, and L. W. Beck, Trans.) (2012). *Kant: Natural Science*. New York: Cambridge University Press.

Kant, I. (R. B. Louden, A. W. Wood, R. R. Clewis, and G. F. Munzel, Trans.) (2013). *Lectures on Anthropology*. New York: Cambridge University Press.

Kerstein, S. (2002). *Kant's Search for the Supreme Principle of Morality*. Cambridge: Cambridge University Press.

Keynes, J. M. (1919). *The Economic Consequences of the Peace*. London: Macmillan.

Keynes, J. M. (1997). *The General Theory of Employment, Interest, and Money*. Maryland: Rowman and Littlefield Publishers.

Kidd, W. (2001). *Culture and Identity*. Basingstoke: Palgrave Macmillan.

Kirkpatrick, R. (1995). *English and Italian Literature From Dante to Shakespeare: A Study of Source, Analogue, and Divergence*. London: Routledge Publication.

Lee, S. (1902). *Shakespeare's Comedies, Histories, and Tragedies. A supplement to the reproduction in facsimile of the First Folio Edition, 1623, from the Chatsworth copy in the possession of the Duke of Devonshire, KG. Containing a census of extant copies with some account of their history and condition*. Oxford: Clarendon Press.

Lees, C. A. (2012). *The Cambridge History of Early Medieval English Literature*. Cambridge: Cambridge University Press.

Libreria Editrice Vaticana. (2019). *Catechism of the Catholic Church*. Second Edition. Revised in accordance with the official Latin text promulgated by Pope John Paul II. Vatican City: Libreria Editrice Vaticana.

Locke, J. (1689). *An Essay Concerning Human Understanding*. London: Thomas Bassett.

Locke, J. (1689). *Two Treatise of Government*. London: Awnsham Churchill.

Locke, J. (R. I. Aaron, and J. Gibb, Eds.) (1936). *An Early Draft of Locke's Essay Together with Excerpts from his Journal*. Oxford: Clarendon Press.

Locke, J. (P. Abrams, Ed.) (1967). *John Locke: Two Tracts of Government*. Cambridge: Cambridge University Press.

Locke, J. (J. L. Axtell, Ed.) (1968). *The Educational Writings of John Locke: A Critical Edition*. Cambridge: Cambridge University Press.

Locke, J. (R. Ashcraft, Ed.) (1987). *Locke's The Two Treatises of Civil Government*. London: Routledge Publication.

Locke, J. (P. Laslett, Ed.). (1988). *Locke: Two Treatises of Government*. Cambridge: Cambridge University Press.

Loughlin, M. (2010). *Foundations of Public Law*. Oxford: Oxford University Press.

Lowndes, W. T. (1857). *A Bibliographer's Manual of English Literature*. First Edition. London: Henry G. Bohn.

Lublin, R. I. (2011). *Costuming the Shakespearean Stage: Visual Codes of Representation in Early Modern Theatre and Culture*. Milton Park: Routledge Publication.

Machiavelli, N. (Q. Skinner., and R. Price, Eds.) (1988). *The Prince*. Cambridge: Cambridge University Press.

Machiavelli, N. (A. Gilbert, Ed. And Trans.). (1989). *Machiavelli: The Chief Works and Others*. Volume 1. North Carolina: Duke University Press Books.

Machiavelli, N. (A. Gilbert, Ed. And Trans.). (1989). *Machiavelli: The Chief Works and Others*. Volume 2. North Carolina: Duke University Press Books.

Machiavelli, N. (A. Gilbert, Ed. And Trans.). (1989). *Machiavelli: The Chief Works and Others*. Volume 3. North Carolina: Duke University Press Books.

Maley, W. (2002). *Nation, State, and Empire in English Renaissance Literature: Shakespeare to Milton*. New York: Palgrave Macmillan.

Mandela, N. (1995). *Long Walk to Freedom: The Autobiography of Nelson Mandela*. Boston: Back Bay Books.

Maslow, A. H. (1943). *A Theory of Human Motivation. Psychological Review*. Volume 50, No. 4, pp. 370–396.

Meron, T. (2017). Shakespeare: A Dove, a Hawk, or Simply a Humanist? *The American Journal of International Law*. Volume 111, No. 4, pp. 936–956.

Miller, J. (Director). (1980). *The Taming of the Shrew.* (Film). The BBC Shakespeare Collection. London: The British Broadcasting Corporation.

Miller, J. (Director). (1981). *Antony And Cleopatra.* (Film). The BBC Shakespeare Collection. London: The British Broadcasting Corporation.

Miller, J. (Director). (1981). *Othello.* (Film). The BBC Shakespeare Collection. London: The British Broadcasting Corporation.

Miller, J. (Director). (1981). *Timon of Athens.* (Film). The BBC Shakespeare Collection. London: The British Broadcasting Corporation.

Miller, J. (Director). (1981). *Troilus and Cressida.* (Film). The BBC Shakespeare Collection. London: The British Broadcasting Corporation.

Miller, J. (Director). (1982). *King Lear.* (Film). The BBC Shakespeare Collection. London: The British Broadcasting Corporation.

Milton, J. (H. Darbishire, Ed.) (1963). *The Poetical Works of John Milton. Volume I: Paradise Lost.* Oxford: Oxford University Press.

Milton, J. (H. Darbishire, Ed.) (1963). *The Poetical Works of John Milton. Volume II: Paradise Regained.* Oxford: Oxford University Press.

Montesquieu, C. (C. J. Betts, Trans.) (1973). *Persian Letters.* New York: Penguin Classics.

Montesquieu, C. (A.M. Cohler, B.C. Miller., and H.S. Stone., Trans., and Eds.) (1989). *Montesquieu: The Spirit of the Laws.* Cambridge: Cambridge University Press.

Moshinsky, E. (Director). (1981). *All's Well That Ends Well.* (Film). The BBC Shakespeare Collection. London: The British Broadcasting Corporation.

Moshinsky, E. (Director). (1981). *A Midsummer Night's Dream.* (Film). The BBC Shakespeare Collection. London: The British Broadcasting Corporation.

Moshinsky, E. (Director). (1982). *Cymbeline.* (Film). The BBC Shakespeare Collection. London: The British Broadcasting Corporation.

Moshinsky, E. (Director). (1984). *Coriolanus.* (Film). The BBC Shakespeare Collection. London: The British Broadcasting Corporation.

Moshinsky, E. (Director). (1985). *Love's Labour's Lost.* (Film). The BBC Shakespeare Collection. London: The British Broadcasting Corporation.

Naughton, M. (2005). Redefining Miscarriages of Justice: A Revived Human-Rights Approach to Unearth Subjugated Discourses of Wrongful Criminal Conviction. *The British Journal of Criminology.* Volume 45, Issue 2, (March 2005), pp. 165–182.

Nietzsche, F. (W. Kaufmann, Trans.) (1967). *The Birth of Tragedy and the Case of Wagner.* New York: Vintage Books.

Nietzsche, F. (W. Kaufmann, Ed.) (W. Kaufmann, and R. J. Hollingdale, Trans.) (1968). *The Will to Power.* New York: Vintage Books.

Nietzsche, F. (1974). *Nietzsche: Philosopher, Psychologist, Antichrist*. Princeton, New Jersey: Princeton University Press.

Nietzsche, F. (W. Kaufmann, Trans.) (1989). *Beyond Good and Evil: Prelude to a Philosophy of the Future*. New York: Vintage Books.

Nietzsche, F. (W. Kaufmann, Ed.) (1989). *On the Genealogy of Morals and Ecce Homo*. New York: Vintage Books.

Nietzsche, F. (1994). *The Birth of Tragedy: Out of the Spirit of Music*. London: Penguin Classics.

Nietzsche, F. (W. Kaufmann, Trans.) (1995). *Thus Spoke Zarathustra: A Book for All and None*. New York: Modern Library.

Nietzsche, F. (R.J. Hollingdale, Trans.) (1996). *Nietzsche: Human, All too Human: A Book for Free Spirits*. Cambridge: Cambridge University Press.

Nietzsche, F. (M. Clark, and B. Leiter, Eds.) (1997). *Daybreak: Thoughts on the Prejudices of Morality*. New York: Cambridge University Press.

Nietzsche, F. (M. Clark, and A. J. Swensen, Trans.) (1998). *On the Genealogy of Morality*. Indiana: Hackett Publishing.

Nietzsche, F. (1998). *On the Genealogy of Morals*. Oxford: Oxford University Press.

Nietzsche, F. (B. Williams, Ed.) (J. Nauckhoff, and A. Del Caro, Trans.) (2001). *Nietzsche: The Gay Science*. New York: Cambridge University Press.

Nietzsche, F. (2003). *Beyond Good and Evil*. London: Penguin Classics.

Nietzsche, F. (R. Bittner, and K. Sturge, Eds.) (2003). *Nietzsche: Writings from the Late Notebooks*. Cambridge: Cambridge University Press.

Nietzsche, F. (2003). *Thus Spoke Zarathustra*. London: Penguin Classics.

Nietzsche, F. (2005). *The Anti-Christ, Ecce Homo, Twilight of the Idols*. Cambridge: Cambridge University Press.

Nietzsche, F. (R. Guess., and A. Nehamas, Eds.) (L. Lob., Trans.) (2009). *Nietzsche: Writings from the Early Notebooks*. Cambridge: Cambridge University Press.

Nietzsche, F. (R. J. Hollingdale, and W. Kaufmann, Trans.) (2016). *Twilight of the Idols: How to Philosophize with a Hammer*. California: CreateSpace Independent Publishing.

Nietzsche, F. (D. Breazeale, Ed.) (1997). *Nietzsche: Untimely Meditations*. Cambridge: Cambridge University Press.

Nightingale, A. (2011). *Once Out of Nature: Augustine on Time and the Body*. Chicago: University of Chicago Press.

Nussbaum, M. C. (1990). *Love's Knowledge*. New York: Oxford University Press.

Nussbaum, M. C. (2001). *The Fragility of Goodness: Luck and Ethics in Greek Tragedy and Philosophy*. New York: Cambridge University Press.

Nussbaum, M. C. (2001). *Upheavals of Thought: The Intelligence of Emotion*. Cambridge: Cambridge University Press.

Nussbaum, M. C. (2019). *The Cosmopolitan Tradition: A Noble but Flawed Ideal.* Cambridge, Massachusetts: Harvard University Press.

Oakeshott, M. (1975). *Hobbes on Civil Association.* Oxford: Oxford University Press.

Payne, A. (2015). *The Global Politics of Unequal Development.* Basingstoke: Palgrave Macmillan.

Pelikan, J. (1975). *The Christian Tradition: A History of the Development of Doctrine. Volume I: The Emergence of the Catholic Tradition (100–600).* Chicago: University of Chicago Press.

Pelikan, J. (1977). *The Christian Tradition: A History of the Development of Doctrine. Volume II: The Spirit of Eastern Christendom (600–1700).* Chicago: University of Chicago Press.

Pelikan, J. (1980). *The Christian Tradition: A History of the Development of Doctrine. Volume III: The Growth of Medieval Theology (600–1300).* Chicago: University of Chicago Press.

Pelikan, J. (1985). *The Christian Tradition: A History of the Development of Doctrine. Volume IV: Reformation of Church and Dogma (1300–1700).* Chicago: University of Chicago Press.

Pelikan, J. (1991). *The Christian Tradition: A History of the Development of Doctrine. Volume V: Christian Doctrine and Modern Culture (Since 1700).* Chicago: University of Chicago Press.

Piaget, J. (1947). *The Psychology of Intelligence.* Abingdon: Taylor and Francis.

Plato. (J. M. Cooper, and D. S. Hutchinson, Eds.) (1997). *Plato: Complete Works.* Cambridge: Hackett Publishing Company.

Pollack-Pelzner, Daniel. (2013). Jane Austen, the Prose Shakespeare. *Studies in English Literature, 1500–1900.* Volume 53, No. 4, pp. 763–792.

Rakoff, A. (Director). (1978). *Romeo and Juliet.* (Film). The BBC Shakespeare Collection. London: The British Broadcasting Corporation.

Rawls, J. (1985). Justice as Fairness: Political not Metaphysical. *Philosophy and Public Affairs.* Volume 14, No. 3, pp. 223–251.

Rawls, J. (1993). *Political Liberalism.* New York: Columbia University Press.

Rawls, J. (1999). *A Theory of Justice.* Cambridge, Massachusetts: Harvard University Press.

Rawls, J. (B. Herman, Ed.) (2000). *Lectures on the History of Moral Philosophy.* Cambridge, Massachusetts: Harvard University Press.

Rawls, J. (2001). *Justice as Fairness.* Cambridge, Massachusetts: Harvard University Press.

Reid, T. (P. Wood, Ed.) (1995). *Thomas Reid on the Animate Creation: Papers Relating to the Life Sciences.* Edinburgh: Edinburgh University Press.

Reid, T. (D. R. Brookes, Ed.) (2000). *An Inquiry into the Human Mind on the Principles of Common Sense.* University Park, Pennsylvania: Penn State University Press.

Reid, T. (D. R. Brookes, Ed.) (2002). *Thomas Reid: Essays on the Intellectual Powers of Man.* Edinburgh: Edinburgh University Press.

Reid, T. (A. Broadie, Ed.) (2004). *Thomas Reid on Logic, Rhetoric and the Fine Arts.* University Park, Pennsylvania: Penn State University Press.

Reid, T. (K. Haakonssen, Ed.) (2007). *Thomas Reid on Practical Ethics.* Edinburgh: Edinburgh University Press.

Reid, T. (K. Haakonssen, and J. A. Harris, Eds.) (2010). *Essays on the Active Powers of Man.* Edinburgh: Edinburgh University Press.

Reid, T. (K. Haakonssen, and P. Wood, Eds.) (2015). *Thomas Reid on Society and Politics.* Edinburgh: Edinburgh University Press.

Reid, T. (P. Wood, Ed.) (2017). *Thomas Reid on Mathematics and Natural Philosophy.* Edinburgh: Edinburgh University Press.

Richetti, J. (2005). *The Cambridge History of English Literature, 1660–1780.* Cambridge: Cambridge University Press.

Rousseau, J. J. (J. M. Cohen, Trans.) (1953). *The Confessions of Jean-Jacques Rousseau.* New York: Penguin Classics.

Rousseau, J. J. (V. Gourevitch, Ed.) (1997). *Rousseau: The Social Contract and Other Later Political Writings.* Cambridge: Cambridge University Press.

Rousseau, J. J. (C. Betts, Trans.) (1999). *Discourse on Political Economy and the Social Contract.* New York: Oxford University Press.

Saint John of the Cross. (2003). *Dark Night of the Soul.* New York: Dover Publications.

Sainsbury, R. M. (1986). Degrees of Belief and Degrees of Truth. *Philosophical Papers.* Volume 15, No. 2, pp. 97–106.

Sainsbury, R. M. (1991). Is There Higher-Order Vagueness? *Philosophical Quarterly.* Volume 41, No. 163, pp. 167–182.

Sainsbury, R. M. (2009). *Paradoxes.* Third Edition. Cambridge: Cambridge University Press.

Schopenhauer, A. (E. F. J. Payne, Trans.) (1969). *The World as Will and Representation.* Volume I. New York: Dover Publications.

Schopenhauer, A. (E. F. J. Payne, Trans.) (1969). *The World as Will and Representation.* Volume II. New York: Dover Publications.

Schopenhauer, A. (1970). *Essays and Aphorisms.* London: Penguin Classics.

Schopenhauer, A. (E. F. J. Payne, Trans.) (1999). *On the Basis of Morality.* Indiana: Hackett Publishing Company.

Schopenhauer, A. (G. Z.ller, Ed.) (1999). *Prize Essay on the Freedom of the Will.* Cambridge: Cambridge University Press.

Schopenhauer, A. (2004). *The Wisdom of Life.* New York: Dover Publications.

Schopenhauer, A. (2010). *The Two Fundamental Problems of Ethics*. New York: Oxford University Press.

Schopenhauer, A. (D. E. Cartwright, E. E. Erdmann, and C. Janaway, Trans.) (2012). *Schopenhauer: On the Fourfold Root of the Principle of Sufficient Reason and Other Writings*. Cambridge: Cambridge University Press.

Schopenhauer, A. (S. Roehr, and C. Janaway, Trans.) (2014). *Schopenhauer: Parerga and Paralipomena. Volume I: Short Philosophical Essays*. Cambridge: Cambridge University Press.

Schopenhauer, A. (C. Janaway, Ed.). (A. D. Caro, Trans.) (2015). *Schopenhauer: Parerga and Paralipomena. Volume II: Short Philosophical Essays*. Cambridge: Cambridge University Press.

Schopenhauer, A. (Cartwright, D. E., Ed.) (Payne, E. F. J., Trans.) (1994). *On Vision and Colors: An Essay*. Oxford: Berg Publishers.

Shakespeare, W. (Condell, H., Droeshout, M., and Heminges, J., Eds.) (1623). *Mr. William Shakespeare's Comedies, Histories, and Tragedies. Published according to the true original copies. Gentle Master Shakespeare. First Folio*. London: Isaac Laggard and Ed Blount.

Shakespeare, W. (1632). *Mr. William Shakespeare Comedies, Histories, and Tragedies. Published according to the true original copies. The Second Impression*. London: Tho. Cotes, for Robert Allot.

Shakespeare, W. (1664). *Mr. William Shakespeare's Comedies, Histories, and Tragedies. Published according to the true original copies. The Third Impression*. London: Philip Chetwind.

Shakespeare, W. (1685). *Mr. William Shakespeare's Comedies, Histories, and Tragedies. Published according to the true original copies. The Fourth Folio*. London: Herringman, H., Brewster, E., Chiswell, R., and Bentley, R.

Shakespeare, W. (1978). *The Plays and Sonnets of William Shakespeare*. Seven Volumes. Pennsylvania: Franklin Library.

Shakespeare, W. (1996). *The Norton Facsimile: The First Folio of Shakespeare prepared by Charlton Hinman*. Second Edition. New York: Norton and Company.

Shakespeare, W. (2015). *The Complete Works of William Shakespeare*. New York: Barnes and Noble, Inc.

Shakespeare, W. (Jowett, J., Montgomery, W., Taylor, G., and Wells, S., Eds.) (2005). *The Oxford Shakespeare: The Complete Works*. Second Edition. Oxford: Oxford University Press.

Shakespeare, W. (J. Kerrigan, Ed.) (1999). *The Sonnets and a Lover's Complaint*. London: Penguin Classics.

Shakespeare, W. (B. A. Mowat, and P. Werstine, Eds.) (2003). *Cymbeline*. New York: Simon & Schuster.

Shakespeare, W. (B. A. Mowat, and P. Werstine, Eds.) (2004). *Julius Caesar.* New York: Simon & Schuster.

Shakespeare, W. (B. A. Mowat, and P. Werstine, Eds.) (2004). *The Merry Wives of Windsor.* New York: Simon & Schuster.

Shakespeare, W. (B. A. Mowat, and P. Werstine, Eds.) (2004). *Shakespeare's Sonnets.* New York: Simon & Schuster.

Shakespeare, W. (B. A. Mowat, and P. Werstine, Eds.) (2005). *Henry IV: Part One.* New York: Simon & Schuster.

Shakespeare, W. (B. A. Mowat, and P. Werstine, Eds.) (2005). *Love's Labour's Lost.* New York: Simon & Schuster.

Shakespeare, W. (B. A. Mowat, and P. Werstine, Eds.) (2005). *Measure for Measure.* New York: Simon & Schuster.

Shakespeare, W. (B. A. Mowat, and P. Werstine, Eds.) (2005). *Pericles, Prince of Tyre.* New York: Simon & Schuster.

Shakespeare, W. (B. A. Mowat, and P. Werstine, Eds.) (2005). *The Winter's Tale.* New York: Simon & Schuster.

Shakespeare, W. (B. A. Mowat, and P. Werstine, Eds.) (2005). *Antony and Cleopatra.* New York: Simon & Schuster.

Shakespeare, W. (B. A. Mowat, and P. Werstine, Eds.) (2005). *Titus of Andronicus.* New York: Simon & Schuster.

Shakespeare, W. (B. A. Mowat, and P. Werstine, Eds.) (2006). *Henry IV: Part Two.* New York: Simon & Schuster.

Shakespeare, W. (B. A. Mowat, and P. Werstine, Eds.) (2006). *All's Well That Ends Well.* New York: Simon & Schuster.

Shakespeare, W. (B. A. Mowat, and P. Werstine, Eds.) (2006). *The Two Gentlemen of Verona.* New York: Simon & Schuster.

Shakespeare, W. (B. A. Mowat, and P. Werstine, Eds.) (2006). *King John.* New York: Simon & Schuster.

Shakespeare, W. (B. A. Mowat, and P. Werstine, Eds.) (2006). *Timon of Athens.* New York: Simon & Schuster.

Shakespeare, W. (B. A. Mowat, and P. Werstine, Eds.) (2007). *Troilus and Cressida.* New York: Simon & Schuster.

Shakespeare, W. (B. A. Mowat, and P. Werstine, Eds.) (2007). *Henry VIII.* New York: Simon & Schuster.

Shakespeare, W. (B. A. Mowat, and P. Werstine, Eds.) (2008). *Henry VI: Part One.* New York: Simon & Schuster.

Shakespeare, W. (B. A. Mowat, and P. Werstine, Eds.) (2008). *Henry VI: Part Two.* New York: Simon & Schuster.

Shakespeare, W. (B. A. Mowat, and P. Werstine, Eds.) (2009). *Henry VI: Part Three.* New York: Simon & Schuster.

Shakespeare, W. (B. A. Mowat, and P. Werstine, Eds.) (2009). *Coriolanus*. New York: Simon & Schuster.

Shakespeare, W. (B. A. Mowat, and P. Werstine, Eds.) (2010). *The Merchant of Venice*. New York: Simon & Schuster.

Shakespeare, W. (B. A. Mowat, and P. Werstine, Eds.) (2011). *Romeo and Juliet*. New York: Simon & Schuster.

Shakespeare, W. (B. A. Mowat, and P. Werstine, Eds.) (2012). *Hamlet*. New York: Simon & Schuster.

Shakespeare, W. (B. A. Mowat, and P. Werstine, Eds) (2013). *Macbeth*. New York: Simon & Schuster.

Shakespeare, W. (B. A. Mowat, and P. Werstine, Eds.) (2014). *The Taming of the Shrew*. New York: Simon & Schuster.

Shakespeare, W. (B. A. Mowat, and P. Werstine, Eds.) (2015). *The Comedy of Errors*. New York: Simon & Schuster.

Shakespeare, W. (B. A. Mowat, and P. Werstine, Eds.) (2015). *The Tempest*. New York: Simon & Schuster.

Shakespeare, W. (B. A. Mowat, and P. Werstine, Eds.) (2015). *King Lear*. New York: Simon & Schuster.

Shakespeare, W. (B. A. Mowat, and P. Werstine, Eds.) (2016). *A Midsummer Night's Dream*. New York: Simon & Schuster.

Shakespeare, W. (B. A. Mowat, and P. Werstine, Eds.) (2016). *Richard II*. New York: Simon & Schuster.

Shakespeare, W. (B. A. Mowat, and P. Werstine, Eds.) (2017). *Othello*. New York: Simon & Schuster.

Shakespeare, W. (B. A. Mowat, and P. Werstine, Eds.) (2018). *Richard III*. New York: Simon & Schuster.

Shakespeare, W. (B. A. Mowat, and P. Werstine, Eds.) (2018). *Much Ado About Nothing*. New York: Simon & Schuster.

Shakespeare, W. (B. A. Mowat, and P. Werstine, Eds.) (2019). *As You Like It*. New York: Simon & Schuster.

Shakespeare, W. (B. A. Mowat, and P. Werstine, Eds.) (2019). *Twelfth Night*. New York: Simon & Schuster.

Shakespeare, W. (B. A. Mowat, and P. Werstine, Eds.) (2020). *Henry V*. New York: Simon & Schuster.

Shakespeare, W. (J. Roe, Ed.) (2006). *The Poems: Venus and Adonis, The Rape of Lucrece, The Phoenix and The Turtle, The Passionate Pilgrim, A Lover's Complaint*. New York: Cambridge University Press.

Shattock, J. (2010). *The Cambridge Companion to English Literature, 1830–1914*. Cambridge: Cambridge University Press.

Smith, A. (E. Cannan, Ed.) (1977). *An Inquiry into the Nature and Causes of the Wealth of Nations*. Chicago: University of Chicago Press.

Smith, A. (K. Haakonssen, Ed.) (2002). *Adam Smith: The Theory of Moral Sentiments*. Cambridge: Cambridge University Press.

Sohmer, S. (2019). *Reading Shakespeare's Mind*. Manchester: Manchester University Press.

Stevens, P., and Loewenstein, D. (2021). *The Cambridge Companion to Shakespeare and War*. Cambridge: Cambridge University Press.

Taylor, D. (1983). *The Two Gentlemen of Verona*. (Film). The BBC Shakespeare Collection. London: The British Broadcasting Corporation.

Tillich, P. (1973). *Systematic Theology*. Volume I. Chicago: University of Chicago Press.

Tillich, P. (1975). *Systematic Theology*. Volume II. Chicago: University of Chicago Press.

Tillich, P. (1976). *Systematic Theology*. Volume III. Chicago: University of Chicago Press.

Tomkins, A. (2003). *Public Law*. Oxford: Oxford University Press.

Tribble, E. (2017). *Early Modern Actors and Shakespeare's Theatre: Thinking with the Body*. London: Bloomsbury Publishing.

Tzu, L. (D. C. Lau, Ed.) (1964). *Tao Te Ching*. London: Penguin Classics.

Weiner, B. (1992). *Human Motivation: Metaphors, Theories, and Research*. Newbury Park: Sage Publications.

Weiner, B. (1995). *Judgements of Responsibility: A Foundation for a Theory of Social Conduct*. New York: Guilford Press.

Whitbourne, S. K. (2001). *Adult Development and Aging: Biopsychosocial Perspectives*. New York: John Wiley and Sons.

White, R. S. (2016). *Shakespeare's Cinema of Love: A Study in Genre and Influence*. Manchester: Manchester University Press.

Wise, H. (Director). (1979). *Julius Caesar*. (Film). The BBC Shakespeare Collection. London: The British Broadcasting Corporation.

Wittgenstein, L. (1965). *The Blue and Brown Books: Preliminary Studies for the Philosophical Investigations*. New York: Harper Torchbooks.

Wittgenstein, L. (Anscombe, G.E.M., and von Wright, G.H., Eds.) (1970). *Zettel*. Berkeley: University of California Press.

Wittgenstein, L. (1975). *On Certainty*. Oxford: Blackwell Publishing.

Wittgenstein, L. (Anscombe, G.E.M., Ed.) (1978). *Remarks on Colour*. Berkeley: University of California Press.

Wittgenstein, L. (1980). *Philosophical Remarks*. Chicago: University of Chicago Press.

Wittgenstein, L. (Rhees, R., Ed.) (1980). *Philosophical Grammar.* Oxford: Wiley-Blackwell.

Wittgenstein, L. (von Wright, G.H., Rhees, R., and Anscombe, G.E.M., Eds.) (1983). *Remarks on the Foundations of Mathematics.* Cambridge: MIT Press.

Wittgenstein, L. (Anscombe, G.E.M., Trans.) (1988). *Remarks on the Philosophy of Psychology.* Volume I. Chicago: University of Chicago Press.

Wittgenstein, L. (Luckhardt, C. G., and Maximilian, A. E. Aue., Trans.) (1988). *Remarks on the Philosophy of Psychology.* Volume II. Chicago: University of Chicago Press.

Wittgenstein, L. (Nyman, H., and von Wright, G. H., Eds.) (1990). *Last Writings on the Philosophy of Psychology. Volume I: Preliminary Studies for Part II of Philosophical Investigations.* Oxford: Wiley-Blackwell.

Wittgenstein, L. (Nyman, H., and von Wright, G. H., Eds.) (1993). *Last Writings on the Philosophy of Psychology. Volume II: The Inner and the Outer.* Oxford: Blackwell Publishing.

Wittgenstein, L. (2007). *Lectures and Conversations on Aesthetics, Psychology, and Religious Belief.* Berkeley: University of California Press.

Wittgenstein, L. (Anscombe, G.E.M., Hacker, P.M.S., and Schulte, J., Trans.) (2009). *Philosophical Investigations.* Oxford: Wiley-Blackwell.

Zussman, R. (1994). *Intensive Care: Medical Ethics and the Medical Profession.* Chicago: University of Chicago Press.

Index

9 780648 981855